Sexuality in Adole

Sexuality in Adolescence: Current Trends considers the latest theory and research on adolescent development, focusing on sexuality as a vital aspect of normal, healthy maturation. Biological changes are discussed within a social context, and the latest research is presented on key issues of our time, including changes in teenage sexual behaviours and beliefs, sexual risk-taking, body dissatisfaction, sex education, teen pregnancy and abortion.

Susan Moore and Doreen Rosenthal explore the roles of parents, peers, the media, social institutions and youth culture in adolescent sexual adjustment. This book covers topical issues ranging from the role of the internet in adolescent romance to the pros and cons of abstinence education versus harm minimization. Issues, such as whether there are male-female differences in desire, sexuality, motives for sex, and beliefs about romance are examined, along with the question of whether a sexual double standard still exists. Maladaptive aspects of sexual development, including sexual risk-taking, disease, unplanned pregnancy, and sexual coercion are also covered.

This fully revised and updated second edition also addresses the crucial issues of:

Sexual minority adolescents
The social determinants of adolescent sexuality
Sexual health as opposed to sexual illness

This book aims to promote sexual well-being, and argues for the importance of the adolescent period as a time for engendering healthy sexual attitudes and practices. It will be valuable reading for students in the social and behavioural sciences interested in adolescent development and the topic of sexuality and for professionals working with young people.

Susan Moore is a developmental social psychologist at Swinburne University Melbourne. Her research focuses on adolescent psychology, risk-taking and the psychology of health and illness. She has published over 100 refereed journal articles, plus several books and book chapters.

Doreen Rosenthal is a developmental psychologist at the University of Melbourne. Her research interests include adolescent psychology, particularly sexuality and sexual health, and the social determinants of health. She has published over 140 refereed journal articles, several books and many book chapters.

Adolescence and Society
Series editor: John C. Coleman
The Trust for the Study of Adolescence

The general aim of the series is to make accessible to a wide readership the growing evidence relating to adolescent development. Much of this material is published in relatively inaccessible professional journals, and the goals of the books in this series will be to summarize, review and place in context current work in the field so as to interest and engage both an undergraduate and a professional audience.

The intention of the authors is to raise the profile of adolescent studies among professionals and in institutions of higher education. By publishing relatively short, readable books on interesting topics to do with youth and society, the series will make people more aware of the relevance of the subject of adolescence to a wide range of social concerns.

The books will not put forward any one theoretical viewpoint. The suthors will outline the most prominent theories in the field and will include a balanced and critical assessment of each of these. Whilst some of the books may have a clinical or applied slant, the majority will concentrate on normal development.

The readership will rest primarily in two major areas: the undergraduate market, particularly in the fields of psychology, sociology and education; and the professional training market, with particular emphasis on social work, clinical and educational psychology, counselling, youth work, nursing and teacher training.

Also available in this series:

Adolescent Health
Patrick C.L. Heaven
**The Nature of Adolescence
(second edition)**
John C. Coleman and Leo Hendry
The Adolescent in the Family
Patricia Noller and Victor Callan
Young People's Understanding of Society
Adrian Furnham and Barrie Stacey
Growing up with Unemployment
*Anthony H. Winefield, Marika
Tiggermann, Helen R. Winefield and
Robert D. Goldney*
Young People's Leisure and Lfestyles
*Leo B. Hendry, Janey Shucksmith,
John G. Love and Anthony Glendinning*
Sexuality in Adolescence
Susan Moore and Doreen Rosenthal
Adolescent Gambling
Mark Griffiths

**Youth, AIDS and Sexually Transmitted
Diseases**
*Susan Moore, Doreen Rosenthal and
Anne Mitchell*
Fathers and Adolsecents
Shmuel Shulman and Inge Seiffge-Krenke
Adolescent Coping
Erica Frydenberg
Young People's Involvement in Sport
*Edited by John Kremer, Karen Trew and
Shaun Ogle*
The Nature of Adolescence
John C. Coleman and Leo B. Hendry
**Social Networks and Social Influences in
Adolescence**
John Cotterell
**Identity in Adolescence
(3rd edition)**
Jane Kroger

Sexuality in Adolescence
Current Trends

Susan Moore and Doreen Rosenthal

Routledge
Taylor & Francis Group

LONDON AND NEW YORK

First published 2006 by Routledge
27 Church Road, Hove, East Sussex, BN3 2FA

Simultaneously published in the USA and Canada
by Routledge
270 Madison Avenue, New York, NY 10016

*Routledge is an imprint of the Taylor & Francis Group, an informa
business*

© 2006 Psychology Press

Typeset in Times by Garfield Morgan, Swansea, West Glamorgan
Printed and bound in Great Britain by MPG Books Ltd, Bodmin, Cornwall
Paperback cover design by Hybert Design

This publication has been produced with paper manufactured to strict
environmental standards and with pulp derived from sustainable
forests.

British Library Cataloguing in Publication Data
A catalogue record for this book is available from the British Library

Library of Congress Cataloging in Publication Data
Moore, Susan, 1945–
    Sexuality in adolescence : current trends / Susan Moore and
Doreen Rosenthal.—2nd ed.
        p. cm.
    Includes bibliographical references and index.
    ISBN-13: 978-0-415-34462-3 (hardcover)
    ISBN-10: 0-415-34462-X (hardcover)
    ISBN-13: 978-0-415-34496-8 (paperback)
    ISBN-10: 0-415-34496-4 (paperback)
    1. Youth–Sexual behavior. 2. Teenagers–Sexual behavior.
I. Rosenthal, Doreen, 1938– . II. Title.
HQ27.M635 2006
306.70835–dc22

                                                        2006009407

ISBN 13: 978-0-415-34462-3 (hbk)
ISBN 13: 978-0-415-34496-8 (pbk)
ISBN 10: 0-415-34462-X (hbk)
ISBN 10: 0-415-34496-4 (pbk)

To the children of our children – adolescents present and future.

Contents

Acknowledgements

We would like to thank our publisher for encouraging us to rethink our understanding of adolescent sexuality in the light of changes in the past decade. Thanks also to our colleagues and institutions (Swinburne University of Technology and The University of Melbourne) for providing the resources that enabled us to complete this book. We are particularly grateful to the research assistants who helped us gather information about adolescent sexuality over many years of research. Special thanks are due to Kathleen Nolan and Katie Symes for their editing skills.

Our picture of what it is like to be a teenager and a sexual being in today's world would not have been possible without the involvement of many young people who contributed to our research and trusted us with such sensitive information. Special thanks go to these adolescents who have talked to us and whose experiences enrich the text and have provided a framework for this book.

Finally, to our families who have endured while we wrote this book, our thanks.

Introduction

There has been an explosion of information and research on adolescent sexuality in the past decade. Yet there have been few attempts to draw this material together and provide an integrated view of adolescent sexuality in its many facets. This book takes account of new research in adolescent sexuality in the last 12 or so years and new issues and debates which have become prominent. These include the greater levels of tolerance in western nations for adolescents' expression of sexuality and sexual diversity (consistent with changes occurring in adult society) and changes in beliefs about sexuality brought about through the power of a globalized youth culture, shaped largely by the media. Debates about sex education – who provides this and how, and what it encompasses – are ongoing and heated. The near universal use of mobile phones and the internet has opened up both positive and negative possibilities for adolescents' sexual lives. Increasingly, although young people across the globe live in different social, cultural and economic circumstances, their sexual worlds reveal commonalities as well as differences. Most of the research we review is from western countries, but we present some studies from developing countries to provide a taste of the wider global context.

We also review issues from the past that remain salient today. There are timeless questions such as how parents talk to their adolescents about sex, how young people cope with the changes of puberty, how the sexual lives of young men and women are shaped by biology and nurture and how social institutions influence young people's sexuality. Additionally, the heavy emphasis on deviance, risk-taking, disease and unwanted pregnancy remains in today's research and discourse about adolescent sexuality.

Sexuality: a critical aspect of adolescent development

Sexual questions, conflicts and crises may begin prior to adolescence and may certainly continue after this phase of life but there is no doubt that, for most people, adolescence is a 'critical period' in the upsurge of sexual drives, the development of sexual values and the initiation of sexual behaviours. The advent of puberty, the power of peer group expectations and the communication of mixed messages about sex from the adult generation make dealing with sexuality a difficult but exciting challenge for adolescents.

For healthy outcomes, adolescents need the information, skills, commitment to the future and, sometimes, protection which will enable them to avoid sex, unplanned unwanted pregnancies and sexually transmitted infections (STIs), especially the life-threatening disease of AIDS. They need the skills to establish healthy and adaptive non-exploitative sexual relationships. Adolescent sexuality need not be defined as problem behaviour. Sexual activity that is non-exploitative and safe, from the point of view of mental and physical health, can make a positive contribution to teenage development through increased independence, social competence and self-esteem. This is not to say that all teenage sexual behaviour is adaptive, healthy and moral. Clearly sexual activity can occur too early and in a context that is inappropriate. The view taken in this book is that sexuality is a normative event in adolescent development with the potential for both positive and negative consequences.

All theories of adolescent development give sexuality a central place in negotiating the transition from child to adult. The sexual urges which emerge at puberty must be blended with other aspects of teenagers' lives and channelled adaptively. It is especially important that the adolescent be able to integrate his or her sexual feelings, needs and desires into a coherent and positive self-identity which contains, as one aspect, a sexual self. Unlike many of the activities we engage in, expression of our sexuality (for the most part) involves a relationship, no matter how limited or fleeting, with another individual. Sexual expression allows, indeed requires, a unique exposure of the self to another. On the one hand there is the possibility of validating one's sense of self-worth and achieving a deeply satisfying intimate relationship. On the other hand, wrong choices can lead to destructive outcomes, to feelings of anxiety and guilt and to a sense of unworthiness. For adolescents who are in the process of forging a satisfying and satisfactory sense of their own identity and their place in the world, dealing with these issues is a crucial part of their development.

As we shall see the task is a complex one. If we are to understand the significance of sexuality during adolescence, we need to consider how it fits into the biological, psychological and social aspects of adolescent development. At the biological level, sexuality is the central feature, marked by the onset of puberty which signals maturation of the reproductive organs, the possibility of becoming a parent and an increasing sex drive. With puberty, changes at the psychological level have to do with readiness for taking on adult roles, including sex and procreation. There is a shift from a primary orientation to one's family to a reliance on peers for providing guidelines for attitudes and behaviour, as well as a clarification of goals and the development of interpersonal skills and attitudes. This occurs within a context of expanded cognitive skills which allow the adolescent to evaluate alternative points of view. At a broader level, social forces shape adolescents' sexuality by establishing and re-establishing values and norms relating to sexuality and expectations tied to gender.

Education enabling young people to develop sexual and relationship knowledge and skills is likely to be most effective if educators take into account the current beliefs and practices of their target audience. Sex education which stresses fear-arousing messages, punitive outcomes of experimentation or value stances considered 'out of date' will fail to reach those most needing intervention. Educators need to know about the different sexual subcultures of youth if their programmes are to be effective. But education about sexuality does not just occur in schools. It is pervasive in our culture through modelling adult behaviour, through the media, through talking with each other and family and through our laws as well as religious and other values.

One major focus for research on adolescent sexuality is documenting sexual behaviours, usually within a biological framework. How many teenagers are sexually active? What are they doing? Are they using contraception? What is the incidence of teenage pregnancy? These are important questions and are addressed in this book. Other research examines the sociocultural underpinnings of sexuality as biological approaches to sexuality have limited explanatory power. They do not fit with observed gender, ethnic and class differences in behaviours and beliefs. Recognizing those aspects of sexuality that are socially constructed enables us to raise questions about the social context and the ways in which this channels teenagers' sexual experiences. Where possible, we draw on the political context to help us explain young people's sexual practices and beliefs. What does it mean, for example, to be a teenager growing up in the USA where, as Wilcox tells us, 'policymakers want to tell adolescents that sex is dirty, so they should save it for someone they love' (1999: 349).

In line with this focus, there have been changes in the methods used to explore aspects of young people's sexuality. Although there is still an emphasis on large-scale quantitative surveys, increasingly qualitative techniques are being used. These enable us to understand better the meanings and motives underlying behaviours and to generate richer explanations of these behaviours. Together these methods allow for educational programmes that are more effectively targeted and take account of young people's own reality.

In the first two chapters, we deal with contemporary sexual attitudes and practices, and with the ways in which sexuality has been theorized in adolescent development. Chapter 1 provides an overview of what young people are doing sexually and the context in which their sexuality is developing. In particular, we note changes that have occurred in the past decade. Chapter 2 looks at theoretical approaches to adolescent sexuality, contrasting essentialist and social constructionist views and explaining why theories are important as a guide to research and practice.

Chapter 3 outlines biological aspects of sexual development in adolescence, and draws out links between behaviours and bodily changes. These changes are considered in context, including a discussion of body dissatisfaction – a condition of epidemic proportions in our society and one with strong repercussions for sexual development and ultimately sexual health. Additionally, the research on early and late timing of puberty has been 'turned around' as new data (and different contexts) prevail.

Chapter 4 describes the influences of parents and peers on adolescent sexuality – in particular, new material on parents' role in sex education is discussed. It is noted that there are significant barriers to parents in presenting sex education to adolescents, even though young people judge their parents as a trusted source. Conflicts between what parents say and what they do sexually are also aired, and the importance of modelling in sexual behaviour and close relationships is discussed.

Chapter 5 allows us to expand on the array of influences young people now experience with respect to sexuality. In particular, media and 'new media' influences such as the internet are considered in terms of their benefits and their perils. Current debates about sex education are considered, including the efficacy or otherwise of 'abstinence only' sex education.

Chapter 6 explores, within a gendered context, the notions of romance, love, lust, infidelity and commitment. Here we capture how socialization influences can make the sexual experience appear so different for young men and women. Chapter 7 provides up to date information about a marginalized group of young people: gay and lesbian adolescents. We discuss the impact of homophobia on these young people's sense of sexual identity and personal safety.

The final three chapters concentrate on potentially negative outcomes of adolescent sexual behaviour. Chapters 8 and 9 deal with two very different consequences of sexual risk, each arising from erratic or non-existent contraceptive practice – STIs, including HIV/AIDS, and unwanted or unplanned pregnancy. These consequences of sexual activity have major implications for the health and well-being of adolescents and for society at large. Chapter 10 focuses on sexual activity which may limit personal growth and threaten psychological health. We discuss unwanted sex in its many forms, including sexual coercion, rape and sexual abuse. Our conclusion draws together themes that recur throughout the chapters and raises some important issues that have not yet been adequately addressed through either scientific or public discourse.

1 Sexuality in the 21st century: adolescents' behaviours and beliefs

New millenium, new mores?

Are adolescents in this new millennium different from their pre-decessors in their sexual behaviours and beliefs? How has the now long-term impact of HIV/AIDS affected young people's uptake of safe sex and their beliefs about sexuality? As we wrote in an earlier version of this book, any understanding of today's adolescent as a sexual being must take account of the historical context. The past decade has seen further changes in social norms that have conse-quences for the expression of adolescent sexuality. Even in countries where premarital sex has long been proscribed and discussions about sexuality taboo, there have been significant changes in the past few decades (Brown *et al.* 2002; Eaton *et al.* 2003).

In western societies, sexually the past was a simpler place than now. Girls became wives and mothers and protected their virginity in order to attract a suitable husband. Boys' lives were career-oriented and they were expected to sow their sexual wild oats prior to taking on their family role of provider. Today, these goals are no longer so well defined. Ideas about 'right' and 'wrong' sexual behaviour are less rigid and boundaries between good and bad girls and boys are less clear. We know, too, that young people are delaying or dispensing with marriage while, at the same time, the age at which puberty begins is decreasing. This extension of the period between physical maturation and the taking up of traditional roles, together with the fact that contraception (including the 'morning after' pill and abortion) is freely available, led to the uncoupling of sexuality, marriage and childbearing in the last few decades of the 20th century. Prohibitions about premarital teenage sex are far less prevalent and difficult to enforce, but there is also a huge diversity of views within the subgroups that make up society. There are many more possible pathways for healthy (and unhealthy) sexual development for today's adolescents than there were in the 1950s or even the 1990s – more possibilities but also more pitfalls. We explore some of these in the subsequent chapters.

Of course teenage sex has always been with us. What is new is the increase in the numbers of young people engaging in this behaviour in the past 50 years. In particular, there has been a dramatic rise over this period in the numbers of teenage girls who are sexually active outside marriage. While historically young boys were more sexually active than young girls, the gap between the sexes began to narrow in the early 1980s. One US study showed an increase in the number of white American 16-year-old girls having intercourse from 7 per cent in 1950 to 44 per cent in 1982 (Brooks-Gunn & Furstenberg 1989). More recent studies confirm this increase, with some revealing that young girls are as sexually active as their male peers (Edgardh 2002; Meekers & Ahmed 2000; Smith *et al.* 2003a; Wellings *et al.* 2001). Nevertheless, the gender gap remains in some populations, for example among the urban minority youth studied by O'Donnell *et al.* (2003).

Undoubtedly the increase in the 1980s was due, at least partially, to the influence of the women's movement of the 1960s and 1970s and the demands for equality of sexual expression and sexual fulfilment which were advocated by members of that movement. More recently, too, there appear to be more opportunities for women to be sexually active. In a review of studies of late adolescents' sexual behaviour from 1900 to 1980, Darling *et al.* (1984) identified three periods, each characterized by different sexual standards. The earliest, which lasted until the 1940s or early 1950s, was the period of the 'double standard', with sexual activity accepted for boys but prohibited for girls. During the next 20 or so years, it seemed that premarital sex was allowed for young people provided that it occurred in a love relationship that was a prelude to marriage. The 'sexual revolution' of the 1960s and 1970s, which was characterized by more permissive attitudes towards sexuality and greater concern for personal fulfilment, brought with it a lessening of the prohibition on premarital sex. The trend towards later marriage may well have contributed since many believe it to be unrealistic to expect teenagers to abstain from sexual activity until marriage. Since then, we have seen a greater tolerance for sex outside of a romantic relationship. Today, young people are likely to live independently or with a partner, expecting to marry later than their parents, if at all. Many young women are now focused on establishing a career rather than a long-term relationship.

Nevertheless, there has been something of a plateau in the rates of sexual activity among teenagers and it would be foolish to expect that all teenagers would engage in premarital sex. A significant proportion of young people advocate no sex before marriage, although it is difficult to assess whether this attitude is consistent with behaviour. Some young people prefer to wait until they find the 'right' person; others do not experience opportunities for sexual engagement because of their family, community or personal characteristics. Current estimates are that about 40 per cent of unmarried 18-year-olds have not yet experienced intercourse, a figure that is consistent across many western nations, although there is variation within groups, the figure being higher for some and lower for others (Rosenthal *et al.* 1990; Smith *et al.* 2003a).

In the remaining sections of this chapter, we examine the sexual behaviour of young people and consider some factors influencing this behaviour.

Patterns of sexual behaviour

Generalizing about the sexual practices of adolescents is a dangerous procedure given the wide range of behaviours included under this rubric, the individual differences that distinguish adolescents from each other and the diversity of societal influences that adolescents in different subgroups experience. No less important are the differences one might expect in comparing the behaviour of 13-year-olds with that of late teenagers. With this caveat in mind, we turn to what adolescents do sexually, with whom and when.

Partnered sexual behaviour

'Falling in love', developing crushes and forming romantic relationships are all part of a sequence which may or may not culminate in sexual intercourse. These aspects of young people's sexual development are dealt with in Chapter 6. Here we focus on specific sexual acts. Several studies have shown the robustness of a sequence of adolescent sexual behaviour which starts at around the age of 13 with embracing and kissing, moving through petting or fondling breasts and sex organs, and ending with intercourse (e.g. Schwartz 1993; Smith *et al.* 2003a). Most adolescents, especially young women, move gradually towards more intimate sexual behaviour – 'heavy' petting and intercourse – through the experience of dating, although cultural variations in this sequence have been described. For example, among African-American girls, sexual intercourse often precedes heavy petting. These experiences provide young people with the opportunities for sexual exploration and discovery, and for acquiring the skills in intimacy which are necessary if one is to establish a long-term partnership. It has often been suggested that premarital petting, especially to orgasm, has been used to protect girls' virginity – an important commodity in many cultures even today. In this way girls can remain technically virgins while experiencing sexual intimacy. There are, of course, other reasons for the observation that many young girls are content to restrict themselves to heavy petting without taking the next step – to sexual intercourse. Such behaviour reduces the risk of pregnancy and, perhaps more importantly, teenage girls' sexual desires may be awakened and satisfied by the direct stimulation of the clitoris which occurs during heavy petting.

The dating behaviour of teenagers and its relationship to sexual behaviour and attitudes has been subjected to some scrutiny. McCabe and Collins (1990) investigated how the sexual desires and behaviours of Australian 16- to 17-year-old adolescents changed as the dating relationship deepened. There was a clear desire for increasing sexual intimacy from first date to going steady, although young boys wanted more intimacy than their female peers at all levels of dating. For example, on their first date, 88 per cent of boys wanted to engage in light breast petting and 41 per cent in stimulation of the girl's genitals, but only 29 per cent and 6 per cent of girls desired this experience on their first date. Boys also showed greater acceleration in their desire for sexual intimacy as they progressed through the dating stages. Desire for intercourse progressed for girls from 2 per cent at the first date to 8 per cent on going steady. Comparable figures for boys were 12 and 45 per cent. The reported behaviour of boys and girls showed similar differences between the sexes although these diminish as the relationship deepens, so that by the time young people are going steady there appears to be mutuality of behaviours.

As might be expected, there is a strong relationship between dating experiences and teenage sexual attitudes and behaviours. Those teenagers who have steady or regular partners are more likely to have premarital sex than are casual daters. In one US study of 6th graders, only 4 per cent had had sex but, not surprisingly, those young adolescents who had an older boyfriend or girlfriend were much more likely (over 30 times) to have ever had sex (Marin *et al.* 2000).

Early dating experience seems to be associated with more permissive attitudes to premarital sex as well as to early sexual experience. For example, in one study (Miller *et al.* 1986), 82 per cent of teenagers who had begun dating at age 12 had experienced intercourse by late adolescence. For those who started dating at age 14, this figure dropped to 56 per cent, and 17 per cent for those whose dating experiences began at age 16. In another study, younger adolescents were less likely than their older peers to have sex with a partner they had met for the first time (Wellings *et al.* 2001).

Sexual initiation

Just how many teenagers are virgins and how many are sexually experienced? We have seen that there was a substantial increase in teenage sexual activity in the last decades of the 20th century. In a UK study of 15- to 19-year-olds interviewed in the early 1960s, Schofield (1968) found that only 20 per cent of boys and 12 per cent of girls had had sexual intercourse. Ten years later, over 50 per cent of teenagers aged 16 to 19 years reported that they were non-virgins (Farrell 1978). In two national surveys of young American women, Zelnik *et al.* (1981) observed that in 1971 30 per cent of 15- to 19-year-old women had had premarital sexual intercourse, a figure rising to 41 per cent in 1976. Most studies in the late 1980s and 1990s, across a number of western countries, suggest that by the end of high school about 35 to 40 per cent of teenagers are non-virgins (Hofferth 1987; Lindsay *et al.* 1997; Rosenthal *et al.* 1990). Australian studies of high school students conducted in 1992 and 1997 showed an increase over that period in the numbers who had ever had sex (Lindsay *et al.* 1997). A third survey, conducted in 2002, found a continuing increase in the numbers of sexually active high schoolers (Smith *et al.* 2003a).

In a study of over 4000 Australian young people (Grunseit & Richters 2000), the median age at first intercourse was 16 years with higher levels of schooling and church attendance related to delaying first intercourse. Similar findings come from a study of New Zealanders (Paul *et al.* 2000). Forty per cent of British adolescents reported their first sexual intercourse at 15 years of age or younger – 9 per cent at 13 years or earlier (Ford & Morgan 1989). Another study of British adolescents (Breakwell *et al.* 1991) found that about 55 per cent of 16- to 17-year-olds had had vaginal intercourse at least once. Manzini (2001) reports that almost half of a sample of 15- to 24-year-olds in one South African study had already had first intercourse at age 16 years.

A trend towards first experience of sex at younger ages is true of most western countries. In Sweden, the age of initiation into sex dropped from an average of 19 years to 16 years in the past four decades. The UK *Sexual Attitudes and Lifestyle* survey showed a decline in age at first intercourse in successive age groups. Among those aged 16 to 24 years, the median age of first intercourse was 17 years, four years earlier than the age at first intercourse for the oldest group (Johnson *et al.* 1994). The second national survey showed that among those aged between 16 and 19 years, the proportion reporting first sexual intercourse before they were 16 was 30 per cent for young men and 25 per cent for young women. The proportion of women reporting first intercourse before 16 years increased up to the mid-1990s but not after (Wellings *et al.* 2001), suggesting that there may have been a stabilization of age at first intercourse among women in the 1990s.

While young people in non-western countries may not be as sexually active as their western counterparts, substantial numbers report engaging in sex. These include young people in sub-Saharan Africa (Gupta & Mahy 2003; Kaaya *et al.* 2002), Nigeria (Odimegwu *et al.* 2002) and Eastern Europe (Gyarmathy *et al.* 2002). Even in Asian countries, where discussion of sex is often taboo and strict traditional prohibitions on premarital sex are still in place, the number who have experienced sex – and it is likely that these numbers are an under-estimate given some young people may be unwilling to disclose sexual activity – is surprisingly high (see Brown *et al.* 2002; Wu 2003; Youn 1996). For example, 23 per cent of male and 10 per cent of female Korean adolescents reported being sexually active (Youn 1996).

It is somewhat misleading to talk of an average age for loss of virginity. There are considerable cultural and subgroup differences among young people. Studies from a range of countries indicate different levels of sexual experience for similarly aged young people from different social, religious, ethnic and racial groups. For example, African-American and Latino adolescents become sexually active at a younger age than American Caucasians (Newcomer & Udry 1983a; O'Donnell *et al.* 2003; Zelnik *et al.* 1981). Several studies note the lower rates of adolescent sexual intercourse (and the later ages of sexual debut) of Mexican-Americans in comparison with their Anglo-American counterparts (Aneshensel *et al.* 1989; Slonim-Nevo 1992).

There is a small but significant number of young people who report intercourse at a very young age, often as a result of sexual abuse. In one American study, 24 per cent of young woman aged 13 years or younger at the time of their first experience of sexual intercourse reported that the experience was not voluntary. Research with 300 18-year-old injecting drug users (IDUs) found that sexual intercourse began at an earlier age for this group than reported for their non-injecting peers (Louie *et al.* 1996). The mean age of first intercourse in this IDU group was around 14 years, an age at which most studies of young people report only low levels of sexual activity.

Our interviews with young people suggest that the majority of adolescents themselves believe that 15 is too young an age to begin intercourse and although the ideal age for loss of virginity 'depends on the person' (their level of maturity), too early sexual initiation can have a damaging psychological effect. In spite of the failure of first sex to live up to the expectations of many young people, most no longer believe that this should wait until marriage (Moore & Rosenthal 1992). Perhaps the most common view can be summed up in the words of a 16-year-old girl interviewed in an Australian study of adolescent sexual attitudes (Buzwell *et al.* 1992: 5): 'It's normal to have sex before marriage. No one waits for the ring these days. That idea is so old-fashioned. No one thinks like that any more'.

Research findings from the UK and the USA indicate that young people, on the whole, prefer to be sexually active within a committed relationship (e.g., Coleman & Hendry 1990; Dusek 1991).

Variety of practices

Just as the numbers of teenagers engaging in sex have increased, at least until recently, and their age of initiation has declined, so too are they becoming more sexually adventurous. Young people are engaging in a wider variety of sexual behaviours than before, and with more partners. The practice of oral sex is now widespread among adolescents and there seems to have been a shift in formerly negative attitudes to less traditional sexual practices. This variety reflects a generational change. Johnson *et al.* (1994) note that while the experience of vaginal intercourse is almost universal in the UK by age 25, there are marked age differences in other practices, particularly cunnilingus and fellatio. In the youngest age group studied (16–24 years), among those who had ever had vaginal sex, 79 per cent reported oral sex in the last year and 85 per cent ever, in comparison with the 45 to 49 cohort for whom only 30 per cent of the women and 42 per cent of the men had had oral sex in the last year. These age differences in practice are reflected in other studies; there is a significant proportion of young people now for whom the practice of oral sex precedes coitus. Smith *et al.* (2003a) found that over half (55 per cent) of their high school students had experienced oral sex but not intercourse with one partner, and 30 per cent with two or more partners, in the previous year.

In Sweden, 66 per cent of high-school students reported experiencing oral sex with no differences between boys and girls (Edgardh 2002). These findings are reflected in Australian studies. Roberts *et al.* (1996) report that the majority of their first-year university students had engaged in oral sex at least once; 78 per cent of sexually active students had both given and received oral sex. Most Australian high-school students surveyed by Smith *et al.* (2003a) reported giving or receiving oral sex in the preceding 12 months. Fifty per cent reported this with one partner and 38 per cent with two or more partners. Although females were somewhat more likely than males to have engaged in this practice, males were more likely to have done so with more than one partner. Of interest is the finding that for both sexes, the younger students were more likely than the older to have had oral sex.

It seems clear that for many young people, oral sex now precedes sexual intercourse in the timetabling of sexual behaviours. An Australian study examining the views of young people about appropriate ages for initiation of sexual practices from kissing to coitus (Rosenthal *et al.* 1998b) found a clear hierarchy, with oral sex coming after genital touching and before intercourse. Oral sex between the ages of 15 and 17 years was deemed to be appropriate activity by over half the participants in the study. There were few gender differences either for age expectations of the practices for boys and girls or between male and female respondents.

The emergence of oral sex as a common practice needs to be recognized, particularly as there is evidence that young people may not equate oral sex with sex (Rissel *et al.* 2003). This separation of oral sex and sex suggests that if young people engage in oral sex without intercourse, they may not recognize the risk of disease transmission. While oral sexual practices are potentially less risky than vaginal intercourse with respect to HIV transmission, it is not entirely safe in this respect (Spitzer & Weiner 1989), and a range of STIs can be spread by these practices particularly if semen, blood or vaginal fluids enter the mouth (Victorian Government Department of Health and Community Services 1993).

The incidence of anal sex, while relatively low, occurs with more frequency among some groups and more often with regular than with casual partners. The incidence of anal sex in three Australian samples was surprisingly high for some groups. Anal sex was relatively uncommon among 18-year-old university students. About 3 per cent regularly and 7 per cent occasionally engaged in this practice, more commonly with regular than with casual partners (Rosenthal *et al.*

1990). In a five-year cross-sectional follow up study of similarly aged university students, the anal sex rates with casual partners had increased significantly (Rosenthal *et al.* 1996). In a UK study (Breakwell *et al.* 1991), heterosexual anal activity was reported by 9 per cent of boys and girls. Johnson *et al.* (1994) indicated that, for their 16- to 59-year-old sample, the highest prevalence of recent anal intercourse occurred among 16- to 24-year-olds who had already experienced vaginal intercourse. Among Edgardh's Swedish high-school students, 10 per cent reported having had anal sex, boys equally as often as girls. Anal intercourse rates are much higher in particular subgroups. In their study of 16-year-olds, Rosenthal *et al.* (1994) found that 25 per cent of homeless girls and boys reported that they engaged in anal sex with casual or regular partners (or both). Of the homeless young people surveyed by Lhuede and Moore (1994), 32 per cent had engaged in anal intercourse with a regular, and 25 per cent with a casual, partner. There was little difference between the anal intercourse rates of homeless girls and boys in either study.

The practice of withdrawal of the penis before ejaculation during vaginal intercourse (known as withdrawal) is often not included as a category separate from vaginal intercourse in adolescent sexuality research. Nevertheless it is an important practice to note from the point of view of both pregnancy protection and STI transmission. The belief that withdrawal eliminates risk is mistaken. Even 'successful' withdrawal – less likely among those sexually inexperienced – still carries risk through possible infection carried in the pre-ejaculate or vaginal fluids. Our own studies have indicated that some young people hold the view that withdrawal does not 'count' as an instance of vaginal intercourse. We found among 17- to 20-year-old tertiary students this practice occurred with regular partners for about half the young women and men, and for a substantial minority with casual partners (Rosenthal *et al.* 1990). In the most recent study of Australian secondary students (Smith *et al.* 2003a), 10 per cent still engaged in withdrawal in spite of education messages about the risks to sexual health associated with this practice.

We need to be cautious in accepting too readily the evidence for an increase in sexual activity and variety. Attitudes to sexuality are more liberal than in previous decades so that the teenagers of today may be more willing to admit to these behaviours than their predecessors. Nevertheless, the generality of these findings across studies in different countries, using different samples and different information-gathering strategies, suggests that real changes have occurred.

Number of partners

To what extent is partner changing a feature of adolescent and young adult sexual practice? Several recent studies suggest that the stereotype of high activity among this age group is not borne out by the data. In the most recent national study of Australian high-school students, half of the young men who had experienced sexual intercourse in the preceding 12 months reported having only one partner as did two-thirds of the young women. It was more common for young men than young women to report having three or more partners – 23 per cent versus 17 per cent. In a review of South African studies of young people's sexual behaviour, Eaton *et al.* (2003) found that the majority reported ever having only one partner, although a small proportion of females (1 to 5 per cent) and about one-quarter of males had more than four partners in the previous year.

From Johnson *et al.*'s (1994) study, the answer is less clear-cut. Men and women in the 16 to 24 age group consistently report the greatest numbers of partners, despite this being the group with the highest proportion of respondents who have not yet experienced intercourse. Among this age group, 11 per cent of men and 3 per cent of women reported ten or more heterosexual partners in the last five years. The researchers argue that these figures represent not only an exploration of several relationships before committing to a long-term partnership (which may have also occurred for older age groups when they were in their teens and 20s), but also a genuine generational change in sexual behaviour patterns. They note the difficulties involved in gaining precise estimates of the number of partners that older people had when they were younger, but believe their evidence points to a pattern indicating that individuals now beginning their sex lives will have, on average, a substantially greater number of partners in a lifetime than did their parents.

In a similar finding that a small minority of young people have more than one partner in a limited period, our studies indicate that 16 per cent of 18-year-old tertiary student Anglo-Australian males and 8 per cent of similarly aged Anglo-Australian females had had three or more sexual partners in the last six months, although most reported no partners or only one. Subgroups differed markedly however, with 43 per cent of Greek-Australian and 30 per cent of Italian-Australian boys reporting three or more partners over the same time period (Rosenthal *et al.* 1990). Outside of the tertiary education sector, it is interesting to note somewhat higher rates of sexual activity among 18-year-olds. In a study of unemployed young people, 90.5 per cent had engaged in penetrative sexual activities (Buzwell & Rosenthal 1995). Most of these young people had had a sexual partner in the preceding six months with 19 per cent reporting three or more partners. In a separate study, 16-year-old homeless young people were questioned about their sexual behaviour and sexual beliefs (Rosenthal *et al.* 1994). The homeless group was significantly more sexually active than the other groups and had more partners. Homeless boys reported an average of 12, and girls an average of 7, partners in the preceding six months, compared with an average of 1 or less for home-based young people.

Solo sex

The focus on changes in young people's sexual behaviours should not allow us to ignore 'solo' sex. We should not forget that sexual behaviours can occur without a partner and that these practices can be intensely gratifying. They can be involuntary, like nocturnal emissions, or behaviours that are deliberately engaged in, like erotic fantasy and masturbation. Perhaps not surprisingly, there is still very little research reported on any of these sexual behaviours, no doubt because they have been and still are regarded as intensely private and somewhat shameful activities. Katchadourian (1990) believes that erotic fantasy is 'by far the most common sexual activity indulged in as such or as part of other sexual behaviours', reporting that 72 per cent of teenagers in one study admitted to having erotic fantasies. He suggests that these fantasies fulfil a number of functions in the adolescent's erotic life. They are a source of pleasurable sexual arousal. They act as a substitute for the satisfaction of unattainable or inappropriate sexual needs or goals, performing a 'compensatory, wish-fulfilment function'. Finally, they provide an opportunity for adolescents to recognize their sexual needs and preferences and to rehearse these in a way that is non-threatening for most teenagers. However, for some, erotic fantasies provoke anxieties and guilt about sexual feelings which may be perceived as perverted or forbidden. So long as sexual fantasies coexist with social sexual ties rather than as substitutes for these, they have a positive, adaptive function.

Unlike menarche, which signals teenage girls' entry into sexual maturity, we know little about the incidence of boys' wet dreams, those disconcerting, involuntary nocturnal emissions which cause so many teenage boys embarrassment and, possibly, guilt in the morning. We know a little more about masturbation – but disturbingly little, no doubt because of the stigma traditionally attached to this practice. Although in some cultures masturbation is accepted as a normal part of human sexuality, there are many cultures in which this behaviour is regarded as unacceptable. Certainly among the great religions of the world, there are prohibitions against this practice.

Western society, in the past, has maintained a strong injunction against this behaviour. At the beginning of the 20th century, physicians, including the Surgeon General of the USA, warned that masturbation was a cause of cancer, heart disease, hysteria, impotence and insanity. On the other side of the Pacific Ocean, in 1906, a review of a New Zealand Borstal institution (which spent considerable time examining the sexual health of the school's inmates) elicited the views of one eminent medical authority of the day. Dr William Henry Symes claimed that masturbation led to imbecility and epilepsy, that 75 per cent of those addicted to this filthy habit could be 'rescued from insanity and probably death' by forcible vasectomies, and that the 'moral defectives' who remained uncured should be put on an island and flogged with the cat-o'-nine-tails.

Even as late as the 1980s, a textbook on adolescent development placed the topic of masturbation in a section entitled 'Special problems of psychosexual development' (Rogers 1981). In spite of these awful dangers, many young people continued to engage, albeit surreptitiously, in this behaviour. It is not difficult to imagine the guilt, conflict, and depression caused by a seeming addiction to such a taboo and dangerous practice. More recently, there has been a shift towards greater openness and acceptance, perhaps reflecting a more general move from a focus on sex for reproduction to sex for pleasure. It is perhaps telling, however, that in popular culture on those few occasions where masturbation is the topic, it is treated as comedy rather than as a pleasurable sexual experience.

Masturbation is the most common source of orgasm in teenagers of both sexes and the source of a boy's first ejaculation in two out of three cases (Katchadourian 1990). There is evidence of a sex difference in masturbatory practices. It seems that young girls begin to masturbate at an earlier age than boys (on average about age 12 compared with age 14) but fewer girls than boys admit to this practice. Whether girls' lower rates of reporting masturbatory behaviour reflect a real difference or simply a difference in willingness to admit to a 'stigmatized' behaviour is not known. Certainly it seems that acceptance of masturbation among boys is greater than for girls. As early as the late 1940s Kinsey *et al.* (1948) reported that observation of peers masturbating was common for boys, prior to their own masturbatory experience. Most knowledge about masturbation among boys comes from their peer group. For girls, masturbation is a more closeted experience. Girls are more likely than boys to report learning about masturbation from books and magazines, or sex education in schools, and less likely to learn from peers (Leitenberg *et al.* 1993).

It is difficult to get accurate figures on masturbatory practices but several studies suggest that most boys and many girls engage in this behaviour. Consistent with changing and more liberal attitudes to a variety of sexual practices, Sorenson (1973), in his important study of adolescent sexuality, found that younger adolescents in his sample reported that they started to masturbate at an earlier age than did the older teenagers, implying a change in cultural norms. It is perhaps significant that few recent studies of adolescent sexuality have information about this topic. In one study in the 1990s, Smith *et al.* found that by age 16 the majority of boys and about 40 per cent of girls reported that they had masturbated, with boys reporting beginning at an earlier age and engaging more frequently in this activity (Smith *et al.* 1996). Interestingly, even as late as the mid-1980s, most teenagers, when asked, retained some degree of guilt about the behaviour and regarded masturbation as shameful, with fewer than one-third saying that they felt no guilt when they masturbated (Coles & Stokes 1985). It appears that teenagers' first sexual anxiety probably revolves around the experience of masturbation.

Although self-stimulation may still cause some anxiety for teenagers, the reality is that masturbation may be both enjoyable and tension-reducing and that it does not cause physical harm. What is particularly injurious is the attitude taken towards this practice. The severe condemnation expressed by many parents when they discover that their teenager (or small infant or toddler) is masturbating can be a disturbing drawback to the young person's psychosexual development. There is no indication that masturbation causes later sexual maladjustment. It may lessen parents' anxiety to know that most researchers have failed to find a relationship between ever having masturbated and engaging in sexual intercourse (Leitenberg *et al.* 1993; Smith *et al.* 1996). Indeed masturbation may have benefits. Thompson gives us a fascinating glimpse into the lives of teenage girls and the role played by earlier masturbation in preparing these young women for their first experience of sexual intercourse. These young women make masturbation part of their story of sexual experience: 'Don't know how I started – it was a combination of curiosity, as in "what does this feel like?" because I have . . . several books about the teenage body and Our Body, Our Selves, and all these things about sex. And I read about masturbation. And I was wondering what an orgasm felt like. So I decided I have to try this'. (Jenny: Thompson 1990: 351).

So masturbation can help inexperienced youngsters learn how to give and receive sexual pleasure and allow for the expression of sexual feelings without entering into a relationship for which the teenager is not emotionally ready. The fantasies associated with masturbation can help the adolescent develop a sexual identity and establish sexual preferences. As with many behaviours, however, excess is potentially problematic. In some cases masturbation may reflect adjustment problems, especially when used not just as a substitute for 'real' sex when this is unavailable but as a refuge from or replacement for satisfactory sexual relationships with peers. It may also be a problem if masturbation develops an obsessional quality, and this may be associated with disturbances of attachment that carry through to adult relationships.

The sexual context

Studies that investigate the age of sexual initiation rarely tell us much about the context in which this significant event occurs. Is early initiation related to regular and frequent subsequent sexual activity? Who are the partners of these young people? Is initiation of sexual activity voluntary? Is it a pleasurable experience or one fraught with negative emotions? It seems that having had intercourse once (and at an early age) does not necessarily mean that the young person maintains a high level of sexual activity. For some young adolescents, sexual intercourse is sporadic and rare, often a one-off experience. However, once the transition to non-virgin is made subsequent acts of intercourse are likely to follow quite quickly.

As might be expected, frequency of intercourse is still related to the nature of the relationship with one's partner – the more committed the relationship (going steady), the more frequent the sexual activity. Young girls tend to engage in fewer acts of intercourse with 'casual' partners or someone they have met for the first time than do boys and are more likely to report that sexual activity occurs with regular or steady partners (Rosenthal *et al.* 1998a; Smith *et al.* 2003a). Of course it is possible that these young girls are avoiding the socially unaccept-able role – at least for women – of taking part in 'one-night-stands' by deluding themselves that the relationship with a new partner will last and is one characterized by love and commitment. Certainly, boys seem to be more willing than girls to engage in uncommitted sex. In one recently reported study, four times as many male than female college students reported having sex with a stranger more than twice in the previous year.

It is not surprising that young women whose sexual experiences begin early report that their partners are older than themselves – on average about three years – while teenage boys report their partners to be the same age as themselves or slightly younger (Smith *et al.* 2003a). An interesting study of a representative group of young Danish late adolescents who reported on the age of their first sexual partner (Wielandt *et al.* 1989) initially confirmed the usual gender differences in partner age but subsequent analyses cast doubt on the validity of this commonly accepted pattern. The researchers were able to cross-check reports of partner age by comparing the self-reported age with the partner-reported age of sexual initiation for couples who were both engaging in sex for the first time. Assuming that self-reported age is correct, it was evident that young women perceived their partner to be older than he actually was, especially so among the youngest (16-year-old) girls. This report bias was not evident for boys. Wielandt *et al.* suggest that the systematic misreporting of the age of their male partners may be due to 'wishful thinking for an older first sexual partner', in line with societal expectations. But sex with an older partner is not always satisfactory for these young women. Abma *et al.* (1998) found that women whose first partner was more than seven years older rated the experience as substantially less pleasurable than those with partners of the same age or younger.

If we turn to the quality of adolescents' earliest experience of sexual intercourse, many young people's first act of coitus is not a pleasurable or satisfying one. Bettelheim captures something of the flavour of the experience, at least for an earlier generation of teenagers:

> American middle-class youth learns about sex in the back seat of a car, or during a slightly drunken party, or because there was nothing better to do to kill boredom . . . The first sexual experience often leaves ineffaceable impressions, marred by a total lack of experience on either side. Both partners feeling anxious and insecure, neither one can offer encouragement to the other, nor can they take comfort from the accomplished sex act, since they cannot be sure they did it well.
>
> (Bettelheim 1962: 68)

The 'surfie chick' in *Puberty Blues*, eager to be initiated into the mysteries of sex, provides a more graphic account of the experience:

Bruce was still trying to screw me. We both took off our clothes. I could see this great, hulking, looming thing in the darkness, with blonde hair and glasses. Then there was a hand on my breast. Knead. Knead. Knead . . . I didn't know how he got an erection. I didn't even know what an erection was. There was just this hard mysterious thing zooming towards me as Bruce mounted and shoved it in. Well, he tried to shove it in. He tried and tried and tried to shove it in. For half an hour he tried . . . It just wouldn't work. What a marvellous sensation! Being split up the middle! . . . I waited in agony to pass out. He gave up.

(Lette & Carey 1979: 40–1)

There is now considerable evidence that young men enjoy first sex more than young women (e.g. Sawyer & Smith 1996) and young women feel pressured by their partner to have intercourse – an important issue that we take up in a later chapter. We know from past research that many young women find the transition from 'virgin' to 'non-virgin' is accompanied by feelings of ambivalence and/or distress. Some regret having intercourse both after the event and subsequently, wishing that they had not lost their virginity at that time. Researchers in the UK survey of sexual attitudes (Wellings *et al.* 2001) found that the earlier first intercourse occurred, the more likely it was that the respondent expressed regret relating to the timing. Among those who initiated sex at age 13 or 14, 84 per cent of women and 42 per cent of men regretted having done so. Even those whose first intercourse occurred at age 17 expressed regret; one-third of these women and 12 per cent of men wished that they had delayed sex.

Among the reasons for regretting having sex and feeling guilty or anxious afterwards are the nature of societal expectations about the acceptability of teenage sexual activity. In one study Schwartz (1993) found that college women from the relatively sexually permissive Swedish culture were less likely than women from the more restrictive US culture to experience negative emotions (guilt, fear, anxiety, embarrassment, regret) after their first sexual intercourse, indicating the powerful effect of cultural norms about appropriate sexual behaviour for young people. Interestingly, many respondents reported that their experience was a positive one – it was romantic, happy, pleasurable, satisfying – suggesting that other factors intervene in determining young people's affective responses to sexual initiation. We take up this important point in later chapters.

A similar duality is shown in an engagingly titled paper, 'Putting a big thing into a little hole' in which Sharon Thompson (1990) retells stories about young girls' sexual initiation. For some, their first experience of sex was 'something that just happened' (p. 343). Their denial of sexual volition or desire is linked to traditional societal (and parental) beliefs that they should not be sexual. As Thompson notes, part of the problem is that coitus, especially among those new to it, is usually a short and unsatisfying experience. Boredom is a common response to first sex. Magazines and movies tell us that sex is romantic and wonderful; the reality for these young people is often painful and certainly uninspiring. As several young women quoted by Thompson tell us:

> It wasn't that I didn't like it. It was just kind of a letdown.

> It didn't really hurt. It hurt a little bit. It was uncomfortable. I was pretty bored actually. I didn't see anything very nice about it at all.
>
> (Thompson 1990: 346)

But for about a quarter of Thompson's young women, first sex was a pleasurable, interesting experience. For them, Thompson relates, early sexual experience is a 'voyage of discovery' (p. 351). These young women tell of being prepared for their first sexual experience, often through childhood sexual experimentation, masturbation or other explorations of their body, or through discussions with parents (usually their mother). Unlike the other young women described by Thompson, these young women knew what they wanted, and had sex at what seemed like the 'right time'. Their first sex may not have been the stuff of movies and magazine stories but they were certainly going to keep trying: 'Oh well, it didn't live up to everything that the romances say it will, but it's worth it. It was fun' (p. 356).

While earlier studies found that, on the whole, young women's (and some young men's) first coital experience is unrewarding, more recent evidence (Smith *et al.* 2003a) suggests that these attitudes may be changing. Generally, high-school students reported feeling positive after their last sexual encounter. Almost all reported that they had wanted to have sex and about half the students reported feeling extremely happy, good or loved and less commonly reported negative feelings. The majority felt not at all upset (82 per cent), used (74 per cent) or guilty (66 per cent). It is true, however, that young women were less likely than their male counterparts to endorse the 'extreme' positive response.

Finally, we know that for a substantial minority of young people the initiation of sex is not voluntary. This important issue is dealt with fully in Chapter 10 (and was noted above). Sufficient to say here that in the recent Smith *et al.* study cited above, about one-quarter of young women and young men had experienced an unwanted sexual encounter. The most common reason for this was that they were too drunk (16 per cent), too high (6 per cent) or their partner wanted them to (13 per cent). While it may be thought that unwanted sex (experienced only by young women and perpetrated by their male partners) provides an excellent example of the gendered power dynamics operating in the sexual world of young people, this study and an earlier one by Arbes-Dupuy (2000) hints at a more complex story. Arbes-Dupuy also showed that young men can be the recipients of unwanted sex, just as young women can be the perpetrators.

The complex interaction of sex and gender is discussed later as another critical influence on the sexual context in which young people enact their sexuality. Here we touch on only a small aspect of the contribution of gender to sexual behaviours. Prior to the 'sexual revolution' of the 1960s, there were strong gender differences in attitudes to premarital sex. For young girls sex was equated with love and was only acceptable in a love relationship. Adolescent boys, on the other hand, were more likely to hold permissive attitudes and be favourably disposed to casual sexual adventures. This double standard extended to virginal status at marriage. Most young boys, while wanting to be sexually experienced themselves, required their wives to be virgins at marriage. There was considerable social support for this double standard, the most prevalent view being that girls 'set the standard' for sexual behaviour and that boys have the right to 'get what they can'. Post-1960s, attitudes as well as behaviours changed. In an early study Yankelovich (1974) demonstrated a change in teen-agers' moral norms around the issue of sex. He reported an increasing consensus that abortion, homosexuality and premarital sex are not morally wrong. Later studies have substantiated these findings. Young people today consider sexuality and sexual behaviour to be a matter of private rather than public morality.

There is, however, clear evidence from a study of Australian teenagers (Moore & Rosenthal 1992) that, at least in the early 1990s, the double standard was alive and well, although unpopular, espe-cially with girls. At least half of the young people in our sample expressed a sexual ideology that reflected a belief that the sexual standards for boys were different from those for girls, a point made by Lees (1986) in her early study of British teenage girls. Girls were equally as likely as boys to hold this view, most compellingly articulated in response to questions like 'How do you feel about girls/ boys who engage in one-night-stands?' (Moore & Rosenthal 1992: 12):

> I would think she is too easy, not a slut but I would say she doesn't feel anything. [Boys?] It doesn't really bother me. It's different. People say we should be equal and the same, but the fact is it is not. For a man to have many sexual partners is okay but for a girl to have many sexual partners, she is considered pretty low and a guy is considered what a man, a stud. He has had some experience, he is great.
>
> (16-year-old girl)

Boys were more likely to be described favourably as 'studs' and girls unfavourably as 'sluts' if they engaged in casual sexual behaviour. Unlike boys, who are not judged simply in terms of their sexual activity (which in any case is likely to enhance their reputation), the social standing of girls is defined by their sexual reputation.

These issues are taken up later; the point here is that while there has been a considerable increase in the extent of teenage sexual activity, the changes in attitudes are neither as substantial nor as clear-cut as might be expected if we use behaviour as an indicator of attitudes.

Determinants of sexual behaviour

If sexual attitudes are imperfect predictors of adolescent sexual activity, what other factors help us understand young people's sexuality? This issue provides a major focus for the remainder of this book. We shall deal with the most important biological, psychological and sociological influences on sexual behaviour in later chapters. These include the impact of puberty as well as factors such as family and peer influences, and the role of cultural norms. For the present, we describe briefly some sociocultural antecedents of teenage sexual activity.

It has been suggested that sociocultural factors determine how adolescent sexuality is expressed through the cultural context which pervades the adolescent's daily life. Social institutions such as the family and religion exert their influence in three ways: they provide the norms for acceptable sexual behaviour; individuals in powerful roles in these institutions use norms as the basis for informal controls; and, finally, there are often formal rules which constrain sexual behaviour through fear of institutional sanctions. In fact, religion –

actually extent of religious belief rather than affiliation with a religion – is strongly related to teenage sexual behaviour (Devaney & Hubley 1981; Grunseit & Richters 2000; Paul *et al.* 2000). Young people who are observant of religious customs and teaching are more likely to refrain from premarital sex than their less religious peers. Those teenagers who are members of fundamentalist religions are less likely to engage in premarital sex than members of other denominations.

There is an interesting question here as to whether there is a direct influence of religion on sexual behaviour or whether the two are part of a general conservatism among some teenagers. A recent study suggests that the effect operates in two directions. More religious adolescents are less likely to engage in sexual intercourse, and adolescents who have started their sexual activity early are likely to become less interested in religion. As noted earlier, there has been a recent upsurge in abstinence approaches to young people's sexuality, particularly in the USA, supported strongly by religious groups. 'Virginity' projects like this fit well with the traditional beliefs towards sexuality prescribed in many of the world's major religions, and campaigns such as the American 'True Love Waits' have now been exported to the UK and to Australia, with some degree of acceptance.

The campaign 'pledge' is: 'Believing that true love waits, I make a commitment to God, myself, my family, my friends, my future mate, and my future children to be sexually abstinent from this day until I enter a biblical marriage relationship' (Henry 1995: 42). There have been reports of attempts to introduce this US solution to the 'sexual epidemic' to the UK's teenagers. The cutely named 'Silver Ring Thing' encourages young people to take a pledge of abstinence before marriage. A similar movement is becoming active in Australia. But, in spite of taking a pledge of sexual abstinence before marriage, a report showed that 88 per cent of 12,000 teenagers in the USA reported having sexual intercourse beforehand (Ellis & Grey 2004). 'Pledgers' also had rates of STIs comparable to their peers who did not take virginity pledges. Of particular concern is that teenagers who had signed pledges were less likely to use condoms when they became sexually active and less likely to seek medical help for symptoms of STIs. So the impact of movements such as these is not clear and, indeed, there may be a negative effect on young people's sexual decision-making.

One of the most powerful influences on adolescents' sexual experience is cultural background. Large black-white differences are regularly reported in the USA. African-American boys and girls become sexually active earlier than white adolescents and at every age more African-Americans than whites are having intercourse. The reasons for this difference are complex. Some writers believe that the socioeconomic differences between blacks and whites account for the disparity in sexual behaviour; others take a cultural norms approach, arguing that there are significant differences in the acceptability of early sexual experience. These two explanations may not be mutually exclusive. Long-term poverty may lead to different outlooks on marriage and childbearing which affect attitudes to early sexual activity. In fact, a recent survey has shown that differences between black and white adolescents persist even when a variety of social class and other social disadvantage indicators are taken into account. One factor that appeared to be important was the composition of the schools attended by these African-American teenagers. There was a higher proportion of sexually experienced African-Americans in segregated schools than in racially diverse schools. Among blacks and whites at these latter schools, there were only small differences in the likelihood of being sexually active. To some extent school segregation is a surrogate for socioeconomic status among African-Americans and reflects the pervasive nature of their social disadvantage.

There is clear evidence for the impact of cultural norms when we look at several Australian studies. Consistent with conservative cultural expectations about sex which make premarital sex an unacceptable activity for the Chinese, we found that a high proportion of young Chinese-Australian teenagers were virgins, whereas their Anglo-Celtic counterparts reported relatively high levels of sexual experience, in keeping with the more liberal views about premarital sex that exist within that culture (Rosenthal *et al.* 1990). Nevertheless, as noted above, the rate of sexual activity among Asian teenagers is increasing (Brown *et al.* 2002; Wu 2003; Youn 1996).

Of particular interest in our study was the relatively high level of sexual activity of boys of Greek descent, and the extremely low rates of premarital sex reported by the Greek girls. Both the high rate for boys and the disparity between the sexes can be explained by the greater sexual freedom given to boys in the Greek culture and the strong emphasis on chastity for girls. We found similar attitudes among younger Greek-Australian teenagers, especially in matters of chastity and fidelity and especially among girls (Moore & Rosenthal 1993: 14):

It is important for a girl to be a virgin on her wedding day. Because [if you were not a virgin] when you did get married and you tried to walk down the aisle wearing white, God would strike you down. In front of everyone!

[Virginity] is something you should take care of, something special. I think it symbolises that you are clean and that there is nothing dirty about you . . . You should keep it for your future husband even though he may have slept around.

Social class has been frequently implicated as a key factor in studies of teenage sexual behaviour (Buzwell & Rosenthal 1995). Living in poverty is associated with early sexual activity, possibly through the impact of poor life satisfaction and even poorer prospects. While many teenagers aspire to good jobs and adequate incomes with all the security that these imply, the reality is that many are trapped in a cycle of poverty. Small wonder that the perceived lack of options and desirable alternatives for the future lead some young people to increased sexual activity as a way of achieving immediate, if short-lived, pleasure. The nature of the inner-city environment may be another reason for the association between poverty and early sexual activity. Living in an environment characterized by poor and crowded housing and serious social disorganization, teenagers are often exposed to a street culture which valorizes male virility, as expressed in a variety of sexual exploits. Certainly the finding that rural youth, usually part of a close-knit homogeneous culture, are less sexually experienced than their urban peers may be interpreted as resulting at least in part from the diffusion of a sense of community among urban young people as well as the increased opportunities for sexual activity.

A final influence to which we briefly allude here is that of education. It seems that higher levels of educational achievement and clear educational goals are related to delayed premarital sex for both boys and girls, as is positive adjustment. The association between educational outcomes and sexual behaviour is mediated by a number of factors including those discussed above. The achieving student is likely to come from a relatively well-to-do family, to place a high value on achievement, to be more goal-oriented and able to plan for the future. All these characteristics may lead to a low likelihood of sexual involvement at an early age. Perhaps involvement in a sexual relationship distracts young people from their studies and, conversely, involvement in studies makes teenagers less interested in a sexual relationship.

We have by no means exhausted the sociocultural factors which are associated with early sexual teenage activity nor have we attempted here anything more than a brief description and a limited explanation of the effects of these factors. Later chapters will place these and other influences in the context of the adolescent's struggle to develop a sense of his or her sexual identity. For now we turn to one other aspect of sexual behaviour which is a source of particular concern, in the light of the increases in activity that have been reported.

Responsible sex? Contraception and STI prevention

The increased sexual activity among teenagers has led to concerns about young women's heightened risk of unwanted pregnancies and, more recently, the dangers of STIs, especially the frightening and lethal disease of AIDS. We might expect, in the light of these threats to adolescents' well-being and sexual health, that young people would have adopted contraceptive methods – and particularly condoms – with great alacrity. What do the figures on contraceptive use show? Alarmingly, whether we take as a measure contraceptive use at first intercourse or the extent to which contraceptives are ever used, there is evidence that many adolescents are ignoring (or not receiving) sexual health messages. This is especially so in developing countries or countries where there is a pervasive impact of poverty and lack of knowledge (Eaton *et al.* 2003; Holschneider & Alexander 2003).

We do not deal here with the wide range of contraceptive techniques available today, although the rates of unwanted pregnancies among teenagers indicate that their contraceptive practices leave them vulnerable. We take up this issue in Chapter 9; here we focus on young people's use of condoms, in the context of increasing rates of STIs, and the continuing threat of HIV/AIDS. Although there has been a considerable increase in young people's acceptance of condoms during the past decade, recent studies of condom use across many countries show that many young people use them inconsistently or not at all (Holschneider & Alexander 2003; Rosenthal *et al.* 1998b; Smith *et al.* 2003a; Sneed *et al.* 2001). In one study of sexually active young people in South Africa, 50 to 60 per cent reported never using condoms (Eaton *et al.* 2003).

The increase in condom use rates appears to have occurred largely because most young people now use condoms 'sometimes'. The meaning of this is complex from the point of view of adolescent sexual health. On the positive side it indicates increased exposure to condoms and the potential for improved skill in negotiating their use. But protection is not consistent. Young people are being influenced by situational factors that occur in sexual encounters, such as high arousal, alcohol and drug use, partner reluctance, making judgements about particular partners ('this partner looks too good to be diseased', 'this partner is someone I love therefore must be safe') and/or sexual situations (bodily fluids are not going to be exchanged in this sexual situation i.e. withdrawal is practised) which lead them to reject the need to use condoms. The most common reason for girls' failure to use condoms was that they were on the contraceptive pill (Moore *et al.* 1996). Some researchers have investigated common misconceptions about condoms (such as the use of Vaseline – which is likely to damage the condom – as a lubricant) and the relationship between these and condom use (Crosby & Yarber 2001), concluding that experience with condoms is an effective counter to these misconceptions. Of concern was the finding by Rosenthal *et al.* (1990) that a small but significant number of students had taken part in anal sex with a regular or casual partner without using a condom, a finding in line with that of Breakwell and Fife-Schaw (1994) in the UK.

However, it is interesting that young people make a distinction between casual and regular partners, and there is evidence to suggest that sexual practices are modified accordingly. Overall, young people, and especially young women, engage in less risky behaviours with casual partners than with regular partners (Abbott 1988; Crawford *et al.* 1990; Rosenthal & Moore 1991; Wyn & Stewart 1991). For example, Abbott's study of adolescent girls in Canberra showed that 55 per cent believed that having sex only with a steady boyfriend was a safe sex option, and this was the main change they had made to protect themselves. But only a very short time span need elapse before a relationship is considered 'steady' and it is a concern that such an indiscriminate, flexible transition point may determine young women's use of condoms.

With greater sexual experience the responsibility for contraception falls on the young woman. There is evidence that many young people stop using condoms when the female partner is on the pill (Kirkman *et al.* 1998a; Lindsay *et al.* 1997; Smith & Rosenthal 1998). Unfortunately the disease prevention role of condoms is either not recognized or is forgotten in favour of protection from pregnancy. It is interesting to speculate about the reason(s) for discarding condoms when the pill is used. It seems that young people are subject to two potentially conflicting discourses around sexual health that are related to condom use. The 'safe sex' discourse is a recent phenomenon, arising out of the HIV/AIDS pandemic. This discourse emphasizes the use of condoms for protection against STIs and HIV. The other discourse ('pregnancy prevention') has been around a lot longer. The

emphasis here is on effective contraception rather than disease prevention and the best way to ensure this is by using a contraceptive pill.
The problem for many young people is that these two become
conflated. Safe sex (no exchange of bodily fluids) equals contraception, but the converse doesn't hold. In one interview study (Kirkman
et al. 1998a) it was common to hear young people insist that their
peers would always use condoms only to realize later in the interview
that they were silently exempting those occasions on which the young
woman was using another contraceptive. Jane answered unequivocally 'yes' to the question whether young people she knew would
use condoms every time they had sexual intercourse. But she added:
'Depending on whether they didn't want to – and whether the girl's
on the pill and they were in a steady relationship . . . and they didn't
want to use one. But otherwise most people would use them'. Other
young people defined safe sex as 'contraception'. One boy, in response
to a question about whether there were sexual issues of concern to
young people like him replied: 'Safe sex mainly, because none of them
want to get pregnant or anything, because most of my friends want to
go on to further education' (Kirkman *et al.* 1998b).

It seems that the term 'safe sex' has been hijacked to mean contraception. Part of the responsibility for this is that the condom has long
been used for contraception and it is only recently that the condom
has been grafted on to the notion of safe sex, namely disease prevention. It shouldn't surprise us that young people, for most of whom
HIV is an abstract 'not-me' phenomenon, have taken the 'condom for
safe sex' message and incorporated it into their own reality – the more
likely danger of unwanted pregnancy.

A number of studies have drawn attention to problems arising from
the inconsistent contraceptive behaviour of male teenagers, their
apparent lack of concern about contraception, and the tendency for
some young girls to rely on the 'contraceptive vigilance' of their
partners. Why are so many young people, especially males, resistant
to contraception? When effective methods of contraception are
readily available and the dangers of unprotected sex, both in terms of
unwanted pregnancies and of potentially lethal or at least debilitating
disease are known to teenagers, why are they so cavalier in their use of
this technology?

There are a number of reasons for contraceptive risk-taking among
adolescents. They may be ignorant about the need for contraception,
they may not know how to use contraceptives, or they may be lacking
in the skills necessary to go about the often embarrassing or difficult
process of gaining access to contraceptive advice and devices. Even

with the appropriate knowledge and skills, teenagers may not like the idea of using contraception or, at best, feel ambivalent about this 'intrusion' into their sexual life. Finally there may be overwhelming structural barriers to contraceptive use. If access to contraception is difficult or if the cost of contraception is beyond the reach of the adolescent then it is likely that, even with the best intentions, contraceptive use will be minimal or absent. Among Latino adolescents in one study, lack of availability and 'didn't think of it' were two most commonly cited reasons for failure to use a condom at first intercourse (Sneed *et al.* 2001).

Another factor which makes decisions about contraception difficult is the often sporadic nature of adolescent sexual activity. Unlike most adult sexual behaviour, teenagers' forays into sexual intercourse are likely to be inconsistent and marked by long periods with no activity. This makes the choice of contraceptive difficult, with 'female' options such as the pill or IUD non-optimal, and the condom a more logical option. But, as we shall see, there are barriers to making this apparently reasonable choice. Concerns about STIs add further complexity to the decision about which contraceptive to use.

One way of understanding contraceptive behaviour in the light of the many possible barriers to contraceptive use is to turn the problem on its head. What factors must be present for adequate contraceptive behaviour to occur? Urberg (1982), drawing from the problem-solving literature, suggests that there are five major steps in the process. First, the individual must recognize that pregnancy (or disease) is a likely outcome of unprotected sex. Next, he or she must be motivated to do something about this. This step involves the belief that one needs to, and can do, something effective as well as the belief that the possible outcome is undesirable. Third, the individual must be able to generate possible solutions to the problem; fourth, these solutions must be evaluated and one chosen; and finally, the chosen solution must be implemented. Each of these steps in the decision-making process is a necessary but not sufficient condition for effective contraceptive use.

How knowledgeable are adolescents about their bodies and the reproductive process and about the relationship between sexual activity and disease? What evidence is there that this knowledge has an impact on adolescents' use of contraceptives? The answer to the first question is encouraging. Many studies have shown that most teenagers, even young ones, have some understanding of conception and how their bodies work, they know that a girl can become pregnant if she has intercourse, and older teenagers are reasonably well informed about contraception. STIs present a different picture. With the exception of HIV/AIDS, teenagers have surprisingly little knowledge of STIs, or of their methods of transmission and ways of avoiding infection. In one study conducted by the authors, more than 50 per cent of a group of Australian university students (mostly young women) had never heard of chlamydia and more than one-quarter had not heard of gonorrhoea. Yet concern about the AIDS epidemic and its potential threat to the well-being of young, sexually active people has led to high levels of knowledge about the importance of 'safe sex' and the role of condoms in minimizing the risk of HIV infection.

For those young people who lack the appropriate knowledge, the solution may appear simple. Contraceptive use can be increased by increasing knowledge. But even when adolescents seem to have adequate knowledge it is clear that effective contraception does not always follow. There is considerable evidence that adolescents do not always have high levels of motivation to contracept. One characteristic that has been attributed to adolescents is the 'personal fable' – a belief that nothing bad or undesirable (including pregnancy or sexually transmitted disease) will happen to them. This perceived invulnerability to nasty events has been well documented in the case of pregnancy (Urberg 1982) and STIs (Moore & Rosenthal 1991a) and is associated with an increase in sexual risk-taking. Another important motivating force is the sense of control that one has over life events. Gendered perceptions of power play a prominent role in young people's beliefs about their ability to control their sexuality, as we shall see in a later chapter. Suffice to say here that many young women feel that they have little power to call the tune when it comes to sexual activity.

Somewhat related to this is the idea of self-efficacy or confidence in dealing with contraception. For those teenagers who have little confidence in their ability to purchase condoms or go to the doctor for a prescription for the pill, contraception looms as an almost insurmountable hurdle to negotiate. Even in this enlightened age when condoms are advertised widely as an important means of avoiding HIV/AIDS and other STIs and are readily available in vending machines, almost half of our teenage respondents, both boys and girls, reported low levels of confidence in dealing with these matters. Such difficulties are likely to lead to avoidance of contraception, putting it in the 'too hard' basket.

Among those teenagers for whom contraception is a perceived option, attitudes vary. For some, using contraception is inconsistent with a view that sex is, or should be, spontaneous and unpremeditated. It is perhaps surprising that in one study young men were more accepting of condoms than young women (Moore & Rosenthal 1991b). For girls even in today's more enlightened climate there is a high psychological cost in acknowledging that they are prepared for casual sex (as might be assumed by the practice of ongoing contraception, such as taking the pill or carrying around a condom 'in case'). Other young people find contraception to be 'messy' or 'unnatural'. Still others say that it interferes with the enjoyment of sex.

Showers in raincoats?

One familiar complaint from both boys and girls is that using condoms is like having 'showers in raincoats' (Moore & Rosenthal 1993: 19):

> They are necessary, but I think they are disgusting things – quite awful.
>
> (16-year-old boy)

> I personally hate the things, they are uncomfortable. They can be fun but it is just a hassle. You start getting into it and you have to stop and put them on. It is less exciting because you have to start all over again.
>
> (16-year-old boy)

> They're alright but I don't really like them. I know they are useful but they say it is like wearing a raincoat and is not enjoyable.
>
> (16-year-old girl)

Most negative attitudes are directed towards male contraceptive methods, an unfortunate view since condoms are an optimal method of contraception among teenagers, certainly at first intercourse. While some enlightened boys today accept that the possible price for not using condoms is too high, for others the benefits do not outweigh the costs. This cost-benefit analysis has been shown to determine young boys' condom use. For example, if they believed that it was the male's responsibility to prevent pregnancy, young boys were more likely to use condoms. If they believed that their partner was on the pill, or that pleasure would be reduced, condom use was inhibited.

Even if a teenager wants to use contraception, the decision usually has to be negotiated with the sexual partner except in those cases where the female has made the decision to use the pill or other long-term devices such as an IUD. Here it is essential that the couple have the social skills which will enable open communication of their wishes and needs. Studies of teenage communication about sexuality and contraception reveal that many teenagers fail to discuss these important issues during a sexual encounter. Girls are particularly diffident about initiating contraception discussions, their lack of assertiveness leaving them vulnerable when their partner is resistant to the use of contraceptives. There is some evidence that girls are expected by boys to take the responsibility for contraception, an expectation which may be unrealistic when considered in the context of the difficulties girls face in asserting their sexual needs. Even when both partners have the best of intentions there can be failure to contracept. Many of our teenagers reported non-use of condoms during a specific sexual encounter, in spite of their previous intention to have 'safe' sex.

What is going on here? With increased exposure to messages about contraception, particularly condoms, in the media and through sexual health programmes in schools, and with increasingly easy access to contraceptives, at point of sale and through family planning clinics, we might expect to see most teenagers acting responsibly in their contraceptive behaviour. Yet this is not the case. Why? Everything we know tells us that much of teenage sex is unplanned and that explanations of teenage sexual behaviour do not fit easily into rational decision-making or problem-solving models of the sort proposed by Urberg and others. At best these give an idealized and partial explanation of the behaviour in question. What needs to be taken into account is the situationally determined and urgent nature of adolescent sex. What sort of relationship does the teenager have with his or her partner? Is it a 'long standing' sexual relationship or a casual 'one-night-stand'? Do alcohol or drugs play a part in the encounter? How sexually aroused are the partners? To what extent are they able to control their sexual urges in the absence of contraception? All these questions and many more need to be asked and answered before we can understand why adolescents fail to take adequate precautions against pregnancy or disease.

A contextual framework

Adolescent sexuality is subject to a complex web of influences, including the physical and psychological characteristics of the individual, the historical period and the ecological setting. The decisions that young people make about their sexuality, the behaviours they engage in, the values and attitudes that they hold – all these are shaped by the particular context in which the adolescent lives his or her life. At any given time, choices about sexual behaviour will reflect the different physical, social, cultural and economic environments in which adolescents live and their personal qualities and life histories. Given the diversity of experiences that young people draw on consciously or unconsciously in determining their sexual behaviours, it is not surprising that we find a remarkable heterogeneity in those behaviours.

Because the choices made by adolescents flow on and affect their sexual well-being as adults, we need to understand the inconsistencies as well as the consistencies in young people's sexual behaviour, the commonalities as well as the differences, and the rational as well as the non-rational bases for that behaviour. Adolescents must make important decisions about sexuality which will reverberate throughout their lives. In this chapter we have considered several of those decisions: the decision whether or not to initiate sexual behaviour and, if sexually active, whether or not to use contraception; the decision about the timing and nature of relationships; and acceptable sexual practices. All these decisions are made in the context of what the adolescent feels is right and proper for him or her to endorse. For some adolescents, there is little difficulty in making these decisions. For others the choices are hard to evaluate. We let two of our 16-year-old girls speak for themselves on the issue of premarital sex (Moore & Rosenthal 1993: 21):

> I think I am a pretty modern girl. I don't believe that you actually have to be married [to have sex]. But you can't do it with anyone. It has to be someone you really love and trust. Someone you have been seeing for a really long time.

> You shouldn't have to wait until you get married to have sex, because people don't get married until they are about twenty-five or something, and you can't be married to the same guy all your life and only have sex with him. You have got to have sex with a few different people.

2 Theoretical approaches: not just what but why?

Coping with sexuality is one of life's essential developmental tasks. In this chapter, we examine theoretical perspectives on the role of young people's emerging sexual behaviours, feelings and attitudes. Literature, history and social science tell us that adolescence is a time of developing sexual attractions to others often accompanied by high emotional intensity and behaviours directed towards coping with these emotions. The role of theory is to assist us in explaining commonalities and differences in these feelings and behaviours, between individuals, groups, cultures and across historical time.

Commonalities are not restricted to biological changes. For example, cultural beliefs about acceptable and unacceptable ways for young people to express their sexuality are usually quite prescriptive, even in sexually liberal cultures. Widmer *et al.* (1998) compared sexual attitudes in 24 different countries and noted that all shared beliefs such as the incest taboo, condemnation of adultery and concerns about regulating sex outside marriage. In addition, concerns about timing and nature of the first sexual encounter and about both sexual licence by and sexual exploitation of young people are shared across nations, cultures and social groupings.

But a good theory of sex must also explain a huge range of differences in sexual beliefs and behaviours. Widmer *et al.* (1998) noted wide cultural differences, even within the developed western world, of attitudes towards value of virginity, the appropriate age to become sexually active and the acceptability of homosexuality.

What accounts for these cultural differences? And within cultures, how are individual differences and gender differences explained – for example, the well-established gender differences in frequency of masturbation and desire for and engagement in casual sex (Oliver & Hyde 1993)? Can non-normative as well as normative sexual preference be adequately explained? Why is sex mostly associated with positive feelings but sometimes linked with aggression and exploitation? Why have taboos and prohibitions built up towards some modes of sexual expression and not others? How do we explain the rituals of court- ship, and their variations across time and place?

To take just one example, the challenge of explaining the different patterns of flirtation and desire in *Little Women* and *Sex in the City* must surely go beyond recourse to simple (or even complex) biological explanations. Biology of course must have its place. There is no denying that one of the basic themes of human history is the desire to mate, and biological explanations of sex drive, sexual development and sex differences play an important part in our understanding of these phenomena. Nevertheless, there are clearly limitations to biology in explaining both 'common knowledge' and research findings in the sexuality domain.

A good theory is usually defined as based on the results of obser- vations and experiments – its propositions amenable to empirical testing, credible in the light of existing knowledge and useful in pre- dicting new knowledge. The theory is more likely to be testable if its concepts are well defined and measurable. The explanations for phenomena should be as simple as possible while still encompassing all the known data. This is Occam's razor – the idea that the simplest logical explanation of any given phenomena should prevail. Theor- etical assumptions – the underlying beliefs on which the theory is based – while not always testable, should at least be overt, so that they can be examined in the light of both science and other processes we use for assessing truth, such as morality and justice. For example, a theory of sexuality that had as an underlying assumption that homosexuality is deviant in the sense of 'bad' as opposed to the sense of non- normative, might lead to propositions which could be supported by empirical evidence (e.g. that homosexuals tend to be marginalized in society). However, we might reject the theory on the grounds that we disagree with the assumptions, rather than disagree with the evidence.

Two major theoretical groupings have been noted among resear- chers interested in the development of sexuality (DeLamater & Hyde 1998). These two groups – essentialists and social constructionists – differ in their theoretical assumptions about the basic explanations for human variability and constancy in matters sexual. Essentialism consists, according to DeLamater and Hyde, of a 'belief that certain phenomena are natural, inevitable and biologically determined' (p. 10). Examples of essentialist theories, according to these authors, are biological, evolutionary, genetic, endocrine, brain function and sociobiological approaches to sexual research. Some psychological theories of sex fit squarely into this camp, such as Freud's 'anatomy is destiny' approach in which a person's sexual nature 'rolls out' with physiological maturity. Although some environmental events may act as triggers or facilitators of change, most of the stimulus for development comes from internal processes. Context is relevant but not pivotal in explaining human nature, according to these theories. For example we learn from our environment, but the direction of learning will be consistent across time and culture, because of the biological underpinnings of human behaviour.

DeLamater and Hyde contrast essentialism with social constructionism, the 'belief that reality is socially constructed' (p. 10), with language playing a major role in the interpretation of experience. What is 'true' about human behaviour in one context is not necessarily 'true' in another. In these frameworks, the power of biology arises from how it is interpreted; it does not have meaning in itself. Social constructionists therefore might interpret sexual orientation (or even gender) as arising out of interactions between people, the way we use language and the 'discourses' or underlying assumptions, of a culture. In these theories, context is the lead player in the drama of how humans unfold, not just a supporting actor. Gagnon and Simon's (1973) notion of 'sexual scripts' is an example of a social constructionist approach to sexuality. Sexual scripts refer to the social prescriptions for sexual behaviour that exist in any society (both explicit and implicit), and the ways we behave in accordance with these prescriptions. Every culture develops scripts for how to behave during courting, for what characteristics are assessed as attractive and desirable in the opposite sex, and generally for how to behave as a man or a woman. The scripts are described as so pervasive that they can program our desires, even reshaping biology to a greater or lesser extent, according to the social constructionists.

We discuss here examples of both essentialist and social constructionist theories of sexuality, and make some evaluation of how they contribute to our understanding of adolescent sexuality.

Essentialist theories

Within essentialist theories, different emphases are given to the relative importance of nature and nurture. Biological approaches stress the role of physiology and hormones in shaping the experience of adolescence. These ideas are discussed in detail in Chapter 3. Evolutionary theories, discussed briefly below, interpret human sexual response as relating to deep-seated drives for survival of the species, while psychoanalytic theories use different metaphors to explain such sexual motivation and behaviour.

Evolutionary theories of sexuality: it's all in your genes

Evolutionary theories of sexuality propose that the driving force behind sexual behaviour is species survival – not individual pleasure or social gain but a hard-wired predisposition to keep the human race viable. By 'hard-wired' we mean innate tendencies that have been bred into the species because these tendencies optimize human survival, or at least they once did. Predominant forms of sexual behaviour are said to have developed because they are successful from a reproductive point of view, and these behavioural strategies are postulated to shape many of our sexual attitudes and customs. The major strategy put forward by evolutionary theorists, beginning with Darwin (1871), is the notion of sexual selection. This refers to the evolution of characteristics that give humans reproductive advantage; that is, they are concerned with species survival rather than only individual survival. Success at winning the right to mate with a chosen member of the opposite sex, either through being more attractive than competing members or more powerful to fight off competitors, leads to reproductive advantage. 'Selected' characteristics might include those that signal higher levels of fertility or childbearing capacity (e.g. 'childbearing hips', full breasts, youthfulness) or those that assist in aggressive competition (e.g. developed musculature) for mating partners. Even though our social situation has changed enormously since the days of prehistoric peoples, evolutionary processes work exceedingly slowly, so the theory claims that we are still largely constrained in our mating patterns by these factors. Maladaptive tendencies, for example attraction to infertile partners, are likely to drop out over the course of evolution, but because evolution is so slow, social changes are unlikely to impinge on our biological/evolutionary predispositions unless they persist over millennia.

A further factor proposed to influence sexual selection is 'parental investment' (Trivers 1972), the effort put into ensuring that offspring survive to maturity. Trivers argued that females will be more choosy about who they mate with because they invest more in parenting. They will favour mating partners who appear to have 'good' genes (such as might be evidenced in health and strength), and who are more likely provide protection and support during major periods of parental investment, such as when children are babies. Males will be more competitive in seeking mating access to partners who provide the best chances of numerous offspring of high quality, and also are likely to provide high parental investment in those offspring (and so give them a high chance of reaching maturity).

More recently, Buss and Schmitt (1993) developed these ideas into 'sexual strategies theory'. A major proposition is that men will devote a larger proportion of their total mating effort to short-term mating than will women, because the minimum level of parental investment is far greater for women than men, by circumstances of biology (e.g. requirements of gestation and lactation). Women can only bear a limited number of infants – their evolutionary 'best strategy' is to ensure those infants are healthy, nurtured and protected. Men can, however, potentially father a very large number of children; only some of these need survive for evolutionary success. Therefore, for men, reproductive success will be maximized through more partners, choice of partners who are readily sexually accessible, fertile, and in whom only minimum commitment and investment is needed (so that the man can move on to the next partner). Youth, attractiveness, health, and a liberal approach to sexuality act as markers (not always reliable ones) for these characteristics. For women, reproductive success will be maximized not through number of partners, but through choice of a partner of high quality (liable to pass on adaptive genes, such as those associated with strength, intelligence and attractiveness), and who is able and willing to invest resources into the partnership on a long-term basis (to enable the protection and nurturance of children). Access to resources, certain personality characteristics (e.g. generosity, trustworthiness) as well as health, strength and attractiveness are clues to assist in these choices.

The theory is successful in predicting or explaining many aspects of human sexuality (Schmitt *et al.* 2003), although critics have argued that a social learning approach, which emphasizes conditioning, behavioural rewards/disincentives and imitation/modelling, could predict many or most of these just as well (Eagly & Wood 1999; Hogben & Dyrne 1998). It is successful in explaining many of the male-female differences in sexual behaviour and attitudes, for example differences in attitudes to and participation in casual sex and infidelity (Oliver & Hyde 1993), but it is less successful in explaining the huge range of individual differences within the sexes with respect to sexual behaviour, for example same-sex attraction and female infidelity. Evolutionary theory is also good at predicting what type of person will be considered 'attractive' – but here again, there are huge social and cultural differences (and differences across time) that are not readily explained. One important feature of the evolutionary theory of mating is perhaps to remind us that our sexual behaviour, the type of person we are attracted to and even our sexual attitudes, are not always under rational conscious control, and indeed may be influenced by ancient and primitive drives. This is something to keep in mind as we try to understand some of the more erratic aspects of adolescent behaviour, given that for young people, part of the task of coping with their developing sexuality involves learning restraint and control of these 'primitive' urges. The psychosexual theorists, discussed next, conceptualize this struggle as played out at a mental as well as a physical level, through their postulation of an 'unconscious' aspect to mind.

The psychosexual theorists: taming the savage beast within

No discussion about adolescent sexuality can omit the influential and early work of psychoanalytic theory. Although rarely used as a basis for current psychological research, psychoanalytic theory has captured popular imagination. Its interpretive frameworks are often employed in literary fiction, biography, art and drama, particularly when the topic is sexuality. The major theorists writing about adolescence from a psychosexual perspective, Sigmund Freud, Anna Freud and Peter Blos, attached great significance to the impact of sexual drives on the psychological functioning of the person. All three viewed the onset of adolescence as a difficult time psychologically because of the increased strength of these drives. This occurs concurrently with the adolescent's developing physical capacities to actually carry out sexual wishes and fantasies – which may come into conflict with social and internalized taboos.

Freud (1924, 1935, 1950, 1953) brought the study of sex into the mainstream with three important ideas. First, he postulated that all behaviours, thoughts and feelings are motivated by biological urges or drives that are mostly unconscious. The sex drive or libido was seen as paramount among these urges. This drive was broader than just the urge to have sex, but involved all desires related to bonding with others and experiencing positive and sensual stimulation. Second, Freud's notion of the unconscious presented a framework for understanding why we sometimes (or often) believe or act in ways that are not consistent with our justificatory statements or logical analyses. This was especially important in trying to explain aspects of sexuality – sexual attraction, sexual beliefs and sexual behaviours – which can appear to defy our rational understanding or even our will. Third, Freud postulated that we develop psychologically through a series of psychosexual stages, each focusing on different bodily functions. Psychosexual development culminates after puberty, at the genital stage.

Freud believed that the psychological conflicts experienced by adolescents and adults arise from failure to satisfy or to express specific wishes during childhood. At any of the childhood stages, sexualized impulses may be so frustrated (or so overwhelmingly gratified) that the person continues to seek gratification of those wishes at later life stages. This is termed 'fixation'. So, for example, anxiety about sexuality in adolescence may lead to a return to oral gratifications, such as binge eating, or to anal concerns expressed as rebelliousness or extreme untidiness. During adolescence, the strength of these fixations and the ability to sublimate and channel sexual drives in acceptable ways will jointly crystallize into the adolescent's life orientation, including their unique pattern of sexual adjustment.

In spite of legitimate questioning of Freud's understanding of sexuality, for example criticism of his research methods and male-oriented perspectives, we should recognize the insights that he has offered about human behaviour in general and sexuality in particular. Freud moved the study of human sexuality to a forefront position for psychologists, opening the way for its legitimacy as a focus for research. He popularized the idea of the unconscious, giving us greater understanding that we can be influenced by motives that we do not always recognize. Nevertheless, many of his concepts were untestable or have not stood up to the scrutiny of more rigorous research.

Anna Freud, Sigmund's daughter, continued her father's work but focused her research energies on adolescent development. She argued that sexual development in adolescence occurs in an atmosphere of unconscious turbulence, which is often reflected in disturbed thoughts and behaviours. Because the hormonal upsurge of puberty leads to an increase in sex drives and this in turn leads to a reawakening and reworking of all the infantile unconscious conflicts, there can be no emotionally painless initiation into adolescence. In fact, one of Anna Freud's most influential articles is entitled 'Adolescence as a developmental disturbance' (1969).

Perhaps the most influential adolescent theorist using a psychoanalytic framework, Blos (1962, 1988) described adolescence as the second individuation process. Adolescent individuation is about learning to sever some of the emotional ties with parents – the recognition that emotional and sexual needs must be met from outside the family. According to Blos, this process has a sense of urgency emanating from the strength of drives, but it is also accompanied by feelings of isolation, loneliness and confusion, so that conflict and swings of emotion are inevitable. Romanticism and falling in love are common as there is a need for these new relationships to replace the intensity of family ties and the feelings of loss that ensue. It is as if teenage romantic love occurs as a rebound from the lost and taboo relationships with family. Like all psychoanalytic theorists, Blos views the physical changes of puberty and the development of mature sexuality as inevitably tied up with conflict and as underlying psychological adjustment at a more pervasive level.

Each of these theorists paints a picture of adolescence as a period in which high levels of unconscious conflict must, perforce, spill over into consciousness. Sexuality is viewed as the basis for this turbulence. Resolution of conflicts is dependent on the development of good coping mechanisms that, in turn, depend on childhood experiences and the adequacy with which earlier conflicts are resolved. Adult maturity and adjustment, in general as well as in the sexual domain, depend heavily on the successful course of adolescence and the young person's ability to learn new coping strategies and to modify child-hood defences. Successful outcomes for men and women are hypo-thesized to be different, as adjustment is measured by these theorists in terms of taking on traditionally defined masculine or feminine roles.

Erikson and adolescent identity

Erikson (1959, 1963, 1968) has had a powerful influence on thinking about adolescence, particularly through his concept of 'identity formation'. His extension of psychoanalytic theories, although taking some account of the social context, still adopts the position that 'anatomy is destiny'. Great importance is attributed to the role of puberty, the upsurge of sex drives and the differences in psychological development of the sexes. However, Erikson does place greater emphasis than the psychosexual theorists on the influence of cultural factors. Erikson postulates that psychological development proceeds through a series of stages across the life span, each stage characterized by a major crisis or conflict to be worked through and resolved. For Erikson, establishing a sense of identity – by which he means a coherent sense of self – is the major task of adolescence. Adolescents who move satisfactorily through this stage have an inner confidence about who they are and where they are going. One important aspect of identity formation is learning to be comfortable with one's body and sexuality. Others involve choice of occupation, establishing values and finding adult ways to relate to friends and family. Erikson argues that sexuality is an important aspect of identity formation for both sexes. By this he means coping with the bodily changes of puberty, developing a sexual ideology, and consolidating one's sex role and sexual orientation. However, it is only at the next stage of young adulthood, labelled 'intimacy versus isolation', that true heterosexual intimacy is established. This is marked by compromise, sharing of goals and 'the experience of the climactic mutuality of orgasm'.

Adolescent falling in love and sexual experimentation is described as contributing to the quest for self-definition, rather than an indicator of true intimacy. Erikson talks about youthful romance as 'projecting one's diffused self-image on another and seeing it thus reflected and gradually clarified' (1968: 132). He cautions against pressure on young people to make permanent commitments too early in life, before an adequate sense of personal identity has been established. When the young person's potential for exploration has been closed off too soon (e.g. by responsibilities like marriage and family), the relationships formed may not survive the test of later personal development of the individuals within the couple. Exploration of self is seen as an important preliminary of genuine intimacy.

One point at issue relates to Erikson's insistence that successful maturation results from a developmental sequence in which identity develops prior to resolution of the intimacy versus isolation conflict. Support for Erikson's position came from early studies such as Orlofsky *et al.* (1973). They found greater capacity for intimate relationships among young people with more fully formed identities. They labelled as 'pseudo-intimate' those with immature identity development who described a particular relationship as central to their lives. These relationships did not appear to be characterized by a high degree of mutuality and were likely to be one-sided and based on overcoming personal deficit ('I am nothing without him').

Of course the route through these stages of development may take different directions for different individuals. Some young people stress the importance of their interpersonal skills in working through both the intimacy and identity stages; for others the interpersonal skills lag behind as individuality develops through mastery and autonomy. The issue of sexual adjustment is one which clearly involves both self-understanding and the ability to relate sensitively to others, so that in Erikson's terms, successful identity and intimacy achievement are important, whatever their mode or pathway of development.

Criticisms of Erikson's model of adolescent development largely concern the separate development hypothesized for boys and girls and his assumption of heterosexuality as the universal goal of mature sexuality. Another attack comes from writers who question the universality and importance of identity development. It has been suggested that issues of identity are paramount only for adolescents from affluent, middle-class groups whose cultural values support individuality, and for adolescents in these groups who are highly intelligent and have the freedom and opportunities to choose the directions their lives will take. It certainly may be the case that aspects of identity formation such as career choice are not relevant to all adolescents. But learning to cope with sexuality and to place sexuality within the context of one's self-identity is an essential task for all adolescents.

Summary of essentialist views

Essentialist theories of sexuality emphasize the crucial role of genetics, hormones, anatomy and other aspects of biological functioning in determining our behaviour. Such theories, while not negating the role of environment in shaping some aspects of the human sexual repertoire, stress the constancy of many features, such as basic sexual drives and motivations. These biological constancies are seen to have implications for sexual behaviour, such as the differential and stereotyped behaviours of men and women, the type of people we are attracted to and, at adolescence, the inevitability of conflict and stress as the hormonal changes swing into play. But these days, even biologically oriented theorists may argue against a purely biologically deterministic perspective on adolescent sexual behaviour (e.g. Halpern 2003). Halpern states that to date, only relatively modest biological effects on adolescent sexuality have been found in research studies, with the variance accounted for in regression models typically ranging between 3 and 5 per cent. It is to a consideration of social factors therefore that we now turn.

Social constructionist interpretations of sexuality

Social constructionist models of adolescent sexuality are by their very nature time- and culture-dependent, emphasizing notions of relative truth. These models postulate that language or discourse provides the basis on which we make sense of the world. Language provides us with the categories that we use to classify events and persons and the means by which we interpret new experience. Because language varies across cultures and even social groups within a culture, it is argued that experience, too, will vary.

Foucault (1978) is perhaps the most famous theorist who has applied social constructionist ideas to sexuality. He argues that sexuality is not merely a biological drive whose character is the same across time and culture, but a social construct. Its meaning is derived from language; each institution in society has a discourse about sex, a way of thinking and talking about the broad array of behaviours and people who are involved in sexual expression. For example, for sexual bodily parts and sexual activity, we have a 'coarse language', a 'romantic language' and a 'scientific language' – possibly others as well. Which one we use will shape our experiences and how others interpret us. The inability to shift from one mode to another will provide us with reduced experiential options.

Various writers have described the sexual behaviours typical of different cultures and attempted to account for these behavioural differences through analysis of prevailing cultural norms and the way these norms are conveyed in language. Some of these norms are explicit and open, with clear guidelines about their enactment. One example of this relates to laws about the age of consent. Other norms are expressed by group members but not necessarily adhered to. For example, in our society we may openly deplore sexual violence, yet much of this behaviour occurs without censure, particularly in a domestic context. There are also instances of conflict between the mores and norms of subgroups within a particular society. While an older generation may value sexual restraint and deplore permissiveness, the younger generation may hold a different view, valuing experimentation and sexual liberalism. As one 15-year-old Italian-Australian girl says:

> My parents were engaged to each other when they were really really young, about 12 or 13. Sex before marriage – no way! It is just the things they believe in, and they put it across to you . . . you just know that is the way you are supposed to act. I don't think I will be like my parents. I will try hard not to be like them.

To confuse the matter further, many social norms and values are implicit and not articulated well or even at all. As a result it may not be possible for many to express clearly what the rule is or why it exists, although the consequences of non-adherence may be severe. An analysis of appropriate courting behaviour in our society provides a good example of this issue. What is meant by 'coming on too strong', for example, and how is it that some individuals can get away with certain sexual overtures while others would be rejected if they engaged in similar behaviours? When is a woman too sexy and when is she not sexy enough? When is it appropriate for a female to take the initiative in courting behaviour? Social constructionists have attempted to understand the subtleties of sexual norms through analysis of inter-views with people about their sexual beliefs and behaviours, or through analysis of written material about sexuality – for example, medical textbooks, women's magazines and 'letters to the editor'. These rich sources of data have led researchers to postulate a range of ideas about how culture and society influence human development within the sexual sphere. Several of these will now be discussed.

Inventionist views of adolescence and sexuality

Is puberty necessarily a time of stress and conflict for adolescents? G. Stanley Hall (1940), influenced by the psychosexual theorists, regarded adolescence as a time of storm and stress in which conflict and confusion inevitably accompany awakening sexual impulses, bodily changes and an increased awareness of self and society. Many theorists, such as Freud, Blos and Erikson, have emphasized the conflict-driven nature of this stage of life, taking the view, implicitly or explicitly, that coping with biological drives is a stressful but necessary accompaniment of adult adjustment. On the other hand, cross-cultural studies have suggested that the level of conflict and stress experienced by adolescents can vary greatly, at least in part as a function of the prevailing cultural norms about sexual expression (Mead 1939, 1950). Although there has been criticism of the validity of Mead's data-gathering techniques so that her conclusions about the relatively stress-free coming of age of Samoan youth must now be considered questionable (Freeman 1983), other writers have also downplayed the conflictual aspects of adolescence.

The view encapsulated by the writings of Lapsley *et al.* (1985) is that stresses and conflicts are undoubtedly experienced by many adolescents, but that these are largely unrelated to the biological changes of puberty. Many writers about adolescence regard this period as a relatively recent cultural invention, produced by economic and social conditions that prolong childhood – ostensibly for the benefit of the individual. Examples of these conditions include the enactment of child labour laws, a minimum school-leaving age, and laws designed to protect children from sexual exploitation. While these may have been implemented to allow adolescents to achieve adult status in a gradual manner – seemingly an advantage in our complex world – these social changes place adolescents in the stressful state of status deprivation. Adolescence is best defined not by the transition to new roles, but by the exclusion from old roles. Adolescents must put away childish beliefs and behaviours but they may not yet begin an autonomous lifestyle. Theorists who adopt this 'inventionist' view (Lapsley *et al.* 1985; Lapsley & Rice 1988) cite historical material to argue that the phenomenon of a prolonged adolescence is not a developmental necessity arising out of biological stresses, but a cultural imposition which causes tensions of its own. The implication of their writings is that the conflicts accompanying sexual maturation may be greatly exaggerated as a result of social norms.

Sexual socialization approaches: learning to be sexual

Various writers have attempted to explain how society influences our sexual behaviour using a learning theory/socialization approach. These theorists apply the principles of learning to our understanding of why biology can work differently depending on the environmental context in which it unfolds. For example, they might use principles of conditioning to explain why some people are strongly attracted to curly hair, while the shape of a well-turned foot in a delicate shoe excites others. Or, painting with a broader brush, they might use reinforcement theory to examine differences between cultures in the strength of sex-role orientations – why in some cultures males are more stereotypically masculine and females more stereotypically feminine, while in others there is a greater degree of overlap between roles and behaviours.

One early theory that used a learning approach to explain a broad range of sexual behaviours, attitudes, traits and norms was developed by Lerner and Spanier (1980). They argued that five aspects of development together comprise the process of 'sexual socialization': (a) development of a sex-object preference; (b) development of gender identity; (c) development of sex roles; (d) acquiring sexual skills, knowledge and values; and (e) development of dispositions to act in sexual contexts. These aspects of development are differentially responsive to the role of nurture, some hardly at all, some extensively so. The first aspect involves the choice of which sex will become the focus of sexual interest. Most people are heterosexual, a proportion of the population is homosexual, and for some the focus of sexual interest will shift at various points through the life span. While Lerner and Spanier and some of the other early learning theorists believed that one's experiences could change one's sexual orientation (e.g. that a homosexual orientation could be changeable with therapy to a heterosexual one), modern research suggests that such change is unlikely to be successful (or even desirable) in most cases (Seligman 1993). The development of gender identity or the identification of oneself as male or female is also resistant to change from environmental forces. The social definition of a child at birth customarily follows the anatomical sex of the child and gender identity is formed over the next few years as the child is reinforced by others in that sexual designation. At the same time, children develop an understanding that their sex is an unchanging feature and that, for example, girls cannot grow up to be 'daddies'. In rare cases there are discrepancies between the person's designated sex and their internal feelings and self-definition, or mistakes in the original designation which do not become obvious until later in life. Gender identity becomes a crisis issue for such individuals, who may wish to cross-dress, live as the opposite sex, or have sex-change operations. While such situations are uncommon, more frequent among teenagers may be feelings of rejection of perceived aspects of their gender identity. For example, a boy may feel uncomfortable about behaving in the 'macho' ways expected of him, or a girl may reject perceived female sex-role expectations to be flirtatious or to act 'dumb' in the presence of boys. These aspects of gender identity are amenable to change, as they relate to aspects of gender that we have learnt 'go with' our designated sex, but they are not in fact an integral part of our biological makeup.

Sex-role development means learning how to be psychologically masculine or feminine within a particular social or cultural framework. Traditional sex roles for females encompass traits such as nurturance, emotionality, warmth, expressiveness, cooperation and dependency, while the corresponding traits for males are independence, assertion, self-sufficiency, competitiveness and instrumental effectiveness. Earlier conceptions of sex roles assumed that the mature, adjusted course of development involved taking on traditional roles, and psychoanalytic models still contain elements of this view (as we have seen in our discussion of Erikson's work).

Bem (1974) was the first to demonstrate that masculinity and femininity were independent traits, an observation that has been confirmed by many researchers. Nevertheless, at least back in the 1980s, feminine traits were not sought after by young men nor associated with valued outcomes, while this was not the case for girls expressing psychologically masculine traits. Has the situation changed? A recent Australian study showed virtually no differences between males and females on self-reported masculinity/instrumentality traits, for young people and adults from Anglo-Australian backgrounds. They saw themselves as equally ambitious, competitive, independent and showing leadership potential. However, females scored much higher than males on relationship orientation/femininity, describing themselves as warmer, more understanding, more compassionate and gentler (Leung & Moore 2003). Although further studies are needed to establish how general this pattern has become among young people, it seems from at least this study that today's women have been socialized to value both instrumental and relationship-oriented traits, drawing into question the validity of sex-role stereotypes for women which reflect research from 20 or 30 years ago.

However, the change for men is not so evident, a finding which aligns with an intriguing qualitative study of adolescent boys from US secondary schools (Watts & Borders 2005). These authors argued that adolescent males experience problems because of gender-role conflicts, which for boys involve restrictions on their possibilities for self-expression. These restrictions can lead to anxiety, difficulties with intimate relationships, negative attitudes towards help-seeking and substance abuse, to name just a few possible outcomes. Watts and Borders found evidence that boys felt uncomfortable sharing feelings or emotions with other males, other than the expression of anger or rage. They mentioned their fathers as modelling such expressive difficulties, even in situations of intense emotional impact, such as the death of a loved one.

Development of sex roles occurs at least partly via the socialization process that encourages and rewards some behaviours and attitudes while discouraging and punishing others. The boys in Watts and Borders' study perceived peer group sanctions on their expression of emotion, and said things like: 'I know that if I share [feelings] with some of my friends, they just laugh in my face. And be like "man you're gay"' (p. 271). In societies with less rigidly defined gender roles, the boundaries between traditional and non-traditional will be blurred, and more traits will be viewed as unrelated to gender. The actual processes by which this happens are not well understood. By adolescence, however, we know that much of what constitutes one's sex role has already been learnt, although there is still opportunity for change.

The next important aspect of sexual socialization in Lerner and Spanier's model, and one of particular relevance to adolescent development, is the acquisition of sexual skills, knowledge and values. Young people are vitally interested in sex and are open to new information, while at the same time questioning values and experimenting with behaviour. Parents and formal channels such as school are important sources of learning about sexuality, but much of this occurs within the peer-group context. The ways in which these social influences operate are taken up in Chapters 4 and 5. What is apparent, though, is that teenagers acquire many myths about sex and learn inappropriate behaviours and values, as well as appropriate skills and positive, safe and life-enhancing values.

In exploring the development of sexual behavioural patterns, Lerner and Spanier point out that teenagers with similar attitudes, knowledge and sexual skills may behave quite differently in similar sexual situations. They suggest that the final aspect of sexual socialization is the development of predispositions to act in certain ways in sexual contexts. Predispositions may relate to social factors, the particular relationship of the moment, or the teenager's past experience. For example, teenage girls are less likely to take precautions against STIs if they interpret their current relationship as 'steady'. Under the influence of alcohol, adolescents may feel more confident about experimenting sexually, or engaging in sexual experiences that they would avoid in a more rational state. Such sexual behaviour patterns have been extensively analysed by the following theorists who talk about sexual scripts and discourses.

All the world's a stage: sexual scripts

Gagnon and Simon (1973) introduced the term 'sexual scripts' to describe the stereotypic and ritualized ways in which we behave sexually and the social prescriptions for this behaviour. They describe scripts as learnt rules of sexual behaviour that consist of directions for what we will do and plans of action for how we will do it, and with whom. They provide guidelines as to who will be judged as attractive and desirable within a particular culture. Adolescents do not, initially, develop their sexual scripts from experience, although their experiences become important later. Rather, early scripts arise out of listening to others talk, absorbing the popular culture through watching movies, videos or television, and reading magazines and books. In this way, teenagers get a sense – not always at a conscious or explicit level – of what is appropriate and inappropriate sexually for someone of their age and gender. 'Official' attitudes of a culture may not reflect the true scripts, which can be ascertained by looking more closely at the behaviours within that society. For example, while premarital sex may be officially disapproved of in the UK and the USA, neither society places many restrictions on its practice. Chaperones are rare and adolescents are left alone in the company of opposite-sex peers. Nor is premarital sex publicly or severely punished in these cultures.

In US society, a common script for sexual development, at least in the past, and currently in more traditional regions, involves elaborate dating procedures, which are approved of by the older generation. These begin at an early age, usually with mixed-sex group activities, and proceed through double and single dates, to 'going steady'. This relationship may culminate in living together or in marriage. During adolescence, however, it is more likely that the relationship will break up with the partners re-forming relationships with others in a process described years ago by Sorensen (1973) as 'serial monogamy'. Similar scripts are often assumed by textbook writers in the UK and Australia (McCabe & Collins 1990; Peterson 1989) but, although there are doubtless similarities, there is also evidence to suggest that different scripts prevail in these cultures. For example, 'dating' was not a concept favoured by Australian youth (Moore *et al.* 1991) who preferred to describe their interactions in looser, less formal terminology and apparently began these interactions at an older age than their US counterparts. Some of their comments about dating were as follows:

> It sounds like something my mum would do – it sounds American.

> I don't really like it, it reminds me of the olden days . . . when they go to a ball or something. I just picture these two people going to a dance or something.

> [I]t used to be when the guy took the girl out and paid for everything, and these days it is less formal.
>
> (Moore *et al.* 1991: 36)

Not only are there likely to be different cultural scripts for prescribing sexual activity, but young people are socialized according to gender-appropriate sexual scripts. Teenage girls have learnt to link sexual intercourse with love and often rationalize their sexual behaviour by believing that they were carried away by love – that the 'magic of the moment', combined with their desire to satisfy the wishes of their loved one, was the reason for having sex, rather than their own sexual needs or desires. As we shall see later, more girls than boys cite being in love as their main reason for being sexually active. Male sexual scripts stress the satisfaction of their sexual desires. The pleas 'If you really loved me, you would have sex with me' or 'You wouldn't make me suffer in this way' suggest that some young men are well attuned to the female sexual script, with the male script allowing for the exploitation of young girls' own needs.

You like potato and I like potahto: sexual discourses

The subtext of Gershwin's lyrics to the song 'Let's call the whole thing off' is not so much about different ways of pronouncing words as it is of the couple's different underlying assumptions regarding romance. These underlying assumptions, reflected in what we say, make up the discourses of sexuality. Discourse in social science is considered to be an institutionalized way of thinking, which affects our attitudes and behaviours without us necessarily recognizing its influence. For example a woman who has had several sexual partners could be described as promiscuous, experienced or liberated – each description conveys a different attitude and could shape the way others act towards the woman.

Two theorists who have studied sexual discourses are Wendy Hollway and Michelle Fine. Hollway (1984) suggests that three discourses represent male-female sexual interactions in western society: the Male Sex Drive discourse, the Have/Hold discourse, and the Permissive discourse. The main assumption of the Male Sex Drive discourse is that strong biological urges propel men in their relationships with women, and women should be subservient to this drive. Men must have sexual release to be healthy and women need to be persuaded into satisfying this male need through a reciprocal arrangement in which female 'needs' for security and to nurture their children are exchanged for sexual favours. If this strategy fails, force or exploitation may be used. This script implies a relationship in which men have power over women, one that is maintained through men's superior strength and in the service of the male sex drive. Women's sex drive is not acknowledged and those women who openly exhibit an interest in sex are considered to be inferior and amenable to exploitation, as loose women who deserve all they get.

In contrast, the Have/Hold discourse involves assumptions that the sex drive should be constrained within marriage, or at least monogamy, commitment to partnership, and family life. The quality of the relationship between partners is compensation for the sacrifice of sexual experimentation and permissiveness on the part of both sexes. Men and women are regarded as equally deserving of satisfaction, but sex is considered as appropriate only within a committed relationship. The Permissive discourse has as its major tenet the proposition that there should be freedom of sexual expression for both sexes, 'so long as no one gets hurt'. While this discourse accepts female sexual arousal and experimentation as legitimate, the implications with respect to sexual commitment are unclear. For example, a sexually unexciting marriage which may be expected to continue within the Have/Hold and the Male Sex Drive discourses (with the husband taking lovers to satisfy his sex drive in the latter case) may break up within the Permissive discourse. For those couples operating within this discourse, there may be pressure to retain sexual excitement which could interfere with some of the other functions of committed relationships such as rearing children, looking after a partner if they are ill (or just having a bad day) and becoming a financially viable family unit.

While Hollway's discourse analysis of sexual politics is a useful and interesting one, it has received little empirical support. Two Australian studies (DiMascolo 1991; Moore & Rosenthal 1992) found that the three discourses described by Hollway failed to account for the complexity of the sexual scripts exhibited by the young people interviewed. These teenagers' sexual attitudes and the principles guiding their sexual behaviour involved a complex and often contradictory mix of themes around issues like romance and love, the perceived intensity of sex drives, standards of behaviour for males and females, the nature of exploitation, and the extent to which it was considered appropriate to question and wonder about sexual values. There were some important differences between boys and girls, for example in their attitudes to permissiveness, but there were many similarities as well in male and female views of sexuality.

More than ten years on we might ask, is there a Female Sex Drive discourse? Holland *et al.* (1998) argue that young women have been 'disembodied' by the power and dominance of masculine sexuality – that female desire is silenced, not just by men's needs but by 'the male in the head'. By this they mean the regulatory norms of a masculinized culture which shape the sexual behaviours of both genders. There are no safe ways for women to express their sexuality other than those approved of by this masculinized culture, and indeed there is not even an appropriate language to enable women to express sexual feelings (without risking the label of 'slut'), according to these feminist theorists. Fine (1988) also discusses this thorny issue of female sex drive in her writing about discourses and their influence on teenage sexuality, and it is to this that we now turn.

It has been suggested by Fine that four themes dominate the public and private discourse about sexuality and these provide conflicting messages about how adolescents should conduct their sex lives. The themes revolve around morality and responsibility, desire, danger and victimization. The discourse of morality, most strongly represented by the parent generation and institutionalized religion, usually focuses on issues such as the moral reprehensibility of sex before marriage. There is a fear among some parents that discussion of sex with young people may encourage increased sexual activity or indicate tacit parental approval, although we know from research (see Chapter 5) that this is not the case. Arguments about the appropriate moral stance can limit the effectiveness of sex education, as contentious material – such as how to use contraception or the discussion of homosexuality – is omitted because some parents object to its inclusion. The morality discourse may, however, also include positive messages to teenagers about responsibility for one's own and one's partner's emotional and sexual health: 'Casual sex is alright so long as no-one gets hurt' or 'Sex before marriage is fine if the two people love each other'.

The discourse of desire is Fine's second theme, one which permeates media portrayals of sexuality but can be ignored in parents', schools' or churches' responses to young people's sexuality. Many adults are embarrassed and uncomfortable about adolescent sexual feelings and, to quote many a parent, 'would rather not know'. The teenager who wishes to articulate and question his or her sexual feelings may find it difficult to find an adult they feel safe talking to. At the other extreme the media can present desire as the main focus of sexuality, with concepts of responsibility in sexual relations rarely emphasized. Feminist researchers (Holland *et al.* 1998) found strong gender differences in the ability to express desire in their interviews with young men and women, such that 'men could access a public language of instrumental sexuality which was inappropriate for women, while women could access a respectable language of romance that did not enable them to communicate practical sexual issues or their own pain or pleasure in bodily contact. Much of feminine language of sex was constituted in silences' (p. 7). Writers such as Ariel Levy (2005) approach the topic differently, deploring the advent of modern 'raunch culture', in which young women flaunt their sexuality through dress and behaviour. Levy argues that this trend towards 'acting like a porn star' is not liberating for young women as it does not reflect their real needs (but is, in fact, merely 'acting'). The vexed question of how young people, especially young women, can safely express desire is taken up to some extent in later chapters in which we consider social influences such as the role of the media on sexuality (Chapter 5) and gender differences in sexual expression (Chapter 6).

The discourse of danger is communicated more frequently to girls, as the possibility of pregnancy, the emotional pain of abandonment and the social disgrace of loss of reputation. There is a sense, however, in which 'risking all for love' is portrayed as exciting. This has certainly been a theme in modern literature and films. In the era of AIDS, educational and public health sources have attempted to instil in young people of both sexes the dangers of unprotected sex. Emphasis on the dangerous aspect of this activity may be to some extent counterproductive, however, as stressing the danger may also stress the thrill and excitement. The idea that there is risk involved may serve to increase rather than decrease the attraction of an activity for some youths, particularly young boys.

Finally, our society provides many sources of messages arising from the discourse of victimization. The power balance in sexual encounters is portrayed as residing with men, who are ready to exploit women in the service of their sexual urges. Hence, women are potential victims and must be protected by parents and by society (e.g. by means of laws against sexual harassment). The message of this discourse is that women have limited power in sexual negotiation, and the implicit corollary is that they also have limited responsibility.

Conflicts between these four discourses lead to confusion for teenagers about the appropriate way to act. For example, young women who accept media messages (and the messages from their own bodies) that desire and sexual feeling are normal, may find themselves interpreted as 'sluts'. Messages which encourage young women to take responsibility for their own sexuality may conflict with their 'victim' role, or the moralistic expectation that this control can only be exercised through self-denial. Men and boys, too, are drawn into these conflicts and ambiguities. Society conveys the idea that 'exciting' men are powerful, reckless and dangerous, yet there are also strong messages to be responsible and sensitive, and to strive for intimate and mutually fulfilling relationships.

Summary of social constructionism approaches

The social constructionism models we have considered range from learning theory through to sociological analyses. They show how sexual behaviour can be heavily influenced by the situation in which an adolescent grows up – including the rewards and punishments meted out in any given society, the underlying messages of a culture with respect to sex, and even political and economic forces. While learning theories try to describe the processes by which such influences occur, there is still much to be understood about individual differences in learning, and the interactive relationships between genes, biology and environment in shaping human behaviour. The idea that we can describe sexual behaviour through recourse to a couple of discourses, or a set number of sexual scripts, is unrealistic. Although such concep-tualizations are useful in guiding our understanding of human sexu-ality, they can lead us to gloss over individual differences, to forget that individuals change over time, and can choose to be different from prevailing social norms. They may fail to acknowledge that some aspects of sexuality are virtually impossible to influence through environmental manipulation, for example gender identity and sexual orientation. Nevertheless, the socializing power of roles, scripts and discourses can be strong and it may be difficult to break away from scripts or stereotypical roles which are unsatisfying or which inhibit or retard emotional growth. The history of the women's movement attests to these difficulties, as do the stresses, outlined in Chapter 7, experi-enced by young people who adopt a homosexual rather than a hetero-sexual life course.

Biosocial views

DeLamater and Hyde (1998) argue that it is not a simple matter to merge essentialist and social constructionist models in an integrated way, because there are philosophical differences between them with respect to the nature of truth. They note that essentialism relies on the notion that some absolute truth can be known through research, while social constructionists see truth as context-dependent, with the func-tion of research being to document and expose (and perhaps even change) these 'relative truths'. However, all current major essentialist and social construction approaches to sexuality acknowledge the influence of both biological and social forces in the shaping of sexual behaviour and mores, but the emphasis is different.

One example of a biosocial approach is that of Edward Smith (1989). He limits his emphasis to the prediction of various aspects of sexual behaviour, such as age of initiation of intercourse, frequency of sexual activity, number of partners, contraceptive practices and the like. While psychosexual theories of behaviour take account of biological influences in a general way only, Smith's biosocial model considers specific, potentially measurable biological aspects of adolescence and uses these to predict sexual behaviour. In addition, he postulates a range of social processes which encourage or discourage sexual involvement, modify the form in which sexual behaviour is expressed and define appropriate sexual partners. Hormonal changes during adolescence are viewed as having both a direct effect on libido (or sexual motivation) and an indirect effect on sexual involvement by changing the adolescent's physical appearance. In this way, external 'signposts' indicate that sexual maturity is beginning, while at the same time producing variations in perceived attractiveness.

As we have already seen, there are various cultural, as well as biological, sources of influence on sexual behaviour and these interact in complex ways. For example, a young person who appears sexually mature and has physical features designated attractive by the prevailing culture may experience more social pressures to act in sexual ways than a late-developing youth or one who is perceived to be unattractive. Peers and potential sexual partners of sexually mature youths may encourage sexual involvement. Praise, popularity and self-esteem may accrue from engaging in sex. On the other hand, parents may be wary of the sexual potential of early maturing teenagers and may offer many sanctions against sex. All of this will be mediated by the young person's own sexual desires and the attitudes and values developed prior to puberty. In Chapters 3 and 4, we discuss research studies in which sexual behaviour is associated with both hormonal changes and social influences (such as best friend's sexual experience). The way these factors interact differs for boys and girls, with evidence that the latter are more susceptible to the social, and males to the biological, influences.

Psychological theories of sexual decision-making

The upsurge of interest in young people's sexual health, largely due to concerns about HIV transmission and unwanted pregnancies among teenage girls, has led to the application of psychological theories of decision-making to specific aspects of sexual behaviour. These models of decision-making describe a number of cognitive factors thought to predict safer sex behaviour, most usually condom use. In this section, we discuss several of the most popular of these. These and other models are described in greater detail in Moore *et al.* (1996). They differ from the previous theories outlined in this chapter in that they are not employed as overarching or 'grand narrative' approaches to understanding sexuality, but as research tools to aid in the prediction and testing of hypotheses about risky sexual behaviour.

The health belief model (HBM)

This model (Becker 1974; Rosenstock 1974) proposes that preventive health action, such as consistent use of condoms, can be predicted by beliefs that one is susceptible to the disease in question (in this case HIV), beliefs that the consequences of the disease are severe, and a balancing of beliefs about the effectiveness of the advocated health measures (benefits of taking action) against the disadvantages of their implementation (barriers to action). In later versions (Janz & Becker 1984) the model was extended to state that the combined levels of susceptibility and seriousness provide the energy or force to act, and the perception of benefits (minus barriers) provides a preferred path of action. However, unspecified 'cues to action' are necessary to trigger the decision-making process as well as a motivational factor, namely the salience of health and illness for the individual.

Most supportive research with HBM has been conducted with adult or child samples rather than adolescents. Few studies have examined the success of this model in explaining the avoidance of unhealthy or otherwise risky behaviours, such as smoking or binge drinking. Research demonstrates that the model's predictive value in the case of safe sex behaviours is limited (Becker & Joseph 1988; Hingson *et al.* 1990). An Australian study (Rosenthal *et al.* 1992) illustrates these limitations. The study demonstrated equivocal results, with the model failing to predict sexual risk with either casual or regular partners for young men or sexual risk with regular partners for young women. Although the model predicted young women's sexual risk-taking with casual partners, the one contributing factor was perceived susceptibility to HIV/AIDS. The authors concluded that rational decision-making models do not capture the essence of adolescent sexual risk-taking, and that these behaviours need to be contextualized before a clearer understanding of this process can emerge. While beliefs about the seriousness of a disease, individual susceptibility to that disease, and the costs and benefits of preventive behaviours may be important, they must be considered alongside the contribution of other factors such as social context.

The theory of reasoned action (TRA)

Ajzen and Fishbein's (1980) theory of reasoned action postulates relationships between engaging in a behaviour and attitudes towards it, knowledge of its likely outcomes and intentions with respect to carrying out the behaviour in question. In this model, intention to perform a behaviour is the immediate antecedent of that behaviour. Intention is predicted by two factors: the individual's attitude to that behaviour and his or her 'subjective norms'. Attitudes are determined by beliefs (or knowledge – both correct and incorrect, explicit and implied) about the behaviour, and the perceived costs and benefits of engaging in it (outcome evaluations), while subjective norms are a function of beliefs that significant others (e.g. family and/or friends) think that the behaviour in question is appropriate, together with the individual's motivation to comply with these perceived norms.

For the example of safe sex behaviour, condom use for any given sexual act would be postulated as predicted by intention to use a condom for that sexual encounter. This intention would be predicted in part by beliefs about the efficacy and desirability of using condoms balanced by the perceived disadvantages of their use, such as messiness, social embarrassment and the like. These beliefs would be mediated by beliefs about the desirability of the outcomes of condom use, that is, protection against HIV/AIDS, STI and pregnancy. Through such beliefs, Ajzen and Fishbein argue, attitudes are formed, in this case attitudes to condoms. Another dimension of influence on intention would be adolescents' ideas about whether or not their parents, friends, sexual partner/s, and other significant individuals or groups thought that condom use was a good thing. These ideas, along with the individual's motivation to comply with the perceived values of significant others, form subjective norms about condoms.

Research using this model tends to indicate what we all know about New Year resolutions – that intention is not always predictive of behaviour. For example, among a group of 112 disco-attending young singles, about a half indicated that their intentions to use a condom in a sexual encounter may not be carried out if they were drunk or drug affected, or because of being carried away by the passion of the moment. Several also indicated that they would lose their resolve if they 'thought their partner was safe', 'no one insisted', or the partner did not want to use condoms (Rosenthal *et al.* 1997).

The TRA has been extended to include other factors such as the extent to which the behaviour in question is under an individual's control. The theory of planned behaviour (TPB: Ajzen & Madden 1986) and its predecessor have been used in several studies of safe sex practice among adolescents, but again with less success than in studies of other health-related behaviours. For example, Boldero *et al.* (1992) asked sexually active young people to state their intentions, as well as answer questions regarding attitudes and subjective norms with respect to condom use. The sample then returned a second questionnaire after their next sexual encounter, indicating (a) whether they had changed their intention, (b) whether they had in fact used a condom in the situation, and (c) aspects of the situation which may have interfered with their intentions, such as alcohol use, type of partner (regular or casual) and level of arousal. The correlation between initial and later intention was very low, indicating that intentions were not stable, and the timing of their measurement is crucial in assessing the efficacy of intention as a predictor of behaviour. Further, there was only limited support for a link between intentions (initial and later) and behaviour, and even less support for the importance of attitudes and subjective norms in determining both intentions and safe sex practices. Contextual features (communication with a partner, level of sexual arousal and condom availability) on the other hand were important predictors of intentions to use condoms and actual condom use, but even inclusion of these situational factors did not fully explain non-condom use among those with intentions to have safe sex.

The authors concluded that, while the model may be useful in predicting behaviours over which individuals have personal control (such as use of the contraceptive pill), and which are private and initiated outside of the 'heat of the moment' of a sexual encounter, this is not so for condom use. Deciding to use a condom usually requires both parties to agree at the time of a sexual encounter and thus cannot be wholly predetermined, and is certainly not private. As with the HBM, failure to take account adequately of both the situational and social context limits the utility of this decision-making model in explaining sexual risk.

Overall, the TRA works relatively well in predicting adult behaviours that are premeditated and rationally governed but, like the HBM, it is less successful in explaining actions in which contextual and emotional factors have a major role. In these cases, intentions are often thwarted or discarded. Such situational factors may be more likely to sway adolescents than adults, because of their lack of experience in dealing with contingencies. It is also possible that adolescents actually define risk differently from adults because they are less able to recognize the persuasive power of situations.

The AIDS risk reduction model (ARRM)

This framework for prediction of health-risk behaviour, unlike the previous two models described, has been put forward specifically to assist in the understanding of risk behaviour relevant to AIDS (Catania *et al.* 1990). There are three distinct stages in the process of changing or reducing sexual risk-taking behaviours: *labelling* involves, for example an awareness by individuals that their current sexual behaviour carries a risk of HIV infection; *commitment* requires them to make a decision to alter high-risk behaviour, for example use a condom during sex; and *enactment* requires that they overcome barriers towards implementing that decision. A fuller description of the ARRM is provided by Sheeran *et al.* (1999). As Sheeran *et al.* note, this last stage provides a shift from considering the individual only to considering sexual behaviour as part of a two-way relationship.

At each point, a range of variables may influence outcomes. For example, recognition of risk is predicted to be affected by knowledge of how HIV is transmitted, perceived susceptibility to AIDS and social norms concerning what constitutes risky behaviour. These variables heavily overlap with or are directly equivalent to some postulated by the HBM and the TRA. Commitment to a decision to alter high-risk behaviour is viewed as consequent on attitudes to high and low-risk activities, that is, a cost-benefit analysis of the positive and negative outcomes of altering behaviour towards safer options. Perceived self-efficacy, too, is a necessary precondition for behaviour change. For example, adolescents must feel confident enough to purchase, carry and manipulate condoms during a sexual encounter before they will commit to the decision to use them on a regular basis. Finally, actual behaviour change, as opposed to change in intention, is enhanced by the young person's sexual communication skills – their ability to discuss condom use with a partner, for example – and the social support available from friends, family and health professionals to reduce risk behaviour.

The ARRM was designed basically to predict adult sexual-risk behaviour and its application to an adolescent population is an empirical question. Research support is available for various elements of the model. The full ARRM model was tested with a small sample of 63 adolescents aged 16 to 20 years by Breakwell and Fife-Schaw (1994), and it accounted for 30 per cent of the variance of condom use. The authors note that the social representations of sex reflected in norms and values override intentions in the explanation of young peoples' prospective condom-use behaviour. Sheeran *et al.* (1999), in their meta-analysis, examined the relationship between a large number of predictor variables and condom use and found that measures of commitment and enactment yielded good correlations with hetero-sexual condom use. They concluded that there was support for 'a social psychological model of condom use highlighting the importance of behavior-specific cognitions, social interaction, and preparatory behaviors rather than knowledge and beliefs about the threat of infection' (p. 90).

Developmental issues

The models described above do not explicitly consider the specific characteristics of adolescence and the particular issues associated with this phase of development. However, there is increasing evidence that such factors make a difference. For example, as we shall see, sex hormones have an important role in the onset of sexual behaviour in males and females (Udry 1985, 1988; Udry & Billy 1987).

Several models have been proposed which integrate adolescent developmental principles with risk factors for the emergence of risk-taking behaviours (Irwin 1993; Irwin & Millstein 1986; Jessor & Jessor 1977). These models take into account intra- and inter-individual processes and influences, as well as the social context and the inter-active nature of these three systems. In their general risk-taking model, Irwin and Millstein posit that biological maturation (the timing of puberty) has an impact on psychosocial aspects of development, including self-perceptions (body image and self-esteem) and develop-mental needs (autonomy, peer affiliation, intimate relationships), on cognitive scope, on perceptions of the social environment (such as the relative influence of parents and peers), and on personal values (such as independence and achievement). These variables are hypothesized to predict adolescent risk-taking behaviour through the mediating effects of risk perception and peer-group characteristics.

The model developed by Irwin *et al.* is a developmental one, dealing with risk in the context of other adolescent developmental tasks. In spite of its complexity, the model is limited for our purposes because it focuses on risk without placing sexual risk-taking within the context of sexuality, broadly speaking. An understanding of young people's sexual risk-taking must include consideration of the nature of sexu-ality (both heterosexuality and homosexuality), the social norms that underpin sexual practices, and the understandings of sex that ensue – in short, social constructions of sexuality, to be discussed in more detail in later chapters.

Letting teenagers speak

The preceding discussion has focused on psychologists' and socio-logists' views of adolescent sexuality and its developmental unfolding and consequences. But teenagers themselves have their own theories of sex and how it impinges on their lives. They express, more or less coherently, both diversity and a similarity of views on these subjects. It is our strong belief that any theory which attempts to explain human behaviour must take into account the experiences and attitudes of its target population – in their variety as well as consistency. To illustrate this point, we conclude this chapter with the voices of young people aged 15 to 18 years from a range of backgrounds, who were asked what they thought about one particular aspect of their sexual lives, namely virginity.

> It's traditional I know. If you're a virgin it means holding yourself back for that one person you're going to marry. When you walk down the aisle with that white dress – and it has to be white – you're that conscious if you've clouded it at all. So you'll be pure. I know that is really old fashioned, but that's how I think it should be.

> For a guy [virginity is] bad. It shows he is weak and can't get it off with a woman and that sort of thing.

> I don't think it exists any more. People usually end up losing their virginity before they are married anyway. So I don't believe in it.

> It is something that you should not take lightly – it is pretty serious. You have to be pretty serious about someone to have sex for the first time.

> I think virginity is a good thing. I don't think you have to prove yourself to people by losing your virginity. I would love to have my virginity back again. The thrill of having sex for the first time and waiting so long would make it so much better. I know a lot of girls who are virgins, and I respect them for that.

> [I] don't know – it is good, but people might pick on you.

> It is just that you are the only one who has made love to her, and if someone else has, and you come along and get married to her, then you come across that person that she has made love with – well, there would still be that bond and you would feel uncomfortable with her.

> A girl should be a virgin, but for a guy it doesn't matter.

Clearly, there is no single sexual culture among adolescents. For example, across the teenage years, young people's sexual worlds are very different, attesting to the degree of change occurring over this age span. But we are on equally shaky ground if we try to generalize across the sexes, or ethnic groups, or socioeconomic status, or possibly even interest groups such as stamp collectors and football fans. The words of our teenagers serve to illustrate some of this variation, which provides a challenge for theory-makers and those working with young people.

We have not attempted, in this chapter, to describe and evaluate every theory that deals with adolescent sexuality. Rather, we have been selective, showing the range of approaches applied to the study of adolescent sex. Research which is summarized in subsequent chapters is usually influenced or motivated by aspects of the models presented, although the researcher may not always be explicit about the assumptions with which she or he is working. Theories and models provide us with new insights and new ways of looking at behaviour. They help us to forge conceptual links between the plethora of data available on teenagers' sexual behaviour, attitudes, knowledge and beliefs. They enable us to understand the antecedents of adolescent sexuality and its expression among the youth of today. Theories can also help in predicting adult sexual outcomes. They link sexuality with other aspects of adjustment and coping skills. What is important is that we view these theoretical approaches not as static, but as developing frameworks that can eventually lead to better integration of research data, case material, common sense and personal experience.

3 Changing hormones, changing bodies

Adolescent sexuality is inextricably tied up with the events of puberty, in which the adolescent's body develops its adult shape and reproductive functioning, and hormonal changes affect sex drives in complex ways. Although biological development does not tell us everything about how and why we behave sexually, understanding of these processes is vital if the whole picture of sexual development is to emerge. In this chapter we describe the biology of sexual development, together with research on the relationships between biology and psychological variables, especially those related to sexual expression and sexual confidence.

Genes, brains, hormones, gender

Puberty's onset marks the beginning of adult sexual development, a process for which biological preparations have been occurring since conception. The single cell that begins life, and arises from the combination of mother's egg and father's sperm, contains 23 pairs of chromosomes. One pair holds the determinants of genetic sex. This pair is either XX, denoting a female, or XY, denoting a male. Each of these genetic configurations provides a blueprint for sexual development of the male or female type but, particularly in the case of the male, does not guarantee this development. Certain conditions in the physiological environment of the uterus must prevail. After birth, although the die is usually cast in a biological sense, conditions of the psychological environment and their interactions with biological features of the individual can influence the ways in which maleness and femaleness are manifest. This influence extends, eventually, to how puberty is coped with and how adult sexuality takes shape. Some of the details of these complex interactions, which are by no means fully understood, will be discussed in this chapter.

For the first six weeks of life, the human embryo is sexually undifferentiated. During the prenatal period, gonadotropin-releasing hormone (GnRH) is produced by specialized neurones in the brain. These neurones intermittently secrete pulses of hormone from nerve terminals in the hypothalamus, which in turn sends signals to the pituitary gland (a small organ at the base of the brain), to secrete the gonadotrophic hormones responsible for sexual differentiation (Sisk & Foster 2004). In the normal course of events, males develop testicles and, somewhat later, females develop ovaries. These structures, termed gonads, themselves produce hormones which further direct the development of male and female internal and external sex organs. Hormone secretion and balance is controlled by the reproductive endocrine system, involving complex interactions between the brain, the pituitary gland and the gonads. Both male and female reproductive systems produce androgen (the masculinizing hormone) and oestrogen (the feminizing hormone), but it is the concentration and balance of these hormones throughout life that determine male or female morphology and, to some extent, behaviour. In utero, testicles produce enough androgen to dominate the oestrogen in the male, while ovaries produce enough oestrogen to dominate the androgen in the female. Once sexual differentiation has occurred, GnRH secretion declines and hormone pulsing rates decrease dramatically and remain that way right through to the pre-pubertal period.

In rare cases when the male embryo does not produce sufficient androgens, or there are problems within the reproductive endocrine system relating to androgen sensitivity, the result is a girl-like appearance of the genitals, in spite of the XY chromosomes. The studies by Money and his associates (1968, 1972) of sexual abnormalities at birth and in childhood led to the conclusion that 'Unless there is sufficient push in the male direction, the foetus will take the female turn at any subsequent fork (of embryonic development). Whether there is a female push or not, nature's first choice is to make Eve' (Money & Tucker 1975: 73). In recent years a good deal of controversy has surrounded this notion, for example Diamond and Sigmundson (1997: 305) argue 'as far as an extensive literature review can attest, there is no known case where a 46 chromosome, XY male, unequivocally so at birth, has ever easily and fully accepted an imposed life as an androphilic female regardless of the physical and medical intervention'.

Money, in his studies of individuals who had their sex reassigned at birth or in infancy (due to genital trauma or ambiguity), leant towards the 'nurture' dimension in his view of sexual development, with the belief that even the influence of genetic makeup could be overridden by environmental factors. Long-term follow-up of some of these sexually reassigned children has however reinforced the power of 'nature' as a force in determining sexual identity, sexual feelings and sexual behaviours (e.g. Colapinto 2000; Diamond & Sigmundson 1999).

Puberty begins when GnRH secretion gradually increases to a high enough level to stimulate gonadotropin hormone (luteinizing hormone and follicle stimulating hormone: LH & FSH) and steroid hormone (testosterone and oestrogen) secretion, resulting (eventually) in sexual maturation. The 'trigger' for this increase in GnRH and so the onset of puberty is hotly debated, and various possibilities will be discussed in a later section. Suffice to say at this point that brain functioning is implicated, and a 'puberty gene' (GPR54) has been postulated (but not yet proven) to drive this neurological change (Seminara *et al.* 2003; Sisk & Foster 2004). The relationship between neural functioning and hormone secretion appears to be a two-way street. Not only does the brain have a role in triggering hormone release, but it has also been postulated that hormonal differences between males and females affect brain structure and function (Bardwick 1971; Kimura 2002; Moir & Jessel 1989).

Both Bardwick and Kimura concluded on the basis of some animal studies that brain differences arise in the prenatal and early infancy stages of life as a result of the effects of the sex hormones on the central nervous system. Male and female brains are predisposed to differentially perceive and respond to stimuli, according to this view, which has been expressed in popular form by Moir and Jessel (1989) in their book *Brainsex*. More recent researchers have also noted the likelihood of circulating sex hormones moderating brain circuits, which in turn may moderate changes in social behaviours, risk-taking and cognitive functioning at adolescence (e.g. Cameron 2004), although there is a recognized need for research to more clearly establish these hypothesized relationships. New technologies such as magnetic resonance imaging (MRI) open up the possibilities of non-invasive mapping of brain structure and function (Tomas 2005), so we can expect to see a great deal of such research in the near future. The outcome of this neurobiological research has been a de-emphasis on the effects of socialization on behaviour, and a re-emphasis on the effects of biology. Like all nature-nurture controversies, the 'truth' is difficult to tease out and the attempt to do so is perhaps not even sensible as biological and social forces are so intertwined. Clearly, biological differences affect the way individuals respond to environmental stimuli. Equally clearly, environment can modify biology. Discussions about the origins of sex differences in behaviour and personality are often more motivated by political than scientific concerns. This may be due to awareness that an overemphasis on biological explanations can be interpreted – incorrectly – as somehow implying the validity of rigid and unchanging sex-role stereotyping.

It is difficult to summarize all of sexual development prior to puberty. Everything that happens to every individual child, in a physiological, psychological and social sense, is relevant. By puberty, much is set in developmental terms. However, there is considerable potential for flexibility and both adaptive and maladaptive change, as at any point in life. Although puberty does not inevitably change amenable children into rebellious, confused, stress-ridden and sex-crazed adolescents, it has particular power as a life-influencing event because of the extent of change which occurs to the individual in a relatively short time span. Teenagers experience change in physical appearance, strength and power, change in feelings, change in others' expectations, change in social pressures and, potentially, change in ways of thinking about the world and about themselves.

Puberty triggers

The word puberty means 'to be covered in fine hair' and is derived from the Latin *pubescere* meaning 'to grow hairy or mossy'. The bodily changes associated with this phenomenon begin when the hypothalamus signals the pituitary gland to release more intense concentrations and more frequent pulses of the gonadotrophic hormones into the bloodstream. These hormones, the release of which precedes noticeable bodily changes by about a year, stimulate increased production of oestrogen and androgen by the ovaries in the girl and the testes in the boy. The ovaries increase their production of oestrogen sixfold in the girl's body, and the testes produce 20 times the amount of the androgen in the boy's body. As we have said, both sexes have male and female hormones circulating in the bloodstream, but the balance is different. During adolescence, a boy's androgen level becomes 20 to 60 per cent higher than that of a girl, while her oestrogen level becomes 20 to 30 per cent higher than his (Nielsen 1991).

What triggers off the signal from the hypothalamus to the pituitary to begin the release of gonadotrophins is largely unknown. Sisk and Foster argue that the timing of puberty will be based on the organism being sufficiently physically developed, socially linked and in an optimal environment to begin the reproductive process. This evolutionary explanation of the onset of puberty is one that relies on signals to the brain from within the body, and from the environment, that the individual is 'ready enough' to develop mature reproductive organs and so be in a position to reproduce. These researchers suggest 'Hope is now fading for finding a single trigger for puberty because of the number and complexity of the variables that determine reproductive success. Rather, we are finding that multiple signals are involved. Thus far, scientists have identified signals that permit puberty to occur or progress, but do not cause puberty. We call these "permissive" signals' (Sisk & Foster 2004: 1041).

Several of these permissive signals have been isolated. Age alone does not qualify, as puberty begins at different times for different people, although most adolescents begin within the age range of 9 to 16 years. For girls, the single best predictor for the onset of menarche is weight (Moffitt *et al.* 1992). More than 30 years ago, Frisch and Revelle (1970) presented the controversial hypothesis that attainment of a critical body weight and a related change in metabolic rate triggers off the decrease in hypothalamic sensitivity to sex hormones which in turn leads to pituitary activation. They cite as evidence the mean weight of girls at menarche (about 47–8 kg) which has not changed over the past 125 years even though the age at which this weight is achieved has declined (Newman & Newman 1986). The recently discovered hormone, leptin, is thought to be involved in triggering the link between puberty and weight. Puberty in mice can be advanced experimentally by increasing leptin levels (Chehab *et al.* 1997). This hormone is secreted in fatty (adipose) tissue, with more adipose tissue leading to more leptin, which in turn is a signal to the body that sufficient somatic growth has been attained to support pregnancy. There is some controversy about whether leptin levels and weight gain are permissive signals for puberty in boys (Ahmed *et al.* 1999). It has been argued from the evolutionary viewpoint that the lack of a clear link between puberty and weight in males is perhaps because males do not have to develop the energy reserves to support pregnancy and lactation (Sisk & Forster 2004).

Precocious or delayed puberty is usually related to disease, the effects of drugs and environmental contaminants, or engaging in practices inimical to physical health, such as excessive dieting or overeating. The average age at onset of puberty has shown a trend towards earlier occurrence – the secular trend – which cuts across geographic and ethnic lines. Herman-Giddens *et al.* (2004) critically reviewed several major studies of pubertal timing published since 1997. They concluded that girls are maturing earlier than they did several decades ago, and that there are substantial racial differences between white and black girls. They quote Freedman *et al.*'s (2002) study which reported the mean menarchal age for black girls had decreased by 9.5 months between 1973 and 1994, with a corresponding decrease of 2 months for white girls. Current estimates from these US-based studies suggest that the mean age of menarche for black girls is approximately 12.1 years and for white girls approximately 12.6 years. The decline in the age of puberty is thought to be due to improvements in nutrition and living conditions and has been linked with diet and weight in early infancy and late childhood. Herman-Giddens *et al.* point out however that earlier puberty is not always indicative of optimal functioning. They note the association between being overweight and earlier puberty as an example, and also refer to studies which suggest links between early puberty and exposure to certain pesticides (Krstevska-Konstantinova *et al.* 2001). Anderson *et al.* (2003) analysed data from the US-based National Health Examination Surveys conducted between 1963–70, and again in 1988–94. They showed that the reducing age of menarche was associated with higher relative weight, even when controlling for race and age.

Social conditions have also been associated with early puberty, although these conditions are often adverse (as with the link between early puberty and environmental contaminants), so any evolutionary significance is difficult if not impossible to explain. For example, girls in father-absent families show a tendency to reach puberty earlier, as do girls in families where an adult male is present who is not the girl's father (Ellis & Garber 2000). Research also suggests that young women from stressed families also tend to reach puberty earlier (Moffitt *et al.* 1992).

The changes

Bodily alterations at puberty include the growth spurt which is accompanied by changes in brain structure and function, strength and body proportion, development of the primary sex characteristics (the external genitalia and internal organs which control their functioning), and of the secondary sex characteristics. These last are features that distinguish males and females but are not directly connected with reproduction, such as facial hair in males, breast development in females and pubic hair for both sexes. Each of these changes will be briefly described in this section.

The brain undergoes dynamic changes during childhood and adolescence. Researchers such as Giedd have conducted longitudinal studies, using MRI technology to scan the brains of thousands of children at regular intervals as they grow towards adulthood. One finding is that grey matter in the cortex (the part of the brain responsible for cognition) has a U-shaped developmental growth pattern. There is an intense period of growth just prior to puberty, possibly related to the influence of sex hormone production (Giedd *et al.* 1999). Grey matter peaks in volume at about 11 or 12 years, then 'prunes back' between about 13 and 18 years. In this process, grey matter is lost as synapses reduce in number, but those remaining are surrounded by white matter (myelin), stabilizing and strengthening neural connections. Neuroscientists believe that the period of pruning is as important as the period of neuronal growth in childhood, because it leads to a consolidation of learning. Giedd argues for the importance of adolescents engaging in activities that stimulate and 'exercise' the brain connections important for cognitive and psycho-motor skills in adulthood, such as those involved in playing sport, academic study and learning music.

The grey matter growth spurt of preadolescence is mostly in the frontal lobe of the cortex, the area most responsible for impulse control, planning, reasoning and decision-making. Functional brain imaging and post-mortem studies suggest that growth of grey matter (and its pruning) continues into early adulthood, with the frontal lobe regions of the brain not reaching full maturity until early adulthood. In one study, researchers looked for differences between the brains of teenagers and young adults, and found greatest differences in the frontal lobes (Sowell *et al.* 1999). Implications of these studies are that adolescents not only experience an extensive remodelling of the body as they reach puberty, but an extensive remodelling of the brain. While this remodelling is going on, some capacities may actually decline temporarily, while others may develop in a more continuous growth pattern. Some brain changes of the teenage years have been shown to be associated with outcomes such as difficulties in reading others' emotions (Baird *et al.* 1999; McGivern *et al.* 2002), and greater sensitivity to emotion-altering recreational drugs (Ehrlich *et al.* 2002). Brain developments are also likely to be implicated in temporary difficulties in impulse control and impaired decision-making among some adolescents. On the positive side, frontal lobe development and myelinization lead to increasing capacity for reasoning, planning and rational thought.

More visibly, adolescence marks the final phase of physical growth, resulting in adult stature and physical sexual maturity. About one year after pubertal hormonal activity has been initiated, the adolescent growth spurt begins. This leads to an average increase in height for girls of 19.6 cm and for boys of 21.1 cm, although there is great individual variation. The growth spurt begins for girls any time between 9.5 years and 15 years, with the average age at about 10.5 years. The peak year of growth occurs at 12 years and the growth spurt is usually completed by age 14. For boys, the growth spurt generally starts later between 10.5 and 16 years – with the average age of commencement being 12.5, peak at age 14 and spurt completion at 16. The average duration of the growth spurt is 2.8 years for both sexes (Tanner 1970).

Growth in height is dramatic during this period. Much of this is in trunk length and the long bones of the legs, contributing to the stereotype of the gangly adolescent. Because of the delay in onset of the growth spurt among boys, 12-year-old girls are on average taller than boys, but this is reversed for all subsequent ages. Weight gains occur also, largely due to increases in muscle and fat, with increases in muscle size contributing to increased strength. Power, athletic skill and endurance all increase progressively and rapidly through adolescence with most boys surpassing most girls on these dimensions. Bodily proportions also alter. Children begin puberty with shoulders slightly broader than hips. For girls, the shoulder width hip width ratio decreases throughout puberty while for boys this ratio increases.

Sexual maturation for girls includes the growth of pubic and axillary hair, breast development and menarche. This occurs usually between 10 and 16 years with a mean age for US and UK populations of around 12.5 years (Tanner 1966). The menstrual cycle introduces a pattern of hormonal variations associated with ovulation, building up of the uterine lining in preparation for fertilization and the shedding of this lining via the menstrual period. Oestrogen and progesterone levels rise and fall in association with these events. The uterus, vagina, vulva, clitoris and other internal structures undergo growth and development so that the teenage girl has a functional reproductive system about 12 to 18 months after the first menstrual period and is physically capable of bearing children.

Sexual maturation for boys involves increased growth of the testes, scrotum and penis, pubic, bodily and facial hair development, and maturation of the internal prostate gland and the seminal vesicles. The first ejaculation of seminal fluid is likely to occur about two years after the beginning of pubic hair growth – either as a spontaneous emission or the result of masturbation. The number and mobility of sperm present in the seminal fluid increases throughout puberty with a corresponding increase in fertility. Other changes include an increase in the size of the larynx, leading to the voice changing to a deeper register and, for boys and girls alike, growth of the sweat glands with accompanying increases in body odour, and enlargement of the pores on facial skin. This last change, accompanied by hormonal changes, leads to the increased likelihood of acne.

It would be surprising if these momentous changes came and went without impact. Brain changes impact through increasing cognitive abilities but apparently also some temporary setbacks in empathy and impulse control. The alterations to appearance, sexualization of the body, increasing hormone concentrations and their effects on mood and libido, uneven growth rates, and inevitable comparisons with one's peers must all be coped with and incorporated into a new, adult body image. Mood swings, embarrassment and self-consciousness are common at this age. Physical awkwardness often results from growth asynchronies. Arms that are 15 cm longer than they were a year ago are apt to knock things over. Teenagers often appear to others as 'all arms and legs'. Other potential embarrassments for the self-conscious teenager include body odours and acne. Many young people worry whether their growth patterns are normal. The peer group can be relentless in its pressure for conformity so being, or even feeling, different in terms of body shape or fitness can be stressful. The effects of pubertal change on body image, the role of perceived attractiveness in adjustment to bodily changes, and the effects of early and late puberty are discussed in more detail in a later section of this chapter.

Adolescents: slaves to their hormones?

Young people are not mere slaves to hormonal changes, but there is no doubt that these changes can have complex emotional and behavioural effects. For example, Rowe *et al.* (2004) found that testosterone levels in adolescent boys were unrelated to the expression of aggression, but were related to non-aggressive conduct disorder symptoms among those boys with antisocial peers. However, if the boys had non-deviant peers, their testosterone levels were associated with leadership abilities and behaviours. This study is just one of many which indicates that the strength of association between hormones and behaviours depends in part on the social context in which the adolescent finds himself or herself.

Buchanan *et al.* (1992) argue that there are four types of hormone-behaviour associations. The first is that increasing or decreasing concentrations of hormones (within the normal range) affect moods or behaviours. Buchanan *et al.* give the example that among adult humans, oestrogen is associated with more positive moods and its lack with depression and negative affect, mainly in women. Among adolescent girls, higher levels of oestrogen have also been shown to relate to more positive mood (Eccles *et al.* 1988). On the negative side, higher androstenedione has been associated with lower energy; and higher testosterone with lower frustration tolerance, in adolescent boys (Nottelmann *et al.* 1985; Olweus 1986). In fact, across a number of studies, oestrogen rises have been associated with positive affect, and testosterone rises with increased aggression.

Additionally, research on neuropeptides suggests that these are affected by levels of oestrogen and testosterone, and relate to experiences of arousal and sexual pleasure. Studies suggest that the neuropeptide oxytocin is associated with pleasure during sexual arousal and orgasm for males and females, while vasopressin is released only during male arousal. As discussed in our chapter on gender differences (Chapter 6), there is also a developing research literature proposing that love and romantic feelings are triggered by higher levels of oxytocin (released in response to oestrogen), while vasopressin, the neuropeptide released in response to testosterone, may be more strongly associated with sexual arousal (Hiller 2004). These studies taken together provide some biological evidence for behavioural and even attitudinal differences between males and females in the domain of sexuality.

The situation is complex however, as similar levels of hormone concentration in different individuals do not necessarily lead to similar behaviours, and indeed correlations between hormone levels and behavioural outcomes are weak (Halpern 2003). Buchanan postulates a second type of hormone effect that relates to individual differences in response to hormonal fluctuations. This is the adjustment required when hormone levels deviate from the levels to which the individual is accustomed, an effect often related to developmental change. For example, while adult women may be used to the effects of hormone-level variations accompanying the menstrual cycle, early-adolescent girls may be highly responsive to these. As an illustration of this, Brooks-Gunn and Warren (1989) found that although oestrogen is generally associated with higher activation and feelings of well-being in animals and adult humans, for girls at an early stage of puberty, high oestrogen predicts depression and lowered impulse control. Nottelmann *et al.* have also shown that high concentrations of certain hormones for one's age are associated with negative moods (1985, 1987). Thus the important determiners of mood are not necessarily hormone levels or even their fluctuations *per se*, but the deviations in concentration from what the adolescent is used to.

A third kind of effect comes about through hormone 'irregularity' or fluctuations in hormone surges that do not follow a standard pattern. Cyclical patterns of hormone activity such as those experienced during the menstrual cycle can occur with unpredictable irregularity during early adolescence when these cycles are establishing themselves. Some evidence that this irregularity affects mood comes from studies of adult women for whom atypical patterns of hormone change have been linked to negative mood and behavioural symptoms (Coppen & Kessel 1963; Dennerstein *et al.* 1984). Buchanan *et al.* (1992) have at present found only limited links between hormone variability (or irregularity) and mood swings in adolescence but this is an area in which there has as yet been little systematic research.

Finally, there are possibilities for complex interactions between hormone levels, moods, behaviours and other biological and social variables. These include an individual's sensitivity to the various hormones, his or her predisposition towards the behaviour of interest, or contextual factors such as strong social sanctions against certain behaviours. For example, the level of circulating testosterone in boys is a significant predictor of sexual arousal, coital activity, masturbation, thinking about sex and future intentions with respect to sexual activity (Udry 1985, 1988). For girls, the adrenal androgens – including testosterone – predict non-coital sexual activity (such as fantasy and masturbation) and arousal. But prediction of actual sexual intercourse depends on social conditions such as best friend's sexual activity, the girl's participation in sports or the presence of father in the home (Udry 1988). It seems that the behavioural concomitants of testosterone for girls are modified by the social forces surrounding the expression of female sexuality, including the influence of significant others.

The ways in which hormone effects in adolescence are conceptualized by Buchanan underscores the importance of studying the relationships between biological variables and behaviour within both a biological and a social context. The biological context refers to the interaction which any hormone change will have with all the other bodily systems, and the relationship of this change to normal patterns of variation and to age and developmental norms. The social context refers to the individual's attitudes, habits, beliefs and past behaviours together with the expectations and norms of significant others, and how this moderates or accentuates the effects of hormones. Among teenagers, these contexts are in a state of rapid change so that while we know that hormone levels affect behaviour, the details of these effects are likely to vary greatly between individuals and even within one individual over time.

Body dissatisfaction: an epidemic of our times?

Tuesday September 8th

Lousy stinking school on Thursday. I tried my old uniform on but I have outgrown it so badly that my father is being forced to buy me a new one tomorrow. He is going up the wall but I can't help it if my body is in a growth period can I? I am only five centimetres shorter than Pandora now. My thing remains static at twelve centimetres.

Friday February 26th

My thing is now thirteen centimetres long when it is extended. When it is contracted it is hardly worth measuring. My general physique is improving. I think the back-stretching exercises are paying off. I used to be the sort of boy who had sand kicked in his face, now I'm the sort of boy who watches somebody else have it kicked in their face.

(Townsend 1982: 177)

One of the most compelling examples of the biological-social nexus comes from teenagers' concerns about their bodies. Early research addressed this by examining adolescents' feelings about their body image and the consequences of physical attractiveness. Most teenage boys and men say that they want to be taller, more muscular and heavier. Many, if not most, teenage girls dislike their bodies, seeing themselves as fat or overweight when in fact they are either average or below average weight for their age and height. A study of nearly 6000 adolescents between 12 and 17 years showed that 70 per cent of the girls wanted to be thinner. The most popular girls were the most concerned about being thin (Duncan *et al.* 1985). Moreover, Dummer's (1987) study of 1000 competitive swimmers whose bodies were fit and trim showed that the teenage girls were more dissatisfied with their bodies than the boys and wanted, more than any other change, to lose weight. Studies from the 1960s to the present day show adolescents are dissatisfied with their bodies and want to change them.

Indeed, at the dawn of the 21st century, body dissatisfaction among young people is a major concern, arguably even more so than at any time in the last 50 or even 100 years. Body dissatisfaction is associated with emotional distress as well as an elevated risk of eating disorders and unnecessary cosmetic surgery (Ohring *et al.* 2002; Stice & Whitenton 2002; Thompson *et al.* 1999). Stice and Whitenton (2002), in their longitudinal study of nearly 500 teenage girls, showed that higher body mass index (indicating greater adiposity or 'fatness'), perceived pressure to be thin, internalization of a 'thin-ideal' and deficits in social support were related to body dissatisfaction measured one year later, even when controlling for initial levels of dissatisfaction. Early menarche, weight-related teasing and depression were not predictive of body dissatisfaction. What is less clear from this and other studies is why social forces have developed which currently elevate the ideal of thinness above most if not all aspects of appearance for girls and women. Some theorists suggest that as economic conditions improve in any society, thinness and smaller waist to hip ratios are perceived as more attractive, while in cultures with limited economic opportunities and wealth, body fat, especially for women, is a sign of desirability (Anderson *et al.* 1992; Pettijohn & Jungeberg 2004). The latter researchers have attempted (with moderate success) to correlate measures of economic 'hard times' in the USA with various physical features of *Playboy*'s Playmate of the Year!

While our knowledge about the 'why' is still somewhat speculative, we have some ideas about how these pressures relating to appearance might develop within an individual. Family attitudes are likely to be important to the adolescent's acceptance of his or her own body. Certain family attitudes may lead to adolescents feeling insecure about their bodies and conflicted about aspects of sexuality and bodily functioning. Families that overstress 'the body beautiful' overreact to slight deviations such as the appearance of a pimple, or even comment on normal development such as pubic hair may lead to young people feeling overly self-conscious or even ashamed of their bodies. Some parents may project their own anxieties about bodies and sexuality onto their children. In these families, for example, sexual motives that are not present may be imputed to the children. Another potentially maladaptive family environment is one in which parents communicate anxieties about their children not growing quickly enough or, in some cases growing up too quickly and becoming too independent.

There is no doubt that how we look affects how people treat us and young people are particularly vulnerable to the pressures to meet culturally prescribed standards of beauty because of their desire to belong. An early study by Lerner *et al.* (1976) found female college students' self-esteem more strongly related to their perceptions of physical attractiveness than to physical effectiveness, that is, fitness and strength. For boys, while self-esteem was somewhat more related to effectiveness than attractiveness, the two ratings were highly correlated. This suggests that the judgements boys make about how good-looking they appear are strongly linked with judgements about how fit they feel. The same study indicated that the two factors contributing most strongly to girls' bodily acceptance were breast development and weight. Weight was seen as more important to girls than to boys in terms of satisfaction with physique. As most girls valued thinness, those more advanced in their puberty (and so heavier) were less satisfied. Prepubertal girls were also more satisfied with their less pronounced facial features and small hands and feet. However, the counterbalancing effect which helped more pubertally advanced girls feel better about their bodies was breast development, which was valued because of its appeal to males. It appears that an 'ideal' female shape for the current generation is that of 'child-woman', in which mature breast development is superimposed on the prepubertal body. Never mind that this is virtually an impossible shape for most women to achieve.

Fashion has increased the stresses on adolescent females with respect to body image and one of the outcomes has been a preoccupation with weight and an upsurge of the syndromes of anorexia nervosa and bulimia. The former is an obsessional and often unrealistic desire for thinness accompanied by excessive dieting to the point of starvation, while the latter refers to regular eating binges followed by purging by self-induced vomiting or laxatives. An illustration of this preoccupation comes from a study by Boocock and Trethewie (1981) of 65 high-school girls who were neither anorexic nor obese. These researchers modified a closed-circuit television so that the girl could project her subjective body image of front and side-on width by adjusting a dial which could stretch or shrink the picture up to 25 per cent wider or narrower than the girl's actual size. A substantial proportion of girls who were underweight in terms of standard age-height norms had a vision of themselves as fat and responded to this by dieting. By contrast, some of the overweight girls were unaware that they had a problem. There is obviously a need to encourage young people to be more realistic about bodily size and shape through education about the contribution of pubertal development to normal weight gain, the importance of a healthy diet and the distorting influences of fashion and media on beliefs about beauty. This is a tall order given that adults are often similarly preoccupied with appearance and weight and do not provide particularly convincing role models.

Body dissatisfaction has a range of negative health-related outcomes. Among young men of college age, Olivardia *et al.* (2004) found body dissatisfaction closely associated with depression, eating pathology, use of performance-enhancing substances and low self-esteem. An Australian longitudinal study (McCabe & Ricciardelli 2004) of nearly 900 13-year-olds tested twice, eight months apart, showed that both girls and boys exhibited high levels of body dissatisfaction, although the rates were greater for girls. In response to bodily concerns, boys were more likely to engage in strategies to increase muscle, such as participating in sport and using food supplements. Both of these strategies have the potential to be either healthy or unhealthy, the former when it involves exercise dependence, the latter when the supplements are dangerous for developing bodies, such as diuretics and steroids. The authors of this study found complex relationships between timing of puberty, extent of body satisfaction and healthy/unhealthy outcomes for boys. For girls, the findings were more clear-cut: both early and late maturing girls were at greater risk (than their on-time peers) of engaging in health-risk behaviours in response to their body dissatisfaction. The strategies they used were focused on weight loss, and included disordered eating patterns and exercise dependence.

Social factors alone may not be sufficient to account for the occurrence of body dissatisfaction including eating disorders like anorexia. A psychoanalytic interpretation of anorexia is that it represents an unconscious flight from sexual maturity through a return to a child-like body state and, usually, the cessation of menstruation when weight reduces to a certain level. Another interpretation involves the idea that anorexia is a way of coping with over-controlling parents, by resisting attempts to make the adolescent eat. Physiological factors have also been implicated. Along with bulimia, anorexia and milder eating disorders are most common among females in adolescence and early adulthood. These body image disturbances are likely to relate to developing sexuality and have effects on relationships between the sexes but in ways which have not yet been explored through systematic research.

While many studies have been concerned with body image in adolescents, few have asked teenagers about their responses to their developing genitals. Is this a source of conflict, pride or anxiety? Does it pass relatively unnoticed? Attitudes to genitals will begin to develop in childhood and be influenced by family attitudes, such as beliefs about modesty, cleanliness and sexuality. How do these attitudes affect young people's responses to the changes in their primary and secondary sex characteristics? From early infancy, parental ways of touching the child, holding him or her, expressing approval or disapproval and reacting to children's activities in relation to bathing, handling of genitals, toilet training and masturbation help to shape the child's body image and beliefs about the 'goodness' and 'badness' or 'cleanness' and 'dirtiness' of various bodily parts. Children in our society are socialized to believe that some bodily parts, notably the genitals, are not the subject of polite conversation nor are they to be viewed or touched publicly. Thus many a 2-year-old touching his or her genitals is told sharply to 'stop doing that'; a command which must be confusing and anxiety-arousing given that the act was probably a pleasurable one. Within this social framework, it would not be surprising if genital growth was a source of adolescent anxiety. The fictional Adrian Mole, quoted at the beginning of this section, kept a graph of the size of his 'thing' (penis) on his bedroom wall and his diary expresses mixtures of pride, mortification, misery and joy about his developing body and sexuality.

Sooner or later: the timing of puberty

The timing of puberty and the psychological effects of this biological event have been widely researched. Unfortunately, comparison between studies is often difficult because different measures are used to assess pubertal status (e.g. bone age, age of menarche, development of secondary sexual characteristics) and due to the use of different standards in the definition of early and late maturers (Brooks-Gunn & Reiter 1990). Results of these studies also depend on the comparison groups used, so that larger differences are found when early and late maturers are compared, than when early or late developers are compared with those maturing within the average or normal time span.

There is not much evidence to suggest that the biological factors associated with timing of puberty lead directly to psychological outcomes. Rather, it is more likely that biological changes affect psychological events both through personal perceptions of these events and through the meanings ascribed to them by family, peers and society. Such mediating variables might be feelings about growing up, conflict with parents or peers, cultural fashions with regard to body shape and social norms concerning sexuality.

The first major studies of early and late puberty, the Oakland Growth Study and the Berkeley Growth Study, found that early maturing boys had advantages over their late-maturing counterparts in self-assurance, poise, confidence, relaxation and popularity – in fact in a range of social and academic performance characteristics (Mussen & Jones 1957; Peskin 1967). Because of their more manly appearance, early developers were more likely to be chosen as leaders, to be popular with peers and to be given responsibility by adults. These are all situations that are likely to increase feelings of self-worth and self-esteem. On the other hand, late-developing boys were perceived to be at a disadvantage in many areas of behaviour and adjustment during adolescence. They are shorter and less strong which means they are less likely to be successful at competitive sport or in winning the admiration of girls, both activities valued highly by the peer group. The advantage enjoyed by early maturers was demonstrated by Mussen and Jones (1957) who found, using projective tests, significant differences in the self-evaluations of early and late-maturing boys. Late maturers completing the Thematic Apperception Test and the Rorschach Test consistently interpreted the central figures in these ambiguous stimuli as foolish or weak individuals, unable to solve problems without assistance and scorned by others. Themes expressed by early maturers were centred on potency and positive self-attributions.

Some of these effects were shown to persist into adulthood (Ames 1957; Peskin 1973) although Brooks-Gunn and Reiter (1990) suggest that later in life the popular, early-maturing boys may be at a disadvantage. The attributes which increased their prestige during adolescence may presage rigid, sex-stereotyped attributes in middle age rather than more flexible, adaptive characteristics. Ames (1957) found that although early maturers had a more active social life in adulthood, late maturers appeared to enjoy the best relationships with their wives and children. To gain popularity with girls, late-maturing boys may have to rely on developing their sensitivity and inter-personal communication skills, characteristics which will hold them in good stead in later intimate relationships.

More recent studies of early and late maturers suggest that the social advantages bestowed on early-maturing boys may no longer be evident, and that results from studies conducted during the 1950s and 1960s cannot be generalized to the contemporary situation. These studies suggest that early-maturing boys are more likely than their late-maturing counterparts to exhibit behaviour problems such as mild delinquency, misbehaviour in school (Duncan *et al.* 1985), drug and alcohol use (Andersson & Magnusson 1990), depression (Alaskar 1992; Susman *et al.* 1991) and even tendencies towards psychopathology (Graber *et al.* 1997). Gi *et al.* (2001), in a longitudinal study of 451 rural families from Iowa USA (the Iowa Youth and Families Project) showed that boys who were more physically developed in grade seven, compared with their less physically developed peers, manifested more externalized hostile feelings and internalized distress symptoms in grades eight and ten. Pubertal timing significantly predicted both external hostility and internal distress (basically depression, anxiety and somatization) even when statistically controlling for grade seven (baseline) maladjustment. Although these effects were small, they certainly lead us to rethink the hitherto supposed advantages of early puberty for boys.

What has changed for boys to lead to this reversal of research findings in a few decades? There is a combination of factors. While physical prowess may bring social prestige to these boys (and indeed research such as that of McCabe and Ricciardelli 2004 suggests they are still advantaged in peer popularity), there are apparently emotional costs which were perhaps not adequately measured in early studies. Today, notions of adjustment may lean more towards a focus on emotional factors than social factors such as status and reputation. Gi *et al.* also argue that the definition of early maturity is important. Their study showed maladjustment associated with pubertal signs in grade seven boys (about age 12), but not grade eight boys. As more peers reach puberty, the stresses associated with 'being different' may dissipate, and corresponding developments in cognitive and emotional maturity may assist young people in handling their physical changes. Another possibility is that the social meaning of puberty has changed over the years. The long apprenticeship associated with adulthood today means that the early-maturing male faces many years of 'enforced' boyhood before he can take his place in society as a man.

Studies have consistently shown that early-maturing does not advantage adolescent girls. These physically mature girls have poorer body images than late maturers (Blyth *et al.* 1985; Duncan *et al.* 1985) and are more likely to experience eating disorders (Brooks-Gunn & Warren 1985; McCabe & Ricciardelli 2004). This may be due to their relatively heavier weight in early puberty, a 'problem' which persists throughout life together with shorter stature. Emotional health may be poorer, with early maturers who experience stress at home more likely to suffer from depression (Paikoff *et al.* 1991; Stice *et al.* 2001). Difficulties seem to extend to school performance. In their longitudinal study, Simmons *et al.* (1983) showed that, at ages 11 to 13, late-maturing girls were doing exceptionally well at school while early maturers received lower marks and had more disciplinary problems than average or late maturers. By age 16, early maturers were dating more and considered themselves more popular with the opposite sex than average and late maturers but there were no differences between groups in same-sex popularity. Simmons *et al.* do not interpret early-maturing girls' popularity with boys in a positive light, regarding it as often accompanied by lowered self-esteem and a lack of emotional readiness. Data presented in a later chapter about early sexual initiation support this conclusion. Peterson (1989) interprets the school achievement differences between the groups as related to differences in opposite sex interest and responses to the stresses of puberty. She suggests that early maturers may be distracted from their studies by a precocious interest in boys. Alternatively, their poorer achievement may relate to the stresses which accompany a body developing at a faster rate than the capacity to deal with emotions. Another possibility is that late-maturing girls compensate for their lack of popularity with boys by concentrating on school work. What is of interest here are the links being made between sexual development and many other aspects of life with precocity, delay and asynchronies in this area affecting other aspects of adolescent development such as school work and popularity.

Not all research shows negative consequences for early-maturing girls. An old study by Peskin (1973) found that by the age of 30, women who had reached menarche early were more responsible, self-directed and objective in their thinking than their late-maturing peers. They were more poised in social situations and more psychologically flexible. These girls, who had faced the stresses of being out of step with their peers, may have developed coping mechanisms which were conducive to later adjustment.

To sum up, the research conclusions are that early maturing provides stresses for both girls and boys, particularly if puberty occurs well before the average age for one's same-sex peers. Late maturing can also be stressful, again more so if the young person is well behind the peer group in his or her physical maturation. Given that girls mature earlier than boys on average, it is the early-maturing girls and the late-maturing boys who are often most out of step with their peers, being most outside of the normative period for pubertal growth and development. Extremely early maturing boys or extremely late-maturing girls would be similarly stressed according to this framework and, in fact, there is evidence that this is the case (Gi *et al.* 2001).

An important caution in the interpretation of studies of early and late maturers is that effects are by no means universal, vary greatly between individuals and are affected by the social context in which puberty occurs. For example, Clausen (1975) found that early maturation was associated with high self-confidence in middle-class girls but lack of confidence in working-class girls. Another example is the finding by Blyth *et al.* (1985) of a relationship between timing of puberty effects and type of school attended. Teenagers' preparation for puberty, the cultural expectations associated with this event, the 'protection' offered by society for those who mature early in body but not emotionally and the opportunities for enhancing self-esteem given to those who are later maturing than their peers – all these factors and many others will influence the nature and timing of the effects of puberty.

Menstruation: curse, comfort or just inconvenient?

The psychoanalytic literature has tended to characterize first menstruation as anxiety-arousing and distressing (e.g. Deutsch 1944), as illustrated by the following quote:

> I had no information whatsoever, no hint that anything was going to happen to me . . . I thought I was on the point of death from internal haemorrhage . . . What did my highly educated mother do? She read me a furious lecture about what a bad, evil, immoral thing I was to start menstruating at the age of eleven! So young and so vile! Even after thirty years I can feel the shock of hearing her condemn me for 'doing' something I had no idea occurred.
>
> (Weideger 1976: 169)

The psychoanalyst Benedek is quoted in Bardwick as viewing menstruation to be the forerunner of 'the pain of defloration and the injuries that will be felt in childbirth' (Bardwick 1971: 50). Some support for this view of menstruation is found in a study by Shainess (1961) who found that women who had no preparation for their first period experienced fantasies of being cut or damaged. As Bardwick points out, negative feelings towards menstruation and the menstruating woman are expressed in all cultures. Menstruating women are also often perceived as unclean or taboo. Holding positive views of one's body is not made easy in the face of subtle or overt social messages that there is something dirty or unacceptable about this natural bodily function. Although tampon manufacturers have worked hard at sanitizing the image of periods via tasteful advertisements of their wares, the social meaning of menstruation in modern western society is still unclear. The association between blood and injury or illness has to be put aside by young women if menstruation is to be accepted as part of healthy, normal functioning.

Menstruating girls must also come to terms with the hassles of periods which include, for some, discomfort and mood swings.

Menstruation, marking as it does the beginning of 'womanhood', may be perceived as having great psychological as well as physical significance by girls and their parents. All the social meanings of being a woman are activated, such as ideas about sexiness, reproductive capacity, 'availability' and pressures towards stereotyping. Parents may feel ambivalent or negative about their child growing up and being potentially sexually vulnerable. Given this confusion of potential responses, it would be surprising if some stresses did not ensue from achievement of this milestone in sexual maturation.

Earlier literature on menstruation suggested a high frequency of negative reactions, but conclusions were often based on retrospective reports of clinical adult samples (Brooks-Gunn 1984; Grief & Ulman 1982). Negative experiences have been associated with lack of preparedness for first menses (Brooks-Gunn & Reiter 1990). It is interesting that the number of women who report being unprepared increases dramatically with the age cohort. Today's young women are far better prepared than their mothers and grandmothers and are likely to have had extensive discussions about this topic with their mothers and girlfriends. But there is still embarrassment and a sense of privacy associated with menstruation, reflecting ambivalent or negative social attitudes. Girls almost never discuss menstruation with boys or their fathers, and even among girlfriends they remain reluctant to discuss the topic immediately after they have their first period (Moore 1995). One study revealed that only a quarter tell anyone other than their mothers when they reach menarche although later on there may be a sharing with friends of tales of symptoms and discomforts (Brooks-Gunn *et al.* 1986).

Perhaps as a result of better preparedness and less socially restrictive attitudes towards matters bodily and sexual – but also possibly because of improved health and fitness – young women in western nations in the 21st century are far less likely, for the most part, to express extremely negative responses to menstruation than were the women of earlier generations. When Brooks-Gunn and her colleagues interviewed girls within two or three months of their first period, about 20 per cent reported only positive responses and about 20 per cent reported negative ones. The remainder felt unsure or expressed mixed emotions. About two-thirds were somewhat frightened or upset although the intensity of these feelings was mild (Ruble & Brooks-Gunn 1982). Nevertheless, with the average age for first menstruation now a year or more younger than it was for their parents, many girls experience their first period while still in primary school, in some cases before any formal sex education has occurred. Silbereisen and Kracke (1997) showed that fast-maturing girls who had experienced early menarche felt unprepared for issues of personal hygiene and did not know how to cope with sports during their periods. An Australian study of Year 6 girls (aged around 11 and 12 years: Moore 1995) demonstrated that knowledge of menstrual changes was poor, with 60 per cent of girls uncertain about whether they could use tampons, most of the sample believing that mood changes were inevitable, and most also greatly overestimating the amount of blood loss to be expected in a typical period. One girl summed up the feelings of many in the following exchange:

Interviewer: Why do you think girls get periods?
11-year-old girl: I don't know. I don't know why we need this. Why don't boys get one?

(Moore 1995: 94)

In Moore's study, attitudes expressed towards menstruation were assessed by asking girls to 'complete the story' in a series of scenarios about menstruation, for example 'Jenny rang Sue to ask her to go swimming. She has her period, what does she do?' In the stories told by girls, attitudes expressed included shame, embarrassment and anxiety. Some examples are:

Hi Sue, how about you come to the pool with me today? Sorry Jenny I am grounded for a week. Why are you grounded? Because I broke the kitchen door.

Sue had her period but she went. She put on a tampon before she went swimming in the water with Jenny. They swam for hours. When she went out of the pool, blood was all over Sue's leg, everyone was laughing at her, she was so embarrassed. Later on she never went in the pool ever again when she had her period.

(Moore 1995: 97)

Brooks-Gunn & Reiter (1990) reject the notion of menstruation as a developmental crisis, viewing it as a challenge to self-definition, an event to be incorporated in the developing self-concept. Certainly, in Moore's study, there were girls who completed stories about menstruation that exhibited a positive, problem-solving approach. For example, in response to a story about Jill having cramps on the first day of her period, one 11-year-old wrote:

Jill goes to the toilet, she has her period and she tells her mum. Her mum buys some pads to take to school and she (Jill) gets on with her life.

(1995: 99)

Girls who successfully meet this challenge and define their menstrual experience within a relatively positive framework will be those who have been best prepared, who do not reach puberty at a much earlier age than their peers, and who receive their information about menstruation from positively valued sources.

Wet dreams

Our knowledge of the psychological meaning of this sign that fertility is developing in boys is far less detailed than our knowledge of the effects of menstruation. First ejaculations may be a source of guilt in boys if they are associated with masturbation (Garbarino 1985) although the severe social condemnation of masturbation and its presumption as the cause of various health problems is largely a thing of the past as we saw earlier. Gaddis and Brooks-Gunn (1985) interviewed a small sample of adolescent boys about their emotional reactions to first ejaculation and found that two-thirds of the sample felt a little frightened by the experience although most had positive responses. Unlike girls, who had mostly discussed their first menstruation quite extensively with their mothers, none of the boys had discussed ejaculation with their peers and only one had mentioned the event to his father. Furthermore, the boys were extremely reluctant to engage in such discussions. Apparently this reluctance does not only stem from the boys. Frankel (2002) asked a small sample of parents of young adolescent boys whether they had communicated with their sons about first ejaculation, or whether they were intending to do so. Parents reported that they had rarely engaged in such communications, the majority (54 per cent) indicating 'I've never thought about it'.

Another issue of interest in the sexual maturation of boys is the problems and difficulties they have in controlling erections – well documented in folklore but not in research. Such events may be embarrassing and humiliating (Garbarino 1985) or coped with readily via joking and humour. We do not really know how most young boys feel about untimely or unexpected erections. Further research on the psychological meaning of sexual maturation in adolescent boys is important but difficult to carry out because boys are embarrassed to talk about these sexual topics in a serious way (Brooks-Gunn & Reiter 1990; Moore & Rosenthal 1991c).

Puberty and sexual initiation

What is the link between pubertal development and the initiation of sexual behaviour? The answer to this question is extremely complex because, although our hormones affect us, we are also strongly influenced by the social lens through which we view sex. Consideration of cultures with very different sexual mores from our own highlights this point. Marshall and Suggs (1971) have described the sexual behaviours of the inhabitants of Inis Beag (a small island off the coast of Ireland) and of Mangaia, an island in the South Pacific. The first of these is a sexually restrictive culture, in which it is reported that a number of sexual activities common to western developed nations are unknown (such as French kissing and hand stimulation of the genitals), sex education is rare, nudity is considered disgusting and intercourse bad for the health. Premarital sex in this society is unknown, yet puberty occurs as it does among all human beings. The physiological changes that accompany puberty do not lead inevitably to sexual experimentation, presumably because hormonally related events are not interpreted in a way which allows for this to happen. In contrast, the Mangaian adolescent is instructed in awareness of his or her genitals, trained in the arts of lovemaking by older women and encouraged to have many sexual experiences with a number of partners before settling down with a marriage partner. Puberty is considered a milestone in development and sexual behaviour is socially sanctioned to occur subsequently.

There is, nevertheless, in western society, a clear association between the signs of pubertal development and the initiation of adolescent sexual activity. After puberty, more and more young people gain sexual experience, usually outside marriage, as we saw in Chapter 1. The relationship between the onset of puberty and sexual debut varies between subcultures and social groups, however. The average time between onset of puberty and first intercourse has also varied across the last two or three decades, with greater approval accorded to premarital sex in the last 20 or 30 years together with an earlier age of sexual initiation, although this trend appears to be levelling off or even reversing in the USA, the UK and Australia (Grunbaum *et al.* 2002; Johnson *et al.* 1994; Rissel *et al.* 2003; Wellings *et al.* 2001).

A study by Smith *et al.* (1985) illustrates the complex interaction between biology and social forces in relation to sexual initiation, and the different pattern of this interaction for boys and girls. White adolescents aged 12 to 15 years were asked about their own sexual behaviour and that of their friends. Close friends' responses could be identified through an anonymous coding system. Respondents were also asked to rate themselves on different aspects of pubertal development. For boys, these were related to androgen-associated changes such as voice deepening and for girls, to oestrogen-based changes (such as breast development and menarche) and androgen-related developments like bodily hair. Boys and girls were both asked to match their pubertal development stage to drawings depicting stages of genital development. In this way sexual behaviour could be linked to both puberty stage and peer influence. For boys, hormonally related changes and best friend's sexual behaviour were both positively associated with their level of sexual involvement. For girls, the results were more complex. They suggested that androgen levels, as measured by pubic hair stage (and reflecting level of sex drive), and oestrogen levels (representing outward signs of sexual maturity) have separate positive influences on sexual behaviour. Best friend's sexual behaviour was also influential. Interactions between these predictors were such that at low levels of androgen development (low sex drive), a young girl was less likely to become sexually involved whatever her friends were doing, while at higher levels of sex drive, friends' behaviour became a positive influence. The extent to which the girl looks sexually developed will also influence sexual involvement, presumably by acting as a signal to potential partners that she is sexually mature.

The results of this and other studies have been interpreted to mean that social influences on sexual behaviour are stronger for girls than for boys. Such studies point to the need to understand simultaneously the roles of both biological maturation and social norms on the initiation of sexual intercourse and the engaging in other sexual behaviours such as fantasy and masturbation. While this chapter has reviewed the role of puberty in sexual development and sexual behaviour, in the next chapter we delineate some relevant social forces. The complex interaction between culture and biology must not, however, be overlooked.

4 Parents and peers: shaping influences

In the next two chapters we examine the effects of some of the social influences on adolescents' thinking about sex, what they do and when they do it. These social factors shape and interact with biology. We learn how to interpret and act out our sexual feelings on the basis of the social attitudes we extract from our cultural contexts. These attitudes are initially formed at home, so that parental models and teachings are important. But increasingly as children get older they are influenced by the contexts provided by the peer group and the wider social arena. We discuss the nature of these proximal family and peer influences in this chapter, and those more distal aspects of the social milieu that impinge upon sexual behaviour and attitudes in the subsequent chapter.

Parents

Taking the adolescents' viewpoint, we asked sexually active young girls from diverse backgrounds about the kind of influences their family had on their ideas about sex (Moore 1994). Responses ranged from the feeling that family had no influence at all to claims that parents passed on values that contributed to shaping sexual development, offering guidance and protection in this difficult area. For example: 'My family has had a big influence on me and so far it has moulded my way of thinking [about sex]'. Other more negative claims were also made including parents curtailing sexual learning by restrictions on freedom and inhibiting young people's moral development by imposing values of their own: 'Our parents have forced into our brains, no sex before marriage . . . I think the ones that are locked up will rebel!'

There is no question that young people take notice of their parents' attitudes and guidance about sexuality, even if it is only to rebel. The 'experts' have also been saying for years that parents are a powerful force in sex education, but they don't always get it right, as suggested in this quote from a medical text from more than 50 years ago:

> Education in sex hygiene is needed to establish better standards . . . The present unfortunate position, where so many gain their first misinformation about sex from some precocious youngster and the furtiveness and indecency which surrounds the whole matter, should be forestalled. Parents may do much by answering truthfully the justifiable curiosity of the young child. The glib lies or stern reproofs, so often employed, are stupid and futile. The later instruction is deferred, the more difficult it is for parents to share the confidences of their young adolescents. Just when they might most help their growing boys and girls, who are just entering a new world of sex, their help is not sought.
>
> (Sutton 1944: 558)

The psychological literature assures us of the profound influence that parents have on the lives of their children. Parents are regarded as the primary socializers of their children, with influence over a variety of beliefs and behaviours. But when we turn to the domain of sexuality, we are dealing with an area of human functioning that has long been surrounded by guilt, mystery, and controversy. How do parents translate their own feelings about sexuality into messages that they give their children? What influence do parents have on the sexual beliefs and behaviours of young people and how are these influences manifested?

What are parents doing about sex education?

Most parents are not trained as educators, let alone as biologists, sex educators and psychologists. Yet many feel that it is important that at least some sex education comes from the home, and try their best to put across information, attitudes and values. Sometimes it's 'too little too late', sometimes it's 'just right' and sometimes what is 'taught' is not necessarily what is 'learnt'. Moore and Rosenthal (1991c) asked sexually active 17- to 20-year olds about what they perceived their parents had communicated to them about sex. Young people on the whole thought their parents disapproved of their adolescent children engaging in sexual intercourse or sex before marriage (about 60 per cent) or having casual sex with several partners (87 per cent). Only 15 per cent of girls and 33 per cent of boys felt they could discuss with their parents any concerns they had about sex, and less than half felt that a substantial amount of their sex education had come from their parents. Very few adolescents of either sex agreed that their parents had discussed contraception with them, or assisted them in arranging for contraception. Fathers were far less likely than mothers to have engaged in any form of sex education with their children.

This is by no means an isolated finding. Nearly 300 high-schoolers completed surveys describing the frequency and importance of mother and father communication about 20 different sex-related topics, in a study by Rosenthal and Feldman (1999). Adolescents reported infrequent communication. When it did occur it was mostly by mothers, and to girls. The major topics discussed were sexual development (such as menstruation and pubertal changes) and sexual safety (contraception and safe sex). Communication about experiencing sex in relationships was even less common, but interestingly, adolescents did not consider these topics to be ones which they particularly wanted to discuss with parents. A range of other studies have shown that despite the widespread belief that parents should be the primary sources of information on sexuality, they usually are not (Abrams *et al.* 1990; Ansuini *et al.* 1996; Rosenthal & Smith 1995).

A study which matched parents' and adolescents' perceptions of parental contributions to the sex education of their children was conducted by Feldman and Rosenthal (2000) with a sample of 209 tenth graders, 156 mothers and 91 fathers. Parents evaluated themselves more highly as sex educators than did their adolescent children, with teens rating their parents as less comfortable with sexual communication, more controlling, more likely to bring up unwanted topics and more likely to avoid important issues than the parents rated themselves. Adolescents' evaluations of their parents' communications about sex were strongly related to ratings of their parents as communicators in general, but less so to frequency of sex-related communication. Quality rather than quantity of communication was an important variable in this study.

Barriers and misperceptions in parent-adolescent communication about sex

While many parents do an excellent job at gradually preparing adolescents for the responsibilities of adulthood and handing them the freedom to shoulder those responsibilities, the task may seem more difficult in the sexual domain. For example, parents often find initiating and sustaining discussions about sexuality with their teenagers extremely 'fraught'. They feel that they lack knowledge, are embarrassed by the topic and may have misperceptions about their adolescent's behaviour. Asked about parents' responsibility for AIDS education for their teenagers, one parent in a study by Rosenthal and Collis (1997: 65) responded: 'I like to think parents should be, but it is my experience that it is a very difficult thing for far too many parents and kids to discuss. Also, many parents prefer to believe their kids are virgins or could not accept their kids might have a homosexual experience. As for drugs!!'

The possibility that there are many misperceptions and miscommunications between parents and their adolescent children about sex is difficult to ignore. Rosenthal and Collis (1997) asked parents of 16-year-old teenagers for estimates about the level of sexual activity among 16-year-olds generally, and received answers reflecting current norms. The same parents, asked their beliefs about their own teenager's sexual activities, were far more conservative in their estimates. In other words, parents found it hard to believe that their own children might have experienced intercourse even though they recognized that similarly aged teenagers were often sexually active. Moreover, parents held more optimistic beliefs than adolescents' teachers about adolescent condom use, knowledge and parent-child communication, and stronger beliefs in parental influence. The data from this study suggests that parents may be seeing what they would like to see, rather than what is. Katchadourian (1990) believes that such misperceptions may arise from the incest taboo. Discussions about sex are a form of sexual interaction and, in the family context, these discussions are often embarrassing, even when both parents and adolescents have liberal attitudes and are comfortable about talking with peers about sexual matters. Furthermore, there may be some adaptive function in parents 'turning a blind eye' (even unconsciously) to adolescent sexual experimentation. Experimentation is one way in today's society for young people to gain a sense of independence from parents, to begin the process of growing up and taking on adult roles. Given that economic independence for teenagers is becoming less possible, the move to independence through sexuality may have healthy elements. Of course it has its risks as well. The concerned parent needs to tread the fine line between respecting an adolescent's privacy and providing information and a values framework so that the teenager can make sensible and well-informed decisions about sexual behaviour.

Another issue is that what parents perceive as meaningful discussion about sex may not impinge on adolescents. Jaccard *et al.*

(2002) reviewed a wide range of studies concluding that about 70 per cent of parents say that they have talked with their teenagers about sex, whereas only about 50 per cent of adolescents indicate that they have had discussions about sex with their parents. Perhaps parents believe they are making an impression because they have made a big effort to broach these topics, but they have not pitched their message to their child's needs, nor checked whether the message was communicated or understood. Jaccard *et al.* suggest that some parents raise the topic of sex education but then do not continue because their adolescents tell them they already know. However, there may not be a follow-up check as to whether this is the case, given that the whole event may be shrouded in embarrassment, with everyone keen to get it over quickly. Conversations may go along the lines of:

Son, I guess it's time we had a talk about . . . you know.
That's OK dad, we did it at school in biology.
You're sure? . . . Your mother's worried you might get in with the wrong company.
No worries dad.
Great, I'm glad we had this chat.

Communication styles

Mothers' perceptions of the style, content and frequency of their communications with their adolescents about sex and sexuality were examined through analyses of semi-structured interviews with 16 mothers of 16-year-old sons and 14 mothers of similarly aged daughters (Rosenthal *et al.* 1998a, 2001). All the mothers assessed themselves to be effective communicators, but their styles differed greatly, in terms of who initiated and maintained the communication (mother or child), the comfort levels of the mother and teenager, the frequency of these communications, the contexts in which they took place and the topics discussed. The researchers isolated five styles of sexual communication: avoidant, reactive, opportunistic, child-initiated and mutually interactive. Avoidant styles were characterized by both the mothers and the adolescents being uncomfortable with discussing sexual topics, and these discussions being avoided, cut short or presented in generalized, non-personal terms when they did occur. Feelings and psychological issues were rarely discussed, the emphasis being on biological or factual material. Mothers using this style tended to reassure themselves that adequate sex education had occurred at school. A typical example: 'I think if he hasn't asked me now, he's probably not going to, so I would presume, you know, or else he's a bit embarrassed to talk about it' (mother of son) (Rosenthal *et al.* 1998a: 732).

Reactive communicators were mothers who only reported one or two sex-related discussions with their teenager, and these were initiated when a pressing need was perceived on the basis of the child's behaviour, for example when the teenager appeared to be 'getting serious' with a romantic partner. Generally, the mothers did not feel particularly confident about these discussions, they feared alienating their teenager, but were concerned to get a message across. They tended to report that the discussions were mainly one-sided, but that this was characteristic of their discussions on a range of topics, not just sex: 'It's a bit hard sometimes to get conversation and things out of him, even just ordinary school work' (mother of son) (Rosenthal *et al.* 1998a: 733).

Opportunistic communicators formed the largest category of mothers – they reported that they were willing to discuss sex-related topics with their adolescents, but did so infrequently. They sought shared occasions to initiate discussions, such as television pro-grammes, family events and the stimulus of sex education occurring at school. They wove their communications in with other activities (such as preparing meals), bringing up issues almost as incidentals, as a way of dissipating anxiety and embarrassment. They talked about feelings as well as opinions, and covered a broad range of topics: 'It's not that we'll sit down and talk specifically about anything, it could just be something that we've seen on TV, something that perhaps they relate to what's happened around them and then we'll sort of have a discussion about it' (mother of daughter) (Rosenthal *et al.* 1998a: 744). Nevertheless these mothers, like the reactive communicators, did not get much response from their children and were largely unaware of what the teenagers were thinking about sexual issues.

Seven mothers were in the child-initiated communications group. These mothers were characterized by a communication style in which they waited until their adolescent brought up the topic before dis-cussion. They believed that when the child was ready to engage in sex-related discussion, the conversations would be more fruitful than if they were parent-initiated: 'Yes, she would probably initiate it [from] something that might have happened at school or something' (mother of daughter); or: 'He does it in layers sometimes. He'll ask a couple of questions and then perhaps go and stew about it and come back and ask some more' (mother of son) (Rosenthal *et al.* 1998a: 736).

Finally, and perhaps most successfully, mothers in the mutually interactive group indicated that sex-related conversations could be initiated either by the adolescent or the parent, and both parties were comfortable about pursuing these conversations. Mother-child communications were generally characterized by openness, intimacy and emotionally based discussions. Mothers worked consciously to promote open communication and make time for their children to bring up issues, and to be good listeners. They were comfortable about setting boundaries and respectful of the child's sensitivities. The authors of this study argued that mothers who were good communicators matched their message to the receptivity and needs of the listener, but also that there may be more than one optimal style for communication about sexual issues to teenagers. Some young people may be more concerned than others about privacy and intrusion into their personal lives as they struggle for autonomy and a sense of self. Some topics may be perceived as 'off limits' or overly invasive, such as discussions about masturbation.

What about fathers? We know they take very little part in the sex education of their children, particularly their daughters, but the reasons appear to be complex and subtle. Kirkman *et al.* (2002) interviewed mothers, fathers and young adolescents in 19 families in which the adolescents were in Year 8 of secondary school (aged about 13 years). Both parents acknowledged that sexuality was a difficult topic, but fathers felt these difficulties more keenly and tended to leave it to the mothers. They expressed puzzlement, confusion and disappointment at this state of affairs, overtly wishing in some cases that they could have overcome the barriers that had been present in communicating with their own fathers. The fathers in this study seemed to have strong, affectionate relationships with their children, but these relationships had been disrupted to some extent by the child's developing adolescence, as if the child's burgeoning sexuality was intruding into the relationship. Fathers felt awkward, nervous even, about broaching sexual topics. One father said that trying to talk to his daughters was like 'talking to a tiger'. The awkwardness was at least in part because the adolescents were embarrassed and often rejected or laughed off their fathers' conversational overtures.

The researchers also found that while most families saw equal mother and father responsibility for communication about sex to teenage children, in practice nearly all the talking was done by mum. This was recognized by all parties, and various explanations put forward such as 'women communicate better' and 'women are better at talking about emotional issues'. There was also an underlying tension about fathers communicating about sexuality, especially to their daughters. Kirkman *et al.* write 'the nature of male heterosexuality is that mothers are safer sexual communicators' (2002: 71). In the families studied this was expressed by discussions of men outside the family as potentially dangerous and sexual predators. For example, one father said, 'I have talked to my daughters about the way a younger fit man is affected by sexual attraction and erections, and how good, common, normal sense can go out the window when he's rampant'. Another commented, 'All they want to do is get in your pants and then they're gone . . . I'm a male and I know what mongrels males can be'. Fathers also warned their sons of getting into 'bad company' with other males who might pressure women into having sex. Families in this study apparently bought into the 'male sex drive discourse' (discussed in a previous chapter) and, in doing so, in effect labelled themselves as dangerous even though their intentions were not so. The attribution of high power and sexual potency to men in general effectively prohibited men as fathers from taking a more caring, emotionally based role in family discussions about sexuality without metaphorically emasculating themselves.

Programmes for parents

On the basis of the kinds of data reviewed above, Kirby and Miller (2002) propose objectives for interventions designed to assist parents to communicate more effectively about sex to their teenagers. They suggest that good programmes will: (a) increase parents' knowledge about sexual issues and also about the sexual behaviours of young people; (b) help parents understand that talking about sex to teenagers is likely to have beneficial effects, and unlikely to increase the chances that their teenagers will engage in sex; (c) help parents clarify their own values about sex and express these in ways that do not 'turn off' the teenager, and thus foreclose further discussion possibilities; and (d) improve parents' skills in talking about sexuality, through increasing their comfort with the material, their listening skills and their skills in initiating discussions. These authors argue that any good programme for parents will acknowledge that being uncomfortable with intergenerational family discussions about sex is normal and acceptable, because such discussions are always in danger of broaching taboo topics and privacy norms. They might also have added that, because of these taboos and norms, it may be appropriate for certain topics to be 'off limits'. In these cases parents may be able to use more subtle communications such as suggesting (or leaving around) particular books, or drawing attention to television programmes or movies that might deal with the issues.

Kirby and Miller, having reviewed many parent programmes, conclude that those most likely to succeed are based around school activities and actively involve the parents in students' homework assignments about sexuality. In this approach, there is a strong motive for parents to be involved, their involvement can be structured in ways that are educative for both parent and child, and parents' expression of values can be sought in ways that are distanced from the stimulus of the adolescents' actual behaviour. Such programmes have great potential to reach a large number of parents (unlike interventions which require mothers and fathers to participate in special programmes outside their homes). Also potentially effective were media campaigns to increase parent-child communication about sex with a view to reducing a public health problem such as teenage pregnancy or HIV transmission. Kirby and Miller note that these programmes, while likely to reach many families, have rarely been evaluated as to whether they lead to changes in behaviour.

Talking Sexual Health: A Parents' Guide (Jones *et al.* 1999) is a best-practice example of a public health initiative in this domain. A small 28-page booklet of light weight (so that it can be inexpensively mailed in bulk) has been developed for parents to assist them in discussion of sexual issues with their children. The book, while providing further reading and resources, is presented in simple language and includes tips for good communication, information about feelings, quotes from young people and research that can act as conversation starters, and basic information about safe sex, pregnancy, contraception and STIs. On the back cover it lists the World Health Organization's (WHO) recommended life skills for young people in the sexual health domain. These behavioural goals help to focus the mind on the really important issues for the sexual health of adolescents, reminding parents that we cannot wrap our children in cotton wool and protect them from the inevitable pains (nor bar them from the pleasures) of growing up. WHO states that young people need the ability to:

- make sound decisions about relationships and sexual intercourse and stand up for these decisions;
- deal with pressures for unwanted sex or drug use;
- recognize a situation that might turn risky or violent;
- know how and where to ask for help and support;
- know how to negotiate protected sex and other forms of safe sex when ready for sexual relationships.

Do what I say, not what I do: the influence of parental attitudes and behaviours

Direct sex education/discussion is not the only way that adolescent sexuality can be shaped by parents. It may indeed have quite a small influence in relation to more indirect factors. According to Thornton and Camburn (1987), parents can influence adolescent sexual behaviour through transmission of attitudes (both directly and indirectly), and through their own behaviours. The marital and childbearing behaviour of parents, including experiences with divorce, remarriage, living arrangements and apparent behaviours towards the opposite sex may provide and support role models for young people. The degree of supervision of young people that parents provide, their discipline practices and parenting style will also shape young people's opportunities for and comfort with various sexual activities and the pace of the behavioural elements of their sexual developmental timetables.

With respect to attitudes, parental approval of adolescent sexual activity is traditionally low. Darling and Hicks (1982) characterized the major parental communications about sex as reflecting these sentiments: 'Pregnancy before marriage can lead to terrible things'; 'No nice person has sex before marriage'; 'Petting can too easily lead to intercourse'; and – the one positive message – 'Sex is a good way of expressing your love for someone'. Have these attitudes changed? The 'me' generations of the 1970s and 1880s who embraced self- (and sexual-) fulfilment as a right are now parents of teenagers. These parents rebelled against the more traditional values of their post-war mothers and fathers, and might be expected to hold more liberal attitudes to their own teenagers' sexual activities. Indeed, parents and teenagers may now collude along the lines of 'Don't let your grandmother know you're on the pill'. The research literature is unclear as to whether these changes are relatively generalized or only evident among particular subgroups. What is clear though is that the attitudinal messages that 'get through' from parents are somewhat different for daughters than for sons.

Darling and Hicks, for example, found that both sons and daughters heard more cautionary messages about sex than positive ones from their parents, but the difference was greater for females. And although sexual discussion with parents was rare in our study of older adolescents (Moore & Rosenthal 1991c), sons were far more likely than daughters to perceive liberal parental attitudes to sex. Further, Moore *et al.* (1986) found that parents who held traditional attitudes to sex and had communicated these to their daughters were the only group whose attitudes had apparently influenced their children's sexual behaviour. In this case, their daughters were less likely to have had intercourse. Boys' sexual behaviours were not associated with per- ceived parental approval of sexual involvement. Sixteen years later, a similar finding comes from a study by McNeely *et al.* (2002), using a very large sample of matching dyads of mothers and their 14- to 15- year-old children. These researchers were unable to predict the timing of first intercourse for boys using a large range of parental psycho- social variables. For girls, mothers' satisfaction with the relationship with their daughters, mothers' strong sense of disapproval of their daughters having sex, and frequency of communication with the parents of their daughters' friends were associated with later sexual debut. These studies provide some support for the notion that the socialization process puts a brake on female sexuality, with parents' rare discussions about sex with their children consisting for the most part of warnings to their daughters. These warnings, implicitly or explicitly emphasize the risks of sexuality; for example the poet, Anne Sexton, writes to her 16-year-old daughter: 'The right thing, the nice thing the kind-to-yourself [*sic*] thing is to wait until it will be something special; not just fumbling on the grass or on a couch or in a car . . . I really think it's better to wait until you're older and readier to handle it' (Payne 1983: 36).

There is more than a little evidence that parent behaviour, of various sorts, has more influence on teenage sexual behaviour than parent talk (Moore & Rosenthal 1993: 65):

> If your parents are divorced or separated, and your mum or dad brings home different people on weekends and each night of the week and stuff, you sort of think that [having sex] is no big deal. It is not special or anything like that. But if your parents are married and stuff like that, you sort of see it as a big deal and should only share it if you love the person.
>
> (16-year-old girl)

Research suggests that general features of family atmosphere and family dynamics (such as parental warmth and family conflict) are relevant to sexuality outcomes for young people. Non-virginity in youths has been associated with non-authoritative parenting (Kandel 1990), permissiveness and lack of parental support (Inazu & Fox 1980). Reports from the US National Longitudinal Study of Adolescent Health (Add Health) conclude that sexual debut among young people occurs at a higher age among families with a high sense of connect- edness, that is, where there is a high perceived degree of closeness, caring, feeling understood, loved and wanted, and where the adolescent feels satisfied with parental relationships (Blum & Rinehart 1997; Resnick *et al.* 1998). Early sexual intercourse and teenage pregnancy were also less likely among families where adolescents and their parents spent time together in joint activities, according to this large US study. In addition, parental presence in the home at 'key' times of day (before and after school, dinner time and bed time) acted as a protective factor against adolescent emotional distress, presumably because these are the times when young people are more likely to seek access to support, either directly or indirectly through angry, withdrawn or agitated behaviour. As any parent of an adolescent is aware, young people will not necessarily discuss their problems (including their concerns about sexuality) 'on cue'. If parents are perceived as available and ready to discuss issues according to the adolescent's emotional timetable, then opportunities for good communication are multiplied.

There is a strong relationship between a mother's own sexual experience as a teenager and that of her adolescent daughter (Newcomer & Udry 1983b). Girls from single-parent families are more likely to become sexually active at an earlier age than those who grow up in two-parent families (Davis & Friel 2001; Newcomer & Udry 1983b). The mechanisms underlying these associations are not clearly understood, however. They may be a function of role modelling, or they may reflect a lack of parental supervision, or they may in some way relate to paternal absence. A study by Longmore *et al.* (2001) does suggest that supervision is a key variable, as indeed did the Add Health study discussed previously. Longmore *et al.* collected data on parental practices of preadolescents, then followed up the children of these families five or six years later, when the children were 14 or 15 years old. Early parental monitoring was assessed by asking whether children were allowed to be home alone after school and at other times, how insistent parents were about knowing their child's whereabouts, and any restrictions they placed on television watching. A clear finding from the study was that parents who monitored their children in preadolescence had teens who delayed the onset of sexual activity. Other parental variables measured at preadolescence, like support and coercive control, were not associated with later teenage dating or sexual practices.

Studies which relate the initiation of early sexual activity to lack of family closeness and lack of parental support suggest that adolescents who seek independence early due to unsatisfactory family relationships regard sex as part of the expression of that independence. On the other hand, it is entirely possible that the causal chain operates in the opposite way. Thus, an adolescent's sexual behaviour may lead to a withdrawal of closeness within a family. Feldman *et al.* (1995) investigated the possibility that parents influence their children's sexual expression indirectly, via the socialization of coping strategies and personality traits. They showed that learnt restraint – incorporating the ability to delay gratification, inhibit aggression, exercise impulse control, be considerate of others and act responsibly – was a factor which mediated between family interaction patterns and adolescent sexual expression for boys. Family environment measures taken when the boys were in grade six (aged 10 to 12) predicted with 70 per cent accuracy those boys who would be virgins or non-virgins four years later. Low-restraint boys were characterized by less supportive families, rejecting fathers, indulgent parents and a greater number of sexual partners at mid-adolescence. Although more research is needed in this area (e.g. to investigate the role of restraint for girls), it is clear that the influence which parents have over their adolescents in the sexual domain is more likely to be indirect than as a result of direct communications.

The range of studies reviewed here indicates that the generality of family atmosphere and the specifics of parental supervision practices have the potential to impact on adolescent sexual development. Parents, it seems, must walk a fine line in providing emotional support and healthy attitudes for the developing sexuality of their adolescent children, while also protecting them or limiting their opportunities for harmful (but not benign) sexual experimentation. Parents need also to be aware of their role as models of behaviour. Given adolescents' finely tuned antennae for hypocrisy, they are unlikely to get away with a 'do as I say, not as I do' approach.

Of course parents influence their children's sexuality through genetic inheritance as well as through their socializing techniques. Parents provide genes that affect appearance, which influences attractiveness, which, in turn, influences opportunities for sexual encounters. Further, there is a genetic aspect to early puberty, and this is associated with earlier sexual experiences, especially for boys. These interactions between biology and socialization need to be considered in teasing out the complex ways in which parents influence their children's sexual development and behaviour.

Other adult models of sexual behaviour

Parents are not the only adult role models available to adolescents. Young people have about them many models of adult lifestyles in which diverse patterns of sexual expression are practised. Examples range through stable monogamous marriages, divorce and recoupling, single parenting, lifestyles characterized by frequent partner changing, and homosexual couples. These days, an adolescent may be almost as likely to watch a parent or other adult agonize about dating and sexual conduct as the reverse. The messages sent by the adult generation about sex are far less clear than they were in the 1950s. Adults seem confused, and their confusion is expressed in worries about relationships, divorce, sexual acting out and sometimes violence. What are the effects of this adult confusion and variety of relationship behaviours on the developing sexuality of young people? One outcome appears to be that adolescents have increased tolerance of sexual diversity and the expressed approval of people 'doing their own thing', even if these behaviours are not engaged in or desired by the adolescent himself or herself (Coleman & Hendry 1990). Beyond this general kind of finding, we know little about the mechanisms by which adult sexual norms affect the youth generation and indeed about the extent of that effect. One way of exploring this further is to examine the influences on young people of various aspects of the wider adult culture, such as the media. Another is to look at the ways in which adults attempt to influence and, to some extent, control adolescent sexual expression directly, through schools, religion and the law. These issues will be taken up in the next chapter. We now go on to explore the second major proximal influence on adolescent sexuality, that of the peer group.

Peers

While peer influence has little impact, relative to that of parents, on young children, there is a shift at adolescence, with peers becoming more important in forming teenagers' beliefs and regulating their behaviour. Peer influence is often cited as an important factor affecting adolescent sexual decisions, and it can operate in a number of ways. Teenagers can obtain information about sex from their friends, which may serve to guide decision-making about sex. This information is, of course, not always accurate, as reflected in long-standing teenage myths about fertility such as 'You can't get pregnant the first time you have sex'. Second, adolescents can accept peer attitudes about sexuality. These can be implicitly reflected in peer behaviour which the teenager may use as a model for his or her own behaviour, or they can be actively proselytized through discussion, questioning, teasing, dares, shaming and the like.

The strong desire of many young people to be like their admired age-mates and part of a group can lead them to engage in the sexual behaviours, and express the sexual attitudes, that they perceive as characteristic of a particular 'hero' or group. It is well to remember that these peer influences are not always negative, as friends and adolescent groups may express and model healthy as well as unhealthy sexual attitudes and behaviours. This issue receives scant attention in current research, where the emphasis seems often to address only adult disapproval of peer influence on adolescent sexuality.

Earlier research about sources of sex information for adolescents showed that peers can be a major influence in this area (Davis & Harris 1982; Dunne *et al.* 1993; Thornburg 1981). In our survey of undergraduate students aged 17 to 20 years (Moore & Rosenthal 1991c), we found that 69 per cent of sexually active young people felt they could discuss any concerns they had about sex with their friends, while only 33 and 15 per cent respectively felt this way about discussing sexual problems with a mother or father. Similarly, 61 per cent agreed that a good deal of their sex education came from friends, with few crediting either parent with providing sex education. Among these older adolescents, 73 per cent had talked about 'many aspects' of contraception with peers, but only 37 per cent had done so with mothers and 15 per cent with fathers. However, although discussion and information-sharing about sexual matters was common among age-mates, it was interesting to note that practical assistance from peers in matters of arranging contraception or encouraging safer sexual practices was rare. Only 22 per cent said that peers had 'helped me arrange for contraception, for example, been to the doctor with me'. Even fewer (17 per cent) said that friends had 'helped me arrange for AIDS precautions, for example, buying condoms'. Parental involvement was even less common. For example, only 5 per cent of fathers had helped their sexually active children arrange for contraception or protection.

Some later research on peer influence suggests that it may depend on what question you ask and which area of sexual information is at issue. Rosenthal and Smith (1995) surveyed about 1000 Year 7, 9 and 11 Australian schoolchildren about where they learnt about diseases you can catch from having sex, who they would prefer to learn from if they wanted more information, and how well they trusted the various sources of information listed. In this domain of sexual disease, peers were not featured highly as used, trusted or preferred sources. Parents and health education were, on the whole, preferred sources, while peers (especially opposite-sex peers) were not particularly trusted, the exception being Year 11 girls who expressed confidence in their girlfriends. Major information sources used by all three year levels were television and other media (these being correspondingly low on trust) and teachers/health education classes, which by and large scored highly as both preferred and trusted sources. These findings may have differed if a less medicalized aspect of sexuality was considered, for example information about normative and emotional aspects of sexuality. In these areas, peers may be a more favoured and believed source.

What are the advantages and disadvantages of sexual information emanating from friends? While it is certainly important for the young person who is establishing values and rehearsing for adult sexuality to have the sympathetic ear and counsel of friends, the sex education provided from this source can be limited when not supplemented by other sources. On its own, this can be a case of 'the blind leading the blind', with incomplete and wrong information being disseminated and with vital elements, like the establishment of non-risky sexual behaviours, neglected. On the other hand, peer education programmes in which young people are supported through adult mentoring and resources to educate each other are a powerful tool in sex education (Moore *et al.* 1996; Sloane & Zimmer 1993). Adolescents are more likely to feel comfortable, ask questions and experience attitude change when the sex education message is imparted by someone they can relate to (Rickert *et al.* 1991).

The role of attitudes in shaping behaviour is at least as important as the role of knowledge. Much of peer influence is likely to work through the transmission of attitudes. Ajzen and Fishbein (1980), in their theory of reasoned action, argued that the perceived attitudes and values of significant others (normative beliefs) have an important effect in shaping an individual's intention to engage in a particular action and, ultimately, on the performance of that action. There has been some support for this proposition in the sexual domain. Daugherty and Burger (1984) found the age of first coitus of undergraduate students was related to the perceived peer approval of premarital sexual intercourse, rather than parents' or the church's perceived attitudes. It appears that there are gender differences in the influence of peers. For example, Daugherty and Burger showed that for young women, but not men, there was a link between their own attitudes to sex, the number of sexual partners they had and perceived attitudes to premarital intercourse of their peers. Young women's, but not men's, use of contraception has been shown to be influenced by peer attitudes and discussions with friends about safer sex practices were more common among young women, but not men, who discussed sexual precautions with their friends (Moore & Rosenthal 1991c).

Examining the longer-term influence of peer attitudes, a US-based large-scale study of urban minority youth by O'Donnell *et al.* (2003) assessed 12-year-olds' (Year 7) attitudes to sex in terms of their beliefs about positive aspects of sexual initiation, for example the idea that sex 'proves you're a man/woman', or that it shows your partner how much you love him or her. In addition, the young people were asked to complete questionnaires about their attitudes to sexual responsibilities and their 'sex refusal skills'. Finally, beliefs about how many of their peers had already had sex were sought, as was information on their own sexual behaviour. At Year 7, those reporting greater peer involvement in sex and more positive sex outcome expectancies were more likely to have initiated sex at a very young age, that is, in their seventh year at school. Longitudinal follow-up of the study sample through to Year 10 (about age 16) showed that these variables were consistently associated with earlier sexual debut. Higher scores on sexual responsibility were associated with delayed timing of sexual intercourse, as were stronger refusal attitudes. In this study, the relationships between variables were similar for males and females, although sexual initiation was on the whole earlier for boys. A similar study by Kinsman *et al.* (1999), using a more broadly based sample of 1389 sixth graders tested at the beginning and end of their school year (mean age at time one was 11.7 years) also showed that beliefs about what their peers were doing sexually were strongly associated with early sexual initiation, as were beliefs about social gains associated with early intercourse.

Halpern (2003), in summarizing studies which assess the relative influences of hormonal and social factors on adolescent sexual behaviour, suggests that while both sexes are likely to have friends with similar levels of sexual experience, boys' experience with intercourse is more likely to be related to hormone levels than the influence of friends, while the opposite is true for girls. Several studies have indicated that girls whose best friends have had intercourse are more likely to also have had intercourse, while for boys, hormone concentration is a more powerful indicator of sexual experience (e.g., Udry 1988, 2000). Widmer (1997) found a different pattern of influence for siblings however. He matched interview data from 183 pairs of cohabiting adolescent siblings from the Philadelphia Teen Study. After controlling for parental attitudes to teenage sex, he used logistic regression to provide evidence that older brothers had an influence on their younger siblings' sexual behaviour. He suggested that this effect acted primarily through a comparative process with older brothers' behaviour, such that both male and female adolescents in families with sexually active older boys were more likely to initiate their own sexual activity at an earlier age. This intriguing finding did not occur in the case of older sisters, suggesting that biological/hormonal explanations were less likely than social/modelling ones. Speculations about the processes by which this apparent sibling influence occurs need to be examined using both longitudinal and qualitative research.

The messages that teenage girls receive from others about sex are more likely to be disapproving than the messages given to boys (Daugherty & Burger 1984; Moore & Rosenthal 1991c). This is particularly true about messages from parents, but also applies to attitudes expressed by friends. In this way the female peer network may, once again, act as a brake on early or deviant sexual activity, while among teenage boys this is less likely to be the case. Feldman *et al.* (1995), for example, showed in a longitudinal study of male adolescents that peer acceptance in Year 6 (ages 10 to 12 years) was related to having experienced multiple sexual partners by middle high school. They speculated that boys who were more popular had more chances to date, and therefore more chances to become sexually experienced. On the other hand, boys who were rejected by their peers in primary schools also showed higher levels of sexual experience in later adolescence, an association which Feldman *et al.* linked to the low levels of self-restraint and general misconduct of these boys. These boys exhibited a pattern of 'acting out' of impulses, including sexual impulses. O'Donnell *et al.*'s (2003) study, discussed above, also showed that even among a highly sexually active and risk-taking group of urban minority teenagers, girls' attitudes to sex were more conservative than boys'. For example, nearly 60 per cent of girls but only 44 per cent of boys disagreed with the statement 'A girl my age who has sex gets respect from other girls'. The same statement in relation to boys ('A boy my age who has sex gets respect from other boys') was, interestingly, only disagreed with by around a third of both sexes. In Kinsman *et al.*'s (1999) study, about half the 11-year-olds thought that a '12-year-old sexually experienced boy gains more respect' while this was only true for 20 per cent of the sample if the sentence was changed to refer to a '12-year-old girl'.

In summary, the role of peers in adolescent sex education is a complex one. Peers talk to each other about sex but do not necessarily believe what they hear. There may be some sexual topics that can be more readily and confidently shared between peers, such as those related to emotional and relationship aspects of sexuality rather than topics where accurate information is required. Indeed, peers can act as important social supports for one another as they go through the highs and lows of romantic relationships and sexual awakening. Also important is that peers influence one another's sexual behaviour through the transmission of attitudes, and through modelling. Much of the 'peer pressure' described in relation to adolescent sexuality seems to relate to beliefs about how others of the same age are behaving. Young people who believe their peers are sexually active are more likely to be so, or want to be so, themselves.

Sexual/romantic partner

One little studied aspect of peer influence on sexual development is the role of the sexual or romantic partner, 'date', boyfriend/girlfriend, 'steady' – whatever the prevailing terminology may be. Partners have the opportunity to have a strong influence on sexual initiation, on the risky elements of sexual behaviour such as contraceptive use, and on the emotions and future attitudes associated with sex. A US-based study by Marin *et al.* (2000) of sixth-graders (mean age 11.5 years) showed that having a boyfriend or girlfriend who was two or more years older was very strongly associated with having had sex, and with reporting more unwanted sexual advances. Miller *et al.*'s (1997) survey of 150 black and Hispanic adolescents showed that first inter-course with a partner three or more years older was likely to be associated with earlier sexual debut and unprotected intercourse in comparison with adolescents whose first partner was roughly the same age. Looking back on their first sexual experience, female college students were significantly more likely than males to have discussed the prospect of sex with their partner before it occurred, considered themselves 'in love', felt pressured by their partner to have sex and 'wished they had waited' (Sawyer & Smith 1996). Finally, our own longitudinal study of contraceptive intentions and actions indicated that communication with a partner about contraception was a major predictor of safe sex behaviour (Moore *et al.* 1993).

Although it is clear that parents and peers do influence teenagers' sexual decision-making in various ways, there is another pervasive set of influences to which we now turn.

5 The social context: from youth culture to globalization

The broader social context in which they live their lives plays a significant role in teenagers' sexual beliefs and behaviour. The nature of that context, and consequently its impact, ranges from the overt and overwhelming world of the adolescent subculture, a world in which teenagers are bombarded by media messages about current (and ephemeral) mores, to the less obvious influence of societal institutions such as school, religion and the law. We address these different contexts in turn, ending with a section exploring an increasingly pervasive global youth culture.

The youth culture in western society

The day-to-day impact of social control on teenagers is reflected in their commitment to perform in ways appropriate to their role. Western societies, by prolonging the transition to adulthood and by segregating their youth, have given rise to an institutionalized youth culture – more or less standardized ways of thinking, feeling and acting that are characteristic of a large number of young people.

The power of the youth culture in shaping teenagers' opinions and behaviours can be recognized when we look around at the conformity of youths to current fashions in clothes, music and leisure activities. The area of sexuality is just as subject to this influence as any other. Adolescents derive much of their information about sexual mores and behaviours from this subculture, which is wider than immediate peers, and which purveys sets of beliefs about what adolescents should be doing, from the point of view of their age-mates. These beliefs are communicated via various media directly targeted at young people. Influences include publications for teenagers, movies and television designed to appeal to this age group, music, songs, rock videos, the internet and various internet games.

Among the print media, magazines (for example; *Dolly or Girl-friend*) and romantic fiction (such as Mills and Boon romances) are popular among adolescent girls, with boys less directed and more varied in their reading (Sachs *et al.* 1991). Writers such as McRobbie (1982) believe that adolescent fiction contributes to the creation of ideologies about relationships between the sexes, sexual expression and power. For girls, she argues, these ideologies deal with the construction of teenage femininity, such as the nature of attractiveness, the desirability of feminine passive acceptance and the importance of attracting a man. Teenage boys' interests in a varied diet of adventure, hobbies, non-fiction and soft porn such as *Playboy* may encourage a wider range of self-definitions and identities which do not necessarily revolve around sexual attractiveness. The recent advent of 'ladmags' such as *Ralph* and *FMH*, and television programmes involving 'makeovers' for men as well as women, do target masculine attractiveness – how to look better, how to be more successful in the dating game – but they tend to be pitched at a somewhat older audience, generally mid-20s to mid-30s. The definition of maleness conveyed by boys' reading matter is mostly one characterized by a sense of agency in the sexual as well as in other life areas, that is, a sense of doing, mastery and control.

Provenzo (1991) noted the same tendency in video games, with boys and men typically portrayed as active, ruthless, aggressive and competitive, and women as victims. Have stereotypes for young women changed over the last ten or so years? Many current television programmes, movies and even computer games have active female heroines as main characters. Nevertheless, perhaps another type of script is emerging that is equally stereotyped. Beasley and Standley (2002) analysed games from Nintendo 64 and Sony Playstation console gaming systems and demonstrated a significant sex bias in the number of male and female characters in the games (only 14 per cent female), and in the way the male and female characters were depicted. Female characters were typically presented with ample cleavage and voluptuous breasts, and they wore clothing that exposed a lot of more skin than the male characters. The scripts being presented to the (mostly) young male consumers of these games may on occasions depict women as exhibiting power and agency, but only highly sexualized women.

Ward (2003) identified at least five recurring (sexuality-based) themes in a content analysis of current magazines (mostly teenage girls' and women's magazines). Many articles revolved around the idea that a focal goal for females is to present themselves as sexually desirable and therefore gain the attention of men. A second theme was depicted by the implication in many articles that the work of relationships is the exclusive domain of women. Third, there was an emphasis on differences in the sexual nature of women and men, these differences corresponding to the double standard. This idea is epitomized by the currently popular *Men are from Mars, Women are from Venus* (Gray 1993) notion, in which communication problems between the sexes are attributed almost entirely to nature, not nurture. Interestingly, and to some extent at odds with the previous theme, a fourth theme depicted female sexuality in ways that were contrary and conflicting, suggesting that the confusion in Freud's famous question 'What do women want?' has not really dissipated much in the last 100 years. Finally, Ward noted that substantial aspects of women's sexuality, such as desire, were absent from magazine discussions. She argued that a distorted reality regarding the nature of women's sexuality continues to be reflected in what women read about themselves (and in what men read about women).

Nevertheless, over the past decade there has been greater recognition of young women's sexual desires and an emphasis on the importance of open and honest communication between the sexes. A recent study of the cultural scripts to which young women in the USA are exposed through the widely read teen magazine *Seventeen* (Carpenter 1998) revealed substantial shifts, particularly in the number of sexual scripts used, over the 20-year period from 1974 to 1994. Newer scripts have been added to the old-time scripts of love and romance – including female desire, ambivalence, homosexuality and masturbation. These offer young people not only information but also proclaim an acceptability of these new ways of thinking and acting.

Teenagers are also presented with role models in the form of current pop stars. Videoclips of pop singers or groups have become popular as a means of promoting careers by persuading teenagers to buy records of their favourites. At the same time, these videoclips frequently give powerful messages about sexuality, not only in terms of their lyrics but also of their behaviour. Popular music and dancing has been likened to a mating ritual, in which rhythm and simulated sexual movements provide sexual release and indicate attraction. Pop groups have names like Machine Gun Fellatio, Lethal Bizzle and Beastie Boys. Of course, complaints about sexual explicitness in music and dancing have been made for hundreds of years, sometimes in relation to activities that seem exceptionally tame by today's standards. Whether high levels of explicitness are a harmful influence

on young people's developing sexuality is probably as much dependent on the attitudes conveyed by such material as on the activities
depicted. Sexual violence, misogyny and exploitation are dehumaniz-
ing and ultimately evil influences. Yet while good taste is sometimes
strained by sexual aspects of the youth culture, much of it could be
construed as youthful rebellion, high spirits and exploration of
boundaries. The debate about benign and harmful effects of media
influences is explored further in the section below, on media models of
sexual behaviour.

Another recent feature of the youth culture in many western
nations is the widespread use of mobile phones and text messaging. In
Australia, one study (Byrne & Findlay 2004) examined sex differences
in the likelihood of initiating 'first moves' (towards relationship
establishment) or a first date via short message service (SMS) text
messaging and telephone calls. Among the approximately 250 young
people surveyed, stereotypy prevailed in that males were far more
likely to initiate first moves or ask for a first date than were females.
Traditional gender-role expectations and preference for telephone
communication were strong when initiating first dates. Nevertheless,
young women used SMS more frequently than young men in initiating first moves, with this mode of communication appearing to have
developed into a new channel for flirting.

There are, of course, complex interconnections among these influences, as well as with the word of mouth wisdom which is passed on
between the 'cliques, crowds and gangs' comprising the set of adolescents in any city, state or country in the western world. Although
there are great individual and group variations in the ways teenagers
think about sex, the subculture provides a popular model of what is
'best', 'right' and 'current', of which most young people are aware.
This complex set of ideas and values is so pervasive, because of the
speed with which ideas are spread by the world media, that young
people need to make conscious decisions on a regular basis as to
whether they accept or reject current trends.

In our highly sexualized society, many of the values and norms of
the youth culture concern sexual behaviour. Consequently this subculture probably has more influence on young people's sexual activity
than it does on, say, their career choices. There have been suggestions
that the pressures inherent in the adolescent subculture may sometimes thrust young people into sexual involvement before they are
physically and emotionally ready to deal with it, almost bullying them
into premature sexual activity. Some indirect support for this idea of
pressure comes from studies which show that the extent of adolescent

sexual activity and the age of first intercourse are related to young people's beliefs about what their peers are doing. For example, Cvetkovich and Grote (1980) report that sexual experience among teenagers is strongly predicted by beliefs about the extent of peers' sexual experience and their perceived level of sexual liberalism. Newcomer *et al.* (1980) conclude that individual sexual behaviour and attitudes are more closely linked to what adolescents think is happening among their peers than what is actually happening. There is a clear belief among some teenagers, at least, that their age-mates are more sexually active than they actually are (McCabe & Collins 1990). Such a belief is likely to affect the behaviours of many young people for whom peer-group acceptance and 'fitting in' are important in the maintenance of self-esteem and the movement towards maturity.

Media models of sexual behaviour

Adolescents spend nearly eight hours per day interacting with the media – mostly television, movies, videos and the internet (Roberts *et al.* 1999). They rank media sources high on their list of informants about sexual behaviour (Andre *et al.* 1989; Rosenthal & Smith 1995). On these media outlets, adolescents see in their own living rooms people expressing the whole gamut of sexual behaviours, including violent sexuality. Indeed, content analysis of television programmes suggests that sexual content occurs in more than 80 per cent of programmes popular with the adolescent age group (Kunkel *et al.* 2003). Many popular modern movies have strong sexual themes. In these movies, sex is explicit and not represented tastefully and discreetly, by waves crashing or reeds blowing in the wind as was the case in the 1940s and 1950s. Today's teenagers are bombarded with scenes of unambiguous sex, the details of which are portrayed with unprecedented precision. As a result, sex is no longer shrouded in mystery. Teenagers know what sex is and how it is enacted at increasingly earlier ages.

Unfortunately, many films and television programmes present stereotyped images of the ways men and women relate, and these have many implicit and explicit messages about what is appropriate sexual behaviour. What are the models of sexual behaviour illustrated by popular media? One prominent finding is that television often emphasizes a casual, recreational approach to sex, where notions of commitment and strong emotions are underplayed (Klassen *et al.* 1989). Ward (1995) also comments on this portrayal of sexual relationships, adding that courtship and romance are often depicted as based on dishonesty and game-playing – indeed as a 'battle of the sexes'. Another feature of media portrayals is the frequent presentation of women and men as stereotypes. The range of stereotypic presentations of women in the media includes 'woman as passive victim'. With good luck, the victim-woman will be saved by a knight on a white charger. She is not saved by her own efforts to take charge of her life, but because she ingratiates the man by providing for his needs – being cute, attractive or good at sex. The popularity of movies and television programmes of this genre attests to the fantasies that they target and activate, a point made persuasively by Walkerdine (1984) and other British feminists.

Another genre focuses on women who express their own sexual needs rather than a desire to please men, and who attempt to satisfy these needs. These women, who are sexual beings on their own terms, are often represented as the epitome of evil, bent on destroying true love and sacred family life. Such films might be said to reflect male fears of women who adopt 'masculine' modes of sexuality, but their popularity with men and women alike is disturbing. The third film genre depicts the teenage male fantasy of women as playthings. Women in these films are not serious and, indeed, are hardly real people. Here, sex is a commodity and no self-respecting man would want to relate to these women for any other reason but to attain sexual release. Men too are presented in a range of limiting stereotypes. One involves the idea of male sexuality as urgent and predatory, with men expected to show little control over their sexual urges (Tolman & Higgins 1996). Another, paradoxically, focuses on men as always in control – the 'rescuing' sex with the answers to all women's problems provided they are willing to submit. The messages conveyed by these films and television shows do not provide strong and positive models of healthy sexual expression for men or women, nor do they reflect sensitive, intimate, relationship-based sexuality as a particularly attractive option for men.

There is an even darker side to what is available in the modern media. Access to pornography, either by choice or accident, is alarmingly easy. Flood and Hamilton (2003a, 2003b) recently examined young people's exposure to pornography through an Australia-wide telephone survey of 16- and 17-year-olds. The findings were disturbing. Their data showed that 84 per cent of 16- to 17-year-olds agreed that watching X-rated videos is widespread among boys of their age. Many fewer (4 per cent of girls and 15 per cent of boys) thought this was true of girls. This belief about boys suggests that watching these videos is considered to be normal, or at least common behaviour – it may give pornography consumption a high degree of social tolerance and acceptability within youth culture. Indeed, 73 per cent of boys admitted watching X-rated videos themselves – 1 in 20 on a weekly basis; more than a fifth watching at least once a month. Similar findings were obtained regarding exposure to sex sites on the internet, with 88 per cent of boys and 83 per cent of girls believing that boys of their age looked at sex sites, but few believing that this was an interest for girls. Accidental exposure to sex sites was high, with 84 per cent of boys and 60 per cent of girls claiming to have been accidentally exposed to these sites. Nearly two in five boys had searched the internet for sex sites. Only 4 per cent reported that they used the internet for this purpose on a weekly basis, but 22 per cent did so at least every two to three months.

The worrying aspect of internet pornography is its hardcore nature. Themes of sexual violence and rape are common. Flood and Hamilton conclude that there is consistent and reliable evidence that exposure to pornography is related to male sexual aggression against women – in terms of attitudes expressed and behaviours. These conclusions are supported by Ward's review of entertainment media discussed previously. She concluded that frequent exposure to sexually oriented genres such as soap operas and music videos was associated with more casual, sexist and stereotyped attitudes about sex and sexual relationships; that media exposure of this sort shapes viewers' sense of sexual reality (such as the prevalence of sex and certain sexual behaviours); and that there is some, although weaker, evidence that media exposure impacts on sexual behaviours. Ward concludes that the media have assumed a prominent role in the sexual socialization of our youth.

It is impossible to avoid sex in the media, and attempts at censorship are rarely successful for very long. What are portrayed are not only overt depictions of sexual acts but many subtle messages about sexuality and relationships. Not all of these are negative by any means. For example, in recent years, several 'teen soapies' have had their characters modelling 'safe sex' messages, and presenting discussion of difficult sexual issues, such as coping with homosexual feeling and identity, sexual harassment and non-consensual sex. The internet too has the capacity to present reliable information on sexuality in ways that are suitable for a variety of age groups, and there are many websites which do just that (Goldman & Bradley 2001; Smith *et al.* 2000).

A site like The Hormone Factory (www.thehormonefactory.com) uses puzzles, quizzes and other novel formats to present sex information to young people and to answer frequently asked questions. The site aims to help children aged 10 to 12 understand the major stages of human development, especially those that relate to sexual maturation and reproduction. As well as covering the physical changes that happen over a lifetime, the information is presented in the context of understanding the emotional and social changes that occur, in particular those that relate to puberty. The tone is friendly and humorous, as well as sensitive to the concern and anxiety often experienced by children and their parents over this topic. For example, the content includes the issues that arise from children developing at different rates and how one might respond to those differences.

Despite the potential for positive sex education provided by the media, some media depictions of sex might lead us to believe that this is an activity in which only the young, firm and beautiful may participate, or worse, that violence and exploitation are normative and acceptable. While sex plays a large part in our lives, media representations can distort its influence out of all proportion. In the words of one of our young interviewees commenting on the media portrayals of sex: 'No one seems interested in how many other things . . . I mean in relation to sex . . . what people do in their lives, like maybe what their career is, or their artistic ambitions, things like that tend to get overlooked I think. Sex is too much of a big deal'.

Social institutions

Sex education in school and the 'abstinence only' debate

Given the apparently limited and difficult role parents have in sex education, the tendency of religions to 'teach only to the converted' (see the next section), and the confusing and often one-sided influence of popular media, there is an important role for schools to play in informing young people and providing a forum for values exploration and clarification about sex. Schools are able to reach most adolescents if sex education is implemented early enough, and there are resources and trusted personnel available to convey information to young people and to facilitate discussion. A problem is that many teachers are not trained to present sensitive and controversial topics, and indeed may feel uncomfortable or anxious about doing so (Kirby 1996; Sanderson 2000). Another barrier to good sex education in schools arises when political pressure is brought to bear on what should and should not be taught. Such pressure is often applied by small, highly conservative but powerful community groups who worry that teaching adolescents about sex will open the floodgates of licentiousness, despite research dismissing any causal association between sexuality education and increased sexual activity (Kirby & Coyle 1997). The Health Development Agency (HDA) of the UK government point out:

> There is good evidence that school-based sex and relationship education (SRE), particularly when linked to contraceptive services, can have an impact on young people's knowledge and attitudes, delay sexual activity and/or reduce pregnancy rates. There is no evidence to support the view that increased provision of SRE increases the onset or frequency of sex, or the number of sexual partners.
>
> (2004: 1)

The importance of overcoming barriers to the provision of school-based sexuality education is emphasized by various surveys of parents, who by and large approve of schools taking on this role, especially as it is one with which they do not always feel at home (Lewis *et al.* 2001; Young 1994).

Starkman and Rajani (2002), reviewing the status of sex education, explain that in the USA, decisions as to whether sex education is included in the curriculum, and if so what is taught, are made by individual states or sometimes school districts. Increasingly, an abstinence-only curriculum is favoured. Supporters believe that by encouraging young people to say no to sex until marriage, teenage pregnancy rates will drop and sexual health will improve. Abstinence education attracts large-scale federal funding and in many US school districts is the only sex education option presented to young people. In the early 1980s, the Adolescent Family Life Act (AFLA) was passed in the USA to subsidize sex education that promoted chastity and self-discipline, in a bid to reduce the high rates of teenage pregnancy. Starkman and Rajani cite data from the Alan Guttmacher Institute (2001) to report that 16 states give local school districts total discretion over whether and how to treat the topics of abstinence *and* contraception, 34 states require that abstinence be covered as a topic in sex education (25 requiring that it be emphasized), and only 19 states require than contraception be included in the curriculum.

These policies do not necessarily reflect the wishes and needs of the adult or the adolescent population. Surveys undertaken by the Sexuality Information and Education Council of the United States

(SIECUS) and other groups suggest that most Americans support the kind of school-based sex education that includes information on both abstinence and contraception. In addition, the American Civil Liberties Union challenged the AFLA in 1983, arguing that it violated the constitutional separation of church and state. A compromise settlement was reached in 1993 in which funded programmes were required not to include religious references and to be medically accurate. In 1996 however, the US Congress added a provision that for sex education programmes to be federally funded, they must teach that sex outside marriage is likely to have harmful physical and psychological effects (Starkman & Rajani 2002).

Controversy rages. For example, a 2002 article in the New Orleans-based newspaper, *The Times-Picayune* (Quick Hits 2002) reported a federal judge ruling that Louisiana's abstinence-only sex education programme veered too far in promoting religion. It was noted that funds had been used to buy Bibles, as well as to conduct prayer vigils at abortion clinics. A further newspaper report from a different state, quoting the Orange County Register of the same year (Quick Hits 2001), told of a group of students in Santa Ana demanding from their school board more comprehensive sex education than that provided by an abstinence-only curriculum. They complained that they were not given enough information to protect themselves against unplanned pregnancies.

While the emphasis on abstinence-only sex education programmes may pose problems for the more liberal minded and, of more concern, have limited research support (see below), it is perhaps an improvement on the state of affairs that we reported in Moore and Rosenthal (1993). Around that time, Nielsen (1991) was describing sex education in the USA as 'too little too late'. Only 60 per cent of students were receiving any sex education before graduating from high school. In 10 states there had been no action with regard to implementation of sex education in schools, and only 7 states required instruction about pregnancy prevention. Only 3 states required sex education in 1980, this increasing to only 17 by 1988.

Does abstinence education work? The answer to this question depends on the criteria chosen to measure effectiveness. Reviews are available in the published, peer-reviewed literature ranging from strongly 'pro' (e.g. Rector 2002; Toups & Holmes 2002) to strongly 'anti' (e.g. Kirby 2002; Starkman & Rajani 2002). First, consider adolescent pregnancy rates. There is evidence that these have been falling in the USA since 1991, around about the time that the movement towards abstinence education began (Sulak 2004). In 2002, teenage pregnancy rates in the USA were reported as being at their lowest level in 60 years (Sulak 2004). Nevertheless, the rates are still much higher than in the UK and other developed nations, where sex education is more varied and broadly based (Mabray & Labauve 2002). Further, research by the Alan Guttmacher Institute (Darroch & Singh 1999) suggests that much of the decline shown in the USA is due to more consistent and efficient contraceptive use among sexually active teenagers.

A second possible criterion of effectiveness is delay of first intercourse. Some supportive evidence is again available, suggesting that teenagers who pledge to remain abstinent until marriage delay having sex about a third longer than comparable non-pledgers (Bearman & Brückner 1999, 2001). Grunbaum *et al.* (2002) presented figures to show that in 2001, 43 per cent of high-school females reported they had had intercourse, compared to 51 per cent in 1991. Abstinence pledges may give young people who wish to delay initiation to intercourse the social support to do so, in line with Sulak's (2004) contention that surveys have consistently shown 'most sexually active adolescents wish they had waited to have sex' (p. S4). It has been argued, however, that the young people influenced by abstinence education may be delayers anyway, given that they are more likely to be religious and, according to some research, more likely to experience later pubertal development, a factor independently associated with older-age sexual initiation. In addition, among teenagers 18 years and older, pledging had no effect, and among the younger teens, the effects depended strongly on the school environment (National Institute of Child Health and Human Development 2001). In short, abstinence-only education may delay sexual debut for some younger teenagers, a factor which may in turn impinge positively on their health and well-being and reduce the adolescent pregnancy rate. There is no evidence that it achieves the goal of abstinence until marriage.

Another possible marker of success or otherwise of abstinence programmes is their role in attitude formation and change. The little evidence existing here is not convincing. Sather and Zinn (2002) surveyed a large sample of seventh and eighth graders from schools in the US midwest. They compared a group who received state-funded abstinence-only education with a group who did not. The abstinence-only group was not significantly different from the control group on values and attitudes regarding premarital sex, nor on their intentions to engage in premarital sex. Indeed, the majority of young people in both groups were against premarital sex, stating that they did not intend to have sexual intercourse while an unmarried teenager, and disagreeing with statements such as 'It is okay for people my age to have sexual intercourse'. A limitation of the study was that the sample, while large, was from a relatively conservative area of the USA; most of the students surveyed were Caucasian and from two-parent families. The abstinence-only education may well have been 'preaching to the converted', and in addition may have targeted adolescents at an age where only a minority were likely to be sexually active anyway, especially within the particular conservative cultural context of the study.

A major concern voiced by critics of abstinence-only sex education is that it does not prepare young people for their sexual lives. It is estimated that by the time they leave high school, nearly two-thirds of US adolescents have had sex, with one in five having had four or more sexual partners (Starkman & Rajani 2002). Those experiencing abstinence-only sex education will not have received school-based information on contraception or safe sex practices. Consequently, it is argued that when abstinence-pledgers do become sexually active, they are less likely to use contraception, either because of ignorance or feelings of guilt and shame (Dailard 2003; National Institute of Child Health and Human Development 2001). Evidence supporting this concern comes from a recent study which has shown that graduates of abstinence programmes have rates of STIs similar to the rates for other young people (Ellis & Grey 2004).

Kirby (2001, 2002) conducted exhaustive reviews of abstinence-only sex education programmes in the USA. He evaluated programmes on the basis of what he described as minimum standards of scientific evidence. These were that: (a) the study compared the abstinence-only group with a well-matched comparison group of young people not receiving this intervention; (b) baseline and follow-up data measuring behavioural variables (e.g. virginity status, frequency of sex, contraceptive usage) were collected from both groups; (c) post-intervention data were collected for a minimum number of months after the intervention (e.g. six months if the study was assessing impact on initiation of sex, or at least two months if frequency of sex or contraceptive usage were the outcome variables); and (d) the study had a sample size of at least 100 and employed proper statistical analyses. Data collected from surveys in which participants were asked to recall if they had been involved in abstinence-only programmes, or had taken the 'virginity pledge', were considered to provide poor data on effectiveness, as recall of these events among young people is notoriously unreliable (Kirby 2002). The conclusions drawn by Kirby were: 'There do not currently exist any abstinence-only programs with

strong evidence that they either delay sex or reduce teenage pregnancy' (p. 6). However, in contrast, Kirby's reviews indicated that
programmes of the 'abstinence-plus' variety – in which abstinence is
presented as a desirable choice but the use of contraceptives is
encouraged among those who do become sexually active – have been
shown to be effective in many well-designed studies (Kirby 2001,
2002).

As suggested by the above, while one of the aims of sex education
may be to encourage adolescents to delay their introduction to sexual
activity, it is clearly not the only aim. 'Harm minimization' is another
educational trend, the philosophy being that if young people are going
to engage in risky activities, better that they know the risks and the
best ways to reduce them. Such an approach is persuasive with sex
education, given that sex has risks (unplanned pregnancy, infection,
emotional outcomes) but is not, in itself, an unhealthy activity, and
indeed is part of the expected and adaptive behavioural repertoire of
most adults. So in teaching young people about sex, we are not
'putting into their minds' something that would not have occurred
anyway (Baldo *et al.* 1993). Nevertheless, critics argue that this style
of sex education privileges information about casual sex and other
styles of sexual relating not conducive to 'traditional' sexual values.

Perhaps the best educational approaches are able to combine these
seemingly incompatible approaches in creative ways, as in the
abstinence-plus approaches discussed by Kirby above. Mabray and
Labauve (2002) present the case for 'a multidimensional approach to
sexual education', in which information and choices are made available to teens who are already sexually active, as well as abstinence
being presented as an option. They recommend the incorporation of
health and developmental aspects of sexuality into any programme,
and the tailoring of programmes to community needs by including
health professionals, parents and young people in curriculum planning. There is some powerful data, also from the Alan Guttmacher
Institute, suggesting that the 'A, B, C' approach to public education
(abstinence, be faithful, use condoms) is working well to reduce rates
of HIV infection in Uganda (Singh *et al.* 2003). Here the emphasis is
to educate to delay young people's first sexual encounter, but also
present clear information on ways to avoid infection once sexual
activity has begun.

Despite the debates and consequent variations and limitations in
the amount and quality of sex education, it appears that young people
nevertheless do gain knowledge of sex from school-linked sources,
although it may not always be on the topics that interest them most,

or are seen as most valuable by parents. As mentioned in the previous chapter, Rosenthal and Smith (1995) found school-based sex education to be a preferred and trusted source of information about sex among young people in Australia. A review from the UK (NHS Centre for Reviews and Dissemination 1997) found that school-based sexuality education could be effective in reducing adolescent pregnancy, particularly if information was included about contraceptive services. There was no relationship between providing information on sexuality and contraception and increase in teenage sexual activity. Grunseit *et al.* (1997) in a meta-analysis, found that sex education in school was related to the postponement of first intercourse and a reduction in sexual risk-taking. While such studies give broad support for the value of sex education, not all sex education fulfils community needs. A survey titled 'Sex Education in America: A View from Inside the Nation's Classrooms' conducted by the Henry J. Kaiser Family Foundation (reported by Melby 2000) found a striking difference between what parents wanted and what was perceived by students to be happening in their sex education classes. For example, while nearly all parents report wanting their children to be taught about safer sex and negotiation skills, many students said these topics were not covered in their school-based courses. Similarly, nearly all parents wanted their children to know what to do if a friend was raped or assaulted, how to deal with pressure to have sex and how to deal with emotional issues/consequences of sex; however only 59 per cent, 79 per cent and 71 per cent respectively of students said they had heard about these topics in their sex education classes.

It is interesting to consider ways that sex education can become more effective. How do we define effectiveness? A closely linked question relates to the goals of programmes. Sex education can range from direct teaching about biological 'plumbing' through to decision-making and value-oriented approaches. The desired outcomes can be an increase in straightforward knowledge about bodily functions, or in sexually responsible behaviour. Or they can combine these and other attitudes to sexuality in a context which provides the adolescent with a script for dealing with sexual relationships. An example of the latter comes from the Scottish Health Education Group's (1990) proposal for health and sexuality education in schools, *Promoting Good Health*. In this model, the topic of sexuality is combined with consideration of relationships, while encouraging an exploratory and discussion-based approach to sexual values and the facilitation of decision-making skills in the sexual domain. The decision process is conceptualized as comprising at least four elements, and teaching in the programme is designed to allow for pupil accessibility to each element. These are: (a) access to, and acceptance of, relevant information; (b) clarification of feelings and related attitudes; (c) investigation of possible alternative actions and probable outcomes for each; and (d) deciding on a course of action that will be right for the individual. The overall aims are outlined below, in order to give an indication of the breadth of focus of the programme:

1   To facilitate communication on sexuality and relationships.
2   To develop knowledge and understanding of physical and emotional development.
3   To develop an awareness of social development and the influences which affect personal choice.
4   To promote responsibility for considerate behaviour and the ability to make informed decisions on sexuality and relationships.
5   To develop skills needed for potential future parents.
6   To increase knowledge of health care services.

(Scottish Health Education Group 1990: 32)

Another best practice model comes from the Australian National Framework for Education about HIV/AIDS, STIs and Blood-Borne Viruses in Secondary Schools – a programme titled *Talking Sexual Health*, of which we have already presented some information regarding the material for parents (Mitchell *et al.* 2000). The framework for sex education is constructed around five key components, which attend to the methods in which the programme is delivered, as well as the content and goals. The programme is built on research that indicates that comprehensive sex education tends to delay (rather than encourage) the early onset of sexual activity, and to increase safe sex behaviours among those who are already sexually active (Baldo *et al.* 1993). The components of the programme are as follows.

A whole-school approach is encouraged along with the development of partnerships with community organizations. As well as implementation of a formal curriculum, such an approach involves evaluation of school policies and procedures, attention to the informal messages conveyed by teachers and in the playground, and support of the curriculum through school policy, student welfare and pastoral care. For example, if issues relating to sexual forcing are raised in class, appropriate supports must be in place for those who may seek counselling or assistance after such discussions. In relation to the 'informal' curriculum, it is not particularly useful to be teaching tolerance of sexual diversity if there are no corresponding moves to eradicate teasing and bullying outside the classroom.

The importance of acknowledging that young people are sexual beings is recognized. Sexual feelings and desires are presented as normal and acceptable, and there is support for informed decision-making about sexual choices. There is acknowledgement of and tolerance for diversity in the programme. For example, it is designed to cater for those who are already sexually active as well as those who are not, and for groups which differ with respect to gender, race, culture, geographic location, socioeconomic background, age, disability, religion and sexual orientation. There is provision for curriculum content that is consistent with public health goals, comprehensive and appropriate to the social context in which it is presented. The curriculum is based around young people's developmental needs and abilities, places decision-making and values clarification activities within their relevant social context, uses a range of teaching methods that engage children, and requires skilled teachers who are comfortable with the material and can provide a classroom climate of safety and trust.

Successful delivery of the programme necessitates professional development of teachers to increase their knowledge, competence and comfort with the material. In addition, there is a need to attend to education of the whole school community – this means keeping parents and community organizations 'in the picture', so that they can support what is happening at a school level.

Programmes such as the ones described have been developed through community, parent and teacher consultation. Although in the past there appeared to be strong parental resistance to sex education programmes (and in some communities that resistance still exists because of cultural norms), current research shows that, although there is still a vocal minority of 'resisters', the majority of parents are in favour of school programmes (Lewis *et al.* 2001; Nielsen 1991). If such programmes are to achieve their aims, parent and community support are important. Equally important is that teaching about sex must be done by trusted and sensitive teachers, secure in their own sexuality and able to cope with discussion of a wide range of views that they do not necessarily share.

Religion

Religiosity has generally been found to be negatively related to premarital sexual behaviour; religious persons regardless of denomination are less likely to be sexually active (Devaney & Hubley 1981;

Spanier 1976). This is not surprising, as sexual values encouraging conservatism and restraint are promulgated by most religions. A position paper on 'rights, duties and obligations' as they relate to sex education, prepared by the Baptist Church states that:

> It is quite clear that sex belongs within a permanent heterosexual relationship. Sexual relations outside this relationship are disobedient to God's intention. Such sexual practices are sinful – whether they are heterosexual, homosexual or bestial practices. They are included for condemnation with other issues of social injustice in Deuteronomy 27: 15–26.
>
> (Carmichael 1995: 1)

Similarly, from the (Australian) Catholic Archdiocese of Melbourne's (2001: 5) *Directives for Christian Education in Sexuality*, comes the statement: 'the prevailing secular and permissive culture of the West must never be used to justify sexuality education which is explicit, premature, or misleading'.

The pledge of the religion-driven 'True Love Waits' campaign (see Chapter 1) emphasizes chastity until marriage, and has been taken up by many young people particularly in the USA, where there is a strong adherence to a religious culture. This pledge is the mainstay of abstinence education, described earlier. Unfortunately, even with the best of intentions, adolescents are not always able to maintain such pledges, and research suggests there may be a good deal of backsliding, as discussed in a previous section (Dailard 2003).

Rebellion against the message is another quite common response as indicated by the following quote from a 16-year-old Australian boy (Moore *et al.* 1996: 16):

> *Interviewer*: What do you think of sex before marriage?
> I have been brought up as a good Catholic, that it is sinful and disgusting; but I have my own personal view that you have to. You don't just walk into a shop with your eyes shut and pick the clothing off the rack and take it home and open your eyes and see it is disgusting. You should sample before you buy.

Overall, adolescents who are devout in their religious beliefs are among those least likely to experience early sexual initiation or multiple partnering. Sexual conservatism among religious youths may not simply be the consequence of religious values *per se*. Religious youths are likely to associate with other religious youths. Thus, the norms of the most salient peer-group work to enforce the values of religion.

Thornton and Camburn (1987) point out that not only does religious participation reduce the likelihood of premarital sexual experience, but the effect works in the other direction as well. Sexual attitudes and behaviour significantly influence religious involvement. Religious instruction which prohibits premarital sex or encourages its delay puts strains on the individual who has begun sexual activity, with the likely effect of diminishing religious involvement. Today's powerful pressures towards adolescent sexual activity militate against their continued involvement in traditional religion, a situation which can leave young people in a spiritual vacuum in terms of developing values about sex and relationships. There is no shortage of other sources of values, as we have seen. Values adopted by the popular media and the adolescent subculture may well fill this vacuum, but these are often materialistic and concerned with immediate gratification, according to Thornburg (1975). It is not surprising that young people are struggling to find a suitable values framework for thinking about their lives, a framework which incorporates the wish to have fun and experiment with sex, while recognizing the powerful emotions which sex elicits and the responsibilities implicit in establishing relationships. Religion may provide this framework for some, but many others will find religious tenets too sexually restrictive and will look to peers, media influences and other social institutions to fill this void.

The law

It would be impossible to review, for all western countries, the laws that deal with adolescent sexual expression. Many countries have such laws, and they provide a broad framework for our decisions about what is deviant adolescent sexuality and what we judge to be normal adolescent experimentation. Age of consent laws, for example, specify an age below which it is illegal to engage in sexual intercourse (usually 14, 15 or 16 years), and indicate punishments related to the perceived scale of the misdemeanour. In England and Wales for example, it is an offence to intentionally engage in sexual touching with a young person aged 13, 14 or 15 years. A person aged 18 or over is liable to up to 14 years imprisonment for this offence. A person under the age of 18 is liable to up to 5 years imprisonment. Intentional sexual touching of a young person under 13 is an absolute offence. This means there can be no defence in such a case that it was believed the person was over 16. Sexual touching which involves penetration of the vagina, anus or mouth by the penis or penetration of the vagina or anus with a part of the body or any object is punishable by up to life imprisonment. Sexual touching not involving penetration is punishable by up to 14 years' imprisonment (Brook 2004).

These laws are a social expression of our beliefs that it is appropriate to protect young people against sexual involvement until they are emotionally and physically ready for it, and that too early sexual activity may be damaging to growth and development. Within such laws, it is often the case that the actions of an older person who has sex with a minor are viewed in a more serious light than, say, the situation in which two minors have sex with each other. In Australia, for example, consensual intercourse with a young girl under 16 years of age was once uniformly unlawful, irrespective of the age of the girl's partner. The law has now been changed so that intercourse with a girl aged between 12 and 16 years may occur lawfully, provided that her partner is no more than two years older than she is.

Another example of the ways in which the law regulates sexuality concerns an individual's right to be treated as medically adult. These laws deal with the rights of a young person to give consent to medical or surgical treatment without the consent of parents, and the requirement of professional confidentiality on the part of the medical profession. In the UK, the legal age for consent in this context has been set at 16 years (17 years in Northern Ireland), one or two years lower than the general age of majority at which, for example, an individual is entitled to vote (Brook 2004). Probably the major implication of this act relates to medical advice and treatment in the sexuality area, such as prescribing contraceptives or termination of a pregnancy. The law, through such acts, recognizes the facts of teenage sexuality, the implicit message being that 'if it's going to happen, let's make sure it happens safely'. The hope is that these legal provisions will ensure that contraception is freely available and that if abortions are to occur they can be carried out by qualified medical practitioners under hygienic conditions.

Of course, one difficulty in attempting to regulate sexuality is that these laws are often unenforced and unenforceable. It is one thing to make sexual intercourse between a 15-year-old girl and a 19-year-old boy illegal. It is another to convince the pair in question that they should cease what they are doing because it is against the law. Nevertheless, there is a sense in which such laws acknowledge the confusions and misperceptions of parents about their children's sexuality by relieving parents of the need to make decisions. Clearly, these laws are not without controversy. For example, the Family Law Reform Act in the UK has been the subject of challenges and subsequent legal guidelines regarding interpretation. Laws against homosexuality and laws about engaging in certain sexual acts such as sodomy or oral sex exist in some countries, or states within countries, and are policed with more or less enthusiasm, depending on the social climate of the region and the times.

What is important in considering the effects of any of these laws on adolescent sexuality is that while they govern behaviour through regulation and punishment, the laws also shape attitudes and are, in turn, shaped by the prevailing social mores. It may be said that the law reflects the overt – but not necessarily the implicit – sexual values of a society. The degree to which laws about sexual behaviour actually affect sexual practice has not been systematically studied. It seems likely, however, that laws which are too out of step with current thinking will be far less likely to be obeyed or to influence sexual decision-making.

Globalization

Many writers point to the increasing commonalities between experiences of young people across the globe – a global youth culture – often accompanied by a shift to western individualism. As the world gets smaller through increasing access to many forms of communication, westernized messages about sex are transmitted across the world. Years ago this occurred through religious missionaries, who tried to limit what they perceived as the sexual excesses of 'foreign' cultures (hence the notion of the missionary position). These days the opposite trend seems to be occurring, in which the so-called sexual excesses of western society, transmitted by media such as television, film and the internet, are often viewed as corruptive forces in less liberal societies. To what extent is sex really being globalized?

In fact, a close look at the social and cultural environments in which young people develop makes it clear that there is still a great diversity in family forms, economic and political circumstances, religious and cultural values, access to schooling and health care, and all those factors which ultimately influence sexuality. This diversity affects sexual health, behaviour, beliefs and attitudes. For example, ideas about gender are culturally specific and have a profound impact on young people's sexual lives. Gender inequalities make young women in many countries sexually vulnerable. We know that in many (most?) countries, young men are seen to be sexual beings and young women are not. This belief is implicated in double standards regarding virginity and has important implications in regard to sexual coercion and sexual exploitation. We know, for example, that 1 million children, mostly girls, are forced into the sex trade every year and that sex workers in all countries start working when they are young (National Centre in HIV Epidemiology and Clinical Research 1998). We know that sexual abuse and rape are experienced commonly by young and not-so-young women in many countries (e.g. Eaton *et al.* 2003; Whitefield 1999).

There is now a plethora of research in western countries that consistently shows a large number of young people are sexually active, use condoms inconsistently or not at all, and that a substantial number engage in practices that put themselves at risk of HIV. This is particularly true of marginalized groups such as homeless young people and those identifying as homosexual, and we have summarized this research in various chapters of this book. We know a great deal about western adolescents, particularly those from the USA, the UK and Australia.

On the other hand, the picture is less clear when it comes to young people in non-western countries. We do know that premarital sex is culturally unacceptable in Asian countries and that there is little open discussion about sexual matters, certainly in the family setting (Hong *et al.* 1994; Moore 1998). And yet, as we saw in Chapter 1, the few studies of young people's sexual practices in a number of Asian countries suggest that premarital sex among adolescents is not as rare a phenomenon as adults may wish to believe (Riono & Jazant 2004; Simon & Paxton 2004; Tarr & Aggleton 1999). While the age of first intercourse may be later in these countries than, say, in Australia, it is clear that a substantial minority of these young people are sexually active prior to marriage.

The 'westernization' of Asian youth is increasing. A recent study (Bennett 2005) examined how western youth culture has been incorporated into the lives of local young people in Mataram, a tourist area of Lombok (Indonesia), with a distinct youth culture emerging. Away from the parental gaze, these young people occupy 'youth spaces' – perhaps in tourist areas, on the beach and in boarding houses for youth. Clearly this has real consequences for the sexual lives of these young people, with opportunities for sexual exploration occurring in these spaces that exclude adults. As others report, the global flow of western youth culture (in its many forms) has led to the spread of what has been referred to as a new kind of sexual infrastructure in the form of bars, discotheques and other venues. The spread of western ways will undoubtedly bring with it some relief from problems like sexual inequality, intolerance of minority groups and lack of contraception. But the two-edged sword of westernization will also result in the breaking-down of some of the traditional values which bind communities, as well as giving young people more freedom to experiment with their sexual lives – no doubt to both their benefit and their cost.

Adolescent sexual development must occur, then, against the back-drop of many and varied social forces, forces which themselves are in a constant state of flux. The way an adolescent balances these forces to produce his or her sexual ideology and behaviour will be unique to each individual.

In the next chapter we move to perhaps the most pervasive social force of all – gender socialization. The implications of this influence on adolescents' sexual lives are examined.

6   Gender, sexuality and romance

Interviewer: What does the word 'sex' mean to you?
Sex is like a need . . . it's sort of like water, and er oxygen, no air and water. I mean it's sort of er physiological need, you know, if you like. Um, sort of you need water to survive, you need food, but you don't really need sex to survive do you?
Interviewer: What do you think of sex?
It's kind of er well like you don't sort of er, your body wants sex, and it's sort of like wanting a glass of water.
Interviewer: Why do you have sex?
Because my spermatozoa accumulate in my testicles and it swells up . . .
(Interview with a young man; Rosenthal *et al.* 1996)

Interviewer: What does the word 'sex' mean to you?
Some type of bonding, I suppose, or coming together as one.
Interviewer: Why do you have sex?
Um, I guess to express those emotions of caring for someone.
(Interview with a young woman; Rosenthal *et al.* 1996)

In this chapter we examine differences in the ways adolescents of both sexes behave and would like to behave, how they think about sex and how they communicate with each other on sexual topics. The quote above suggests there is a gap between young men and women in how they think about sex – how general is this difference? We address the impact of social conditioning and biological sex on gender-specific motives for sex and attitudes to permissiveness, as well as gender differences in 'libido' and in intimacy development. We focus on ideas about romance, and how these vary between young men and women, and across cultural groups. The debate about whether a double standard of sexual behaviour still exists is aired and we conclude by discussing the implications for sexual communication of the differences that are observed.

In earlier times, traditional gender roles for men were seen as worker, primary breadwinner and head of the household. Men were supposed to be assertive, confident, brave and independent. The female gender role was to bear and nurture children, run the household and care for people's feelings. Consequently, women were expected to be warm and expressive, tender and dependent. Sexually speaking, man was to be the 'hunter' and initiator of sexual activity, the one with the more powerful and demanding sex drive and the strong figure in a heterosexual relationship. The traditional woman played her role through being agreeable, cooperative, placating, flirtatious, and attending to her appearance and the pleasure of the male, while retaining a respectable and ladylike demeanour in public. To some extent, we know that modern life has become less rigid in terms of the presentation of stereotypes and the pressure to conform. On the other hand, in the domain of sexuality, there has been less change than might be expected, especially for young people, as we shall see in the following sections.

Motives for sex

Do gender differences include differences in motives expressed for having sex? Leigh (1989) studied the reasons for having or not having sex among 1000 adults and found men attached significantly more importance to pleasure, pleasing a partner, conquest and relief of tension than did women who were significantly more likely to rate emotional closeness as an important reason for having sex. Among reasons for not having sex, men rated fear of AIDS and fear of rejection more highly than women, while the converse was true for fear of pregnancy, lack of interest and lack of enjoyment. Also in the 1980s, several investigators showed that teenage girls, more than boys, reported being in love as the main reason for being sexually active (Cassell 1984; Zelnik & Shah 1983). Nielsen (1991: 370) summed up these views on gender differences:

> Boys are more likely to see intercourse as a way of establishing their maturity and of achieving social status, whereas most girls see intercourse as a way of expressing their love and of achieving greater intimacy. As a consequence, boys are more apt to have

sex with someone who is a relative stranger, to have more sexual partners, and to disassociate sex from love. Even in their sexual fantasies, boys are more likely to imagine sexual adventures detached from love and emotional intimacy.

Recent writers have pointed out a gender convergence towards expressed motives for sex and attitudes towards sexual encounters. Woody *et al.* (2003) asked sexually experienced 19-year-olds to recall their emotions and motivations preceding first intercourse. The most common motives for boys were (in order): 'I was curious to see what it felt like' (curiosity), and 'I felt turned on sexually and wanted to do it for more pleasure' (pleasure). For girls, curiosity was also the highest rated motive, although to a lesser extent than for boys. The second highest rating was for the statement 'I felt emotionally mature enough'. For both girls and boys, 'healthy' motives far outranked unhealthy ones such as 'I did it to escape from problems or bad feelings', or 'I did it because I was high on alcohol and drugs'.

Woody *et al.* also asked the young people about their feelings towards their partner. Here there were only a few gender differences. Attraction was the strongest feeling for both sexes, followed for boys by desire to please, being in love, and feeling safe and cared for by the partner. For girls, the order of ratings was slightly different, with feeling safe and cared for rated second highest, followed by 'in love', then wanting to please. Eyre and Millstein (1999) however did find gender differences when they asked male and female adolescents aged 16 to 20 years to generate reasons for having sex rather than responding to a checklist of reasons as in the study by Woody *et al.* Eyre and Millstein showed that male adolescents indicated sexual arousal as a reason for having sex whereas female adolescents did not. Nevertheless, 55 per cent of the reasons to have or not to have sex were shared across the total group, with 'love' a major motive reported by all age, gender and ethnic subgroups in the sample.

Our own studies have also shown that ideas of love and romance are important aspects of sex for both adolescent boys and girls, who expressed positive evaluations of these aspects of relationships (Moore 1994; Moore & Rosenthal 1992). The desire to experience a loving relationship with 'the right person' is shown by their responses to the question 'What do the words "romantic love" mean to you?'

> I see romantic as roses, candlelit dinner, holding hands, walking down the beach – stuff like that. Someone to talk to, to love, basically.

From movies and things, I see it everywhere. When you think you have the right person, and you have someone forever, and you don't want to break up. You love them and they love you, and you think there is nothing wrong and you are perfect for each other.

When you are really involved with each other and you don't think about anything else except the other person and you are really close.

I think it is more when you have a strong friendship with someone like a girlfriend or your wife or your fiancée . . . it is much different to sex although there might be sex in it, it is different. Romantic love is more sensual and more deep; and it comes from deep inside, where[as] sex – you just want to get it done and it might be over, like a one-night stand.

(Moore & Rosenthal 1993: 90)

'Loving, caring and affection' were the primary motivations for having sex among most boys and girls in our middle-class Anglo-Australian sample although physical pleasure or fun was the major motive for some boys and girls. The picture was different for our group of homeless teenagers, with clear differences in the responses of boys and girls. Most of these vulnerable young girls (71 per cent), but few boys (15 per cent), elected loving, caring and affection as their major reason for engaging in sex. The preferred motive for these boys was sex for physical pleasure or fun (53 per cent). Few homeless girls (8 per cent) used sex to satisfy these goals. Teenagers in our ethnic minority group had yet a different pattern of motives. Sex for pleasure played no part in the girls' sexual behaviour but was the primary motive for some boys (19 per cent). Clearly, among these last two groups of teenagers, there was a mismatch of expectations, with girls looking for something that their likely partners were not wanting or able to give. Many of the homeless boys responded to the harshness of their lives with an unequivocal rejection of romantic values, although this cynical split between romance and sex was not restricted to the most disadvantaged of our male teenagers. What did romantic love mean to these boys?

I try to keep away from all that. Romance is alright I suppose, but fuck the love.

Airy-fairy stuff.

> Can't see myself answering that question. Romantic isn't a word
> to me. You are sexually attracted to them and that's it. There's no
> romance and all that crap that people say – it's all garbage and
> it's all bullshit.
>
> (Moore & Rosenthal 1993: 90)

While some homeless girls shared their male peers' views about
romance and love, most wanted sex with friendship, consideration
and love. These girls appeared to have accepted the full complement
of middle-class ideals about partnerships, only more so. Their expression of neediness, and thus vulnerability, coupled with the data we
have about the views of sex of their potential partners, does not augur
well for these young women's future satisfaction in relationships. Our
picture of these girls is that their search for love is enacted through
sexual encounters, many unsatisfying and not enhancing their sense of
self-worth, leading to a cycle of further neediness. The plight of these
young girls is poignantly expressed by one 16-year-old's response to
the question of why some girls 'sleep around':

> I think some of them are searching for love and they get their
> wires crossed, in having a sexual partner – that that is what they
> are getting from that person. Or they are drunk or on drugs and
> don't know what they are doing, and it happens. There are
> different forms of why friends have different partners. For
> instance one of my friends does it because she is making money . . .
> but [it] depends, really. Mainly I think not being in control, being
> under the influence of drugs, often makes my friends have many
> sexual partners. I don't think if they were sober or straight they
> would do it as often.
>
> (Moore & Rosenthal 1993: 91)

Research on motives for sex reveals that, among certain groups of
teenagers, there are strong differences between boys and girls, while
among middle-class and probably more educated teenagers, some
gender convergence is occurring, with young boys including relationship-oriented motives for sex more often, and girls acknowledging the
contribution of arousal and pleasure as reasons underlying their
sexual activity.

Libido: is the sex drive different for boys and girls?

Differences between males and females in their beliefs about sexuality, modes of relating sexually and perceived motives for sex have been at times attributed to differences in strength of sex drive, or libido. In this section we explore the evidence that such differences do exist, and the extent to which they are related to biological sex differences (such as hormone levels) or to socialization processes.

It is difficult to disentangle the role of hormones from that of social factors in sexual arousal. The fact that levels of testosterone in boys are associated with their sexual activities, including masturbation, provides evidence that hormones affect drive or arousal. Testosterone levels in females are only about one-tenth of those in males. Furthermore, some have argued that female sex hormone levels are not directly linked to libido, for example, Smith (1989) cites studies in which female libido is decreased after surgical removal of the ovaries and adrenalectomy, but not when ovaries alone are removed. However, more recent research on the role of neuropeptides in arousal and sexual pleasure suggests the situation is more complex than these early studies indicate. The neuropeptides oxytocin and vasopressin are secreted by the pituitary gland, their secretion regulated by the hormones oestrogen and testosterone respectively. Hiller (2004), reporting on laboratory investigations into hormonal release during human sexual activity, argues that oxytocin is associated with the experience of pleasure during arousal and orgasm in both sexes, while vasopressin is released only during male arousal. Feelings of love, attachment and protectiveness are also associated with oxytocin (a hormone associated with pregnancy and childbirth). This neuropeptide (brain affecting hormone) is secreted by both men and women during sexual activity, but more so by women, leading some theorists to argue that this is why love and sex are more associated among women than men (Diamond 2004). Vasopressin has been linked with male craving, persistence and sexual assertiveness but there is speculation, based on animal studies, that increases in this neuropeptide for women lead to a loss of sexual interest (Hiller 2004).

Clearly there is much still to be learnt about the role of hormones and arousal. A complicating factor is that hormone levels interact with social factors in the prediction of sexual activities. For example, testosterone levels in girls are associated with sexual interests (masturbation, thinking about sex) but not behaviours (Udry *et al.* 1986). We could infer from this that girls act out their libidinal wishes to a lesser extent than boys. Whether this greater social restraint of sexual expression is also accompanied by changed perceptions of arousal is not clear, as studies which show sex differences in permissive attitudes and motives for sex have not included measures of hormone levels. Goggin (1989) did find differences in self-reported arousal among a group of 18- to 25-year-olds. Young men scored higher than young women on a measure of sexual interest and arousability, which included items such as 'I have a lot of sexual energy', 'I feel quite frustrated if I don't have sex regularly', and 'I have very strong sexual drives'. But writers like Deborah Tolman (2002) claim that teenage girls are wary about admitting to their sexual desire even in this day and age because of worries about reputation. More research is needed to tease out the physiological predictors of sexual arousal among adolescents, and their interaction with social factors.

Early feminists such as Millett (1972) and Koedt (1973) took a different slant on the issue of male and female sex drive. They argued that female sex drive only seems less strong because the power differential between the sexes leads to sexuality itself being defined as activities and feelings that are more exciting to men. In the *Myth of the Vaginal Orgasm*, Koedt presents a case that female sexuality has been structured around men's convenience, denying the physical basis of women's sexual pleasure. Hite (1977) also criticized the 'reproductive model' in which sex is defined as penetration, intercourse and male orgasm. Activities such as foreplay and female orgasm are devalued. Women's lack of power in this phallocentric model of sex leads them to take more passive roles and in fact to being less interested in the whole activity. More recently, Holland *et al.* (1998) argue that there is no socially acceptable way for women to express their sex drives; indeed there is not even a language that can be suitably employed to talk about these drives. From their interviews with young women, this group report that formal and parent-driven sex education is about warning daughters of the pitfalls of unrestrained sexual desire and teaching a surveillance system ('the male in the head') to provide guidelines on what constitutes sluttish behaviour. Although these feminist writers underplay the role of biology in gender differences, their perspective is valuable in its attempt to break through social conditioning and change the lens through which we view male-female relationships.

We can address the question of gender differences in sex drive from the perspective of behavioural rather than physiological evidence. As previously reported, adolescent boys report more masturbatory and other sexual activity than girls. Additionally, they are more likely to be aroused by a wider variety of sexual stimuli (Canli & Gabrieli

2004; Oliver & Hyde 1993). In 1991, Dusek suggested that the sex drive for girls is more diffuse and is likely to be displaced into other areas such as close friendships, and that the quality of intimate relationships is more important in sexual expression for girls. Dusek characterized the first sexual experiences of males and females thus:

> The modal male will engage in his initial sexual intercourse with someone with whom he has no particular emotional attachment. He will have sex with her a few times, and then never again. The modal female will be in love with her initial partner and will likely be planning to marry him. The relationship will last some period of time and may result in marriage.
>
> (Dusek 1991: 202)

The truth or otherwise of this characterization today is still open to debate. We do have evidence that adolescent boys and girls are becoming more similar in their sexual behaviours and attitudes, although clearly differences remain, some no doubt related to biological makeup and some to social conditioning. Added complexity comes from the knowledge that girls or young women may still be more reluctant than their male counterparts to admit to their sexual behaviours, given that more social disapproval attaches to sexually adventurous females.

Can boys control their sex drive? The persistence of a dangerous myth

There appears to be a strong belief in society that male but not female sex drive is largely uncontrollable once aroused. In our research, young people of both sexes readily expressed this conventional view. Boys' sexual urges were seen as able to be controlled by only 37 per cent of our sample of teenagers, although 87 per cent agreed that this was possible for girls (Moore & Rosenthal 1993: 93).

> No, the only way they can control it is if they use their hand a lot.

> No, I think if any guy has a chance to root a girl, and if they liked her and she wasn't exactly ugly, they would do it. I think the majority of guys would say 'Yes, go for it', but there might be a small minority that says no. I haven't met that minority yet.

Another illustration of male sex drive supremacy beliefs comes from excuses given for forcing sex – 'she led me on' or 'if she didn't want sex she shouldn't have dressed like that'. Such excuses imply that once aroused, men must be satisfied. These ideas are not yet a thing of the past, as is shown in recent newspaper stories (in the UK, the USA and Australia) of elite footballers accused of rape, gang rape and other sexual violations, not just once but on several occasions (e.g. 'AFL [Australian Football League] standing still on spate of sex assaults', *The Australian*, 15 September 2004; 'Degrading culture knows no boundaries', *The Australian*, 3 March 2004). These young men at the peak of their physical fitness and energy can find themselves in situations where there is an explosive mix of free-flowing alcohol, peer (or team) pressure and strong sexual temptation. The adulation of young women is flattering, and can lead to a sense of entitlement that any kind of sexual behaviour will be tolerated. Indeed, this attitude is widespread, as epitomized by a university official investigating rape allegations directed at football recruits at a US university. This investigator was quoted as saying about the alleged victims: 'The question I have for these ladies in this is why they are going to parties like this and drinking or taking drugs and putting themselves in a very threatening or serious position' (*Detroit Free Press*, 9 February 2004). The implication is that restraint and respect for women cannot be expected once the boys are aroused, and it is the responsibility of the girls to keep control. It's probably what many parents fear they must teach their daughters, despite the unfairness of such an attitude and the way it treats female desire as both an aberration and an excuse for punishment.

What did the young people in our study think about female sex drive? Most thought that girls had greater control over their sex drives because they were more responsible or because their drives were weaker in the first place. There was, however, some recognition of exceptions to the general rule. Boys could be restrained and girls could be uncontrolled:

Interviewer: Can women control their sexual urges?
I know girls that can, and I know girls that can't. It depends on the girl really. I think that most girls can control it more than guys, definitely. With girls it is different. Guys reach a stage where they don't mature any more, and I think girls keep maturing, that's the main difference. Girls are more emotional than guys. I think because girls mature more they come to realise that there is more to life than just sexual relationships.

(Moore & Rosenthal 1993: 93–4

In summary, our evidence suggests first that hormonal and physiological studies point to the possibility of a stronger libido in males,
but more needs to be done to clarify the differential role of hormones
in human male and female arousal and attachment. Second, gender
differences in arousability exist but, as social conditions change, there
is evidence that young women are admitting to being aroused by a
greater range of stimuli than was previously thought. Third, the sex
drive manifests itself in different sexual behaviours for teenage boys
and girls but some or even all of these may be a function of the
different social learnings experienced by the sexes and the power
differential between them. Finally, adolescents perceive and accept
gender differences in levels of sexual control in ways which do not
square with a healthy and sexually responsible society.

Is there still a sexual double standard?

Perhaps not surprisingly in the light of the above discussion, a review
of 30 studies published since 1980 found evidence of the continued
existence of different standards of sexual permissiveness for men and
women (Crawford & Popp 2003). These writers reviewed studies
which used a range of methodologies, including experimental studies
(e.g. rating the behaviour of men and women in hypothetical sexual
scenarios), ethnographic studies (e.g. observing sex education classes
in secondary schools) and interviews/focus groups with men and
women. Most of these studies were conducted with young people in
their middle or later teenage years. The authors comment on the
continuing power of the epithet 'slut' as a way of controlling female
sexuality. They note that beliefs that the double standard would fade
away as a result of the women's movement and the sexual revolution,
'may have been overly optimistic' (p. 22).

Eder *et al.* (1995) also argue that the discourse on adolescent
sexuality still overwhelmingly reflects a double standard. In a three-
year ethnographic study of middle-school peer culture, Eder *et al.*
showed that girls but never boys could be derogated if they showed
interest in sex or sexual assertiveness. Making 'the first move' was not
tolerated for girls, with the sanctions against female sexual agency even
including negative comments about dressing attractively. In Orenstein's (1994) ethnographic study of middle schools, girls described
their fear of the slut label, and Moffat's (1989) participant observation
of peer culture on a university campus also came to the conclusion that
women were classified as 'good women' or 'sluts'.

According to Lees (1993), reputation is a major issue for girls, so that sexual desire can only be expressed in the context of romantic love and commitment. There is an expectation that both sexes will engage in premarital sex, but girls have to make sure they do so in a circumspect way whereas boys are encouraged to be as active as they like and their reputations are enhanced by more encounters. Girls respond by romanticizing their sexual encounters, so they can be interpreted as expressions of caring and love, not as expressions of sexual desire. Such idealization of sex, while enjoyable and appropriate for certain relationships, is less appropriate for casual and short-term encounters as it renders the romantic young woman highly vulnerable to hurt and disappointment and reduces the likelihood of her being able to take responsibility for her sexual life. 'He will look after me because he loves me' is an all too common refrain among young women, and one which can lead to a mismatch of expectations and perceptions about sexual encounters.

Holland *et al.*'s (1998) work also supports the notion of double standards in sexual behaviour for men and women. They state: 'Behaviour that made him successfully masculine, a real man, caused her to lose her reputation – to be seen as loose, slack, a slag – a reputation policed just as forcibly by women as by men' (p. 11). They theorize this phenomenon as, in a sense, being what is meant by heterosexuality – a set of norms and behaviours which, by the power of masculine culture (and supported by both sexes), allows sexual freedom for young men but not young women as part of their identity development.

But the situation is complex. Sexual attitudes are more permissive across the board than they were in the mid-20th century. Martin (1996) found that adolescent girls who had sexual intercourse were not necessarily negatively evaluated by their peers, as once may have been the case. But 'too much', 'too many partners' or 'too young', and the slut label was used. Data from our own studies (Moore & Rosenthal 1992) provide evidence that while some aspects of sexual inequality are less common, others remain. We found that more than half of our 16-year-old teenagers had the same reaction to girls or boys who 'sleep around'. This occurred independently of the sex of the judges and reflected views ranging from approval to strong disapproval (Moore & Rosenthal 1993: 97):

Interviewer: What do you think about girls who sleep around?
I think it is okay. Most of my friends think it is okay. Maybe some girls would think it is not acceptable. It depends on who

they are sleeping around with. If they had been in a few relationships, and slept with the guys that they had been with, that would be alright. But if they were just sleeping with anyone, it probably wouldn't be accepted as much. [Boys?] Similar to females. [It] depends on who they are having sex with.

(Boy)

[Girls?] Personally, I think it disgusting. I know girls who do that, but I feel really different to them. No, I don't like it. It makes her reputation go down from there. Keep away from them. [Boys?] The same. Equal rights. If a guy does it, a girl can do it too.

(Girl)

Of those who did judge 'sleeping around' differently for boys and girls, virtually all saw this activity as far more detrimental for girls than boys. The double standards applicable to sexual behaviour are clear in these young people's responses. Sadly, both boys and girls held these views equally (Moore & Rosenthal 1993: 98):

[Girls?] Sluts, basically. Because they have a mattress on their back, they like having sex. That's the way I look at it, no two ways about it. [Boys?] A stud. Good luck to him. It's OK for a guy to be like that. I don't have to have sex with a guy, so I don't care. That's what the difference is.

(Boy)

[Girls?] I think they are sluts basically. [Boys?] They are different to girls because they like competing against others, like [a] peer group pressure type of thing. When a guy does something, the other guys do it too. They also like bragging, I think.

(Girl)

Interpretations of sexual experience tell us something of the workings of the double standard. In a survey of about 2000 older adolescents aged 17 to 20 years (Rosenthal *et al.* 1990), we found that young women were more likely to define their sexual encounters as occurring with a regular or steady partner than with a casual partner, while young men were more likely to regard what must be essentially the same encounters as casual. We are aware that the real pattern of adolescent sexual relationships is one of very loosely defined serial monogamy. Teenagers tend to have a succession of partners, with relatively short lead-ups to the start of new relationships (around six months on average in this group, but varying from 'a few hours' to 'a few years'), so in fact the male interpretation of what is going on may be closer to reality. The girls are interpreting, as an indication of love and commitment, encounters which will often turn out to be short term.

Views about fidelity are also relevant here. Almost all the girls in this study expected themselves and their partners to be faithful in a long-term relationship, with this pattern consistent across different ethnic groups we tested. Among the boys, most (86 per cent) expected their partners to be faithful, but expectations for their own behaviour were far less stringent and varied quite markedly across groups. On average 75 per cent of young men said they would try to be monogamous in a steady relationship, but for some groups the figure was considerably lower. Teenage boys, while easier on themselves in terms of standards of fidelity, were more likely to take an aggressive approach to partners who strayed. Most respondents of both sexes said they would either 'talk it over' or 'get angry' if they found out that their partner was unfaithful. There were, however, some disturbingly vengeful responses, all from boys, to the question 'What would you do if your partner was unfaithful?': 'Beat the shit out of them. Get a bit upset'; 'Beat her up because she was a fucking slut'.

While most boys reported some sort of active response to a partner's infidelity – whether it be a reasoned attempt to discuss the matter or aggressive behaviour – some girls (15 per cent) adopted a stereotyped passive role, replying that they would 'do nothing'. This suggests either a greater tolerance for partners' lapses than was evident for boys or (and possibly more likely) an acceptance of the lesser power that girls hold in these sexual relationships. Whatever the underlying dynamics, it is clear that the meaning of fidelity in steady relationships differs for adolescent girls and boys, with the norms of behaviour being viewed less stringently among boys for themselves but not for their partners.

Summing up, we can say that while the double standard may be weakening, it has certainly not died altogether, especially among some adolescents such as those from lower social-class groups (Lees 1993) or those from cultural groups in which sex roles are emphasized (Rosenthal *et al.* 1990). Even among groups who pay lip service to sexual equality, if one scratches the surface, there are still subtle – and not so subtle – pressures for girls to restrain their sexuality. Of course from an evolutionary, psychoanalytic and a biological perspective, it is possible that double standard reflects innate differential needs of the sexes. From these theoretical approaches it could be argued that social conditioning may be able to moderate but never entirely eradicate gender differences in the expression of sexual desire.

Romance

Adolescent sexuality is not all bad news, inequality, risky behaviour and a war between the sexes. Young people can enjoy the awakening of desire, the fun of flirting and the fulfilment of relationships as part of their sexual development. One aspect of this is romance, a topic once neglected by psychologists but recently subject to a flurry of research. Love, romance and courtship are rites of passage for young people in western society, and according to Robert Johnson (1987: xi), 'Romantic love is the single greatest energy system in the Western psyche'. This topic has already featured in several sections of the book – for example, we have discussed Erikson's notions of the role of adolescent romance as assisting identity formation (Chapter 2) and earlier in this chapter presented information on male and female perceptions of romantic love and the nomination of 'love and romance' as motives for having sex. In this section, we consider research on both the pitfalls and positive outcomes of adolescent romantic relationships, as well as studies that indicate different styles of romantic relating may be associated with personality characteristics, developmental experiences and cultural context.

First, we present data on the frequency and nature of adolescent romantic relationships from the National Longitudinal Study of Adolescent Health (Add Health), a US study of thousands of young people aged 12 to 18 years at school (Carver *et al.* 2003). Approximately 65 per cent of both boys and girls had experienced a romantic relationship, with higher percentages, not surprisingly, in the older age groups. Many of the romantic relationships were long term, more than half being a year or more in duration. A small number of boys and girls (2.2 and 3.5 per cent respectively) nominated same-sex romantic partners. More girls than boys reported having sexual intercourse with their romantic partner, reflecting the usual pattern of girls more likely to have intercourse within what they perceive as a romantic context. The social connectedness of these adolescent relationships was indicated by data showing that parents had met the partners of approximately three-quarters of the romantically attached adolescents, and a similarly large percentage had told others 'they were a couple', and gone out together in a group. Clearly, romantic relationships are normative among middle and older adolescents, but there are also significant numbers of young people who have not yet experienced them.

Adolescent romantic relationships have the potential to provide positive learning experiences about the self and how to relate intimately to others. They can contribute to overall self-esteem (Harter 1999) and to beliefs about attractiveness and self-worth (Kuttler *et al.* 1999). They can assist young people in renegotiating and developing more mature relationships with their parents, raise young people's status in the peer group and offer a safe environment for learning about and experimenting with sexuality. On the other hand, romantic relationships can sometimes hinder identity development through closing off options (such as may occur with early parenthood) or through exposing the young person to abusive and violent interactions (Shulman 2003) or unwanted or coerced sexual activity (Wekerle & Avgoustis 2003). In addition, romantic break-ups among young people are often associated with depression (Welsh *et al.* 2003) and have been cited as the most common trigger of the first episode of a major depressive disorder (Monroe *et al.* 1999). What is it about the desired state of being in love or romantically attached that can have so much potential for positive and negative outcomes?

One answer revolves around characteristics of the individual in love, another around the nature of the relationship and yet another around the ways we socially construct love and romance. At the individual level, various studies indicate that insecure attachment styles are implicated in less satisfactory romantic partnerships. What does this mean? Attachment theory suggests that infants form various kinds of bonds with their carers, and the quality of these bonds affects adult relationships, especially close or romantic relationships (Bartholomew & Horowitz 1991). Securely attached people are 'good at' relationships; they learn to trust in others and to manage a healthy 'give and take' in their intimate associations. Insecurely attached individuals are either overly anxious and 'clingy' about their adult relationships (anxiously attached) or relatively indifferent to others (avoidantly attached). Bogaert and Sadava (2002), in a large-scale study, found that anxiously attached young people saw themselves as less physically attractive, had an earlier first intercourse, more sexual partners and were more likely to be unfaithful than those with secure attachment styles. Interestingly, this anxious group was more likely than the securely attached to express very strong love towards their romantic partner, even though they were also more likely to be

unfaithful. Tracy *et al.* (2003) also found anxiously attached adolescents reported being in love the most times. If they had sex, fear of
losing their partner was more likely to be given as the motive than it
was for secure young people. Another example of the role of attachment comes from a study by Moore and Leung (2002). They showed
that securely attached adolescents were less stressed, less lonely and
more academically satisfied than those with insecure attachment
styles, regardless of relationship status. These securely attached adolescents were more resilient to relationship break-up, or to being
currently 'single', that is, without a romantic partner.

Relationship characteristics also impact on the outcomes of romantic relationships in adolescence. Welsh *et al.* (2003) list situations like
unrequited love, infidelity of one's partner, sexual coercion and
breaking up as potentially associated with depression in young people.
In the case of unrequited love, fantasies about the other can be
intense, sometimes leading to misinterpretations that the feelings are
reciprocated. In extreme cases this may result in maladjusted acting
out behaviours such as stalking, but usually the distress is turned
inwards. Self-esteem can be damaged and would-be lovers may feel
humiliated, unattractive and inferior (Baumeister *et al.* 1993). A study
by Smith and Hokland (1988), assessing psychological and physiological correlates of adolescent love, showed that requited love was
associated with self-confidence, interest in the environment, better
immunity response and good general health. Unrequited love on the
other hand linked with depression, lack of relaxation and recent
hangover. Interestingly, not only disappointed lovers feel bad,
according to Baumeister, whose study showed that rejectors often
felt guilty about hurting another's feelings, as well as aversive feelings
of being hounded.

Unfaithfulness also has the potential to be devastating to young
people, especially if their expectations have been for an exclusive
relationship. In an earlier section we discussed some of these expectations and noted that adolescents are not particularly good at living
up to their own standards. Feldman and Cauffman (1999a, 1999b)
suggest that this may relate to the competing and conflicting developmental demands of adolescence. The identity task of exploring the
world of adult experience is facilitated by variety and the challenge of
new relationships, while the developmental task of achieving intimacy
proceeds through practice in mutuality and commitment, learning
what it is like to really get to know another person. Such conflict is
expressed by these 16-year-old Australian girls, when asked 'Are you
always faithful to your partner?':

> Yes and I would expect the same from him (but) if we were going
> steady and this gorgeous hunk came up . . . it depends on how far
> the relationship had gone. It depends on how committed you are.

> No, he got boring.

Trying to balance these tasks is difficult enough for adults let alone
young people, and their failure to do so can lead to negative emotions
for the 'betrayer' as well as the 'betrayed'. In the first quote below, a
16-year-old boy, asked about his response if a partner was unfaithful,
expresses his likely feelings of hurt. In the second quote another
adolescent boy admits to shame at his own perceived infidelity:

> *Interviewer*: What would you do if your partner was unfaithful?
> I'd be upset at the fact that they didn't tell me. Because it should
> be a relationship where you can talk to people about what is in
> your mind, and share. It is like all of a sudden that person hasn't
> shared this with you, and you feel, 'what have I done, what's gone
> wrong, how come they don't want to talk to me about it?'

> *Interviewer*: Are you always faithful to your partner?
> No . . . I feel a bit ashamed, if she was just a normal girl I
> wouldn't, but because I like my girlfriend a fair bit I feel like a
> dirt-bag now.

Of more serious concern are adolescent relationships characterized
by abuse, violence or conflict. Carver *et al.* (2003), from their large
national US sample, found about 12 per cent of young people in
romantic relationships reported being insulted by partners in front of
others, nearly 20 per cent were sworn at, 8 per cent pushed or shoved
and around 3 per cent threatened with violence by their partner. Boys
were as likely to report abusive behaviour as girls. Several studies
have suggested that both victims and perpetrators of teenage dating
violence are more likely to have experienced childhood maltreatment
and/or had substance abuse problems (Wekerle & Avgoustis 2003).
Alcohol abuse has a prominent role in dating violence, a topic discussed in more detail in Chapter 10.

Finally, social constructions of romance influence how young
people feel about falling in and out of love, and how they act on those
feelings. While choosing a partner and partnering for love are

regarded as a vital component of romantic love in the West, they may not be so important in all cultures. For example, according to Robert Moore (1998), adolescents in the People's Republic of China view romance and love as subordinate to the needs of the group (typically the family). Love and romance are considered in the light of responsibility towards parents. Spontaneous expressions of love, especially in terms of non-marital sexual activities, are not regarded as appropriate. Youth from collectivist cultures generally appear to display more conservative attitudes to sexual expression and less commitment to romantic passion than is common in the West. To illustrate this point, Dion and Dion (1996) demonstrated that Asian students in the USA endorsed companionate/friendship and altruistic views of love to a greater extent than their Caucasian counterparts. These authors argued that such views are consistent with a collectivist rather than an individualistic framework.

Beliefs about the specific nature of romance differ across cultures. In a two-culture study of university students, Puerto Rican youth showed different ideas about romance from those in the USA. Puerto Ricans saw 'holding hands' as more romantic than Americans, while Americans viewed saying 'I love you' as more crucial (Quiles 2003). A more detailed analysis by Knee (1998) identified five components of romanticism. These are the beliefs that (a) love conquers all, (b) there is only one true love for each person, (c) the beloved will live up to high expectations, (d) love at first sight is possible, and (e) one finds true love through the heart, not the mind. Medora *et al.* (2002) explored the existence of these attitudes across US, Asian-Indian and Turkish young adults. Americans had higher romanticism scores than Turks, who in turn scored higher than Asian-Indians. Medora *et al.* argued along the same lines as Moore that romance is less valued in collectivist, traditional and less industrialized cultures. In traditional cultures, these authors suggest, familial obligations and social expectations dictate attitudes to romance and there are constraints on choice of a marriage partner. Such constraints are not realistically consistent with the ideas of romanticism as suggested by Knee above. It is worth considering whether these beliefs about romance are so unrealistically idealistic that they may also contribute to the high levels of dissatisfaction and relationship breakdown in the West.

One does not have to cross nations to find different cultures of romance. Young men and women are socialized differently with respect to romance, particularly the relationships between sexual behaviour and romance, as we saw earlier in the chapter.

Intimacy and commitment

Erikson (1959, 1968) wrote that the development of the capacity for intimacy, and its culmination in the formation of a life partnership was a vital psychological task for young adults. He was referring to emotional as well as physical intimacy – the ability to share feelings with another, to self-disclose and to listen, to set mutual goals and to compromise individual desires in order to work towards 'couple' goals – as well as to share one's body in harmonious and mutually satisfying sexuality. Intimacy and falling in love are closely associated. Intimate relationships or expectations about their development are often initiated in the charged emotional climate of falling in love. Youth and falling in love seem to go hand in hand but the outcome is not always intimacy. One common developmental path begins with the hero worship and crushes of the early teenage years. Price-Adams and Greene (1990) argue that crushes on celebrity figures can form an important part of the process of self-concept development. The adolescent projects an ego ideal onto the object of the crush. Crushes can be explored through fantasy in ways not involving high risk to self-esteem. Eventually fantasy objects (in the sense that they are unattainable) are replaced by a 'real' love object in which partners share a romantic vision of their relationship.

Do young men and women differ in the ways in which they deal with issues of intimacy and commitment? It seems that they do. Young men frequently interpret their initial sexual experiences as learning and experimentation, and as contributing to their sense of self-definition, rather than as a way to become emotionally close to another. In some cases, sex may be used as a way to ward off emotional closeness, as expressed by the 'love them and leave them' stereotype associated with some young men's behaviour. Young women, on the other hand, often assume that commitment will accompany physical intimacy, and that sex and love automatically go together. These divergent perceptions are likely to give rise to frustration, confusion and hurt as teenagers explore their sexual feelings. It may be true that a 'permissiveness with affection' morality is becoming the norm among young people, reducing differences between the sexes in their attitudes to intimacy. Our research suggests this is not always the case, at least among some groups of adolescents.

In developmental terms, girls at adolescence may be better equipped to handle intimate relationships as a result of their experiences with same-sex friends. Analysis of adolescent friendship patterns shows that, while girls and boys may have a similar number of friends at preadolescence and during their teenage years, girls' friendships are characterized by more self-disclosure, discussion of problems, sharing of emotions and mutual support than boys' friendships (Moore & Boldero 1991). We can describe the difference this way. Boys do things with their friends – they play sport, go on outings, ride bicycles, kick a football. When they talk to each other, it is 'agency' talk – what we are going to do and how we are going to do it. The nearest these boys get to becoming intimate is through shared banter and joking. Girls also have activity-oriented friendships, but their talk is likely to be different. It is about who they are, how they appear to others, how they feel and how others feel – in other words, intimate, relationship-oriented talk. When romantic relationships begin, girls may have a head start on boys with respect to talking about emotions but are likely to be unprepared for boys' inability and/or unwillingness to express closeness in this way. There is considerable evidence that these mismatches of communication between the sexes are not only features of adolescence but last well into adulthood (Tannen 1990), suggesting an ongoing problem in sexual understanding.

Negotiating the sexual encounter

Negotiating the sexual encounter requires that partners are able to communicate with one another about sex. Sexual communication is vital because good communication can enhance people's sex lives by enabling them to understand each other's needs, to avoid misunderstandings – such as the idea that 'no' means 'yes' – and to talk to each other about precautions against pregnancy, STIs and AIDS. Boldero *et al.* (1992) found, for example, that among young people, feeling comfortable communicating about condoms with a sexual partner was associated with a greater likelihood of condom use. Such communication is not always straightforward. It can be undermined by embarrassment, defensiveness, fear of rejection, the desire to exploit or by simply misunderstanding one's partner.

In the area of self-confidence about sex, or sexual self-efficacy, interesting gender differences emerge. Rosenthal *et al.* (1991) found 31 per cent of late adolescent boys, compared with only 9 per cent of girls, were unable or very uncertain about being able to refuse a sexual advance by a partner. Boys also felt less confident of their ability to have a sexual encounter which did not necessarily lead to intercourse. That is, they felt less able than girls to control themselves sexually, to ask a potential partner to wait for sex if precautions were unavailable, to refuse to do something sexually which they did not feel comfortable about, to reject an unwanted sexual advance and to admit sexual inexperience to experienced peers.

While girls claimed that they felt relatively confident of their ability to 'say no' to unwanted sex (a somewhat surprising finding in the light of concerns about girls' lack of power in the sexual situation), this was not matched by their confidence in expressing sexual drives and wishes, or in taking the initiative in relationships. They were less confident than boys about asking someone (other than a 'steady' partner) for a date, or asking a partner to stimulate them sexually. These young girls also had poorer sexual self-esteem, assessed by perceptions of self-worth on items such as 'I feel comfortable with my sexuality' and 'I am comfortable being affectionate with dating partners'.

There were other problems experienced in sexual communication, as these young girls' responses to the question 'Is it hard to say no to sex?' illustrate (Moore & Rosenthal 1993: 100):

> When you are in that situation, I think it is hard to say it. I think you would have to. I wouldn't say it in words; but I would act it out, like move away or whatever. It is very difficult to say no, though.

> Yes. Because you are letting the guy down, you are showing him you don't want him as much as he thinks you do. You feel bad.

Mitchell and Wellings (2002: 393) point out that lack of clear communication between young people puts them at risk of having sex that is 'unwanted, unanticipated or regretted'. Following focus groups and semi-structured interviews with young people in the UK, they concluded that ambiguity was a key feature of sexual communication, and indeed served useful purposes. Ambivalent or ambiguous signals during flirting and in sexual contexts may protect individuals from the embarrassment of rejection, or guard against them making false assumptions about where the encounter is headed. For example, a young man may prefer not to directly ask a young woman if she is interested in having sex, rather he may rely on her bodily signals to decide whether to proceed with the encounter. The young woman in the situation may not wish to have sex but may also be reluctant to reject the advances outright. She may wish for a continuing relationship, and want to take things more slowly. Or, like one young woman in the Mitchell and Wellings study, she may want to protect her self-esteem, as in: 'You're not going to come out with . . . "I'm not going to sleep with you tonight", because that makes him think you thought you could'.

These defensive communications serve a purpose but they ultimately make 'negotiated sex' extremely difficult. Both parties can readily misinterpret what is happening, due more to their hopes and fears than the reality of the situation.

Another element of relationships in which communication falls short of ideal is the maintenance of honesty about other partners. According to Mays and Cochran (1993), dishonesty is an intimate feature of dating life. Their study indicated that 47 per cent of male and 42 per cent of female college students would not admit to a new partner the number of partners they had in the past. Of the men, 34 per cent said they had lied about their sexual history in order to convince a potential partner to have sex. In addition, 22 per cent of the men and 10 per cent of the women would not disclose the existence of another partner to a new partner, and over a third of both sexes would not admit to their partner if they had been unfaithful. Why is this so? Presumably there is a desire to maintain the relationship and a belief that this will be very difficult if the partner knows too much about past and concurrent boyfriends or girlfriends. The illusion of the exclusivity that most see as important to love and romance is maintained through subterfuge. As well, both sexes, but perhaps particularly young women, may see such practices as protective of their reputations. But while non-disclosure of other partners may work for a time, keeping relationships 'happy in ignorance' , there is great potential for strong negative emotions of jealousy, betrayal and hurt, not to mention implications for safe sex practice (no need for condoms if you believe you are the exclusive partner). For teenagers, these can be difficult life lessons to learn.

Research on the way adults talk to each other can enlighten us further on the difficulties which can occur in communication about the emotionally laden topic of sex. Tannen (1990) concludes that men and women use conversation differently. Women talk to negotiate closeness, to give and seek confirmation of themselves, and to work out ways to gain consensus. Men's talk on the other hand is designed to disguise feeling or vulnerability and to assert power, control and independence. The sexes misunderstand each other's 'talk motives', leading them to non-communicative strategies such as dismissing the talk of the other as trivial ('She's just rambling on as usual'), not registering what has been said because it is couched in tentative language ('Why didn't you come straight out and tell me all this before?'), or interpreting the lack of 'feelings' talk as indicating a genuine lack of feelings rather than an inability to discuss them ('Whenever I bring it up he makes a joke, or walks away'). Others have studied male-female discussions and note that men are more likely to set the topic of conversation, to interrupt, to ignore women's conversational initiatives and to make assertions. Women are more likely to defer to male conversational opening gambits, to 'work' to keep the conversation going and to be tentative and questioning in their speech.

Maccoby (1990), in her review of sex differences in behaviour, concluded that differences in communication style emerge primarily in social situations and are particularly evident in mixed-sex groups. If men and women have different motives for their talk to one another, if they misinterpret each other's conversational styles and if they use different strategies when they engage in discussion, it is no wonder that misunderstandings so often occur. Such misunderstandings are much more likely in the highly emotionally charged domain of sex, in which myths and fantasies about what the opposite sex is like can be exacerbated by differences in communication styles. Adolescents, because of their inexperience, are probably even more vulnerable than adults to communication breakdowns in the difficult area of sexual negotiation.

In fact, there are few systematic studies of what young people say to one another during courting, sexual preliminaries or during sexual activity but it is an area ripe for research. Unfortunately, our major sources of information – films, television, books, magazines – are likely to perpetuate sex stereotypes and sexual misunderstanding. Understanding more fully the nature of sexual communication may help young people to explain to each other their point of view. In this era of HIV/AIDS, effective communication about safe sex has become a crucial issue. Sex education in schools has a potential role to play here in the facilitation of discussions about sex in which girls and boys can share their values, misunderstandings and myths as well as learn about their sexual plumbing.

We conclude this chapter by noting that young men and women tend to construct their sexual worlds in different ways, possibly because of biological (and/or evolutionary) differences, certainly because of socialization practices and the power differential between the sexes, and probably because of interactions between these sets of influences. Adolescents face the complex task of coming to terms with their own sexuality, learning the 'rules' of romance and courtship as well as how to relate to a partner in a sexual way. All this is set against the background of helpful and unhelpful aspects of sex-role stereotyping, issues of power, conflicting social and cultural mores, and constantly changing rules for romance and sexual expression. It is to the great credit of teenagers today that most of them are able to steer a path through this minefield to a point where they can establish positive and fulfilling relationships with one another.

7 Issues for gay and lesbian adolescents

I was 15 years old and I was going through a pretty hard time and stuff. I was feeling pretty low about myself. One day I said I've got to meet someone else like myself. I've got to meet other people because I was in a very isolated position from my family, from the guys at school, as I was going to an all boys' school. My parents didn't have any gay friends, I had no gay relatives that I knew of. And I just felt, Oh my God! I'm a freak or something, and I think that was doing a lot of damage to me. So I decided I had nothing to lose and I joined a group and met some other young gay guys. Through accepting myself and my sexuality, I've become proud of myself, happy with myself, more confident about who I am.

(Thomas, 16 years: MacKenzie *et al.* 1992: 13)

When we wrote *Sexuality in Adolescence* (Moore & Rosenthal 1993), including a chapter on gay and lesbian adolescence, was a novel and brave venture. Very few texts recognized the existence of homosexual young people let alone attempted to deal with the issues that gay and lesbian adolescents confront in their daily lives. At a time when the sexuality of young people has remained a cause for concern, the focus has almost exclusively been on what makes for an acceptable, desirable heterosexual sexual life. Indeed, the normative nature of heterosexuality is constantly reinforced in the media, in popular culture, in societal institutions as well as in academic research (Wilton 2000). In recent years, however, there has been a burgeoning interest in young people's same-sex desire, mostly framed as a health issue and largely driven by concerns about the potential impact of an AIDS epidemic. Academics, public health professionals and those working with young people now recognize the need to understand homosexuality as well as heterosexuality among adolescents in order to provide a positive and safe environment in which young people can live their lives. As Hillier and Rosenthal (2001) wrote in their introduction to a special issue of the *Journal of Adolescence* dedicated to gay and lesbian youth, it is important to promote research that is devoted to this group because we 'need to better understand and theorize young people's sexuality in all its diversity' (p. 1).

The recognition of how homosexuality develops in childhood and adolescence is gradually evolving from a past of myths and stigma, towards understanding, support and acceptance. While the origins of homosexuality are still poorly understood, it is now generally believed by most researchers and health professionals that there is no evidence that homosexuality is pathological in nature but rather is a variation in human sexual behaviour (Bell *et al.* 1981; Bidwell & Deisher 1991; Kimmel & Plante 2004; Remafedi 1987, 1990; Wilton 2000).

The 'love that dared not speak its name' has now become a source of television entertainment, with an increasing number of programmes including gays or lesbians as key characters, either in romantic rela- tionships or as 'experts' who can sort out the lives of others (e.g. the hugely successful *Queer Eye for the Straight Guy*). Although society's attitudes towards homosexuality have slowly shifted, the old stereo- types prevail. Being gay is still regarded by most as unnatural, as deviant and as problematic. Young gay people are far more than troubled youths whose 'problems' cause them to exhibit deviant behaviour. Rather, growing up with an awareness of same-sex attrac- tion is an enormous and undeniable personal challenge in the face of pervasive social stigma. We know from emerging research that these negative attitudes are reflected in the youth culture and played out in schools, as these quotes taken from Wilton (2000) illustrate:

> In our school the anti-sex business was so colossal that almost everything was successfully tabooed . . . I didn't regard myself as a homosexual, I never thought of this word, nobody knew such a word.
>
> (David: Porter & Weeks 1991: 42)

> I spent most of my time outside of school alone in my room, secluded from a world that I thought hated me. I was sure of this because I hated myself. I hated being different. I hated myself for being alone.
>
> (Rhonda: Holmes 1988: 44)

As Wilton comments, this 'cultural silence' about gays and lesbians is interpreted as reflecting shame and disapproval of behaviour that is too awful to put into words. Worse than silence are the attitudes and behaviours of many heterosexuals directed to gays and lesbians. We know that non-heterosexual young people still face discrimination and abuse that impacts negatively on their physical and mental health. But the picture is not as bleak as it was a decade ago; increasingly, for many young people, personal acceptance of a gay or lesbian identity as a positive and fulfilling lifestyle is possible.

The dominant themes of adolescent homosexuality are explored in this chapter. What is homosexuality and how prevalent is the expression of homosexuality during adolescence? Does homosexuality develop from biological or environmental influences? How do young girls and boys come to grips with a sexual orientation other than heterosexual? How do they develop a sexual identity and 'come out' as lesbian or gay? How do they deal with experiences of homophobia? What impact does their sexual orientation have on the physical and mental well-being of gay and lesbian young people? What changes have occurred that should lead to greater understanding of homosexual adolescents in our society?

A historical overview

For a young person, understanding how society will react to a disclosure that 'I'm homosexual' is important. Beliefs that homosexuality is a crime, an illness or a sin against God have been, and among some sections of the community still are, pervasive. Young people who are attempting to understand their sexual orientation still grapple with the historical stigma attached to homosexuality.

For centuries, homosexual acts were regarded as criminal activities. For example, the English Act of 1533 made buggery (anal intercourse between men) punishable by death (Brown 1989). Historically, what we call 'homosexuality' was not considered a unified set of acts, much less a set of qualities defining particular persons. As Weeks (1977: 12) describes it, 'There was no concept of the homosexual in law, and homosexuality was not regarded as a particular attribute of a certain type of person but as a potential in all sinful creatures'.

Largely, lesbian sex was seen as unimaginable. Most civil laws against same-sex relations were quite explicit about the acts committed by males but did not specifically mention women: 'Compared with the frequency with which male homosexuality is mentioned, in canon and civil law, especially after the thirteenth century, in penitentials and confessional manuals, in popular sermons and literature . . . the handful of documents which cite the love of women for one another is truly scant' (Brown 1989: 70).

Homosexuality, or at least male homosexuality, was considered a crime and remains so within some jurisdictions. Within some Christian (and other religious) frameworks, homosexuality was, and is still considered, a sin, a violation of God's law.

From the early 20th century, homosexuality became increasingly regarded as a medical illness. As physicians took over the responsibility for managing this socially unacceptable behaviour from the law and the Church, homosexuality was defined as a pathological condition to be investigated, treated and cured. With the early failure of biological explanations and cures for homosexuality, psychoanalytic and behavioural theories proliferated and homosexuality was classified as a psychiatric disorder.

Influenced by political pressure from the gay movement, the American Psychiatric Association removed homosexuality in 1973 as a psychiatric disorder from its official register of psychopathology. The era of homosexuality as an illness was officially over. But biomedical theories of sexual orientation are still with us and the search for a 'gay' gene or a specific brain function is still on. Those adopting a biomedical approach share a belief that sexuality is an innate element of individual biological inheritance, unchangeable and fixed. At the same time, there has been a plethora of social explanations of homosexuality, spurred on in part by feminism and gay liberation (Wilton 2000). Rather than viewing hetero- and homosexuality as fundamentally different in kind, social scientists take the view that sexuality is enmeshed in diverse and complex sets of social and cultural environments that are constantly evolving. The consequence of this for 'homosex' is that gay and lesbian sexuality is played out in different ways in different cultures at different times (see Wilton 2000 for an extended discussion of theoretical explanations).

In the last decades of the 20th century, with more liberal social attitudes towards sexuality, homosexuality was widely decriminalized, openness about homosexuality increased, and gay and lesbian communities developed throughout urban western countries such as North America, Europe and Australia. These changes and the advent of HIV/AIDS altered the social environment in which young people were coming out and the questions that were relevant to ask about lesbian and gay adolescence. For instance, interest in effeminate childhood behaviour in boys as predictive of homosexuality has been replaced by more pressing concerns such as understanding sexual practices and condom use, and examining the impact of HIV/AIDS in intensifying gay stigma. In these changing social contexts, however, lesbian and gay adolescents are still one of the most under-researched groups of adolescents and the most poorly understood in terms of sexuality.

What is homosexuality?[1]

Homosexuality involves not just sexual contact with persons of the same sex but also romantic feelings, emotional attraction, fantasies and a sense of identity. A homosexual person is an individual 'whose primary erotic, psychological and social interest is in a member of the same sex, even though that interest may not be overtly expressed' (Martin & Lyon 1972: 1). The label 'homosexual' carries with it substantial stigma, with an emphasis on sexual behaviours. In an effort to create labels that are more positive and inclusive, 'gay' and 'lesbian' have become the preferred terms. 'Gay', in western culture, is generally used to describe self-identified homosexual identity. Because of the visibility of male homosexual communities and the relative invisibility of lesbian culture, the word 'gay' has become synonymous with male homosexuality. While some are satisfied that the words 'gay' or 'homosexual' include gay women and men, others are not. With the symptomatic neglect and ignorance of lesbian experience, most gay women prefer 'lesbian' as their label of definition.

It is important to distinguish between three aspects of sexuality: sexual orientation, sexual identity and sexual practices. Sexual orientation describes a person's underlying sexual preferences, whether heterosexual, bisexual or homosexual, and has been defined as a consistent pattern of sexual arousal towards persons of the same and/ or opposite gender (Spitzer 1981), encompassing fantasy, conscious attractions and emotional and romantic feelings (Klein *et al.* 1985). Sexual identity refers to how a person describes his or her sexual self and how that person expresses that self to others. Usually sexual identity will be an expression of a person's underlying sexual orientation. For example, a young woman is romantically and sexually attracted to women. For many years she experiences intimate friendships with other girls. Some of the friendships have become sexual at

---

1 We have restricted our discussion of homosexuality in this chapter to western nations. We do not deal here with the variations in the meanings and enactments of male to male sexual behaviour that occur in many cultures.

times and these experiences have been pleasurable and satisfying. Her experiences tell her that she is lesbian and she desires a long-term romantic and sexual relationship with another woman. Because she had always assumed she was heterosexual, these feelings for other women are in conflict with her heterosexual identity. Through a process of coming out (from her presumed heterosexual identity), described later in this chapter, she begins to describe herself as lesbian to herself and others. Through romantic and sexual experiences she has come to develop a sexual identity that matches her sexual orientation.

Sexual orientation and sexual identity do not always match. A young man has grown up in a large family. All his siblings are married and he, too, desires marriage and a family. This is how he has always planned his life. He believes, as his upbringing has taught him, that these are the experiences that will bring him happiness. Yet, throughout his adolescence he has had intense crushes on other boys at school, sometimes leading to sexual experimentation. Sexual experiences with girls lacked intensity, pleasure and romantic attraction. Though he is aware of his sexual attraction to men, he discounts this as a passing phase. The idea that he might be gay is abhorrent. Eventually he marries; the marriage is without passion and lacks sexual interest. Children add fulfilment to his desire for a family but he remains dissatisfied and troubled. He chooses to suppress his attraction to men and adopts a conventional heterosexual identity. Would we describe this young man as heterosexual, homosexual or bisexual? None of these categories is entirely satisfactory.

Sexual orientation is commonly viewed as an either/or choice – one is either heterosexual or homosexual. Yet, the sexual practices individuals engage in, as distinct from sexual orientation and identity, are not infrequently sexual acts with both opposite-sex and same-sex partners. This is particularly so in adolescence, when it is assumed that sexuality is fluid and there is considerable transient sexual experimentation typical of early adolescence. Indeed, studies of fantasies, behaviours and sexual identity show that uncertainty over sexuality is common for adolescents.

As many adolescents questioning their sexual orientation wonder if they are bisexual or homosexual, it is important to understand the difference between bisexuality and transitory homosexual experiences (of the sort that may occur in single-sex boarding schools, in prisons and among male sex workers who work with both men and women). Bisexuality refers to a natural attraction to both sexes that continues into adulthood. A bisexual individual might or might not be sexually active with partners of both sexes at any time but would continue to have feelings of attraction to both sexes. There can also be a transitional state or temporary identity (Cass 1979), in which a person is changing from one exclusive orientation to another and engages in sexual acts with both men and women:

> I had led a traditional life with a husband, two kids and community activities. My best friend and I were very active together. Much to our surprise, we fell in love. We were initially secretive about our sexual relationship and continued our marital lives, but then we both divorced our husbands and moved away to start a life together. The best way I can describe being with her is that life is now like a colour TV, instead of black and white.
>
> (Crooks & Baur 1990: 320)

Finally, 'bisexuality' may sometimes be an attempt to deny exclusive homosexual interests and to avoid the stigma of homosexual activity (MacDonald 1981).

Crucial for adolescents is the distinction between transitory same-sex sexual acts and homosexual identification. We are all familiar with the extent of schoolgirl crushes on female teachers or senior students. A heterosexual girl who has an incidental sexual experience with another student may feel that this one act makes her homosexual. Because she equates having sex with another woman as being homosexual, she may wrongly ascribe to herself a lesbian identity, causing considerable and unnecessary distress. As the following discussion shows, homosexual activity, homosexual fantasies and confusion about sexual orientation are fairly common among adolescents. Only a small minority of adolescents, however, actually develop sexual identities as gay or lesbian. Thus, while homosexual activity may help predict who is gay or lesbian, it does not determine sexual identity. It appears that homosexual activity is integral, but not sufficient in itself, to the development of a homosexual identity.

Troiden (1989) postulates the development of a homosexual identity as a series of four stages: sensitization, identity confusion, identity assumption and identity commitment. In the sensitization stage, which occurs before puberty, lesbians and gay males typically report social experiences during their childhood that serve later as the bases for seeing homosexuality as personally relevant. As two young lesbians report: 'I felt different: unfeminine, ungraceful, not very pretty, kind of a mess'; 'I didn't express myself the way other girls would. I never showed feelings. I wasn't emotional'. Similar comments come from young gay males: 'I couldn't stand sports, so naturally that made me different. A ball thrown at me was like a bomb'; 'I was indifferent to boys' games, like cops and robbers. I was more interested in watching insects and reflecting on things' (Bell *et al.* 1981: 74–86).

Identity confusion begins during early adolescence when young lesbians and gays reflect upon the idea that their feelings and/or behaviours could be regarded as homosexual. This confusion is caused by a number of factors including the stigma surrounding homosexuality and inaccurate knowledge about homosexuals and homosexuality:

> I'm not sure who I am. I'm confused about what sort of person I am and where my life is going. I ask the question, 'Who am I? Am I homosexual? Am I really heterosexual?'
>
> I feel that I probably am homosexual, although I'm not definitely sure. I feel distant or cut off from other people. I'm beginning to think that it might help to meet other homosexuals but I'm not sure whether I really want to or not. I prefer to put on a front of being completely heterosexual.
>
> (Cass 1984: 126)

Typical responses to the uncertainties of identity confusion about sexual orientation are to adopt one or more of a range of strategies: denial, repair, avoidance, redefining and acceptance:

> I figured I'd go straight and develop more of an interest in girls if I got even more involved in sports and didn't spend so much time on my art.
>
> I hated dating. I was always afraid I wouldn't get erect when we petted and kissed and that girls would find out I was probably gay.
>
> Situational reasons also become a justifiable excuse. 'It only happened because I was drunk'; 'I was at boarding school and everyone did it'.
>
> (Troiden 1989: 56, 57)

According to Troiden, in the third stage, identity assumption, homosexual identity becomes both a self-identity and a presented identity, at least to other lesbian or gay friends. The young person regularly socializes with other lesbians or gay males, experiments sexually and explores the lesbian or gay subculture. Contexts of self-identification as homosexual vary between lesbians and gay males. Most girls who self-identify as lesbian do so in situations of intense affectionate involvements with other women (Cronin 1974; Schafer 1976). For gay males, sociosexual contexts are the usual places of homosexual self-definition – gay bars, clubs and saunas, parties and public places where men meet for sex (e.g. parks, beaches, public toilets). Initially, being gay or lesbian is tolerated rather than accepted:

> I feel sure I'm gay and I put up with this. I see myself as gay for now but I'm not sure about how I'll be in the future. I'm careful to put across a straight [heterosexual] image. I feel like I want to meet others like myself.

> I'm quite sure I'm lesbian. I'm happy about this. I'll tell a few people I'm gay but I'm careful about who. I try to fit in at work and home. I can't see the point in confronting people with being lesbian if it's going to embarrass all concerned.
>
> (Adapted from Cass 1984: 126)

There are now new possibilities of learning how to cope with discrimination, feeling good about being gay, neutralizing guilt feelings and beginning to understand the range of identities and roles open to lesbians and gays (Gerstel *et al.* 1989; Troiden 1989). Undesirable homosexual experiences, however, may prompt attempts at rejection and abandonment of both identity and behaviour (Troiden 1989).

Finally, commitment involves adopting homosexuality as a way of life. For the committed homosexual it becomes easier, more attractive and less costly to remain a homosexual than to try to function as a heterosexual (Troiden 1989): 'I'm prepared to tell almost anyone that I'm gay. I'm happy about the way I am but I don't feel that being gay is the most important part of me. I mix socially with gay people and straight people, all of whom know I'm gay' (Cass 1984: 126). At this stage there is a fusion of sexuality and emotionality, feelings that homosexuality is a valid and satisfying self-identity and increased happiness after self-identifying as homosexual. A relationship may become a manifestation of this synthesis between emotionality and sexuality (Coleman 1982).

While models of development of a homosexual identity such as Troiden's are informative, a common criticism is that they are essentially a developmental psychology of the remembered past (Boxer & Cohler 1989). The sense of being different as a child or adolescent may be an adult interpretation of earlier life events. The true chronology of events may be obscured by the passage of time (Remafedi 1987). Little is yet known about how gay and lesbian adolescents experience their lives as they are living them, rather than as they are remembered. There is a clear and urgent need for longitudinal studies of coming out that trace the experience of young gays and lesbians as they grow up and develop new sexual identities.

Homosexuals: born or made?

The origins of homosexuality have long been a source of fascination for scientists and, traditionally, the search for the cause of the disease 'homosexuality' went hand in hand with the search for a cure and the subsequent eradication of homosexuality. Now the question is more sensibly posed as 'What are the biological mechanisms and the environmental experiences that are involved in the development of homosexuality?'

The search for a physiological cause, beginning in the late 19th century, failed to pinpoint a congenital deficit or find physical differences between heterosexual and homosexual men. Nevertheless, medical treatments to 'cure' homosexuality abounded. At the turn of the century these included castration and vasectomy (Minichiello 1992). Later, in the 1930s and 1940s, hormone therapy (consisting of androgen supplements) was used, without significant changes in sexual orientation (Money & Ehrhardt 1972). Treatment of homosexuality with electroconvulsive therapy (ECT) persisted into the 1960s.

There have been two influential physiological explanations for homosexuality: the role of 'sex' hormones and brain structure. Hormonal theories explain homosexuality in terms of underexposure to male hormones or overexposure to female hormones during development. While the search for a hormonal basis for homosexuality continues, the evidence is scant and contradictory, and the studies have been widely criticized for methodological deficiencies.

The search for the gay brain has been led by Le Vay (1991) who claims to have discovered a difference between homosexual and heterosexual brains, by demonstrating that cells in the interstitial nuclei of the anterior hypothalamus (which participates in the regulation of typical male sexual behaviour) are more densely clustered in gays. Subsequently, Allen and Gorski (1992) found that a cluster of nerves connecting the two sides of the brain, called the anterior commissure, is around 34 per cent bigger in gay males than straight males. Though provocative, the links between these structural differences in the brain and their effect on the development of sexual orientation need to be demonstrated. Most recently, there has been an attempt to link the development of homosexuality to genetic factors. The search for a 'gay' gene (e.g. Hamer & Copeland 1994) has not to date provided a credible outcome (Terry 1997).

In fact, it is interesting to consider why theories such as these have taken hold in spite of the lack of solid evidence to support them. As Wilton (2000) notes, it is not surprising that some members of gay communities are willing to adopt an approach that deflects blame for their 'condition' onto forces beyond their control, and so offers a defence against powerful groups in society who wish to eliminate, or at least cure, homosexuality.

A different approach to the origins of homosexuality adopts a range of psychosocial explanations. Based on the fact that sexual practices and customs vary from place to place and time to time, these theories look to different life experiences and societal factors for explanations of the development of homosexuality. There is no space here to outline the wide range of theoretical positions taken by those who propose environmental origins (for an excellent description see Wilton 2000); rather, we note just several of the most influential accounts.

An early, and mostly discredited approach, was based on Freud's speculations about homosexuality. Freud (1924, 1935) maintained that the relationship with one's father and mother was a crucial factor. He believed humans to be innately bisexual, passing through a homoerotic phase in the process of establishing a heterosexual orien- tation. Fixating at this homoerotic phase could occur, especially if a male had a poor relationship with his father and an overly close and binding relationship with his mother. While some research supported the theory of a close-binding intimate mother and a distant father (Bieber *et al.* 1962; Saghir & Robins 1973), others found no such childhood experiences for male homosexuals (Robertson 1972) or differences between homosexual and heterosexual males in their rela- tionships with their mothers (Bene 1965). Indeed, Boxer and Cohler (1989) conclude that these relationships may be a result rather than a cause of homosexuality. Reviews conclude that there is no particular phenomenon of family life that can be singled out as especially consequential for either homosexual or heterosexual development (Bell *et al.* 1981; Ross 1988).

The sociology of deviance was the source of another important approach to the development of homosexuality. Labelling theory proposes that while acts may be labelled as deviant, what is critical is that the person engaging in the act believes him/herself to be deviant for doing so. If sucking a man's penis is regarded as a deviant act for a male adolescent, then that young man may either dismiss this act as an experiment – a transient practice – or he may begin to think of himself as homosexual and take on a homosexual role (Wilton 2000).

A third influential approach is taken by social constructionists. Social construction theory has been dealt with in an earlier chapter but it has specific implications for our understanding of homosexuality. The emphasis here is on deviance but focuses on the way in which homosexuality is produced by means of social relations and social actions (McIntosh 1968). A key outcome of this approach is, as Wilton (2000: 73) states:

> It becomes possible to investigate how sexual desire and activity between members of the same biological sex came to be called 'homosexuality', how the idea of homosexuality is maintained, which groups have a vested interest in maintaining it and which in challenging it and what the implications are for the categories of people created by this idea (namely, homosexuals, heterosexuals and the residual category of bisexuals).

Implicit in some psychosocial explanations of homosexuality is an assumption that it is a less permanent condition than heterosexuality and thus may be reversible. Some therapists have provided therapeutic intervention for homosexuals or bisexuals who are distressed by their orientation and want to change (e.g. Masters & Johnson 1979). Such programmes have been heavily criticized for their claim of converting so-called homosexuals to heterosexuals. Currently, most therapists agree that changing the sexual orientation of people who are homosexual is not only unlikely to succeed but is also undesirable (Crooks & Baur 1990). Rather than assuming that their homosexual clients must be cured, therapists have made it an objective to assist them to love, live and work in a society that harbours considerable hostility towards them (Milligan 1975). This change in therapeutic practice is significant in that it defines the problem as society's negativity towards homosexuality rather than homosexuality itself (Crooks & Baur 1990).

Homosexual orientation and same-sex attraction among adolescents: what does the research tell us?

Statements like 'All a lesbian needs is a good lay' and 'He just needs to meet the right woman' reflect the belief that homosexuality is a poor second choice for people who lack satisfactory heterosexual experiences (Crooks & Baur 1990). In fact, one study showed about 45 per cent of gay adolescents had at least one sexual experience with a female (Davies *et al.* 1992), while 70 per cent of gay and lesbian adults have had heterosexual sexual experiences (Herdt 1989; Martin & Lyon 1972; Troiden 1989). Gay young men and lesbians did, however, feel differently about dating, tending to engage in fewer types of heterosexual activities with fewer partners than heterosexuals and finding them less satisfying. Another myth is that homosexuality begins with seduction by an older person. In fact, typically, young gays' and lesbians' first homosexual encounters are with a partner about the same age. Homosexuals are less likely than heterosexuals to have had initial sexual encounters with a stranger or older person (Bell *et al.* 1981).

In recent years there have been a significant number of studies of adolescent sexuality that have included questions about sexual orientation. Notwithstanding problems of definition and comparability, we now know that a substantial minority of young people do not define themselves as exclusively heterosexual or attracted to those of the opposite sex. In Australia, this figure was 9–11 per cent in a study of 1200 rural youth (Hillier *et al.* 1996) and 8–9 per cent in a large national study of 3500 senior high-school students (Lindsay *et al.* 1997). This latter figure was slightly higher than that obtained in a similar national study of 2388 students in 2002 (Smith *et al.* 2003a). In the USA, findings by Russell *et al.* (2001) from the nationally representative Add Health Study showed that 7.4 per cent of boys and 5.3 per cent of girls reported same-sex romantic attraction. In an earlier study of all secondary students in Minnesota (Remafedi *et al.* 1992), 11 per cent were unsure of their sexual orientation. Remafedi *et al.* found that uncertainty about sexual orientation gradually shifted to heterosexual or homosexual identification with the passage of time and/or increasing sexual experience, with a steady decline in uncertainty with age from 25.9 per cent in 12-year-olds, to 5 per cent in 18-year-old students. Youths who were unsure were more likely to entertain homosexual fantasies and attractions and less likely to have heterosexual sexual experience.

Since Kinsey it has been assumed that the incidence of female homosexuality is less than the corresponding male figure. In Remafedi's study, male-female differences in homosexual identification were less evident and, in fact, a larger proportion of young women than young men reported homosexual attractions and fantasies. Dempsey *et al.* (2001) comment on the under-representation of young women in the research and report research documenting important differences between same-sex attracted young men and women. Young women experience attractions for other women at a later age than young men and are older when they act on these attractions and/or begin questioning their sexual identities (Bell *et al.* 1981; Rosario *et al.* 1997; Savin-Williams 1990). In their internet study of 'difficult to reach' (e.g. rural), isolated young people who were not linked to gay communities, Dempsey *et al.* found significant gender differences among their 749 adolescent respondents. They conclude:

> Overall, young women displayed more fluidity with regard to their sexual feelings, behaviours and identities. Young women were more likely to be engaged in private explorations of lesbian-ism, concurrent with participation in heterosexual sex and rela-tionships . . . The invisibility of lesbianism as an identity or practice led to confusion about what feelings meant for the future.
>
> (2001: 67)

While longitudinal research is needed to verify their conclusions, Remafedi *et al.* (1992) paint a picture of undifferentiated sexuality in early adolescence with low homosexual identity leading to greater certainty about sexual orientation by late adolescence. Clearly, by late adolescence most teenagers identify as heterosexual. Only a minority of young people with homosexual fantasies, attractions or behaviours reported a homosexual identity during adolescence. Many, however, especially young lesbians, take until their early 20s or longer to openly acknowledge these feelings and self-identify as homosexual (Barbeler 1992; Herdt 1989; Troiden 1989).

In the recent upsurge of research on young people who identify as gay or lesbian, there has been less attention paid to the desire of these young people to have intimate and romantic relationships with their peers. We know that establishing such a relationship helps the young person to feel accepted, supports his or her chosen identity and enhances self-esteem. As we saw in Chapter 6, these are exactly the outcomes of romantic relationships for heterosexual young people. Furthermore, contrary to the stereotype of young gays and lesbians as failing to commit to relationships and seeking a sequence of partners, a long-term relationship is seen as the ideal state, just as it is for heterosexual young people (Savin-Williams & Cohen 1996). But Savin-Williams notes that, in addition to the normal complexities of establishing and maintaining romantic relationships, many of these young people have to keep these relationships hidden at a time when romance looms large in adolescent life. Nevertheless, even though these young people find it particularly difficult to maintain a visible same-sex romance in school, many of them do so.

What has been lost, to some extent, in the focus on establishing difference – or counting numbers of gay and lesbian adolescents – are the similarities. In many (most?) respects, these young people are no different from their heterosexual peers. They are good or bad at school, they are funny or serious, they cherish friendships, they care about family. What sets them apart is their sexual orientation or identity and the treatment they receive as a consequence. We deal with homophobia and some of its consequences later; first we discuss a key milestone for most young gay or lesbian identified young people.

Coming out

An important task for most young people who identify as gay or lesbian is the process of coming out. Disclosure of a gay or lesbian identity to significant others, notably family and friends, is one aspect of the process; the other is self-acceptance of that identity – 'becoming' a gay or lesbian person (Flowers & Buston 2001). Some gays and lesbians, fearful or anxious about the outcome of such disclosure in the face of stigma and discrimination, attempt to conceal their sexual orientation, seeking to pass as heterosexual. Others may partially come out, selecting a set of trusted individuals with knowledge of their sexual orientation. Yet others are open to all, often actively supporting reform to minimize discrimination.

Flowers and Buston describe how Nicholas' acceptance of himself was dependent on others' acceptance of him as a gay man: 'It was almost as if you'd actually accepted it yourself for the first time . . . when you actually said it . . . I felt like saying "No, shut up!" but once I'd told that one person, you know, a lot of weight, a sense of relief almost that somebody knew and she didn't think "Oh my God, he's a leper" or something' (2001: 58). Brent's experience in telling his father was less positive: 'Well I knew from an early age I were gay anyway. And when I were 16, I actually got the guts to tell my parents. Anyway, I told 'em and me dad says "If you're gay you are going to get kicked out", so I thought "I'll hide it. I'll hide it then"' (2001: 59).

The experience of coming out can be risky as Brent's experience shows; it can also be confusing and frightening as young people consider how and whether to tell their family, their friends, their school or workmates. Perhaps not surprisingly, most young people's first disclosure is to a best friend rather than parents (Hillier *et al.* 1998; Savin-Williams & Diamond 2001). In one innovative study, Hillier *et al.* (1998) found that young people often used the internet to come out. Nearly half had told 'everyone' on the internet about their sexual identity and almost all (90 per cent) had told at least one person they met on the net. Young people also reported better support on the net. Hillier *et al.* conclude that 'The Net clearly provides an important "rehearsal space" for coming out in real life'.

As we shall see in the next section, the pervasiveness of homophobic attitudes makes coming out a particularly difficult act. Fortunately there are now gay organizations which provide support in the form of well-produced 'how to' booklets (see e.g. *Out There*, a sexual health guide for young men produced in 1998). Parent support groups such as PFLAG (Parents and Friends of Lesbians and Gays) play a major role in helping parents understand their gay and lesbian adolescents better and encouraging acceptance of their sexual orientation.

Homophobia

Centuries of public and religious opinion that homosexuality is unnatural, and irrational fears of gay people (homophobia) underlie public attitudes that affect the psychological, educative, legal and political treatment young gays and lesbians currently experience. Despite the greater understanding of sexuality in all its forms that exists in some sectors of society, for many, coming out as gay or lesbian is not a safe experience. Homophobic harassment and assault, sometimes leading to murder, is common (Plummer 2001) so it should come as no surprise that serious health consequences follow. We know these young people are over-represented among homeless populations (Hillier *et al.* 1997; Irwin *et al.* 1995) and many turn to alcohol and illicit drugs (Hillier *et al.* 1998; Smith *et al.* 1999). Bullying (frequently in school), homophobia and victimization are frequent experiences for gay and lesbian young people (Bagley & Tremblay 2000; D'Augelli & Hershberger 1993; Remafedi & Deisher 1991), leading to feelings of guilt, shame, depression and isolation – all factors that have been linked to suicidal behaviours (Rivers 1995).

Australian research indicates that gay or lesbian identified young people may be up to six times more likely to attempt suicide than the population in general, with most attempts occurring after self-identifying as gay but before having a sexual experience with someone of the same sex (Nicholas & Howard 1998). In another study, worry about sexual orientation was a predictor of deliberate attempts at self-harm, including suicide attempts for 14- to 18-year-old female students (De Leo & Heller 2004). In 1993, one US study showed that 42 per cent of gay and lesbian young people surveyed reported attempting suicide (D'Augelli & Hershberger 1993). Similar over-representation in suicide attempts has been reported in studies in three states in the USA (Morrison & L'Heureux 2001).

An exploration of hate language gives us a window onto the experience of young homosexuals. There is considerable evidence that homophobic verbal abuse is widespread, particularly in schools (Thurlow 2001). Thurlow found that terms like 'poof' or 'queer' accounted for 10 per cent of the 'taboo' words used by students, but homophobic verbal abuse was rated much less seriously than other abusive terms. He concludes: 'Sticks and stones may be more likely to break their bones but the relentless, careless use of homophobic pejoratives will most certainly continue to compromise the psycho-logical health of young homosexual and bisexual people by insidiously constructing their sexuality as something wrong, dangerous or shameworthy' (2001: 36).

David Plummer (2001) adds to our understanding of the power of language by unravelling the meanings attached to terms such as 'poofter' and 'faggot' among boys from an early age. He concludes that initially these terms do not refer to homosexuality: 'If it looks a bit different, a bit tacky, pathetic or anything like that, it's "gay"!'; 'The one's that weren't playing sport . . . more interested in collecting bugs, reading . . . The one's that weren't sort of in the "in crowd" were [called poofters]'. It is only at a later stage that sexual connotations are attached to these terms. Nevertheless, words like poofter and fag carry deeply negative and offensive meanings: 'If you really, really, really wanted to offend somebody you call them a poof' (Plummer 2001: 17, 18, 19). The powerful effect of these precisely targeted homophobic terms, even if they have their beginnings in a non-sexual sense, pro-vides a hostile context for the development of a homosexual identity.

More subtle expression of homophobia is apparent in careful avoidance of any behaviour that might be perceived as homosexual. Same-sex friends or family may refrain from spontaneous embraces, people may shun unfeminine or unmasculine clothing or a woman may decide not to support feminism because she fears being called a lesbian. The effect of homophobia on the depth of intimacy in male friendships may be quite significant, although these attitudes can change over time:

My own reaction to learning that one of my school mates was gay was discomfort. I increasingly avoided him. I am sorry now that I didn't confront myself as to why I felt that way. I was homophobic. And because I didn't deal with that then, it kept me from developing closeness with my other male friends. I lost something in those relationships because I was afraid that being physically and emotionally close to another man meant that I, too, was homosexual. I finally began to explore why I felt so uncomfortable touching or being touched by another man. Today, I am no longer threatened or frightened by physical closeness from another man. I am secure enough to deal with that honestly.

(Crooks & Baur 1990: 326)

There is now considerable evidence that schools are a powerful site for homophobia to flourish. Hillier *et al.* (1998) found that of the large number of same-sex attracted young people who had been physically or verbally abused, 70 per cent were abused at school. In other studies, homophobia among students, especially boys, was common (Buston & Hart 2001). Not surprisingly, Russell *et al.* (2001) reported that sexual minority adolescents had more negative attitudes to school, more school problems and lower grades than their heterosexual peers. Importantly, supportive teachers helped to forestall school difficulties for these minority young people.

Teachers were sometimes complicit in homophobic behaviours, either directly, for example by inappropriate jokes, or by failing to rein in the behaviours of their students (Buston & Hart 2001). Part of the problem lies in teachers' inability to understand the issues for gay or lesbian adolescents or to counsel them effectively. Warwick *et al.* (2001) describe the confusion and lack of knowledge expressed by teachers in UK schools. As one headteacher told them: 'We're clear for racist abuse . . . it really has to be an issue that the school takes a very strong stand on and so the children are suspended for two days if they call a Black child a nigger or Paki, whatever. We would try to be consistent on that . . . I think we're still thinking about how we should respond to homophobic bullying' (2001: 135).

So far we have painted a disturbing picture of the difficulties faced by gay and lesbian young people but the situation is not altogether grim. Luckily there have been researchers, teachers, parents, policymakers and others who work with these young people who have spoken out about the stigma and discrimination faced by gays and lesbians. Perhaps more importantly, young gays and lesbians are doing this work themselves.

Creating change

Encouragingly, and testimony to their resilience in the face of a hostile environment, most gays and lesbians do not abuse drugs nor do they attempt suicide or become depressed. In one study, 60 per cent said that they felt great or pretty good about their sexual feelings and only 10 per cent felt pretty bad or really bad (Hillier & Harrison 2004). One strategy used by these young people is to 'find, subvert or create and inhabit safe spaces in which they feel comfortable' (Hillier & Harrison 2004). Some attest to the internet as a safe space to work through issues related to a homosexual identity. Others find activities, such as sports, provide opportunities to test their sexuality safely. In a study of young women participating in women's football, one respondent commented:

> When they started they were known as the team of straight girls and it wasn't until some time later that people in the rest of the league sort of started to find out that perhaps they all weren't . . . And it's just not an issue in this club, and everybody's made to feel that their sexuality, regardless of what it is, is not an issue, and is supported. And even like there's so many young people coming through and some of them are even unsure of their sexuality, but they're never pushed one way or another. They're supported and they're given the opportunity of identifying their sexuality.
>
> (Cath, 16 years: Hillier 2006: 60)

The ability to resist the negative discourses associated with homosexuality – as illness, as evil, as unnatural, as a phase rather than the real thing – is described in a fascinating paper by Hillier and Harrison (2004). They tell how young people report finding the 'fault lines' in these discourses, positioning themselves as normal and healthy. So 19-year-old Sandy was able to co-opt thinking about the normalized practice (heterosexuality) and apply this to homosexuality, thereby exposing double standards: 'How many parents say to their straight children I think you should have sex with someone of the same sex before you decide that you are straight? I'd say none, but swap it around to being queer and all of a sudden you don't know your own mind and have to justify yourself constantly' (Hillier and Harrison 2004: 90).

Happily, this change at the personal level is accompanied by the beginnings of structural change. In Australia, there has been a significant shift in attitudes to young gays and lesbians among policy-makers, professionals who work with young people, researchers and communities – from a moral issue to one of safety and rights. This was aided, in part, by concerns about young gays' vulnerability to HIV at a time when there was widespread public education about safe sex (see Chapter 8). An Australian sex education curriculum, *Talking Sexual Health*, based on this framework, is described in Chapter 5. The curriculum, for secondary students, includes discussions of sexual diversity and homophobia and also provides opportunities for teacher education to reduce ignorance and fear of classroom discussion. In the UK, government policy has promoted 'healthy schools', recognizing the importance of good health and social behaviour as well as citizenship (including human rights), in achieving positive academic outcomes. As Warwick *et al.* (2001: 139) note: 'These twin sources of impetus towards health and citizenship – towards on the one hand good physical and mental health, and on the other a respect for personal integrity and worth – offer encouragement for the future'.

It's clear that progress has been made towards shifting the hostile environment endured by many gay and lesbian young people. There is still a long way to go. Let one 19-year-old lesbian, Lina, have the last word: 'It makes me feel uncomfortable. I have felt this way for as long as I can remember, but it still doesn't feel normal. Only my family knows. They reacted so badly, I haven't told anyone else (Hillier & Harrison 2004: 85).

8   Sexually transmitted infections: an increasing problem

In this chapter we address some outcomes of unprotected sexual intercourse among young people – STIs, including HIV. We note the increase in STIs, the continuing concerns about HIV/AIDS and some myths which lead young people to take unwarranted risks in their sexual encounters. We ask whether there are obstacles to safe sex and why good intentions often fail. We conclude the chapter with a look into the future and suggest some new and exciting approaches to minimizing the potential of STIs among young people.

An increasing problem

Most of the focus of sexual health promotion messages has been on disease prevention, and especially prevention of HIV/AIDS – not unreasonably given the appalling swathe that the pandemic has cut through young people worldwide. The impact of other STIs on young people's health has been ignored until relatively recently. These infections have been recognized from ancient times and there has long been a moral agenda added to concerns about the public health implications of STIs (Moore *et al.* 1996). This has been mirrored in the early approach to HIV when sex workers were singled out as 'vectors' of infection. The public condemnation of STIs as dirty and shameful – beliefs that persisted even among young people at the end of the 20th century – meant that treatment was often delayed or deferred, exacerbating the problem (Smith *et al.* 1995).

In an earlier volume (Moore *et al.* 1996) we outlined the scope of the problem, noting the increasing incidence of some STIs and their potential dangers to young people's health. Little has changed a decade later in spite of the development of many education programmes designed to encourage 'safe sex' behaviours that reduce or eliminate infection. In fact, there has been a disturbing increase in the rates of some STIs, especially among young people. Although the actual incidence of STIs in the community is difficult to ascertain accurately, the surveillance data that exist make it clear that STIs, in western society, are predominantly diseases of adolescents and young adults. Indeed, more than ten years ago in the USA it was estimated that one in five adolescents would have acquired an STI by the age of 21 (Ellickson *et al.* 1993; Rosenthal *et al.* 1998b). STIs were then among the major causes of mortality and morbidity among young people, with approximately 86 per cent of all STIs occurring among 15- to 29-year-olds. More recent data put the number of sexually experienced 13- to 19-year-olds who acquire an STI each year at one in four (Coyle *et al.* 2004). It is argued that approximately 3 million teenagers become infected with an STI each year, with 15–19-year-old women being most at risk (Berman & Hein 1999; Meade & Ickovics 2005). The significant burden of STIs among young people is not limited to health outcomes as a study of the direct medical costs of these infections among US youth shows (Chesson *et al.* 2004). The estimated cost of the 9 million new cases of STIs, including HIV, that occurred among 15- to 24-year-olds was a staggering $6.5 billion.

Among STIs other than HIV (which we discuss later in this chapter), chlamydia is one of the most prevalent. It is difficult to estimate the number of new infections accurately because chlamydia can be asymptomatic, with up to 75 per cent of those infected not realizing that they are infected. Australian data show that there has been a rapid increase in infection rates with a threefold increase in the ten years from 1991 to 2001. By 2001, chlamydia notifications for young people aged 12–24 represented 59 per cent of all notifications (Communicable Diseases Surveillance Australia 2001). This increase is mirrored in figures from the UK (Health Protection Agency 2004, cited in Coleman & Schofield 2005: 67) where the increase in infections over an eight-year period from 1995 to 2003 was about 250 per cent for 16- to 19-year-old women and a staggering 400 per cent for young men of the same age.

Chlamydia can have serious potential long-term health consequences, especially for young women – who are much more likely than young men to be infected. The most common complication of chlamydia for young women is the spread of the infection to the upper genital tract leading to pelvic inflammatory disease (PID), the major cause of tubal damage resulting in ectopic pregnancy and infertility. A review of PID in the USA (Igra 1998) reported that one in five cases of PID occurs among young women younger than 19, with these young women having the highest age-specific rates of PID among sexually active women. The risk of developing PID for a 15-year-old sexually active girl is estimated to be ten times that of a 24-year-old woman, in part because of their biologic vulnerability.

Other common STIs include genital herpes simplex and genital warts (human papilloma virus – HPV). Genital herpes is being diagnosed with increasing frequency and has been reported since the 1970s as affecting as much as 15 per cent of the population (Gallois & Callan 1990). In young women, genital herpes is a significant problem because, like chlamydia, it may be asymptomatic and there is a strong likelihood that the infection will be transmitted from mother to infant if the infection is in an active phase during birth. A similar possibility exists for HPV, another STI whose incidence is increasing. Of particular concern is the association now known to exist between HPV infection and the development of carcinoma of the cervix. The development of a vaccine for HPV (Garland 2002) is one beacon of light in the battle to reduce the burden of STIs. Finally, there is an equally worrying increase in the incidence of gonorrhoea, with rates doubling over the decade of the 1990s among Australians with the highest number of infections occurring among 15- to 29-year-olds (Communicable Diseases Surveillance Australia 2001). Infections have increased dramatically in the UK (Health Protection Agency 2004) with a nearly threefold increase in infections among 16- to 19-year-old women in the period 1995–2003 and a fourfold increase among young men.

Apart from the health consequences of specific STIs, there is now considerable evidence that infection with an STI makes individuals more vulnerable to HIV infection. Unfortunately, there is still no vaccine available for HIV, although the existence of highly active retroviral drugs appears to have turned this inevitably fatal virus into one which can be controlled over a long period of time for those able to access and afford this expensive drug therapy and maintain the complex treatment regimen. So HIV infection remains the most destructive STI threatening the lives of millions of young people. In the next sections of this chapter, we focus on HIV/AIDS, bearing in mind that the factors which make young people vulnerable to HIV infection may also make them vulnerable to other STIs.

HIV/AIDS: an ongoing epidemic

In 2002, UNICEF and UNAIDS estimated 11.8 million young people between the ages of 15 and 24, worldwide, were living with HIV/AIDS

(UNICEF 2002). They accounted for more than 50 per cent of new HIV infections, with nearly 6000 young people in this age group becoming infected every day. Young women accounted for two-thirds of those infected (7.3 million) but this pattern of greater risk for young women was not consistent worldwide. The African and South Asian epidemics were female dominated while young men were more likely to be infected in the industrialized countries of the West as well as Eastern Europe. Heterosexual and homosexual unprotected sex is still the single most important factor in the spread of the disease in most countries, but transmission via injecting drug users is a significant contributing factor to the rise in infections in some countries such as those in Eastern Europe, through rapid spreading to a wider population of occasional drug users and their sexual partners.

At the end of 2002, in sub-Saharan Africa, there were nearly 10 million young people between ages of 15 and 24 and nearly 3 million children under 15 living with HIV/AIDS. It is estimated that, at existing levels of infection, one in five South African women currently aged 20–24 will die of AIDS. More than 11 million children under the age of 15 in sub-Saharan Africa have lost at least one parent to HIV/AIDS. More than half of those orphaned by HIV/AIDS are between the ages of 10 and 15. In parts of Asia, children and young people are facing unprecedented risks from HIV/AIDS. In the Asia and Pacific region, UNAIDS estimates that about 2.1 million young people aged 15 to 24 years are living with HIV, with widening epidemics in many countries in the region. In Australia, by contrast, there has been a total of about 500 cases of HIV infection among 13- to 19-year-olds (representing 2.4 per cent of the total number of infections), and 7122 among 20- to 29-year-olds (34.6 per cent of the total number of infections). These numbers reflect only a tiny proportion of the population in this age range.

The hardest hit group of young (and not so young) people among those infected with HIV in the western world has been male homosexuals:

> I want to feel joy again but I don't think I can. You can't turn it [the thought of being HIV positive] off, it's always there to take the edge off things. Being carefree, buoyant, feeling how it is to be alive, I'm envious of that in my friends. I want to be normal but fundamentally my base mood is grey, sad, withdrawn. What do I want? A normal life and all the shit that goes with it. Not just the prospect of getting sick and dying. There is this pressing sense of urgency. You have to work it all out before you die. So

I work and work on trying to figure life out. But the payoff is that you die.

(Goggin 1989, personal communication)

These young gay men's lives may have changed with the advent of new effective drugs that stave off progression to AIDS and death; nevertheless the current epidemiological picture strongly suggests that young gay and bisexual men remain one of the highest risk groups for HIV infections in western countries. Infections among young gay men (younger than 24 years) in Australia and the UK represent about 19 to 20 per cent of all HIV infections in those countries. Worryingly, studies of gay adolescents aged 20 and younger in Australia, the UK and the USA (Davies *et al.* 1992; Gold & Skinner 1992; Remafedi *et al.* 1992) suggest that young gay men are less likely than their older peers to have taken an HIV test. Under-reporting of new HIV infections among gay male adolescents therefore seems probable. The primary mode of new HIV infections among these young gay men is unprotected anal intercourse, although needle sharing is not uncommon and concerns about transmission through oral sex persist. There is also evidence that a substantial number of young gay men engage in unprotected anal intercourse and with more partners than older gay men.

Early studies showed that being in a relationship was a major predictor of unsafe sexual behaviour for gay adolescents and young gay adults (Hay *et al.* 1990; Remafedi *et al.* 1992) – findings similar to those among heterosexual young people, discussed below. Choosing relationships as a protection against HIV remains a questionable strategy. From this research, the imperatives for educating gay adolescents are emphasizing the pleasures of non-penetrative sex, exploring the pitfalls of unprotected anal sex in relationships and promoting awareness of the dangers of unsafe sex occurring when drugs or alcohol are used.

The need for education and counselling of young gay people in the face of discrimination continues. Although there are grounds for believing that more tolerant community attitudes are forming, the social climate of stigma and oppression towards gays prevails in many countries. As discussed in Chapter 7, recent research has considerably enhanced our understanding of the sexual lives of homosexual adolescents (see e.g. a 2004 special issue of the *Journal of Adolescence* on gay, lesbian and bisexual young people).

Early in the epidemic it might have appeared that HIV was a 'gay' disease in western countries but it is now clear that the heterosexual community, and especially young people, are vulnerable to HIV infection and AIDS. Although the number of adolescents among diagnosed AIDS cases is low (about 1 per cent in western countries), the highest incidence of AIDs occurs among those in their 20s. Given the long lead time from infection to diagnosis, the inescapable conclusion is that many were infected in their teens. Among 15- to 24-year-olds in the USA, AIDS deaths increased a hundredfold between 1981 and 1987.

It is not surprising, then, that the theme of adolescent vulnerability has been taken up forcefully by the popular press, with anxiety-arousing headlines such as 'AIDS message fails to make impression on youth' and 'Warning: teens, the new AIDS risk group'. Dramatic claims such as these may overstate the likelihood of HIV infection among young people since they fail to do justice to the variability among adolescents in terms of their sexual behaviours and ideologies. This is a view put compellingly by Warwick and Aggleton (1990) in their analysis of researchers' representations of adolescence and their review of themes in research studies of adolescents and AIDS. Rosenthal (2004), too, draws on others in her analysis of public 'at risk' discourses around young people and how these result in a belief that adolescents are a homogeneous population exposing themselves to considerable health risks. These analyses are supported by even the most cursory reading of studies which document the importance of context in the development and nature of young people's sexual beliefs and behaviours.

Nevertheless, there are grounds for concern about the potential for risk of STIs, including HIV infection, among some adolescent sub-groups. To what extent are adolescents engaging in sexual behaviour that puts them at risk of infection? Are they heeding messages about safe sex – particularly the need to use condoms as protection against HIV infection? Do adolescents perceive themselves to be at risk? If not, why not? Can adolescents be persuaded to change unsafe practices which may leave them at risk of AIDS?

As we have seen in an earlier chapter, recent studies in a number of western countries show a trend to sexual liberalism among adolescents – more young people are having sex and the age of initiation of sex is declining. By the 1980s and 1990s premarital sex had become normative by the end of high school although there is wide variation among young people in the age at which they begin to be sexually active. The fact of relatively high levels of sexual activity does not, in itself, give cause for alarm. Coupled with this, however, is the finding that many sexually active adolescents have multiple partners and that unprotected intercourse or inconsistent use of condoms is common, especially with partners who are regarded as 'steady' or long term. It is to this apparent failure of some adolescents to take on board the messages of safe sex, now being targeted at them via mass media and school education programmes, that we now turn.

Myths and stereotypes

Why do so many sexually active young people engage in behaviour which appears to place them at risk of STIs? In fact, it is clear that STIs other than HIV are not on young people's radar, with most knowing little or nothing about chlamydia, HPV or any other STI (Smith *et al.* 1995). Add to this the focus of most programmes on HIV/AIDS which lead young people to believe that HIV is the only STI that 'counts'. So these behaviours are, in part, explained by inappropriate beliefs or myths about sexuality and HIV/AIDS. The first of these we have called the 'trusting to love' myth. Many young people appear to justify their non-use of condoms with the belief that condoms are unnecessary because their current relationship is mono-gamous and promises to be long term. For example, Gallois *et al.* (1989) found that a majority of their sexually active heterosexuals kept themselves safe from infection by having sex only within what they believed to be an exclusive, monogamous relationship.

Other studies (Crawford *et al.* 1990; Holland *et al.* 1990; Rosenthal *et al.* 1990) reveal that young people are less likely to use condoms with regular than casual partners, with young women using this strategy more than young men. These consistently higher levels of risk-taking with regular partners suggest that adolescents may have acknowledged the HIV/AIDS threat in casual encounters but have yet to realize that in the fickle world of adolescent relationships, sex with regular partners may also entail a high level of risk. It is clear that the meaning of a 'regular' relationship varies, both in terms of duration and fidelity. Among our samples of adolescents, the period defining a relationship as regular ranged from one month to marriage, with a modal time of six months. For some adolescents, serial monogamy – or a succession of 'permanent' relationships – is the norm. There were also alarming cultural and gender differences in beliefs about mono-gamy in so-called steady relationships. While girls held firm views about their own and their partner's fidelity, at least 25 per cent of boys, and more in some groups, expected their partner to be faithful but did not require the same commitment of themselves.

It appears that girls, in particular, operate with rose-coloured glasses, taking the view that sex is about romance and love, and therefore trust. Trust becomes a significant element in making decisions about using condoms (Moore & Rosenthal 1993: 128): 'Are there any situations when you wouldn't use a condom?' 'Yeah, if I've been with a partner for a very long time. I know him. I know what he's all about'; '[Yes] Once it is a relationship and it has been going on for a while and you really care about them . . . It is more serious'.

Sobo's research on poor black women in the USA described a 'monogamy narrative', similar to the trusting to love myth. In this narrative, the idealized heterosexual union is one of faithfulness and trust. Admitting one's partner could be unfaithful damages self-pride and social position: 'Disinclined to experience pain or lose status, women deny the possibility of adultery in their relationships. Condomlessness helps them do this as it implies fidelity' (Sobo 1993: 471).

A further complicating factor associated with particular types of relationship is the reluctance of young girls to describe themselves as having casual sex, for fear of the harm to their reputation which may result from this breaching of culturally approved feminine behaviour. The other side to this dilemma is the expectation and hope held by many young girls that relationships of short duration will last. If young girls' relationships are conceived of as steady until proven otherwise, condom use is unlikely or, at best, will be inconsistent. Compounding the problem is the fact that few young people consider that the issue is relevant to their own lives (Moore & Rosenthal 1993: 128):

> *Interviewer*: Do you consider the risk of AIDS?
> No, I'm not involved in that sort of scene.
>
> All of the people that I have gone out with before, I have known beforehand and have known that they haven't been into that sort of thing. That they are pretty clean.
> (Two sexually active homeless 16-year-olds)

This is a common theme among heterosexual adolescents in their responses to the threat of HIV/AIDS – the 'not-me' myth. It is clear that most adolescents have not personalized the risk, perceiving HIV/AIDS as a threat to others, not themselves. Adolescents' belief that 'it can't happen to me' has been shown to influence risk-taking in a variety of health-related situations including smoking and contraceptive use. In a study of UK adolescents, Abrams *et al.* (1990) found high levels of concern about the presence of the HIV virus in the community, but little evidence of concern about their own levels of risk. In our own work with Australian adolescents, it is apparent that not only do many feel themselves to be invulnerable to the threat of AIDS, but also that concerns about HIV infection rarely figure in their decision-making about whether or not to have intercourse.

Closer exploration of the reasons underlying the failure of these adolescents to take on board the messages of safe sex suggests a number of processes are at work. In part, what seems likely to be happening is that these young people have linked HIV/AIDS to risk groups rather than risk behaviours. Moore and Rosenthal (1991a) showed that those young people who perceived themselves to be least at risk have a strong stereotype of an AIDS 'victim'. Given that social representations of HIV/AIDS include theories about the type of person who will become infected (homosexuals, drug users, sex workers), and in the absence of personal knowledge of someone who is infected, this stereotyping serves a distancing function by allowing individuals either to ignore the possibility that some or even many of those who are infected may not fit the stereotype, or to see fundamental similarities (such as in sexual behaviours). The illusion of invulnerability may also be fostered by engaging in risky acts which have no (immediate) negative consequences. Thus, adolescents who repeatedly engage in unsafe sex without becoming infected are likely to deny the riskiness of that behaviour. Perceptions of risk are also influenced by beliefs about control. Most of the adolescents in our studies believe that they can completely control their risk of HIV/ AIDS. However, those who perceived themselves to be most at risk of HIV/AIDS were those who believed themselves to be least able to control the risk of infection. Plainly, issues of personal mastery and the ability to take responsibility for one's sexuality are touched on here, a point we shall return to later.

While the notion of personal invulnerability provides a compelling and frequently invoked explanation of adolescents' risk-taking behaviour, we must be careful not to assume a simple and direct relationship between low perceptions of risk and actual risky behaviour. In fact, there appears to be only a weak link between the two. For some adolescents, perceptions of low HIV/AIDS risk are associated with risky sexual behaviour; for others, there seems to be a realistic appraisal of low risk, based on their safe sexual activity. A third group, which we have labelled 'risk-and-be-damned', are cause for concern because of their risky behaviours and their realistic perceptions of relatively high levels of risk. What is of interest is that this group – mostly males – doubted their control over avoiding AIDS. It is clear that characterizing adolescent risk-taking merely as resulting from beliefs in invulnerability is to oversimplify the processes at work in determining their responses to HIV/AIDS.

Adolescents' confidence that they are not at risk may stem from another misconception – that 'you can tell by looking' whether or not people are infected. Use of physical characteristics as a justification for unsafe sexual behaviour has been found in studies of young homosexuals as well as heterosexuals by Gold *et al.* (see Gold *et al.* 1992 for a review). It seems that inferences about the likelihood of infection of one's partner, based on that partner's healthy, clean and/ or beautiful physical appearance, are not uncommon among these young people. It may be that adolescents are drawing on the socially constructed equation of beauty with good health – a link reinforced endlessly by the media. Whatever the basis for their misconception, it is vital that adolescents learn to look beneath the external packaging to the realities of transmission of HIV.

Moore *et al.* report an all-too-long list of other stereotyped ideas that are implicated in young people's failure to protect themselves against disease. These include the belief, generally shared, that 'boys can't help themselves' (discussed in Chapter 6). This view of male desire as unstoppable accords young men positions of power and as the knowledgeable partners in sex. Young women are expected to accept this traditional masculine view and to act accordingly. Furthermore, for some young people, the idea of 'safe sex' goes against their sense that sex should be dangerous and exciting – a view not limited to young people! As Moore *et al.* note, 'no one ever talks about safe sex and sexual excitement in the same breath. In fact, more common is the link between "risking all for love" (danger) and thrilling, passionate sex (desire)' (1996: 87). The fantasies inspired by movies and novels do not incorporate condom use, which in turn can be construed as boring and conservative, especially by young people who are still experimenting with their sexual lives.

A further barrier is that young people don't really want to talk about sexual protection. In spite of its ubiquity in the mass media, intimate sexual behaviour is still considered to be a difficult topic to open up for discussion among young (and older) people. Negotiation about sex, including condom use, is a source of embarrassment, or concern that this will impede the passage of true love (Moore *et al.* 1996).

A final myth – better described as a misunderstanding – is that condoms are unnecessary if a young woman is on the pill. There is now considerable evidence that many young people, when they do use condoms, use them for contraception rather than disease prevention. Why is this so? Young people are subject to two potentially conflicting discourses around sexual health related to condom use. The 'safe sex' discourse is a recent phenomenon, arising in the mid-1980s out of the HIV/AIDS pandemic. This discourse emphasizes the use of condoms for protection against STIs, including HIV. The other discourse ('pregnancy prevention') has been around a lot longer – the emphasis here is on effective contraception rather than disease prevention and the preferred mode is the pill. The problem is that these two discourses become conflated. Safe sex (no exchange of bodily fluids) equals contraception, but the converse doesn't hold. We argue that adolescents (and others, often researchers) are using the term 'safe sex' to include contraception.

When asked, 'What do you think of when you hear the words "safe sex"?' the answer is almost always 'condoms'. However, when we asked young people to elaborate, or when we probed, the following sort of response occurred: 'Um, that's [condoms] the first thing that comes into my mind. Um, you know, then you've got stuff like the pill, and, you know, diaphragms, and stuff like that'. In one interview study, it was common to hear students insist that their peers would always use condoms, only to realize later in the interview that they were silently exempting those occasions on which the young woman was using another contraceptive. Jane answered unequivocally 'yes' to the question whether young people she knew would use condoms every time they had sexual intercourse. But she added: 'Depending on whether they didn't want to or – yeah. And whether the girl's on the pill and they were in, like, steady relationship, been going out for ages, and they didn't want to use one. But yeah, otherwise most people would use them' (Kirkman *et al.* 1998b: 26).

Other young people actually defined safe sex as 'contraception'. One boy, in response to a question about whether there were sexual issues of concern to young people like him replied: 'Safe sex mainly, because none of them want to get pregnant'. It seems that the term 'safe sex' has been hijacked to mean contraception. Part of the responsibility for this is that the condom has long been used for contraception and it is only recently that it has been grafted on to the notion of safe sex, initially packaged for gay men.

Are there real obstacles to safe sex?

We have seen that, for some adolescents, responses to HIV/AIDS are influenced by misconceptions about themselves and their partners.

Are there other, reality-based obstacles to their adoption of safe sex practices? In addressing this question, researchers have assumed that sexual behaviour, like other behaviours, can be predicted from an individual's attitudes, beliefs and values. Thus, adolescents' sexual behaviour has been conceptualized as arising out of a process of rational decision-making. For example, adolescents who have good levels of knowledge about HIV transmission will avoid unsafe behaviours; the adolescent who perceives that there are high costs in using condoms is less likely to use condoms than one whose attitudes are positive. When we check these assumptions, we find that they do not provide an adequate or indeed accurate explanation of adolescent sexual behaviour.

Early surveys of adolescents' knowledge of HIV transmission (e.g. DiClemente *et al.* 1986; Strunin & Hingson 1987) suggested that substantial numbers of teenagers had misconceptions about the ways in which HIV is transmitted and that these misconceptions were more apparent among minority group youths and those who were poorly educated. Knowledge levels were independent of whether or not teenagers were sexually active or used drugs. By the late 1980s, it seemed that almost all the American youths surveyed had learnt the major modes of HIV transmission and misconceptions had diminished, although some remained (Hingson & Strunin 1992). Somewhat worryingly, these studies revealed that the few teenagers whose knowledge was inadequate were found disproportionately among groups where the risk of exposure to the virus is high.

Like their American peers, Australian youth appear to be well informed about HIV/AIDS although there is evidence of uneven knowledge in some groups. As in the USA, ethnicity plays a role in levels of knowledge. Not only were there lower levels of knowledge among youths of non-English-speaking backgrounds but also in these groups young women were less well informed about HIV and safe sex practices than their male counterparts.

While it is clear that accurate information about AIDS and transmission of HIV is important, it appears that knowledge is a necessary but not sufficient cause for action. Of considerable concern is the increasing evidence that knowledge is not reflected in these adolescents' behaviour. Several early studies showed that higher levels of knowledge are substantially unrelated to safe sex practices (Keller *et al.* 1988; Richard & van der Pligt 1991; Turtle *et al.* 1989). In an interesting study, Turtle *et al.* gave parallel questionnaires to two sets of students selected at random, one asking about behaviours, the other about AIDS beliefs. They found a marked discrepancy between knowledge and performance of safe sexual behaviours, measured by questions about condom use in casual sexual encounters, and about drug use and blood transfusions. For example, 92 per cent of their 'beliefs' group answered 'always' to the question 'Should you use a condom as a safeguard against AIDS in vaginal sex with a casual partner?' In their 'behaviours' group, only 26 per cent had actually done so. Of the beliefs group, 86 per cent thought that a potential partner should be asked questions about IV drug use; only 6 per cent of the behaviours group had done this. Of course, we do not know if Turtle's beliefs group would actually follow up their intentions with the appropriate behaviour, but this sort of discrepancy is in line with other findings which imply that knowledge and beliefs are not necessarily clearly linked with behaviour.

One of the key AIDS prevention messages is the importance of consistent condom use. Unfortunately, condoms have not been regarded positively in the past. Attempts to socialize the condom (encapsulated in Australia by the catchy slogan 'Tell him if it's not on, it's not on') have been designed to reduce resistance to their use. While dislike of condoms is still reported by many teenagers, there is some evidence that negative attitudes are breaking down, and that the benefits of condom use are being recognized. Despite this, and although *both* positive and negative attitudes to condoms are associated with *intentions* to use condoms in the future, it seems that whether or not condoms are *actually* used depends on young peoples' negative attitudes to their use (Boldero *et al.* 1992), a finding that is particularly clear for young girls. Another belief about condoms that relates particularly to sexual risk-taking with casual partners is an unwillingness to take personal responsibility for AIDS precautions. Teenagers in this study who held the view that this responsibility lay with one's partner and who were more likely to make excuses for not initiating a discussion about condoms or other precautions were engaging in more risky behaviours. It appears that casual sexual situations may be characterized by less comfort about communication. This is particularly problematic, as participants in casual encounters usually know less about each other than do those in regular relationships.

Why good intentions fail

The message that condoms are an acceptable (and indeed important) accessory to sexual intercourse appears to have been only partially acted on by today's adolescents. What, apart from their own negative attitudes, are the factors that intervene between adolescents' good intentions to use condoms and their frequent failure to do so?

In attempting to answer this question, some researchers have drawn on the concept of self-efficacy (e.g. Bandura 1982). Just as a perceived sense of mastery in other health-related domains is predictive of healthier patterns of behaviour in that domain, it is expected that a sense of sexual self-efficacy or mastery will be associated with safer sexual practices. In fact, as we noted earlier, many adolescents lack the confidence necessary to deal with condoms. For example, only half of our 18-year-olds felt confident that they could purchase a condom; half that they could discuss the use of a condom with a potential partner; and less than half felt that they could carry a condom with them 'just in case'. Lack of mastery of their sexual world is evident in other ways. We found two particularly important areas where levels of confidence varied. These were adolescents' ability to be assertive about their sexual needs (including communicating the desire to use a condom), and the ability to say no to unwanted sexual activity (including refusing to have unsafe sex). In both areas a sense of sexual self-efficacy or perceived competence was related positively to safe sex practices. In a similar vein Breakwell *et al.* (1991) explored young virgins' perceptions of three aspects of sexual control or mastery – choice of a trustworthy sexual partner, condom use and confidence in dealing with sexual relationships. They found that perceived control in the first two areas predicted intentions to use a condom, especially for female virgins. While these findings are encouraging, we must remember that, in the area of condom use, there appears to be a wide gap between intentions and behaviour. We do not know whether Breakwell's young virgins would retain their sense of control if put to the test in an actual sexual situation. Our strong hunch is that many of them would not.

One interesting aspect of Breakwell's study is that these young girls felt themselves to be more in control of partner choice and condom decisions than did the young boys. To some extent this unexpected sex difference in favour of perceptions of greater control by girls was confirmed by sexually experienced young people in another study (Rosenthal *et al.* 1991). In this study, it became clear that there were differences in the skills needed to deal with sexual matters. Young girls' sense of sexual mastery appears to be based on being responsible about the consequences of sex and being able to say no to unwanted sexual activity – perhaps because they have more experience of saying no to sex than do young boys. On the other hand, the boys were more able than their female counterparts to assert their sexual needs and to initiate sexual activities, a finding consistent with gender differences in norms and experience.

These findings might suggest some flaws in one of the most commonly held views about the process of sexual negotiation, namely that girls have less power or control over this process than do boys and this makes it difficult for them to insist on safe sex. Before rejecting this view of a gendered power imbalance in favour of one of gender equality, we should remember that the girls in one study were virgins whose sense of control reflected a guess about a hypothetical situation, with no assurance that their control would survive the reality of a sexual encounter. In the second study, most girls were well educated and middle class. It is possible that their competence in the sexual domain would not be matched by their less privileged sisters.

Perhaps the most important aspects of the everyday social context for adolescents are the beliefs about and attitudes to condom use of family and peers (see Chapter 4). Indeed, most models of decision-making (see examples in Chapter 2) take account of the potential influence of individuals' subjective norms for 'good' or 'correct' behaviour, derived from their perceptions of the attitudes and practices of salient others. Studies of sexual behaviour using Fishbein and Ajzen's (1975) early model report that positive normative beliefs about the importance of contraception are related to young women's intentions to use the pill as a contraceptive. More recent studies have shown that the importance attached to using condoms by parents and friends did not predict adolescents' actual use of condoms.

Why were these adolescents, contrary to expectation, not influenced in their behaviour by perceived social norms about condom use? We speculate that condom use usually requires both partners to communicate and to agree before the behaviour occurs. Using a condom is not a private act, carried out well in advance of a sexual encounter – unlike taking a contraceptive pill. The negotiated, shared aspect of using condoms is likely to add considerably to the difficulties in dealing with condoms that we have already described for some adolescents. Because of this, the immediate context of the sexual encounter may have a more powerful influence on adolescents' sexual decisions to use a condom than any distal normative influences.

It is not surprising, then, that there are difficulties in applying general models of decision-making, albeit ones that have been successfully used to explain a variety of illness or health-related behaviours, to sexual behaviour. As we have seen in Chapter 2, one other popular model of health behaviour that has been extended to the study of sexual risk-taking is the health beliefs model (HBM) (Janz & Becker 1984). The hope here is that the factors which appear to govern positive, health-sustaining or health-promoting responses to illness will produce safer sexual practices. According to the model, people make a rational cost-benefit analysis in deciding whether to adopt preventive behaviour.

Unfortunately, it is becoming clear that concerns such as the seriousness of the illness and the individual's susceptibility to that illness (key components of the HBM) may have considerable explanatory value in many areas of health-related behaviour – but not in the less predictable and less rationally governed world of sex (see e.g. Rosenthal *et al.* 1992).

Taking context into account

Plainly, sex is more than a matter of making rational decisions in advance of the act and independent of its context. As further evidence for this we can consider the regrettable gap between good intentions and actual behaviour. Why is it so hard for some young people to maintain their professed intentions at the critical moment? We have identified several determinants of condom use which arise out of the immediate context. As might be expected, high levels of sexual arousal at the time of the encounter seem to reduce the likelihood of using condoms. It may be that sexual arousal operates in a similar fashion to the effects of arousal on other tasks. For highly aroused young people, the encounter becomes the focus and the issue of whether or not to use a condom receives little or no attention. For some young people the difficulties in dealing with condoms may be overcome if they are taught to negotiate about and use condoms in sexual situations almost as if they were on automatic pilot.

A second significant contextual factor is the ability to communicate with a partner about his or her past sexual history and about using condoms – not an easy task, as we have seen, especially for adolescents brought up in cultures where discussion of sexual matters is, or has been, taboo. Asked about their willingness to discuss a partner's sexual history, these 16-year-olds responded as follows.

> If you have just met her that night, you don't want to say have you gone to the doctor or whatever before we have sex. It is a bit hard to say that sort of thing.
>
> (Boy)

Probably not. Because it is embarrassing. What do you say? Usually I sleep with people I know and I know they haven't got any diseases.

(Girl)

Condom use is reported more often by those adolescents who communicate with each other, highlighting our earlier point that the decision to use a condom involves both partners. We know that many adolescents report disturbingly low levels of confidence in their ability to discuss the use of condoms with their partners and many believe that they are unable to take the initiative in expressing their sexual needs. It is important, then, that adolescents be taught the skills which will enable them to communicate confidently and accurately in a climate of mutual acceptance.

What of the future?

What have we found out about young people's sexual behaviour in an era when their sexual health may be increasingly at risk? We know that young people's sexual behaviour does not follow a rule-governed script but is strongly influenced by the moment-to-moment context and by beliefs about unequal gendered relationships. Their behaviour is governed by many factors, some rational, some less so. As we saw in Chapter 6, the reasons given by young men and women for engaging in sex differ. In spite of apparent changes in society, young men are still more likely than young women to have multiple partners, to regard themselves as needing sex, to approve of casual sex and to seek sex for physical pleasure. Young women, on the other hand, stress the need for emotional commitment to a sexual partner and feel uncomfortable about sex with a one-night stand. It appears that love and romance are still potent forces in the sexual world of the female adolescent. Small wonder, then, that young people engage in sexual behaviour that does not seem to be rationally governed in the light of current knowledge about AIDS. If adolescents are to take sexually responsible decisions, they must be aware of the meaning and obligations attached to love and relationships. They must understand that communication with a partner about his or her sexual history and about using condoms is crucial and does not imply a questionable past. Given that trusting one's partner is likely to lead to less cautious sexual behaviour, it is important that such trust is not misplaced, and that the information received is accurate.

An exciting new approach to prevention of STIs among young people has been to document their sexual networks in the hope that this will bring home to adolescents the importance of one's partner's sexual history and allow for the development of suitable health promotion programmes. The structure of sexual networks as a critical factor in spreading STIs has been long known (see e.g. the work of Friedman *et al.* 1997), and is exemplified in an early Australian HIV/ AIDS health promotion campaign that featured many young people in bed together. But it is only recently that researchers have taken an interest in mapping the sexual rather than social networks of young people. Bearman *et al.* (2004) examined the structure of adolescent sexual networks in one US high school over an 18-month period. Somewhat to their surprise, they found that these networks had a different structure from that expected. The idea of a 'core group' of individuals who are responsible for infecting many others has been a key theme among epidemiologists. In this study, rather than finding a core group of sexually active young people, with many partners, the sexual networks created long chains of connections, with few students sharing partners at the school. The researchers report that one part of the network linked 288 students – more than half of those who were sexually active – to each other in one long chain. This finding has important implications for policy and practice interventions. Bearman *et al.* point out that with a 'core' network structure it is vital to reach members of the core group; with a 'chain' structure, it does not matter which individuals are reached. Breaking the chain is possible if the behaviour of only some individuals is changed. Their exciting work demonstrates 'how having an accurate sense of the real structure of a network matters for the effectiveness of an intervention' (2004: 80).

What of the future? It is possible that as the impact of STIs increases, adolescent sexual behaviour will become more conservative. Fewer partners and more frequent use of condoms are possible options. Alternatively, adolescents may return to the pre-1960 days of premarital chastity, when non-penetrative sex was a preferred and often-used substitute for sexual intercourse. Whatever their chosen path, today's adolescents live in a world where STIs, including HIV, are a realistic threat; their sexual decisions must be guided accordingly.

9 Having a baby: choices and outcomes

Teenage pregnancy emerged as a major concern in the 1960s and 1970s, with policy-makers and the public alike in many western countries expressing dismay at the number of teen pregnancies. Although some writers questioned whether the perceived 'epidemic of teenage pregnancies', so named by the Alan Guttmacher Institute (1976), was a reality, others continued to fuel anxieties. Even a decade later, there were dramatic and disturbing figures produced by writers such as Trussell (1988) in the USA, recording about 837,000 pregnancies, plus another 23,000 among those aged 14 and younger: 'One out of every 10 women aged 15–19 becomes pregnant each year in the United States. Of the pregnancies, five out of every six are unintended – 92 per cent of those conceived premaritally, and half of those conceived in marriage' (Trussell 1988: 262).

Another report (Richmond 1979) claimed that births to adolescents were one-fifth of all births in the USA. Other writers at the time attempted to put this anxiety into context: 'Teenage mothers are not a significantly large group, nor are they a particularly increasing "problem" in this country, but their lives are quite different to those of other girls of the same age without children' (Sharpe 1987: 10). Sharpe argued that teenage mothers were no more numerous than their sisters of yesteryear. Phoenix (1991), in her analysis of demographic trends in teenage motherhood, made the point that accurate data are difficult to obtain. In calculating and interpreting teenage conception and birth rates, Phoenix, in England, and Siedlecky (1984), in Australia, reminded us that inaccuracies are likely to arise. For example, in the case of pregnancy rates, the incidence of abortion in the population, where this is available, is included in calculations but not that of spontaneous miscarriage. We need also to make the distinction between wanted and unwanted pregnancies and pregnancies that occur within a committed relationship and those that do not. Some (many?) young people plan a pregnancy and are delighted with this outcome; some find the positive experiences of parenting present an opportunity for their own development. For example, only half the African-American women aged 14–20 years in one study (Crosby *et al.* 2003) described their pregnancy as unplanned or unwanted, although this was more likely for those who were under 18 years. Nevertheless, the magnitude of the numbers of pregnancies and births to teenagers that are reported gives cause for concern. Whether they imply a 'baby boom' is less clear.

The negative consequences of young (and often single) motherhood for both infant and mother have been the focus of public and policy concerns as have the outcomes for pregnant young women who choose alternative paths to that of motherhood, such as abortion or adoption. In the context of societal worries about the care and cost of teenage pregnancies, it is essential that we understand the dynamics underlying early pregnancies as well as the outcomes of these pregnancies.

Facts and figures: then and now

A glance at the early research literature reveals inconsistencies in the reported figures for pregnancies and births. Trussell (1988) reported that the proportion of pregnancies in the USA had changed little in the previous 15 years. Other researchers have suggested that, in fact, there has been a fall in teenage fertility rates since the 1970s when the so-called epidemic of teenage parenthood first came to public attention (Furstenberg *et al.* 1989; Phoenix 1991). Teenage pregnancies and births occurred far less frequently in other industrialized countries than in the USA (Trussell 1988; Werner 1988). In England and Wales, Phoenix reported birth rates for teenagers were not much higher in the 1980s than they were in the 1950s with a rapid fall from a peak in the mid-1970s. She concluded that early motherhood was now less common in these countries and in the USA than it has been for most of the past two decades. In Australia a similar picture to that in the UK emerged. There was a steady increase in teenage birth rates between the 1940s and early 1970s, with a subsequent decline until 1982. By that time there had been a 50 per cent reduction in births to teenage mothers – from 55.2 per 1000 girls to 27.4 (Siedlecky 1984).

What do current trends suggest? In western countries the number of births to teenage women is still highest in the USA. Henshaw and Finer (2003) report that nearly half a million American teens give birth each year. Kirby (2001) puts it somewhat differently, noting that 40 per cent of teenage girls become pregnant at least once before they reach the age of 20; this amounts to nearly 900,000 teen pregnancies each year. The birth rate for under 20s in the USA is 52.2 per 1000 (UNICEF 2001) and, in a 1999 report, around 11,500 babies were born to mothers aged 15 or younger (Cheesebourgh *et al.* 1999). Vinovskis (2003), in an interesting historical analysis of adolescent pregnancy in the USA, notes that the teen birth rate declined substantially between 1990 and 1999: by 30 per cent among African-Americans and 24 per cent among whites. Teen birth rates in the UK are second only to those in the USA (UNICEF 2001), although conception rates have been declining (Coleman & Schofield 2005). By contrast, Wellings *et al.* (2001) reported that the proportion of 18 to 44-year-old women in their study who reported having a child before 18 years of age was constant across their sample, although the younger women reported termination of pregnancy more frequently than did older women. Finally, Australia's teenage birth rate has decreased considerably over the past 30 years (Australian Institute of Health and Welfare 2003). In a nationally representative sample of Australian women (Smith *et al.* 2003b), the percentage who reported becoming pregnant as a teenager declined from 22.8 per cent of women aged 50–59 to 16.9 per cent among women aged 20–29. Nevertheless, Australia is still high on the 'league table' of teen births, with a teen birth rate of 17.1 per 1000 females under 20 years in 2002 (Australian Bureau of Statistics 2003). It has been estimated that the probability of an Australian female teenager becoming pregnant is one in five (Condon *et al.* 2001). Worldwide, there is a consistent trend in western countries towards lower rates of teen pregnancy. This trend is mirrored in some but not all developing countries (Blum & Nelson-Mmari 2004). Adolescent childbearing has decreased by about a quarter to a half in North Africa but increased in other African countries. It should be noted that the decline in teen births in western countries has occurred in the context of declining fertility across all age groups in these countries.

Along with this general decline in teen pregnancies, there has been a rise in the proportion of babies born to adolescents outside of marriage. Early research (Bury 1984) showed that in the decade of the 1970s in the UK, the number of pregnant teenagers who married was halved. By the late 1980s, teenagers had become the first age group in the UK, as in the USA and Canada, in which the majority (over 70 per cent) were single when they gave birth. In the USA, too, young women are less likely than in the past to marry in order to legitimate their baby's birth. Trussell, writing in the late 1980s, suggests that about 75 per cent of 15- to 19-year-olds will deal with their pregnancies outside the context of marriage, a figure that rises to almost all younger pregnant teenagers. This is in stark contrast to the early 1950s when less than a third of babies born to teenage mothers were conceived out of wedlock (Furstenberg *et al.* 1989). These figures are confirmed by Australian data where there was a marked increase in conceptions and births outside of marriage over this period (Siedlecky 1984).

This trend has continued. In the early 1970s, 67 per cent of Australian teenage mothers were married; in 2002 only 8 per cent were (Australian Bureau of Statistics 2003). Even when *de facto* relationships were taken into account, in 1999 it was estimated that around half of new teenage mothers were single (Nassar & Sullivan 2001). Similar increases in births to unmarried young women have been shown in the USA and the UK (Arnett 2001; Boonstra 2002; Wellings *et al.* 1999). Vinovskis (2003) reports that out-of-wedlock births among American teenage women increased from 69 per cent in 1990 to 79 per cent in 1999. Wellings *et al.* estimated that by the end of the 20th century, about 90 per cent of British teenage mothers were not married. Although these figures should be interpreted in the context of considerable increases in adult out-of-wedlock pregnancies, they add fuel to the concerns about teenage pregnancies, as we shall see.

To talk about a plateau or decline in the teenage birth rate may mask important social features of the phenomenon. We shall deal with these in later sections of this chapter. It is sufficient to refer briefly here to some likely contributing factors. The decline in birth rate may have occurred because of teenagers' increased access to a wider range of contraceptives (including the 'morning-after pill'), or to abortion as a means of dealing with an unwanted pregnancy. Another reason sometimes offered is that a higher rate of sexual abstinence rather than increased contraceptive use is responsible for the drop in numbers of teen births. This explanation is unlikely in view of the data we presented in Chapter 1 regarding increases rather than decreases in sexual experience among young people. A further consideration is the need to take demographic factors into account. For example, it is quite possible that there are two opposing trends among teenagers. In some groups – the well educated or affluent – there may still be a declining birth rate; in others – the unemployed or socially disadvantaged – rates of teenage pregnancy and birth may actually be increasing.

Inspection of the data available for the USA and the UK confirms that the incidence of teenage pregnancy is unevenly spread over different groups of teenagers. As Hudson and Ineichen (1991: 42) observe: 'Teenage motherhood remains overwhelmingly a working class affair'. Particularly at risk, it seems, are adolescents who are poor and adolescents of colour. The association between low socio-economic status and teenage pregnancy has long been noted (e.g. Shearer 2000; Turner 2004). Trussell (1988) estimated that about 77 per cent of births among teenagers will occur to those whose family incomes are well under the poverty level. The high levels of teenage pregnancy and motherhood among African-Americans in the USA (Arnett 2001) may also have their genesis, at least in part, in the poverty that prevails for many of these people.

In addition to social class and race, we need to take into account the differences in pregnancy and birth rates between younger and older teenagers. Although the pattern of declining birth rates in recent years applies to all cohorts, there are more births to older than to younger adolescents (UNICEF 2001). In Australia, the birth rate for young women aged 20–24 was three times that for 15- to 19-year-olds (Australian Institute of Health and Welfare 2003). In part, these differences can be accounted for by the greater proportion of termi-nations of pregnancy in the latter group, an issue we take up later in this chapter. Of course as we have seen, older adolescents are more likely to be sexually active and thus have more opportunities to become pregnant.

What can we conclude about teenage pregnancy and motherhood from these figures? It appears that the decline in teenage births that we reported over a decade ago has continued, as has the incidence of births within marriage. There are, however, considerable national and subcultural differences within this context of an overall decline in teenage pregnancy. In most western, industrialized countries the number of teenagers who conceive and become mothers is relatively low. In the USA the numbers are much higher and enough to be regarded as a significant social problem, especially among the poor, people of colour and the otherwise socially disadvantaged. Why do these differences exist? We turn now to the reasons why some young girls become pregnant.

Contraceptive options

Uptake of, and access to, contraception are key to reducing rates of teen pregnancy. Both uptake and access vary in different countries. While condoms are increasingly being used to prevent infection with HIV or other STIs (see Chapter 8), we have noted the tendency for young people to discontinue using condoms when other forms of contraception are being used. Of the many contraceptive strategies other than condoms now available, including IUDs and hormonal implants, the contraceptive pill is by far the most commonly used. In Australia, 70 per cent of women under 24 years choose the contraceptive pill for contraception (Williams & Davidson 2004). Oral contraceptives were used by more than a third of sexually active girls in year 10 and over half of those in year 12 in one national study in Australia (Lindsay *et al.* 1997). Nearly half of 18- to 24-year-old women reported using the pill in another study (Australian Bureau of Statistics 2002). Data from the US Youth Risk Surveillance study (Grunbaum *et al.* 2002) showed that only 21 per cent of sexually active female students reported using birth control pills before their last sexual intercourse. In the UK, among young women attending family planning clinics, the 'pill' was the most commonly used contraceptive especially among older (16- to 24-year-old) women. Of those under 16, 34 per cent were using the pill compared with 51 per cent of 16- to 19-year-olds (Coleman & Schofield 2005).

Of particular interest is the increasing availability and use of emergency contraception (EC) or the 'morning-after pill' as it is commonly called. EC has a very low failure rate when taken within 24 hours of conception, is simple to use and has relatively few side-effects (Fairley & Sawyer 2003). Many of those presenting for EC have experienced contraceptive, specifically condom, failure (Evans *et al.* 1996). Knowledge of EC among sexually active young people is high (Crosier 1996; Kosunen *et al.* 1999; Ottensen *et al.* 2002), with high levels of use by young people. Young people have been major users of EC in Australia, in part because of the unplanned nature of much of their sexual activity (van der Klis *et al.* 2002). No less important is the ready access to EC, which is available in Australia over the counter at pharmacies without a prescription, and its relatively low cost. This situation exists in countries like Holland and the UK but not in the USA.

Why do teenagers become pregnant?

Why do so many teenagers fail to use contraception or use these methods inefficiently? And why do some teenagers have more than one pregnancy? Two stereotypes have been commonly called upon as explanations of teenage pregnancy. The first is that the pregnancy is planned, but as a deliberate manoeuvre to get some sort of financial benefit or material gain such as welfare payments or subsidized housing. The second is that teenagers become pregnant accidentally because they are incapable of planning contraception adequately. Neither stereotype captures accurately or completely the reality of teenage pregnancies. In several UK studies reported by Phoenix (1991) it was rare for young women questioned about why they wanted to have a baby to supply a reason relating to material gain. In a study of Australian pregnant teenagers, not one gave such a reason for her pregnancy (Littlejohn 1996). The incentive of welfare is likewise insufficient as an explanation in the USA where there is little or no support for the belief that young women have babies in order to be eligible for welfare.

The second stereotype – teenage pregnancy as the unwanted outcome of incompetent or non-use of contraception – appears, on the face of it, a more likely explanation. And yet the evidence we have suggests that this is an oversimplification of what occurs. Indeed, for some young women their pregnancy is not accidental and unwanted. Rather, having a baby is a planned and deliberate choice. For these young women the decision to become a mother is often influenced by social factors such as having a mother who had her own first child earlier than average, having friends who are themselves young mothers and having a stable relationship – which may or may not be marriage – with a partner.

Some young girls admit that getting pregnant is a planned strategy which enables them to avoid sex! If sex is seen as an unpleasant but unavoidable activity, if your boyfriend treats you as his sexual possession, free to use you sexually as and when he pleases, then being pregnant is a way of buying some status as well as temporary 'freedom'. As one 15-year-old mother, quoted by Hudson and Ineichen (1991: 42), put it: 'It was great when I's pregnant – wouldn't let him near me and he respected that – I dunno if he went anywhere else for it. I didn't care anyway. I was glad to have meself to meself . . . I wouldn't mind getting pregnant again – just to have the peace and quiet'. Other young women, it seems, do not even have that choice. Recent research has shown that both a history of physical abuse by a partner and current involvement in a physically abusive relationship were associated with becoming pregnant (Roberts *et al.* 2005).

As we have noted, research tells us that most teenage pregnancies are not planned. For example, Phoenix (1991) reports that 82 per cent of pregnant adolescent girls in one study had not 'planned' to get pregnant. When she explored attitudes to conception of these young mothers-to-be, Phoenix found that the majority held one of two positions. The first group had not thought about the possibility that they might conceive; the second did not want to conceive when they did. Among the former we would expect to find those teenagers with a limited understanding of the reproductive process who failed to use contraception at all. In some ways, these young women are reminiscent of the 'invulnerable' adolescents described in a previous chapter. In her Australian study, Littlejohn (1996) found that 20 per cent of pregnant teenagers did not think they needed to use contraception because they couldn't get pregnant.

Members of the second group, the 'inconvenient' conceivers, are likely to include those young people for whom contraception had failed, one way or another. For some, inadequate knowledge about reproduction and/or effective contraception is a problem (Evans 2000; Shearer *et al.* 2002); for others, negative attitudes to contraception or problems associated with obtaining contraceptives are a deterrent (Zabin *et al.* 1993). But there is another group for whom an unplanned pregnancy occurs. These are the contraceptively 'unprepared' young people for whom sexual activity is regarded as – and often is – a spontaneous, unplanned event. A substantial number of adolescents report that they did not use contraception because they were not planning to have intercourse.

The reasons why some young people use effective contraception and others do not are many and varied. What factors are associated with effective contraception? Among the plethora of reasons identified by researchers in the past decade or so as 'risk factors' for teen pregnancy is age of sexual initiation (Hockaday *et al.* 2000; O'Donnell *et al.* 2001; Woodward *et al.* 2001). The older the adolescent girl at the time of initiation, the more likely she is to use contraception and to use it effectively. When there is a stable and committed male-female relationship, contraceptives are more likely to be used than when there are no romantic ties between sexual partners. Although this finding is inconsistent with that reported for condom use in the previous chapter, a partial explanation may be that adolescents in committed relationships are more likely to use oral contraceptives. There is substantial support for the view that girls who have clear educational goals and those who are achieving well in school are more likely than their less achieving and ambitious peers to use effective contraception. Finally, girls who feel good about themselves, who feel that they have some degree of control over their lives, who have a sense of equality with their male partners – in short those who have high levels of 'ego strength' – are likely to be good contraceptors.

One reason for failure to use contraception is related to policy decisions within each country. In the USA, Wilcox (1999) notes the emergence in the early 1980s of attempts to restrict girls' access to the contraceptive pill. Although this proposal to limit young girls' contraceptive autonomy was successfully challenged, there have been continuing attempts to pass this bill and its amendments through Congress.

We have no space here to do other than list some, but not all, other antecedents of teen pregnancy which have been documented by researchers. These include poverty, low levels of education, sexual abuse, having a mother or sister who is a teenage mother and dysfunctional family relationships. One important risk factor can be defined as problematic family environments, including single-parent families, poor parental monitoring, low levels of closeness between parents and child, and parental drug use or crime (Christoffersen & Soothill 2003; Ellis *et al.* 2003; Jaccard & Dittus 2000; Russell 2002). A second set of potential risk factors is significant mental health problems (e.g. Kessler *et al.* 1997; Quinlivan *et al.* 2004). Some longitudinal studies have found that depressive symptoms in adolescence place young women at greater risk of becoming pregnant (Fergusson & Woodward 2002; Miller-Johnson *et al.* 1999) although other studies have not confirmed this relationship. However, relationships between anxiety and/or adolescent conduct disorder and early pregnancy have been consistently demonstrated (Hockaday *et al.* 2000; Quinlivan *et al.* 2004; Scaramella *et al.* 1998; Woodward & Fergusson 2001; Yampolskaya *et al.* 2002).

Resolution of teenage pregnancies: 'making the choice'

Today's pregnant young women (and their partners) have available to them a number of possibilities. They may choose to continue the pregnancy or not. If the former, they may decide to keep the infant or relinquish it. The ready availability of legal abortions has enabled more young people to choose termination of pregnancy as an option. Today, pregnant teenage girls are more able than their peers of the previous generation(s) to choose to keep their child and rear it either alone or with the support of their partner. Alternatively, they may avoid motherhood by choosing either abortion or adoption. Each of these choices depends on a variety of factors and each brings with it different consequences.

Abortion

Legalization of abortion that occurred several decades ago in many parts of the world brought with it a substantial increase in the number of terminations of teenage pregnancies (Bury 1984; Phoenix 1991). Hofferth (1987) estimated that the percentage of teenage pregnancies terminated by abortion in the USA almost doubled between 1974 and 1980, with a levelling off in abortion rate since then. A similar trend was reported among Australian and British young women (Hudson & Ineichen 1991; Siedlecky 1985). In the late 1980s, it was estimated that roughly 40 per cent of pregnancies to teenagers in the USA ended in abortion (Hayes 1987), one of the highest abortion rates for teenagers in any developed country.

More recent research suggests that many young people continue to terminate their pregnancies. Edgardh (2002) reports that teenage abortion rates in Sweden increased by about a third in the last half of the 1990s. Blum and Nelson-Mmari (2004) claim that the total estimates of abortions among women under 20 in developing countries range from 1–4.5 million each year. In one report (Kittelson & Howard-Barr 2005), of the 1.3 million women who decide to have an abortion in the USA, approximately 20 per cent are 19 years old. In Australia, Siedlecky (1996) reported a continuing increase since her earlier figures. In the only state in Australia which records reliable data for abortions, in 1997 54 per cent of teenage pregnancies ended in abortion (Australian Bureau of Statistics 1999). These figures are similar to those reported in the UK (Coleman & Schofield 2005).

The large number of adolescents who opt for abortion leads us to ask why they make this choice and what are the consequences of the decision to terminate a pregnancy for these young women? It appears that now, as in the past, younger teenagers are more likely to choose abortion as an option than those who are older. For example, in South Australia in the period 1995 to 1999, the younger the female, the more likely that her pregnancy would be terminated: 83 per cent of pregnancies in 13-year-olds ended in abortion compared with 47 per cent among those aged 19 years (Australian Institute of Health and Welfare 2003). Similar findings are reported in the UK, where, in 2002, 56 per cent of 13- to 15-years-olds terminated their pregnancy compared with 40 per cent of 15- to 19-year-olds (Coleman & Schofield 2005). There are also substantial regional differences in rates of abortion, with some areas in England reporting up to three-quarters of teenage pregnancies being aborted while in other regions the abortion rates were about a fifth of pregnancies.

Who is likely to choose abortion? Teenagers who choose to have abortions are more likely than those who carry their pregnancies to full term to be contraceptive users, single, have high educational or occupational aspirations and to be of higher socioeconomic status. A review by Hayes (1987) supported these conclusions, noting also the significant impact of religion as well as parents', especially mothers', attitudes to abortion. Positive peer (and boyfriend) attitudes to abortion are related to pregnant teenagers' decision to abort, while adolescents who report knowing other unmarried teenage mothers are less likely to make this choice. Although there are claims of substantial racial differences in abortion rates, with black adolescents less likely to abort than their white peers, it has been argued that this black-white difference varies according to age, with similar ratios for 19-year-olds and higher rates of abortion for older black women than whites.

Young women provide a range of reasons for terminating their pregnancy. The most common reasons are lack of money, a belief that she is too young or immature to have a baby, or unwillingness to take on the responsibility of a baby at this time (Addelson *et al.* 1995). Less commonly, young women say that they don't want their parents to know that they were pregnant, that they have problems in their relationship with the baby's father or that they don't want to be a single parent. Whatever the reason(s) for their decision, and even within a social context in which abortion is seen as a legal option for teenagers, there are grounds for concern about the health consequences of this decision. Teenagers are less likely than older women to obtain abortions in the safer, earlier months of pregnancy. This delay is likely to result in increased health risks. While young women who have chosen to terminate their pregnancy do not, in general, appear to have a higher incidence of negative health outcomes than do older women, there is evidence that these young women are at greater risk of cervical trauma which in turn may have long-term negative implications for future conception and pregnancy outcomes (Siedlecky 1985; Strobino 1987).

Few studies examine the psychological consequences of abortion for young girls. There is something of a paradox in the situation where abortion is now readily available to most young women in most western countries but it still stirs strong negative feelings among teenagers. Girls, and working-class girls in particular, are the ones who have the least positive attitudes. This would suggest that the decision to abort an unwanted pregnancy is likely to engender conflict for many of these young girls. It appears that abortion can be a major stressor but for most this stress is short term with no long-term psychological distress, although there may be short-term, transient episodes of guilt or depression (Bradshaw & Slade 2003; Pope *et al.* 2001). For the small number of teenagers who experience negative emotions, underlying factors are varied and include lack of support from partner or family, being pressured into having an abortion, having prior psychiatric histories or strong religious beliefs (Adler & Smith 1998; Congleton & Calhoun 1993; Pope *et al.* 2001).

It is also true that the impact of having an abortion may be dependent, at least in part, on the social context. Even in cultures where abortion is legal there is often a highly vocal opposition to this procedure, usually couched in 'pro-life' terms and, in some cases, accompanied by violence towards providers of abortion services (Kittelson & Howard-Barr 2005). As with attempts to regulate young people's access to contraception in the USA, there has been a long-term effort to restrict access to abortion through policies that require parental consent or notification (Wilcox 1999). At the time of writing, Wilcox noted that half the states in the USA had such laws in place, with others on the way. He points to one study (Ellertson 1997) which showed that parental involvement laws may increase the likelihood that young people will access abortions in states that have no such laws.

In spite of potential difficulties such as these, for some teenagers the decision is easily made and has no negative consequences; for others, abortion is an event replete with ambivalence. This letter to one dispenser of advice to young girls captures something of the dilemma faced by teenagers:

> Six weeks ago I found out I was pregnant. [My boyfriend and I] spent the next day crying together. I decided the only thing I could do was have an abortion . . . Ray was totally against the abortion. He said I was being selfish. Then he gave me a choice; me, him and the baby or just me. After a million tears, I chose just me . . . he paid for half the abortion . . . He also said he didn't love me anymore, would never forgive me and that we had no future together. I was so hurt I wanted to die. I trusted him and couldn't believe he turned on me . . . We're back together now, but I feel so guilty for having the abortion . . . Every time I see a baby, I cry.
>
> (Weston 1988: 190)

For young women who do choose abortion as the means of dealing with an unwanted pregnancy, access to good counselling support is essential so that the decision whether or not to abort can be made after a careful, informed and thoughtful appraisal of the situation. For some, the process is akin to one of mourning in which the natural stages of grief and loss must be worked through. The teenager who chooses to terminate her pregnancy needs to feel that that decision is the right one for her.

Giving up the baby: choosing adoption

Adoption of a baby was long the option of choice for teenagers facing unwanted pregnancies. However, since the advent of legalized abortion and a reduction in the social stigma attached to unwed motherhood, adoption has become rare in western countries. There is some evidence that the numbers of young women who gave up their babies for adoption declined in the 1970s (Bachrach 1986). By 1982, only 7.4 per cent of white teenagers and less than 1 per cent of blacks reported having given up a child for adoption.

The consequences of adoption are likewise little researched, although one small study indicates that relinquishing one's baby may be less problematic for teenagers than choosing to continue in the parenting role (McLaughlin *et al.* 1988). On the other hand, several studies report that giving one's baby up for adoption results in long-term feelings of loss and guilt (Condon 1986; Evans 2003).

Keeping the baby

Why do some teenagers choose to continue with a pregnancy and to take on the responsibilities of parenthood, often without a partner to provide emotional and material support? Taking a broad sociological perspective, we could argue that unwed parenthood is associated with changes in society which have led to the two-parent family becoming less important for the economic well-being of parents and children. Equally, changes in cultural norms have resulted in out-of-wedlock children – and their mothers – no longer being stigmatized as they once were, although a recent study by Wiemann *et al.* (2005) found that two out of five adolescent mothers did feel stigmatized by their pregnancies.

There is also considerable research to suggest that race plays a significant role in a teenager's decision to keep her child. Although the rate of childbearing among unmarried white teenagers in the USA is increasing, the figure has always been high for black teenagers. In fact, in the early 1980s almost all births to black teenagers under 15 and nearly 90 per cent to those aged between 15 and 19 occurred outside of marriage. This high rate of ex-nuptial births may be attributed to the high rates of sexual activity of these young women and their greater reluctance to use abortion as a means of dealing with an unwanted pregnancy (Hayes 1987). There is a suggestion that these girls perceive motherhood as a rare gratification in a life devoid of opportunity. When life offers little but continuing unemployment poverty and difficult family circumstances, it would not be surprising if teenage girls sought comfort in the prospect of bearing and rearing a child. Before we accept this appealing hypothesis too readily, we should note, however, that the implied link between bleak social and economic prospects and contraceptive behaviour has not been supported.

One factor that does seem to have a complex impact is the availability and source of financial assistance to unwed mothers-to-be. Several studies have shown that the decision to carry a premarital pregnancy to term is influenced by the availability of financial aid from the young woman's family of origin as well as the availability of public aid. However, as we noted earlier, the weight of evidence suggests that unmarried teenage girls do not get pregnant in order to receive public assistance. Rather, it is likely that unmarried mothers are drawn from the ranks of low-income, female-headed families, many of whom are receiving welfare assistance themselves. It has been suggested that if welfare assistance is available, many young women will choose to continue with a pregnancy rather than contemplate a termination. Again, the evidence for this conclusion is thin with at least one study (Moore & Caldwell 1977) revealing little evidence for any connection between the availability of welfare and choosing single parenthood over other options.

Apart from issues of class, race and economics, young girls give many reasons for keeping their babies. Becoming a mother may not be a real matter of choice. Some young girls fail to realize, perhaps because they have erratic periods, they are pregnant until too late to do anything but have the baby. Some may deny the pregnancy, hoping that 'it will go away' if they don't think about it. Others may be frightened of telling people until after the time when an abortion would be possible. But motherhood is seen by some young girls as having positive (although possibly short-term) consequences for their lives. Apart from having an object to call their own and to love, for some young girls a baby may be seen as a means of keeping a boyfriend's interest, of complying with his wishes to keep the baby, or of achieving status because of their new 'adult' role as mother.

One particularly disturbing reason for the young teenager to involuntarily choose motherhood is because of poor or inadequate medical advice. While most doctors do their best to help the young girl decide among the options open to her, others are less helpful. In one study reported by Hudson and Ineichen (1991), patients claimed that 21 per cent of all doctors consulted made no effort to help teenage girls obtain abortions. A second study revealed that 20 per cent of the pregnant girls who continued with their pregnancy had wanted an abortion but were either too late or had their wish thwarted. Given these difficulties, it would not be surprising if some teenage girls had little confidence in the medical profession as a source of guidance and assistance.

Choosing parenthood: consequences for teenagers

While we have relatively little research to draw on in determining the consequences for teenagers of choosing abortion or adoption as the outcome of an unwanted pregnancy, the decision to keep the baby and the consequences of that decision have been the focus of considerable research. Here we discuss these consequences only briefly.

Teenage motherhood

In line with the negative view of young mothers' life chances that prevailed until relatively recently, Arthur Campbell, an influential expert of the time, asserted more than 40 years ago:

> The girl who has an illegitimate child at the age of 16 suddenly has 90 per cent of her life's script written for her. She will probably drop out of school; even if someone else in her family helps to take care of the baby, she will probably not be able to find a steady job that pays enough to provide for herself and her child; she may feel impelled to marry someone she might not otherwise have chosen. Her life choices are few and most of them are bad.
>
> (Campbell 1968: 238)

These dire predictions have not been strongly supported by subsequent research. In terms of pregnancy and birth outcomes, pregnant teenagers do have higher rates of complications, maternal morbidity and mortality, premature and/or low birthweight babies and perinatal deaths than older women (Australian Institute of Health and Welfare 2003; Chang *et al.* 2003). But when we turn to the consequences of teenage motherhood, the picture is more positive although some researchers maintain a focus on poor outcomes for mother and child:

> When teens give birth, their future prospects become more bleak. They become less likely to complete school and more likely to be single parents, for instance. Their children's prospects are even worse – they have less supportive and stimulating home environments, poorer health, lower cognitive development, worse educational outcomes, more behavioural problems, and are more likely to become teen parents themselves.
>
> (Kirby 2001: 3)

In spite of this, many studies now have shown positive outcomes for some young mothers (Fessler 2003; Leadbeater 2001; Swann *et al.* 2003). It appears that teenage pregnancy and motherhood are not in and of themselves as incapacitating as once thought. Rather, contextual factors such as socioeconomic status and social supports predicted well-being better among their pregnant and non-pregnant, parenting and non-parenting adolescents than did parenting status.

Nevertheless, economic adversity and educational difficulties are perhaps the most common outcomes of becoming an adolescent parent. Teenage mothers do find it difficult to re-enter school and to complete their education (Littlejohn 1996; Milne-Holme *et al.* 1996; Moffitt & The E-Risk Study Team 2002). Since education substantially influences later life chances through income and occupational opportunities, this is a particularly important issue. But impending or actual motherhood may not be the sole or critical factor operating here. There is now good evidence that pregnant teenagers have lower grades and lower school motivation before becoming pregnant than their non-pregnant peers. Some researchers have noted that some of the characteristics of teenage school dropouts (such as being impulsive, lacking in long-term goals and coming from unhappy families) are similar to those which lead to becoming an unmarried adolescent mother.

There is no question that the interruption to schooling or termination of education that often follows pregnancy and early motherhood has implications for the economic well-being of these young women. Most studies show that teenage mothers are less likely than older mothers to find stable and well-paid employment. Once again, we should be wary of assuming a direct link between early motherhood and poor job prospects. Several writers have pointed out that the employment of young women is just as dependent on the conditions of the labour market and personal characteristics as it is on high educational attainment. Nevertheless, it is true that teenagers who begin childrearing at an early age are economically disadvantaged and more likely to be dependent on welfare. Although the differences in income between early and later childrearing decrease over time, these teenage mothers are at greater risk of poverty throughout their lifetime.

To what extent is the interruption by premature parenthood of the normal maturational cycle of workforce experience before 'marriage' and childrearing likely to affect these young women's intimate relationships and marital outcomes? We know that many teenage mothers raise their children as single parents (Bennett *et al.* 1995; Furstenberg *et al.* 1987; Quinlivan *et al.* 1999). It seems that, for some, early childbearing accelerates the pace of marriage or cohabiting. It also accelerates the pace of separation and divorce. But premarital pregnancy or childbirth does not necessarily prevent a stable, happy relationship, be it marriage or cohabiting. Furstenberg's work shows that marriages are most likely to last if the couple had a longstanding, committed relationship prior to the child's birth.

The children of teenage mothers

There appear to be considerable health risks for children of teenage mothers. Infants of these young women have a higher likelihood of low birthweight and of dying within the first year of life than those of older mothers (Australian Institute of Health and Welfare 2003; Jolly *et al.* 2000). Indeed, the prevailing wisdom has been that these children face a bleak future with increased risk of parental neglect, child abuse, abandonment and other forms of parental mistreatment. The reasons for this, it is argued, are to be found in the young mother's immaturity, lack of parenting skills and inadequate financial resources.

In support of this, Hayes (1987) concluded that the developmental disadvantage of having a teenage mother does not decline over time. The developmental disadvantage of children born to teenage mothers compared with those of older mothers is reflected in deficits in cognitive functioning, in problems in social functioning (e.g. higher levels of aggression and lower self-control) and later school motivation and achievement. These difficulties appear to persist into adolescence and may be more pronounced for sons than daughters.

A less pessimistic view of the outcomes for children of teenage mothers comes from work in the UK. Phoenix (1991) suggests that the deleterious effects of a mother's youthfulness disappear or diminish when other important social and economic characteristics are controlled for, although she concedes that children of very young mothers are likely to be at risk, both from the point of view of their health and their subsequent social and psychological development. Reporting the findings of a rare longitudinal study of young mothers, Phoenix concluded that the responses of many of these teenagers to pregnancy and motherhood were not very different from those of older women. On the whole, the children were well cared for by their young mothers, most of whom took full-time responsibility for child care. These mothers were not ignorant of the need to provide a stimulating environment and good nutrition so that their children could develop to their maximum potential. When the children's developmental status was assessed, test scores revealed normal variability and were related to the usual sorts of factors, such as cooperativeness of the child and satisfaction with motherhood.

Researchers are now turning to the task of identifying risk-protective factors, especially those features of the mother's environment which serve as a buffer against negative outcomes. One promising area is the relationship between children's outcomes and the timing and sequence of events in the lives of their mothers. For example, resuming education and entry into a stable marriage appear to influence positively the child's later academic performance. Quite clearly the outcomes for children of young mothers are determined by a complex set of issues. To argue that these outcomes are inevitably negative is to overlook the possibility that teenage mothers can reclaim their lives.

Programmes to reduce teen pregnancy

Not surprisingly, in the light of the concerns about the number of teen pregnancies and the potential for negative outcomes for mother and child, increasing attention is being paid to this issue. The UK has developed a teenage pregnancy strategy and there have been many programmes in western countries designed to reduce teen pregnancies. For the most part these are incorporated in broader sex education programmes (see earlier for a description of school-based programmes). Kirby (2001) reviewed programmes in the USA and Canada, examining three categories: those focusing on sexual or nonsexual antecedents or both. Among the former he included school-based abstinence programmes discussed earlier in this book, as well as family- and clinic-based programmes. Among the latter were youth development programmes such as vocational education and employ-ment programmes. As might be expected, there was great variability in the success of these programmes. The most effective programmes had a number of characteristics, including an emphasis on non-sexual aspects of young people's behaviour, consistent with 'best practice' school sex education programmes described earlier. The most effective of all the programmes he reviewed, asserts Kirby, had a positive effect on sexual practices, pregnancy and births among girls for three years. The multifaceted Children's Aid Society-Carrera Program included reproductive and sexual health education, academic and employment assistance, arts and sporting activities and comprehensive medical care. Not surprisingly, this programme is 'long-term, intensive and expensive' (p. 15) and few communities would have the resources to replicate it. Nevertheless, there is much to be learnt from the finding that a comprehensive programme such as this is the most effective protection against unplanned pregnancy.

What about the fathers?

It seems that fathers, young or old, have long been invisible par-ticipants in the act of procreation and parenthood. In the case of partners of teenage mothers, there are particular difficulties involved in researching and writing them into the family formation process. Most pregnant young women become known to service agencies because they seek medical help. The fathers of these babies are some-times unknown or, if known, may be fearful of disapproval or reluctant to accept responsibility for ongoing support of mother and child. For these reasons, they are likely to be wary of contacts with service providers or even researchers. In a rare review of research on teenage fathers, Parke and Neville (1987) argue that we need to recognize that male partners of adolescent mothers represent a wide range of ages and are not necessarily adolescents themselves. Never-theless we shall limit our brief analysis to teenage fathers while acknowledging that this oversimplifies the issue.

A substantial minority of teenage fathers never acknowledge their paternity, partly through ignorance, partly through disbelief and partly because they refuse to accept the responsibilities of fatherhood. Furstenberg reports that in one study many young fathers doubted their ability to support their new family, either financially or emo-tionally. In another of the few studies of partners of teenage mothers, Simms and Smith (1986) were able to locate 59 per cent of the young men six months after the birth. The fathers interviewed presented a somewhat rosy view of parenting, no doubt because the least satisfied young men did not participate, but they also added to the depressing picture of ignorance about, and apathy towards, pregnancy and contraception that is characteristic of many young mothers.

When the pregnancy is carried to term and the baby arrives, it is too often the case that boys continue to behave in ways that have been socially conditioned. They may find it difficult to deal with the demands of a dependent infant and an inexperienced young mother. Some resolve this problem by leaving, escaping from their new responsibilities. Several studies have shown that only about a quarter to two-thirds of fathers are still involved with their children two to three years on and less than a third provided financial support (East & Felice 1996; Fagot *et al.* 1998). Turning once again to Phoenix's longitudinal study, we find little cause for optimism about the role of these young men in the lives of their young families. Phoenix reports that a sizeable minority of relationships come to an end during the pregnancy and that most male partners did not provide the emotional and material support that the young women desired. Before condemning those young men who fail to support their partners, financially or emotionally, we need to acknowledge that mothers (and their parents) can function as gatekeepers. For some fathers, access to their infants and children may be restricted, thus limiting the degree of paternal involvement in infant and childcare even when they keenly desire the opportunity to participate in childrearing.

There are many unanswered questions about the consequences of teenage fatherhood – for the young fathers themselves, for their partners and for their children. Why do some young fathers accept their family responsibilities and obligations? How effective are these young men as parents (and as partners)? What is the effect of these young fathers on their children's development? These and other questions need to be addressed before we can fully understand what it means to father a child while still a teenager.

Teenage pregnancy: what can we conclude?

Our discussion of teenage pregnancy and parenthood has highlighted the variability of outcomes for those concerned. It is clear that, for some, pregnancy is unplanned and the baby unwanted. For others, the decision to have a baby at an early age brings in its wake a series of negative consequences. Teenage parenthood may prove to be a difficult and disruptive choice, resulting in serious and permanent limitations to life's opportunities. But not all teenage parents, especially mothers, experience difficulties. A substantial number complete their schooling, marry (and do not divorce), find rewarding employment and their children develop along patterns which are not different from those of children of older parents. In spite of the very serious hurdles that these young people encounter, they are able to realize their ambitions and life plans.

What are the factors that protect these successful young parents from difficulties and distress? We have mentioned some of these in passing. The importance of adequate social support in mediating the stress for young mothers, whether this comes from the child's father, parents or other family members, has been well documented. Not surprisingly, the socioeconomic level contributes substantially. To be poor and undereducated is likely to decrease significantly the likelihood of well-being for these young parents and their offspring. One factor to which we have not yet paid attention is the interpretation given to teenage pregnancy within the society. Is teenage pregnancy seen to be a normative phenomenon or is it assumed to be disruptive of young people's normal life trajectory? In some cultures, it is clear that parenting at a youthful age is accepted and incorporated into everyday life. The African-American culture in the USA provides an example, among western countries, of this process. In many studies, we find that parenthood at an early age is less disruptive of their everyday lives for young black women than for their white counterparts.

In other cultures, teenage pregnancy and parenting are seen to require special programmes to assist these young parents and their children. Considerable funds are spent to prevent teen pregnancy as well as providing services to ameliorate problems after conception occurs. These include provision of family planning services, antenatal care, health and parenting programmes, and a variety of comprehensive care programmes (see e.g. Frost & Forrest 1995; Vinovskis 2003). There are some programmes which have been directed to promoting educational or occupational opportunities, including the provision of alternative schools for pregnant girls. It is not possible for us to outline in detail the variety of programmes designed to overcome the negative health, social and economic consequences of early child-rearing. Rather, we wish to make the point that the responses to teenage pregnancy are, to some extent, culturally bound as well as dependent on individual characteristics.

What is striking about the research findings is that teenage parents are not a homogeneous group. Clearly many of the problems that beset these young people are not a function of their premature parenthood but are shared by their non-parenting peers. Moreover, we still know too little about the impact of early pregnancy and parenthood. We have mentioned the dearth of research on teenage fathers. More than a decade ago, we wrote that missing from the research are the voices of these young mothers and fathers. This is still true today. In spite of the plethora of books dealing with teenage pregnancy, contemporary researchers have neglected the phenomenology of early motherhood and fatherhood. We have little idea of what it actually feels like to become a mother or father when one is little more than a child. We know, from a reading of early UK researchers' interviews with pregnant teenagers and young mothers that individuals experience these events in many different ways. Teenage pregnancy and/or parenthood may be a monumental handicap to well-being and achievement. Even when this is the case, many young women, while regretting lost opportunities, cannot imagine themselves without their children and are happy as parents, as the words of this young mother testify:

> Sometimes I say to myself I wish I never had her. Maybe I would probably have had a boyfriend . . . Sometimes when I've got money problems I say to myself if I didn't have her I'd probably be well off now . . . but then when I think of her I say no. She's mine, and I'm happy she's here. You know I can sit down and play with her and give her the love I never really had from my father when I was small . . . and I'm two parents in one really.
>
> (Phoenix 1991: 242)

10 When sex is unwanted

Some aspects of adolescent sexuality can be described as maladaptive, troubled or troubling. Or they may reflect a desire to escape from unpleasant experiences, to fit in with peer pressures, satisfy a drive for dominance or submissiveness, express a pathological need or reflect the presence of self-destructive urges or alienation from society's institutions. These worrying aspects of sexuality may be self-regulated, as in early onset of sexual activity, or be the result of external forces over which the adolescent has little or no control, as in rape. Whether the impetus is internal or external, voluntary or involuntary, the common feature of these behaviours is that the outcome for the teenager is inimical to current and future life adjustment generally, and sexual adjustment in particular.

Making the transition 'too early'

Adolescents' propensity for risk-taking, their experimentation with adult behaviours, their drive towards autonomy and their openness to peer influences have been thought to make them vulnerable to maladaptive sexual behaviours. These include sexual intercourse that occurs before the young person is emotionally or physically 'ready', or in a way that does not allow the adolescent to be an informed and equal decision-maker in whether or not to have sex. Although engaging in sexual activity becomes normative with increasing age, for young adolescents it is behaviour that for the most part the adult generation does not condone. Why is this the case? The particular focus on initiation of sexual activity is due to its special place as transition behaviour. Like many behaviours which reflect the transition from child to adult, sexual activity, if ill-timed or otherwise out of step with developmental needs, may be detrimental to the psychological, emotional and social well-being of the adolescent.

It is not only teenage sexual behaviour that raises parents' and society's anxiety levels. Other adolescent behaviours which cause concern include substance use, drinking, smoking, truancy and delinquency, as well as further forms of antisocial behaviour. Some researchers have argued that these behaviours have a common aetiology, and form part of a syndrome of deviant behaviours, in what has come to be known as problem behaviour theory (Jessor *et al.* 2003). In a longitudinal study of high-schoolers and college students, Jessor *et al.* found a positive association between problem drinking, marijuana use, delinquent behaviour and early participation in sexual intercourse for both age groups. These behaviours were found to correlate negatively with measures of conformity and conventional behaviour such as church attendance and school performance, and positively with personality measures reflecting unconventionality. From these findings, the researchers concluded that early transition to non-virginity was linked with the transition to other problem behaviours. In later studies, this group also showed that there were strong correlations between sexual risk-taking (defined as not using contraception), other health-compromising behaviours and psychological adjustment problems among young people.

Another framework which presents adolescent sexual activity as deviance is the stage termination model (Peskin 1973). This model assumes that movement to the next stage of psychosocial development requires a minimum level of maturation to have occurred if the transition is to be successful. If transitions occur 'too early' there are negative consequences for future development. Thus, if the virginity transition occurs early in adolescence, or adolescents engage in sexual behaviours for which they are not emotionally prepared, subsequent development may be compromised. The stage termination model predicts not only that early and 'unprepared' sexual activity will be associated with delinquent behaviours, but that it will, in itself, lead to later problems of adjustment.

Bingham and Crockett (1996), in a longitudinal study of school-aged adolescents, tested both the problem behaviour model and the stage termination model. They contrasted outcomes for young people who had experienced early, middle and late timing of first intercourse. Timing was defined differently for boys and girls because girls in their sample became sexually active on average ten months later than the boys. Early loss of virginity was defined as having sex before the median age of the sample (15.5 years for girls and 14.8 years for boys). Middle timing was loss of virginity by grade 12 but at ages above the median for the boys and girls respectively. Late-timers were those who had not had sex by grade 12. Forty per cent of the sample were early-timers, 38 per cent middle- and 22 per cent late-timers using these definitions. There was support for problem behaviour theory: drunkenness, drug use, minor deviance and poorer family relationships were associated with early intercourse, while late-timers were higher on church attendance, school marks and had more positive academic plans. However, the stage termination model was not supported: early sexual intercourse did not lead to later poorer psychosocial outcomes over and above those predicted from baseline measures of psychosocial adjustment. This interesting finding suggests that early sexual intercourse *per se* need not have negative consequences – it is only its association with other indicators of poor adjustment that is problematic, as these indicators do predict later adjustment.

Some other interesting aspects of the Bingham and Crockett study suggest the need for caution in labelling all adolescent sexual experimentation as problem behaviour. First, there were no relationships between timing of first intercourse and either self-esteem or positive affect. Second, while those who postponed intercourse had, in the main, the most adaptive psychosocial profiles, there was one area where they reported less well-being. The early intercourse group (especially the boys) rated their peer relationships more highly than the virgins. A study of 18- to 20-year-old Australian young people (Moore & Buzwell 2002) showed similar findings, with general well-being not related to age of first intercourse, but those young people who were virgins at the time of the study reporting lower social self-esteem, less satisfaction with romantic relationships, less certain sexual identity and more worries about sexual health than the non-virgins.

Another twist to the issue of whether we should be worried about adolescent sexual behaviour comes from the idea that a certain amount of so-called deviance and rebellion in adolescence may indeed be a healthy sign. Experimentation with risky behaviours can sometimes be associated with a positive, constructive form of teenage unconventionality, reflecting independence and creativity. Of course such behaviours can also be destructive and the associated risk-taking can lead to a range of outcomes potentially harmful to healthy development. Chassin's study of health-related behaviours such as smoking and participation in sport and/or exercise suggests that 'constructive' and 'destructive' deviance can be regarded as independent, representing different pathways to adolescent health-related behaviours. They concluded that: 'one type of adolescent at risk for substance use is unconventional, creative, independent, and assertive. However, these adolescents are not in rebellion against traditional socializing agents such as the family and the school and they also engage in relatively higher levels of health protective behaviours' (Chassin *et al.* 1989: 261).

We do not know if these alternative pathways, via a positive, constructive independence or a destructive, rebellious anti-conformity, operate for early sexual behaviour but there is some evidence that there are both positive (through peer acceptance) and negative (through peer rejection) paths to early multiple partnering (Feldman *et al.* 1995). This evidence is suggestive of the distinction that Chassin *et al.* wish to draw and which downplays the maladaptive aspects of sexual precocity and other 'deviant' expressions of teenage sexuality. But, although we may wish to focus on the more positive features of some teenage sexual behaviours that have been defined as undesirable, there is little question about the harmful nature of the behaviour to which we now turn.

Sex unwanted: abuse and victimization

The high attractiveness of youth, coupled with their low power and status targets them as frequent victims of sexual violence and abuse. A recent large-scale study of sexual experiences in Australia revealed that more than 20 per cent of women and almost 5 per cent of men have experienced some form of sexual coercion, defined as being forced or frightened into unwanted sexual activity (de Visser *et al.* 2003). US data from nearly 1000 college women in 1992 (Tanzman 1992) found about 7 per cent of women agreeing that they had experienced unwanted sexual activity, while more recently, also in the USA, the National Survey of Youth found that nearly 12 per cent of female students and 6 per cent of male students reported being forced to engage in intercourse at least once in the past year (Youth Risk Behavior Surveillances (YRBS) 2004). Accurate prevalence rates are difficult to ascertain due to under-reporting and different definitions of what constitutes sexual forcing or coercion. In particular, men's reluctance to report is undoubtedly related to both the stigma associated with male-to-male sexual contact and the high degree of shame for men in admitting victimization.

There is evidence that most sexual molestation is committed by someone known to the victim and many cases involves incest or rape by a known and trusted adult. Incest is often much harder to deal with than sexual abuse by a stranger outside the home. The following quote in a letter to her mother from a survivor of teenage incest poignantly illustrates the breach of trust experienced by this young woman and her feelings of self-blame:

> It was in the context of a loving, trusting relationship. My father was somebody who represented right and wrong to me, which is why it was so difficult to understand what was happening to me at that age. One grows up with the idea that male sexuality, male passion, is somehow a woman's fault, something you're responsible for. As a little girl, I can remember being taught not to sit in a certain way, not to stand in certain ways – and it's very complicated to learn all those things, because you're supposed to be sexy and attractive to men; at the same time you're not supposed to lead them on, you're supposed to know what the balance is. Of course, I now realise that men must take responsibility for their own sexual feelings . . . One of the things I resent most is how it damaged my relationship with my mother. It put such a barrier between us.
>
> (Payne 1983: 59)

Abuse by a stranger involves one incident; incest usually involves many incidents over a long period of time, and is shrouded in secrecy. Victims feel they have no one to turn to and fear that they may not be believed – a fear that is often justified. They believe that they will cause family break-up or be rejected by other family members. In the case of sexual abuse by a parent, victims may feel betrayed by their non-abusing parent, who may be perceived to be powerless as a protector, or even as colluding in the abuse. In children and adults, more severe symptoms have been consistently associated with incest by a father compared with other perpetrators (Browne & Finkelhor 1986; Naar-King *et al.* 2002).

> I have to remind myself that it is not I who brings this pain into our lives.
>
> (from a poem by a teenage incest survivor: Payne 1983: 59)

While abuse by a stranger is traumatic, it is a situation with which people close to the victim are more likely to empathize and offer support than in incest cases. Stranger sexual abuse is also a situation in which the victim can readily interpret the perpetrator as evil and hated – therefore different from normal people. This interpretation is far more difficult, and may be impossible, when the perpetrator is a family member, with long-term consequences for psychological adjustment. In such cases the issue of who can be trusted in life is likely to loom large.

Research studies and case material examining the effects of sexual abuse on psychological functioning suggest that, together with violent stranger rapes, long-term incest beginning in childhood has the most damaging effects. The clinical literature suggests that sexual abuse in childhood is associated with both negative short-term outcomes such as guilt and anxiety, and longer-term effects including drug and alcohol abuse, somatic problems, depression and suicide (Bergen *et al.* 2004; Naar-King *et al.* 2002). In addition, childhood sexual abuse is a risk factor for being a victim of subsequent sexual assault (Krupnick *et al.* 2004; Noll 2005). Sexual maladjustment has also been shown to result from sexual abuse in childhood and adolescence. Outcomes include a greater likelihood of starting sex at a younger age, having multiple partners, exchanging sex for money, suffering sexual dysfunction in adulthood and becoming a perpetrator of sexual abuse oneself, a topic we will discuss in greater detail later in this chapter (French & Dishion 2003).

It is useful to be aware that sexual abuse does not necessarily lead to long-term psychological maladjustment. There are protective factors in adolescents' lives which are associated with resilience, the ability to work through and eventually cope with trauma. Chandy *et al.* (1996) compared over 1000 sexually abused teenager girls with the same number of teenage girls without a background of abuse. As expected, sexually abused young women had higher rates of suicidal involvement, disordered eating behaviours, pregnancy risk and drug use, as well as poorer school grades, than non-abused girls. But protective factors were present which reduced the likelihood of adverse outcomes for the young women with a history of sexual abuse. These included higher degrees of religiosity, perceptions of being cared for by adults, living with both biological parents and the presence of a clinic or nurse at school. Factors which raised the risk for the abused girls were perceived substance use in school, mothers' use of alcohol, major family stressors in the past year and worry about sexual coercion.

Childhood and adolescent rape and sexual abuse are too common and their effects devastating and often long-lasting. Their consequences are costly for the community in terms of the health, social adjustment, and relationship quality and stability of its members. There is both an economic and humanitarian argument for increasing the resources currently being devoted to victims of sexual violence and the training of those who work with them. Preventive efforts are also important, and take two forms, working with potential victims and with potential perpetrators. Examples of the former include programmes which alert children and adolescents to potential dangers and raise discussion of what is appropriate and inappropriate touching. One of the aims of these programmes is often to provide a safe space for young people to air their concerns about their experiences, to let them know that they are not to blame for another's abusive behaviour. Another type of preventive effort targets education and treatment of those who engage in sexually abusive behaviours. The message in many such educational or training programmes is about the inappropriateness (and criminality) of violating another's boundaries. Such interventions may be targeted at the community in general, for example media campaigns that remind us that 'no means no', or that children and young adolescents are not in the position to give informed consent to sex. Less successful are programmes to 'retrain' known abusers and paedophiles, posing a huge community problem of how to assimilate such people back into the community once they have served jail sentences. Research into the topic of adolescent sexual abusers (discussed in a later section) may be particularly important in informing more effective interventions than we currently have in our social armoury.

Sex unwanted: coercion, manipulation, miscommunication

Childhood sexual abuse and rape are serious crimes that often have severe consequences for the victims. But unwanted sex also occurs in ways that have less potential for subsequent trauma but can still lead to long-term negative effects on psychological health and relationships. It is clear that there is a great deal of sexual activity occurring among young people that is not consensual, or where consent has been obtained through dishonest, manipulative or fear-arousing strategies. Humphrey and White (2000) in their longitudinal US research found that a huge 70 per cent of college women had experienced sexual coercion at least once from the age of 14 years. Coercion includes being talked into unwanted (or regretted) sex through 'seductive' or manipulatory techniques as well as forced sexual activity. Examples include sex occurring when one partner is not in the position to give informed consent, such as when they are under the influence of alcohol or drugs, or where partners are in a situation where the power balance between the couple is highly uneven, such as a teacher seducing a student. Peer pressure to have sex, fear of losing a partner's interest, or miscommunications between couples about the signals of consent can all lead to sexual activity where one partner feels used, violated, or at the very least regretful.

For young people, the dating or 'going out' encounter has been described by O'Sullivan (2005) as an 'intensified exchange' – a situation of high emotional charge. So too are other situations in which young men and women meet for the purposes of potential romantic or sexual relationships, for example pubs and clubs. The intensity of charge within these situations is heightened by drugs and alcohol, and by strategies which both sexes use to increase their attractiveness such as seductive dress, flirtatious presentation and displays of status and confidence designed to mask any underlying insecurities. This heady cocktail of youth, hormones, needs and alcohol can be great fun but there is potential for unwanted and unhealthy outcomes, such as forced and coerced sex. How common are these occurrences?

A study by Waldner-Haugrud and Magruder (1995) of 422 male and female college students aged 19 to 24 years showed, in their terms, 'a phenomenal amount of sexual coercion', with such behaviour being so common as to be considered normative within the age group. Tactics such as detainment, persistent touching, lies and being held down were commonly experienced by young women, with the outcome often being unwanted (though not necessarily refused) sexual intercourse. Vicary *et al.* (1995) found similar types of coercive strategies being used to force sex or sex play on young women. These included making false promises, physical restraint, physical threats, verbal threats, name-calling or pursuing physical contact and ignoring a woman's requests to stop. Unwanted outcomes for young men were also evident in the study by Waldner-Haugrud and Magruder, though less common than for women. Tactics used in sexual coercion of young men included blackmail and threats, and these were more likely to result in milder forms of unwanted behaviour such as kissing or touching than in intercourse. Krahe *et al.* (2003) detailed a similar range of strategies used by young women to coerce young men into sexual activity, finding such occurrences to be relatively common and rated by the men as moderately upsetting. A qualitative focus group study of school-based and college adolescents in Australia (Crowley *et al.* 2004: 29) showed that unwanted sexual activity was perceived as an issue for boys as well as girls, but boys indicated they felt more able to either avoid it or cope with it, as expressed tentatively by this 18-year-old male:

> there may be some guy who could innocently be attracted to a girl and, you know, and buy her some drinks and she gets drunk or,

you know, just under the effects of alcohol or something and she's, you know, making advances on him that are, you know, unwanted, um, but I would, and this is again such a stereotype, such a generalisation, but um I would probably say that guys probably would be more prone to just be like . . . probably be more open if they, if they didn't want those advances or whatever and to get out of the situation, than girls would, and that's, that's probably something that our society has done, you know, kind of empowered men more so in the sexual arena than, than women.

The boundaries of what constitutes sexual coercion are not always clear. Some feminists have argued that all male-female sexual intercourse is rape, because the lower power and status of women means they can never be truly consenting parties – they are always constrained by social pressures and fears. But this is not a commonly held or popular view, even among liberated women and certainly not among adolescents. Nevertheless, young people are aware that sexual situations can provide high levels of ambiguity, as well as the potential for impulsive action that is later regretted. In a study of American high-school students, adolescents expressed confusion over who should be blamed in a date rape situation in which the victim had consumed alcohol (Mandelblatt 1999). In focus groups with young people (Crowley *et al.* 2004: 3) adolescents discussed whether sexual activity with someone who was too drunk to make an informed decision could actually be called rape. Some young people clearly did not define it as such and were, as in the US study, inclined to 'blame the victim'. For example:

> Some girls . . . when they're passed out, people sort of move in. And they pretty much . . . there's no doubt that a lot of those cases would be unwanted, but there's not really any great deal they can do about it.
> *Interviewer*: The girls?
> The girls, yeh. Cause if they're passed out or close to it, then, like, it wouldn't be really considered rape 'cause they're not sort of doing anything to stop it, but obviously alcohol has put them in that situation.

Another worrying trend is the idea that some young people (girls in particular) 'deserve what they get' because they dress or behave provocatively, or they already have a 'reputation'. Sexual coercion is justified by the perpetrator through the rationalization that the girl is 'asking for it', not directly or verbally, but through signals that mean different things to different people. The following quotes from adolescents illustrate these ideas (Crowley *et al.* 2004: 26, 28) and show that they are not confined to males.

> Yeah well I reckon, I don't know, I mean if a girl wears a really short skirt and like, you know, a belly, a top that, you know, shows everything, um I reckon um you're a bit asking for it.
>
> (Young man)

> *Interviewer*: Do you think there are some people who are more prone to being taken advantage of?
> Outgoing people, I mean I've got that certain friend who's you know she's er blonde, big tits and very extroverted um and she does get drunk on occasions and she's just a really nice person, very extroverted, but gets into the situations where the other people think she, like, well yeah she likes him, and that's in a situation where it can get taken advantage of because they just go for it and she's so lost that she doesn't know what she's doing. Um, so I definitely think if you're out there, sending, you know, not negative messages, um but anything you're more likely to be noticed.
>
> (Young woman)

It seems that the impression of sexual availability, through dress, appearance and behaviour, can still, for young women, be dangerous to reputation and indeed to safety. The impression may or may not relate to the young woman's sexual wishes and desires. It may be a reflection of male projection, or a flirtation tactic designed (sometimes unconsciously) to lead to greater closeness, perhaps romance and love, perhaps sex, but perhaps not. In Chapter 6 we discussed the sexual double standard and the socialization pressures limiting the ways women can express their sexuality. Arbes-Dupuy (2000) talks of it as 'the silencing of women's desire'. For young women it seems it is sometimes easier to abdicate responsibility for their desires and let the 'magic of the moment' take over. Sometimes the moment does not turn out to be all that magic – the encounter goes 'too far', the sex is cursory and unromantic, the priming with alcohol means things get out of control. But the lack of a (verbal) language for young women to express their sexual needs adds to the ambiguity of sexual encounters, increasing possibilities for unwanted outcomes. Communication issues between the sexes were also mentioned in Crowley's (2004: 28) study as contributing to misunderstandings about expectations, which may then lead to unwanted and later regretted sexual activities:

> I've definitely been in a situation where um, you know, a person's been saying no but eventually I talked to them afterwards and they said yeah, 'I didn't mean that', and that puts me in a bit of a weird situation where, you know, I don't know where to draw the line, you know. Some people say no and mean it, some people say no and don't, um so I mean if you had 10 girls in a row who said no and they really want it, and you get the one girl off, I mean, it's just, I guess, experience and you need to try and read the calls, read the signs, and some people just read them wrong.

Additionally, in the high arousal states of a sexual encounter, the non-verbal aspects of sexual communication are easy to misinterpret when a decision has to be made about whether to proceed with sex or slow down. Research suggests that there tends to be very little verbal communication during the transition from sexual intercourse being a possibility to it becoming a reality (Kent *et al.* 1990). Couples often do not decide to have sex verbally, but through action. The ambiguity may be perceived as reducing embarrassment (and in some cases personal responsibility for the decision to go ahead) or heightening romance and spontaneity. The desire for such ambiguity, seen by some as part of the 'magic' of sex, may therefore militate against the more prosaic discussion of whether this encounter is really wanted by both parties. Jenkins (2000) talks about the popular media tendency to romanticize women's submission to men in sexual situations. This reminds us of the popularity among young women of the literary genre known as 'bodice rippers'. In these stories, women say 'no, no' to a man's advances but the subtext is 'yes, yes', and afterwards there is satisfaction and often 'true love' for both partners. But in real life if some young men and young women believe this is the way the game is played, but some do not, the potential for feeling used and abused on the one hand, or unfairly accused on the other, is tremendous.

A related issue is withdrawal of consent (O'Sullivan 2005). Some incidents of reported sexual forcing or coercion occur when permission has been given (either overtly or tacitly) to begin a sexual encounter but one party has a change of mind. Usually the mind-changer is depicted as the female, but men can and do change their minds as well. Partners may reject this change of mind for a range of reasons. They may not understand the communication if it is not clear, they may interpret it as sex play, or they may become angry, either forcing the sex to continue or expressing their anger through physical or verbal violence or sarcasm. Teaching young people about sexual communication must include education about being clear about what is wanted and accepting the rights of a partner, including the right to a change of mind, even if these are very difficult things to do in some situations.

A complicating factor is that adolescents can consent to unwanted sex because of peer pressure, the desire to belong, or as a way of maintaining a relationship. Impett and Peplau (2002) asked the question 'why do women comply with requests or pressure for unwanted sexual activity?', that is, why does 'yes' sometimes really mean 'no'? They tested an ethnically diverse sample of more than 100 college women who had consented to unwanted sex with a dating partner at least once, using attachment theory as a framework for their study. Anxiously attached young women were the most willing to consent to unwanted sex, often giving the reason that they feared their partner would lose interest if they did not comply. Avoidantly attached young women gave different reasons for compliance, indicating more passive reasons such as 'It was easier than saying no' and 'I felt obligated'. In Crowley *et al.*'s (2004: 27) focus groups, adolescents mentioned that their peers might say 'yes' when they meant 'no' so that they could gain approval from the group, or because they succumbed to pressure from a boyfriend, for example: 'I guess I would have thought unwanted sexual activity could also mean, like, um just pressure from boyfriends or friends or something like that . . . A friend has said to me [about her boyfriend] "he keeps mentioning it, he keeps mentioning it, brings it up all the time", that sort of thing'. Some girls talked about the pressure to perform sexual activities to 'hold on' to boyfriends who were losing interest, but wanted to resist that pressure. They recognized the potentially negative outcomes to reputation, self-esteem and ultimately to the relationship they were trying to maintain:

> *Girl 1*: Like if I was losing him I'd be oh well I'm not gonna perform tricks 'cause he's not gonna stay 'cause I do something once, and I yeah, I don't want to be involved in something continual all the time, and it . . . 'cause that's ridiculous, and quite frankly you can find someone else.
>
> *Girl 2*: And usually guys, if you do perform it, usually guys will go and tell their friends that you're easy, and they will come along and ask you out and act all sweet and then get that off you 'cause they don't want to lose you, it's like a never ending line, just trying to keep a guy. It's stupid.

In a study by Rosenthal (1997), boys and girls aged 15 to 17 years were administered a questionnaire that contained scenarios depicting 16 situations with two protagonists where sex may or may not ensue. The scenarios were designed to vary in the extent to which the desire to have or not have sex was clearly articulated, where sex did or did not occur, and whether pressure was exerted by one individual on the other. All scenarios were worded so that responses could refer to same- or different-sex partners, and to males or females, so that there was no assumption of either heterosexuality or exclusively male coercion. The young people in the study were asked to rate clarity of communication in the scenario, amount of pressure being exerted and how acceptable they found the scenario. Results showed that the absence of discussion was often interpreted as clear communication, and that scenarios where sex actually occurred, with or without discussion, were assessed as exhibiting clearer communication than scenarios where discussion occurred and one person said 'no'. Such a finding reflects some of the potential for communication confusion discussed above, where 'no' in sexually charged situations may not be interpreted as a clear message for a whole range of reasons, or where words do not speak as loudly as actions, despite the fact that the latter may be far more readily misinterpreted. Further, while the study did show that perceived pressure to have sex was associated with higher ratings of unacceptability, there was wide variability among young people as to which scenarios were acceptable, pressured and unclear. The variation was not particularly along gender lines, with few sex differences found in the research.

The studies described above suggest that while young people may be able to label coercive sexual scenarios as unacceptable, they are confused about the issue of informed consent in 'real life' sexual matters. They sense there are problems with taking advantage of alcohol-fuelled situations but make excuses for those who do so. They recognize that people have sex when they do not really want to, and that sexual messages are easy to misunderstand. On the positive side, young people are often able to develop strategies which help them to deal with these ambiguities. It is to these we now turn.

Minimizing risk of unwanted sex

In Crowley *et al.*'s study, there were some strategies and techniques nominated by young people as ways of avoiding unwanted sex. The major strategy could be summarized as 'watch out for your friends' by socializing in groups and keeping an eye on any group member who seemed to be getting drunk or taken advantage of. The strategy was seen as both a way of protecting yourself and a way of protecting your friends. The following example demonstrates that in certain groups watching out takes the form of a peer-group norm which protects the young people who are too drunk to look after themselves:

> If they're just that, flat out on the floor, we sort of try and put them away, push them away on the corner or something. It's not like someone will start jumping on them and make them do something they didn't want . . . Amongst our friends it's sort of understood that if a girl's really drunk, um and, like, can't really make decisions and you get with her, you sort of get a really bad reputation and like, 'cause you've taken advantage of someone who's drunk, so everyone sort of bags you . . . I think a lot of guys would be scared to go any further than kissing a girl, like, if you kissed a girl fine, and if you did anything further then, it's just really really bad, everyone would really hate you and like all the girls would hate you.
>
> (2004: 30)

Another peer-related strategy was the technique of socializing with a non-drinking friend such as a 'designated driver'. Such a friend was seen as someone who might intervene, not necessarily in an assertive or protective way, but in a way that might break the nexus between drinking and getting into trouble, through, for example, a suggestion that it was time to leave: 'A designated driver helps me a lot because sometimes I feel like I'm just getting started, and, like, "no, it's time to go home", like, you know, I feel like, well I don't want to pay for a cab, alright let's go!'

Maintaining control of potentially out-of-control situations through counting drinks, watching (or 'nursing') drinks to ensure they were not spiked, or only getting drunk in familiar environments (presumably therefore perceived as safe) were also mentioned. Boys particularly liked the idea of 'knowing your limits', while girls were concerned with keeping an eye on their drinks to ensure they were not tampered with.

> Watch out how many drinks you're actually having as well because you wouldn't wanna . . . be so out of control that you can't stop something happening.

> About a year ago I went to like a girls' night party, so the guys rocked up later, and I left my drink just for two seconds, and I

only had one and I know that I don't throw up over one drink and later in the night I was just violently ill, and ever since then I've never left my drink. Like I didn't drink much after that either, because I don't think I can hold my alcohol either half the time.

(Crowley *et al.* 2004: 31)

Being clear about your intentions, expecting to have 'no' taken seriously, and not taking advantage of someone who was drunk were also mentioned relatively frequently by girls, but rarely if at all by boys: 'Regardless of what your friends do or what you think the acceptable practice when you go into a club is, if you're not comfortable with something, you know, no matter where you are, it's OK for you to say, "no! I don't want you to do that"'.

Boys and girls also mentioned social, educational and institutionalized means to minimize risk in the sexual domain. There were four approaches suggested: changes and improvements to school-based sex/relationship education, changes within the family and on the part of parents, general social changes and improvements in the assistance available to young people through counselling and support services. Educational/school-based suggestions were requesting more information on certain topics, guest speakers, more discussion and role play, and education about communicating to others about one's needs and wishes: 'More communication about how to say no and how, like, um just because you've said yes to one thing doesn't mean you have to go all the way and, so people can say no and um, they don't have to um lead into other things just 'cause, just 'cause they said yes earlier'.

Parental/adult/family changes varied from suggestions that parents take more responsibility by supervising parties to a greater extent, to the opposite view of parents allowing young people to have more responsibility through teaching them about alcohol and sexuality, and generally being more open about these issues: 'Trying to get some kind of awareness to parents even, like they need to be open-minded that it's not 1970 any more and you're not having sex [only] when you're married, and that their openness allows us to be safer because we talk to them about it'. Compared with:

If there's more boundaries at parties, and more um supervision and stuff then I don't think a lot of that stuff would happen. 'Cause um, like, I know some people that you know . . . as soon as there's a party, some bedrooms, they leave the rest of the party . . . but if there's parents there then people are restricted to one area, then nothing can happen. I think if you take out food, it's definitely sort of a subtle way of checking what's happening.

(Crowley *et al.* 2004: 32, 33)

Changes to society were about large-scale attitude change in the community, a difficult task particularly in our highly sexualized and alcohol-driven culture. Some examples were:

> I think, like, definitely role models are good, like, when you hear on the news or something that . . . footballers go out to nightclubs and get pissed and get beat up in fights and stuff, that definitely, like, doesn't set a good example.

> If you could make some sort of magazine that um gives examples of such, that maybe you could, you could have fun without drink, or maybe um just experiences, that someone could read or you could learn by others' mistakes, or maybe just a magazine that showed good stuff and then people might say, 'oh yeah, they seem to enjoy it, it's cool'.

(2004: 33)

Suggestions regarding counselling and help-seeking were largely along the lines of making these services more confidential and accessible: 'I think sort of counsellors at schools might . . . be feared by kids . . . like, "I don't want to go to him, he's only for crazy people or something like that"'.

In summary, sexual coercion and unwanted sexual experience are widespread for girls and certainly not unknown for boys. They can and do occur through violence and forcing, but the more common scenario is through peer or relationship pressure and communication misinterpretations. While young people have developed some risk-reduction strategies to avoid unwanted sex, they appear confused about their rights and the rights of others in sexually charged situations. The sexual double standard, which devalues female sexual desire but valorizes it in males as a sign of masculinity, leads to communication difficulties when a decision is to be made about whether to go ahead or not go ahead with sex. The media presentation of sexuality as the basis to popularity and happiness adds further confusion for young people who need to negotiate ways to express themselves sexually that are healthy and growth-promoting, rather than degrading, unpleasant and inimical to psychosocial health. This task has proven too great for the next group we discuss – adolescent sex offenders.

Perpetrators: adolescent sex offenders

Many experts in sexual coercion and rape argue that the focus of prevention should not be on risk-reduction strategies for women (although these are clearly important), but on identifying and managing the perpetrators of sexual violence (Rozee & Koss 2001). Sheridan *et al.* (1998) report that in the USA adolescents make up at least a third of the sexually abusive population, and similar data are evident from UK statistics (Glasgow *et al.* 1994; Kelly *et al.* 1991). Davis and Leitenberg (1987) more specifically report that about 20 per cent of all rapes and 30 to 50 per cent of all cases of child sexual abuse in the USA can be attributed to adolescents. Farr *et al.* (2004) argue that these data are likely to be an underestimation, due to under-reporting.

A significant number of adult sex offenders (possibly more than 50 per cent) report that their first sexual offence occurred during their teenage years (Abel *et al.* 1985; Sciarra 1999). Offences range from rape through indecent assault (sexual fondling or touching, usually short of penetration), sexual assault, exhibitionism, voyeurism, to obscene telephone calls. However, adolescent sex offenders do not necessarily progress to adult sex crimes. Nisbet *et al.* (2004) followed up 303 males who had been assessed by the Sex Offender Program of the New South Wales Department of Juvenile Justice in Australia. All had either pleaded guilty to or had been found guilty of a sexual offence that occurred when they were between the ages of 11 and 17 years. First assessment was at 16 years, on average, with a mean follow-up period of seven years. About a quarter of the young men received additional convictions for sexual offences before they were 18 years, but only 5 per cent received convictions for sexual offences as adults (with a further 4 per cent charged but not convicted). The authors concluded that transition from adolescent to adult sexual offending is the exception rather than the rule, but it could also be argued that a longer time frame is needed to be confident of this prediction. One particularly interesting finding of this study was that non-sexual recidivism was very high – more than 60 per cent of the young men received convictions for non-sexual offences as adults. In addition, having a prior non-sexual offence in adolescence was associated with almost a threefold increase in the odds of being charged with sexual offences as an adult. Both these findings indicate a strong element of antisocial behaviour (over and above, and possibly independent of, sexual deviance) associated with sex crimes.

Whatever the precursors of adult sexual offences, there is no doubt that treatment of adolescents who commit sex crimes is desirable, to reduce the probability of reoffending, to lessen the likelihood of escalation of crimes, and to intervene at a developmental period when antisocial behaviours may be less entrenched and more amenable to change. Edwards and Beech (2004) reviewed the effectiveness of treatment programmes for adolescents who commit sexual offences, focusing on drop-out and recidivism as their measures of effectiveness. They indicated that (a) the drop-out rates are very high, with often fewer than 50 per cent of adolescents completing the programmes, and (b) future offending is associated with drop-out, which in turn relates to older age and impulsivity. The implication was that current programmes are not meeting the needs of the adolescents who attend them. Edwards and Beech claimed that different personality subtypes showed different patterns of recidivism and that each subtype has correspondingly specialized treatment needs. For example, they cited Worling's (2001) study, in which cluster analysis was used to identify four personality-based groups – antisocial/impulsive, unusual/isolated, over-controlled/reserved and confident/aggressive. The antisocial/impulsive group comprised the majority of the adolescent sexual offenders, but it is difficult to isolate the risk factors that discriminate between this group and general delinquents, according to Edwards and Beech. They may require interventions that stress impulse control and aggression management, while other subtypes may benefit from more emphasis on channelling deviant arousal, or understanding the rights of others.

Most adolescent sex offenders are male and are known by their victims (Becker 1988; Davis & Lee 1996; Manocha & Mezey 1998). Carr and VanDeusen (2004) suggest four main risk factors for male sexual aggression, and although their research is confined to college campuses in the USA (and thus a late adolescent-young adult population), these factors may also apply to younger adolescents. The factors are male sex-role socialization, alcohol abuse, personality traits, and child abuse and neglect. Kilmartin (2000) and Rozee and Koss (2001) suggest that male sex-role socialization in which dominance and aggression are stressed can lead to what has been termed 'hypermasculinity', characterized by beliefs of entitlement in relation to the male sex drive, high levels of sexual aggression, belief in rape myths such as that rape can be justified under certain circumstances, and adversarial sexual beliefs. The role of male peer support in sexual coercion, forcing and violence has been noted in environments such as university campuses and sporting clubs, where sexual conquest of women can be valorized, but attitudes towards women, particularly women who express their sexuality, are hostile. Farr *et al.* (2004) compared hypermasculinity levels of 44 male adolescent sex offenders with 57 non-offending adolescent males, using an adapted version of the Hypermasculinity Inventory (Mosher & Sirkin 1984). They found the young offenders scored significantly higher than non-offending boys on two subscales, 'callous sexual attitudes towards females' and 'adversarial attitudes towards females and sexual minorities', but they did not differ on 'violence as manly' or 'danger as exciting'. This suggested to the authors that hypermasculinity *per se* may not be the culprit, but rather what characterized adolescent sexual offenders were their negative and hostile attitudes to women.

The role of alcohol abuse in sexual coercion has already been discussed in relation to victims of unwanted sex, but it also plays a key role in perpetration. Alcohol use may act as a precipitant of and an excuse for sexually aggressive and coercive behaviour. A number of studies have found that, among sexual assaults perpetrated by males against females, at least half involve the consumption of alcohol by the perpetrator or the victim (e.g. Muehlenhard & Linton 1987; Ouimette 1997; Zawacki *et al.* 2003). Interestingly, women (victims) are consistently rated as more culpable for acquaintance rape when they have been drinking (Carr & VanDeusen 2004), and women who drink are perceived as more sexually available than those who do not (Abbey *et al.* 1996). This is even more unfair when considered in the light of a study by Tyler *et al.* (1998), which showed that 23 per cent of college men admitted to getting a date drunk or stoned to engage in sexual intercourse, and 23 per cent of women reported a date getting them drunk or stoned and engaging in unwanted sex. A confounding issue is that alcohol consumption is part of the social context for many teenagers. Sheehan and Ridge (2001) argue that drinking with friends, despite its dangers, serves several healthy developmental needs for young people. It provides opportunities for bonding as a group, and for sharing stories and secrets about fun, friendships, adventure and sex. Their study using focus groups with year 9 and 10 female students found that reasons for drinking included fun, relaxation, to be popular and to forget worries, as well as 'to pick up guys' or to 'get with someone' (p. 354). Greater control of alcohol use at teenage social events may be an important element in reducing unwanted sex but, by itself, will not be enough to eliminate the attitudes and beliefs that underpin sexual aggression and coercion.

Drink spiking is a special issue related to unwanted sexual activity that has been reported with increased frequency in recent years (*The*

Herald-Sun 2003). Drink spiking occurs when illicit drugs are added to a person's drink without their permission. The motive is often to obtain sex while the victim is in a confused or even comatose state. Drink spiking occurs not only in licensed venues, but also at private parties, with so-called 'date-rape drugs' like Rohypnol producing symptoms mimicking over-indulgence in alcohol or drugs. Victims may have difficulty gaining assistance from others, who believe they are drunk.

Alcohol use may be associated with personality characteristics and attitudes among certain types of perpetrators. For example, Gross *et al.* (2001) demonstrated that even with low doses of alcohol, men in an alcohol consumption condition rated a female in a hypothetical dating scenario as being more sexually aroused than their counterparts in a non-consumption condition. Zawacki *et al.* (2003) compared the personality characteristics, attitudes and experiences of men who had not committed sexual assaults with those of men who had done so, either with or without the involvement of alcohol. Among their sample of male college students, 31 per cent reported they had verbally coerced a partner to have sexual intercourse, 9 per cent admitted to forced sexual contact short of intercourse, 4 per cent to attempted rape and 14 per cent to completed rape. Among these men, about three-quarters reported alcohol involvement, mostly of both victim and perpetrator. Compared to non-perpetrators, men who had sexually coerced were more likely to have a history of delinquency, exhibit aggressive and dominant personality traits, and have experienced incidents in which they misperceived a woman's friendliness as sexual interest. They also had stronger attitudes supporting violence towards women. Alcohol-involved perpetrators were more impulsive than the other two groups, and were more likely to believe that alcohol enhances sex drive and that women's drinking signifies sexual interest. The authors suggest these types of perpetrators would benefit from interventions that challenged and provided corrective feedback about the inaccuracy and potential destructiveness of such beliefs.

We conclude that sexual coercion is so widespread as to be part of the social environment in which adolescents find themselves, some features of which we will now discuss.

Rape myths, victim blame and coercion tactics

It is well known that those who engage in sexual abuse often avoid conviction because of the difficulties associated with proving, beyond reasonable doubt, that they have been guilty of an offence.

Compounding the difficulty is the fact that many sexual crimes are unreported because of victims' fear and shame, and the further trauma that physical examination, questioning and court appearance involves for those who have been raped. The unfortunate (and still present) tendency for society towards victim-blaming in cases of rape can make court appearances even more traumatic for the assaulted person and render conviction of the assailant unlikely unless there is overwhelming evidence available. Society's readiness to endorse a position of blaming the victim arises from a complex rape mythology. One element is the belief that women with a sexually active history are always willing to consent to sex or that they forfeit their right of choice. Other pervasive beliefs are that women who dress in a so-called provocative way are considered to be 'asking for it', that women enjoy men forcing them to have sex, and that the rules of courtship decree that when a woman says 'no' to sex she means 'yes'.

Myths about rape, together with sexist attitudes and beliefs, provide a framework for justifications of sexual coercion and force. Even if the myths are not completely accepted, elements of victim blame remain, even among the well educated. A study by Wallis (1992), surveying community attitudes to child abuse, found that about a quarter of the randomly selected adults believed that, in some cases, blame rested with the child. Men were twice as likely as women to hold this attitude and, although it was more prevalent in blue-collar workers, this view of diminished perpetrator responsibility pervaded all social classes and education levels. Hollway's male sex drive discourse (discussed in Chapter 2) describes a social context which legitimizes sexual coercion. The belief that masculine biological urges are so strong that they must be satisfied at any cost, together with the corresponding belief that those who do not exhibit such strong sex drives are not real 'men', puts pressures on men to display their sexual prowess and their ability to 'score'. Further, this discourse encourages the interpretation of male-female encounters as basically sexual, with other options such as friendship or non-sexual intimacy not taken seriously. Young men socialized according to this discourse who find their sexual drives thwarted may feel justified in expressing anger and forcing their partners to engage in unwanted sexual behaviour.

Not surprisingly, those who hold these myths about rape are more likely to engage in victim blame. Distressingly, these myths are held by both sexes but are more common among young and adult men than among girls and women (Blumberg & Lester 1991). A study of Australian young people (Roberts 1992) found that one in three 14-

year-old boys surveyed by Brisbane's Domestic Violence Resource Centre believed it was reasonable to rape a girl if she 'led him on'. About 10 per cent thought rape was acceptable if 'they had dated a long time' or if 'the girl was stoned or drunk', while 14 per cent believed that a girl who had had intercourse with other boys was a permissible rape target. Twenty-three per cent were similarly inclined if the girl 'says she is going to have sex with him then changes her mind'. Many of these young boys believed that a girl meant yes when she said no to sex, using spurious justifications for their beliefs such as 'she was smiling when she said it'.

Among a sample of 16-year-old boys from all social classes interviewed by the authors (Moore & Rosenthal 1994: 12), there was clear evidence of exploitative views about sexual relationships as well as aggression towards girls who were not prepared to be sexually accommodating. Disturbingly, young girls who were perceived to be sexually liberated, in that they engaged in the same activities as their male peers, were the frequent targets of aggressive attitudes on the part of these same young men. They were regarded as fair game for exploitation or even rape. Many boys who might not consider rape or physical force were not averse to strong persuasion in order to get their own way sexually. A variety of techniques such as shaming, teasing, trickery and perseverance were considered appropriate:

> What I would do is carry on for a little bit by saying 'come on, come on, are you sure?', and I would tease them and shit like that . . . and after about half an hour or so, and they still say no, I would let up. I would say 'don't worry, give me a blow job or a hand job instead'.

> Yes, I would try to convince her. In a short term relationship, you would tell her she is not normal, and everyone else is doing it.

> I would try to persuade her, maybe with a bit of force. I wouldn't rape the girl, but kiss her and so on, touch her vagina; her bosoms, try to stimulate her, and if she didn't want to, I would give up and just talk to her and see what is wrong.

> Yes, probably try to get her drunk and talk her into it.

Many young men saw sexual persuasion as part of the game of male-female interaction and failed to recognize that their persistent attempts at sexual conquest could be regarded as more than gentle seduction. The following two example answers to the question about sexual persuasion illustrate this point: 'Most definitely, it is all part of the game. I would say "come on, come on, it's not that big". You have to say those things to virgins because they are scared'; 'Morally, I would say no, but really I would say yes. It's like yes and no. I would just keep on with what we were doing, and give her a bit of time'.

In all, over two-thirds of the teenage boys interviewed said they would try to convince a reluctant female partner to have sex. They appeared to regard their partner's reticence as a weak barrier to intercourse, one which it was part of the male role to overcome. While seduction is very different to rape, there is some sense of a continuum in the boys' methods of achieving their sexual goals. Methods ranged from seemingly harmless persistence and titillation through to the clearly unacceptable techniques of derogation and force. Our data unfortunately do not address the issue of whether these young women accepted this male behaviour, although the boys themselves, not surprisingly, seemed to believe that girls both expect and encourage it. Previously discussed studies of perceived sexual victimization suggest that this is certainly not always the case.

The message is clear that we need to resocialize many young men to think differently about sex, as shared experience rather than exploitation. Young women, too, need assistance in learning to express their sexual needs – whether this be for different forms of sexual activity or no sex at all – and in understanding the social forces which often place them in the role of sexual victim. There are programmes which have been effective in other areas and which could be adapted to resocializing teenagers' views of sex. These include work with families and school populations to reduce sex-role stereotyping and assertion training for women and children, such as the protective behaviours programme in which children learn the difference between 'good' touching and 'bad' touching. More directly, interventions which encourage men who are perpetrators of violence towards women or sexual abusers to relearn appropriate sexual relationship skills and to handle their violence more effectively are being carried out. However, as previously discussed, recidivism and drop-out rates suggest there is still much to learn about how to conduct such interventions.

Conclusion

What's changed, what's stayed the same?

The conclusions we draw today are in many respects similar to those we drew in our 1993 book, *Sexuality in Adolescence*. Sex in the 21st century remains a powerful force in the lives of young people. Even though patterns of sexual behaviours and attitudes change in a changing context, there are constant threads. Young people still have crushes, fall in love, struggle to maintain or lose their virginity, desperately want to find a girlfriend or boyfriend, experience relationship break-ups, have fun with sex and agonize about it, depending on the day. Parents still find it difficult to communicate with their adolescents about sex, despite wishing otherwise. Along with adolescent idealism, hopes for commitment to another and moves towards sexual equality we still see evidence of sexual manipulation, coercion and the double standard. The power of the epithet 'slut' remains. In the early 1990s we warned against overgeneralizing about adolescent sexual behaviour because of the wide range of differences between young people concerning what is 'normal' or 'average' sexual behaviour and that warning still stands. The need for tolerance of difference remains today, as we have seen with marginalized groups such as gays and lesbians. Perhaps most importantly, we emphasized then and do so now the many positive outcomes of sexual activity, including its role in contributing to mature development – as a step towards independence and contribution to an individual's sense of self or identity. Sex can enable people to feel lovable and provides an opportunity to express love, enhance closeness and sharing, and experience intimacy.

In the last dozen years we have learnt more about both the biology of sex and the impact of the social and cultural environment on its expression, but the two are still closely interconnected in determining the ways young people play out their sexuality. What is perhaps most interesting in comparing the last couple of decades is the demonstration of the power of social influence through noting the change in these influences and the corresponding changes in attitudes and behaviours that follow. New technologies provide both positive opportunities for sex education and research, and even socializing, but correspondingly dangerous possibilities. As we have seen, the internet enables young people to access information that addresses their sexual worries and misperceptions. But the internet also allows young people access to violent and hardcore pornography, wittingly or unwittingly, and potentially to be victims of sexual predators. Another emergent change is the recognition that sexual abuse is not a rare phenomenon. As a result, there is more help and protection available to young people who are at risk of being abused (or already have been), but this too comes at a cost. There is a danger that the panic that has arisen around sexual abuse will interfere with adults taking positive mentoring roles with young people. Already some men are diffident about expressing physical affection or talking about sex in an educative way to their children, lest these behaviours be misinterpreted.

In the conclusion of our earlier book we touched on the need for research that would broaden the study of sexuality and sexual behaviour, noting the importance of moving away from the dominating idea of adolescent sexual behaviour as risky and deviant. We also stressed the value of recognizing that sexuality is not just about intercourse, but comprises a wide range of attitudes and behaviours that influence and interact with many, if not most, other aspects of life. To some extent we have taken up these challenges in the current book by including new sections (and further development of previous material) on topics such as sexual communication, romance, sex education and sexual diversity. But there is no escaping the fact that the explosion of research on adolescent sexuality since the publication of that first book has mostly been in response to concerns about sexual health arising from the worldwide HIV/AIDS epidemic. For this reason there is still something of an emphasis on sexual health and sexual risk in the current text. The development of a book that surveys research on adolescent sexual well-being and presents careful studies on the consequences of different sexual decisions, behaviours and beliefs on sexual adjustment is still some time in coming.

In 1993 we wrote that we knew little about the relationships between adolescent sexual behaviour and lifelong sexual development. This is still the case today. There have been very few longitudinal studies of sexual behaviour in the last decade. We know very little about sexual developmental pathways for young people. What makes for an easy and positive transition from a non-sexually active to a sexually active person? What are the factors that enhance or inhibit young people's capacity to achieve a fulfilling sexual life? We have not asked young people about their sexual histories and the meanings these have. We assume that the experience of 'doing sex' must influence subsequent experiences but we do not know how the accumulated knowledge, risks, practices and beliefs become incorporated into the sexual histories of young people. The concern was, and still is, that sexuality research has been decontextualized from normal development. It is embedded in concerns about health rather than linked with the other key changes at adolescence, such as cognitive and emotional growth, achieving a sense of power and control over one's life, independence from family, and identity formation. How and where does sexual development fit with all these other important developmental shifts and transitions?

The importance of listening to what young people were saying – of considering adolescent perspectives on sexuality – was another recommendation to researchers in our earlier book. At that stage, most adolescent sexuality research was based on paper-and-pencil surveys administered to college students. One of the strengths of this book is the incorporation of recent research using a broad range of innovative methodologies. Young people's own voices are heard through the medium of interviews and focus groups. Qualitative methodology has allowed us to move beyond testing researcher-generated models and adult-centred frameworks of behaviour and helped us 'get inside the heads' of young people. Marginalized and difficult-to-reach young people have had opportunities to contribute to knowledge about sexuality through the use of internet-based data collection. More and more, young people are participating in the planning and design of research, to ensure that questions relevant to them are included. So when a young girl talks about sexual health as follows she reminds us that sexual health is more than the absence of disease (Moore 2002): 'Sexual health, I see that as a little bit different, as not putting yourself in a sexual situation where you will come out feeling that your self-esteem has been violated in some way . . . Having sex within a relationship where there is no respect is very damaging'.

A concern for sex researchers has always been the politicization of sexuality research. Governments, funding agencies, schools and the like have set limits on what may and may not be asked of young people and what topics are 'off limits'. Questions are asked about whether the researchers are attempting to gratify their own voyeuristic tendencies, or even whether conducting sex research *per se* has some kind of corrupting influence on the participants. Of course these sensibilities have to be taken into account to ensure that the best interests of research participants are served, but the search for knowledge can be hampered by attitudes based on prejudice and fear. Udry (1993), discussing the politics of sex research in his address to the Society for the Scientific Study of Sex, commented that emotions run high on the matter of researching the sexual behaviour of the populace. He quotes a Congressman who told the US Senate: 'These sex surveys have not . . . been concerned with legitimate scientific inquiry as much as they have been concerned with a blatant attempt to sway public attitudes in order to liberalise opinions and laws regarding homosexuality, paedophilia, anal and oral sex, sex education, teenage pregnancy, and all down the line' (p. 107).

Negative and derogatory attitudes on the part of politicians and policy-makers have the potential to bring adolescent sex research to a standstill. That this kind of influence seems to be increasing rather than waning in the 21st century should remind researchers that we, too, need to be opinion leaders and policy influencers. In other words, we need to be able to show how research into the sexual lives of young people can lead to improvements in adolescent sexual well-being, through, for example, better health care, better education and ultimately better relationships.

What's missing?

Information on the sex education of boys

One significant gap that still exists is an understanding of how boys get to learn about sex. Boys are encouraged to be sexually active while at the same time there is a dearth of information about sexuality directed at these young men, so that they are left confused and uncertain about how to behave. We commented in an earlier chapter that fathers take very little part in the sex education of their children. When they do, the 'education' they provide is not always appropriate or acceptable to their teenage sons, as shown by these interviews with young men remembering key experiences with their fathers: '[I remember] my father getting me to jerk him off while looking at a porno. As he "taught" me how to masturbate at 11 years old, I felt disgusted, shamed, degraded, and revolted. I have no memory of a positive experience' (Gruenert 2003: 150). On the other hand, fathers can be effective educators, sometimes by actions as much as words:

I remember when I broke up with my first long-term girlfriend my father sat me down and placed his hand on my knee and told me that I was a worthwhile person that deserved better and life would get better. The physical contact and reassuring words from him made me feel good about myself and about my relationship with my father.

(Gruenert 2003: 149)

Many media sources that present information for girls are not accessed by boys. Male readers of *Wheels* are unlikely to pick up sexual tips about 'how to', unlike young female readers of *Dolly* and *Girlfriend*. It is not surprising that a recent study reported a substantial percentage of young men 16–19 years of age felt anxious about their sexual performance and worried during sex about whether their body looked unattractive. As one male colleague poignantly put it: 'The encouragement of boys to be sexually active is doubly endowed with a desperate quest for knowledge and information in the face of silence about their sexuality' (Dowsett, personal communication).

A cross-cultural perspective on adolescent sexuality

While we have written a little about globalization, the data presented in this book are still largely dealing with western adolescents. In part, this is due to the dearth of information about young people in other cultures. As Mackay (2001) points out, although sex is a universal experience, there is no central depository for global sex information (in contrast to the WHO's databank on health statistics). Sex research, where it exists, is mostly fertility-based rather than oriented towards differences in attitudes and behaviours. Political impediments to sex research, not unknown in western countries as we have mentioned, can be so powerful as to be totally prohibitive in some nations. So there is still much to learn about how young people negotiate puberty, sexuality and sexual relationships in different countries and cultural groups. Additionally, a comparative analysis of adolescents across the globe is a huge undertaking in itself and one we felt was beyond the scope of this text. Such a study would need to discuss the many global differences in sexual laws, mores, values and practices, but also acknowledge that even the concept of adolescence, which we have mostly accepted as a 'given' in this book (although see Chapter 2 for some discussion of this issue), is by no means universal.

Longitudinal studies of sexuality across adolescence and young adulthood

Sexual development is a lifelong process, not a task that begins at 12 and finishes at 20. This is true biologically as well as psychologically. Reproductive powers peak then fall away, sexual drives wax and wane, and social expectations shape how sexuality manifests itself at different ages and stages of life. Individuals learn through successes and mistakes to incorporate sexuality into their lives. There is time for adolescents to experiment and make mistakes, yet still 'get it right' in the end. One relevant feature of the 1990s that has extended into the 21st century is a worldwide trend against marrying young. There is now a chance for young people to learn more about themselves and others, to experiment sexually, and to be able to make more mature choices about whether to partner and with whom. Arnett (2004) talks about 'emerging adulthood' as a new life stage worthy of study, an extended adolescence in which transitions of marriage and parent-hood are postponed, and there is more time for exploration of different possibilities in love and work. But this opportunity also has its negative aspects. The risk of HIV/AIDS or other STIs is increased if experimentation is not accompanied by safe practice. High or even unrealistic expectations about a life partner and unwillingness to compromise individual goals for couple goals are other risks. So, while sexual development was once seen as culminating at the end of adolescence with marriage and childbearing, today young people in their 20s and 30s may still have many sexual decisions to make before they choose a relatively stable path. Few studies examine how sexual beliefs and practices change between adolescence and emerging adult-hood, and the relative influences of these life periods on relationship choices, sexual satisfaction and life adjustment.

Why bother?

Adolescent sexuality is here to stay in spite of parents and politicians who may wish otherwise. Continuation of sexuality research is important because the more we know about what young people are saying, thinking, feeling and doing about sexuality, the more we can provide them with sex education that speaks to their current concerns and with sexual health care that is non-judgemental, freely available and effective. We can better shape our public health interventions to reduce unwanted pregnancy and sexual disease. We can teach young people what works best for satisfying relationships and how to develop skills in communicating with sexual partners. We can encourage tolerance of sexual diversity, and lobby for better and fairer laws about sexual conduct. But first we need to know about young people's lived experiences and what influences these. We hope this book provides some of the answers.

References

Abbey, A., Ross, L. T., McDuffie, D., & McAuslan, P. (1996). Alcohol and dating risk factors for sexual assault among college women. *Psychology of Women Quarterly, 20,* 147–69.

Abbott, S. (1988). AIDS and young women. *The Bulletin of the National Clearinghouse for Youth Studies, 7,* 38–41.

Abel, G. G., Mittelman, M. S., & Becker, J. V. (1985). Sexual offenders: Results of assessment and recommendations for treatment. In M. H. Ben-Aron, S. J. Huckle, & C. D. Webster (Eds), *Clinical Criminology: The Assessment and Treatment of Criminal Behaviour.* Toronto: M & M Graphics.

Abma, J., Driscoll, A., & Moore, K. (1998). Young women's degree of control over first intercourse – an exploratory analysis. *Family Planning Perspectives, 30,* 12–28.

Abrams, D., Abraham, C., Spears, R., & Marks, D. (1990). AIDS invulnerability, relationships, sexual behaviour and attitudes among 16 to 19 year olds. In P. Aggleton, P. Davies, & D. G. Hart (Eds), *AIDS: Individual, Cultural and Policy Dimensions.* Lewes: Falmer Press.

Addelson, P. L., Frommer, M. S., & Weisberg, E. (1995). A survey of women seeking termination of pregnancy in New South Wales. *The Medical Journal of Australia, 163,* 419–22.

Adler, N. E., & Smith, L. B. (1998). Abortion. In E. A. Blechman, & K. D. Brownwell (Eds), *Behavioural Medicine and Women: A Comprehensive Handbook.* New York: The Guilford Press.

Ahmed, M., Ong, K., Morrell, D., Cox, L., Drayer, N., Perry, M., & Dunger, D. (1999). Longitudinal study of leptin concentrations during puberty: Sex differences and relationship to changes in body composition. *The Journal of Clinical Endocrinology & Metabolism, 84,* 899–905.

Ajzen, I., & Fishbein, M. (1980). *Understanding Attitudes and Predicting Social Behavior.* Englewood Cliffs, NJ: Prentice Hall.

Ajzen, I., & Madden, T. J. (1986). Prediction of goal directed behaviour: Attitudes, intentions and perceived behaviour control. *Journal of Experimental and Social Psychology, 22,* 453–74.

Alan Guttmacher Institute (1976). *Eleven Million Teenagers*. New York: Author.

Alan Guttmacher Institute (2001). *State Policy Makers Provide Minimal Guidance on Sexuality Education Policy* (press release).

Alaskar, F. D. (1992). Pubertal timing, overweight, and psychological adjustment. *Journal of Early Adolescence, 12*, 396–419.

Allen, D. M., & Gorski, R. A. (1992). Sexual orientation and the size of the anterior commissure in the human brain. *Proceedings of the National Academy of Science, 89*, 7199–202.

Ames, R. (1957). Physical maturing among boys as related to adult social behavior: A longitudinal study. *Californian Journal of Educational Research, 8*, 69–75.

Anderson, J. L., Crawford, C. B., Nadeau, J., & Lindberg, T. (1992). Was the Duchess of Windsor right? A cross-cultural review of the sociology of ideals of female body shape. *Ethology and Sociobiology, 13*, 197–227.

Anderson, S. E., Dallal, G. E., & Must, A. (2003). Relative weight and race influence average age at menarche: Results from two nationally representative surveys of US girls studied 25 years apart. *Pediatrics, 111*, 844–50.

Andersson, T., & Magnusson, D. (1990). Biological maturation in adolescence and the development of drinking habits and alcohol abuse among young males: A prospective longitudinal study. *Journal of Youth & Adolescence, 19*(1), 33–41.

Andre, T., Frevert, R. L., & Schuchmann, D. (1989). From whom have college students learned what about sex? *Youth & Society, 20*, 241–68.

Aneshensel, C. S., Fielder, E. P., & Becerra, R. M. (1989). Fertility and fertility-related behavior among Mexican-American and non-Hispanic white female adolescents. *Journal of Health & Social Behavior, 30*(1), 56–76.

Ansuini, C. G., Fidler-Woite, J., & Woite, R. S. (1996). The source, accuracy and impact of initial sexuality information on lifetime wellness. *Adolescence, 31*, 283–9.

Arbes-Dupuy, V. (2000). *Dupes or collaborators? Young adults' sexual encounters*. Unpublished PhD thesis, The University of Melbourne, Melbourne, Australia.

Arnett, J. J. (2001). Conceptions of the transition to adulthood: Perspectives from adolescence through midlife. *Journal of Adult Development, 8*, 133–43.

Arnett, J. J. (2004). *Emerging Adulthood: The Winding Road from Late Teens through the Twenties*. New York: Oxford University Press.

Australian Bureau of Statistics (1999). *3301.0 Births, Australia*. Canberra: Australian Bureau of Statistics.

Australian Bureau of Statistics (2002). *Catalogue 3301.0: Births Australia, 2001*. Canberra: Commonwealth of Australia.

Australian Bureau of Statistics (2003). *Catalogue 3301.0: Births Australia, 2002*. Canberra: Commonwealth of Australia.

Australian Institute of Health and Welfare (2003). *Australia's Young People: Their Health and Wellbeing 2003. AIHW Cat. No. PHE 50.* Canberra: Australian Institute of Health and Welfare.

Bachrach, C. A. (1986). Adoption plans, adopted children, and adoptive mothers. *Journal of Marriage and the Family, 48,* 243–53.

Bagley, C., & Tremblay, P. (2000). Elevated rates of suicidal behavior in gay, lesbian and bisexual youth. *Crisis: The Journal of Crisis Intervention and Suicide Prevention, 21*(3), 111–17.

Baird, A. A., Gruber, S. A., Fein, D. A., Maas, L. C., Steingard, R. J., Renshaw, P. F., Cohen, B. M., & Yurgelun-Todd, D. A. (1999). Functional magnetic resonance imaging of facial affect recognition in children and adolescents. *Journal of the American Academy of Child and Adolescent Psychiatry, 38*(2), 195–9.

Baldo, M., Aggleton, P., & Slutkin, G. (1993). *Sex Education Does not Lead to Earlier or Increased Sexual Activity in Youth.* Geneva: World Health Organization Global Program on AIDS.

Bandura, A. (1982). Self-efficacy mechanism in human agency. *American Psychologist, 37,* 122–47.

Barbeler, V. (1992). *The Young Lesbian Report.* Sydney: Report by TwentyTen, Gay and Lesbian Youth Refuge.

Bardwick, J. M. (1971). *The Psychology of Women: A Study of Biocultural Conflicts.* New York: Harper & Row.

Bartholomew, K., & Horowitz, L. (1991). Attachment styles among young adults: A test of a four-category model. *Journal of Personality & Social Psychology, 61,* 226–44.

Baumeister, R. F., Wotman, S. R., & Sitwell, A. M. (1993). Unrequited love: On heartbreak, anger, guilt, scriptlessness and humiliation. *Journal of Personality and Social Psychology, 64,* 377–94.

Bearman, P. S., & Brückner, H. (1999). *Peer Effects on Adolescent Girls' Sexual Debut and Pregnancy.* Washington, DC: National Campaign to Prevent Teen Pregnancy.

Bearman, P. S., & Brückner, H. (2001). Promising the future: abstinence pledges and the transition to first intercourse. *American Journal of Sociology, 106*(4), 859–912.

Bearman, P. S., Moody, J., & Stovel, K. (2004). Chains of affection: The structure of adolescent romantic and sexual networks. *American Journal of Sociology, 110*(1), 44–91.

Beasley, B., & Standley, T. (2002). Shirts vs. skins: Clothing as an indicator of gender role stereotyping in video games. *Mass Communication & Society, 5,* 279–93.

Becker, M. H. (1974). The health belief model and personal health behavior. *Health Education Monographs, 2,* 326–473.

Becker, J. V. (1988). The effects of child sexual abuse on adolescent sexual offenders. In G. E. Wyatt, & G. J. Powell (Eds), *Lasting Effects of Child Sexual Abuse.* Newbury Park, CA: Sage.

Becker, M. H., & Joseph, J. G. (1988). AIDS and behavioural change to reduce risk: A review. *American Journal of Public Health, 78*, 394–410.

Bell, A. P., Weinberg, M. S., & Hammersmith, S. K. (1981). *Sexual Preference: Its Development in Men and Women.* Bloomington, IN: Indiana University Press.

Bem, S. L. (1974). The measurement of psychological androgyny. *Journal of Consulting and Clinical Psychology, 42*, 155–62.

Bene, E. (1965). On the genesis of male homosexuality: An attempt to clarify the role of parents. *British Journal of Psychiatry, 111*, 803–813.

Bennett, L. R. (2005). Patterns of resistance and transgression in Eastern Indonesia: Single women's practices of clandestine courtship and cohabitation. *Culture, Health & Sexuality, 7*, 101–12.

Bennett, N. G., Bloom, D. E., & Miller, C. K. (1995). The influence of nonmarital childbearing on the formation of first marriages. *Demography, 32*, 47–62.

Bergen, H. A., Martin, G., Richardson, A. S., Allison, S., & Roeger, L. (2004). Sexual abuse, antisocial behaviour and substance use: Gender differences in young community adolescents. *Australian and New Zealand Journal of Psychiatry, 38*, 34–41.

Berman, S. M., & Hein, K. (1999). Adolescents and STDs. In K. K. Holmes *et al.* (Eds), *Sexually Transmitted Diseases.* New York: McGraw-Hill.

Bettelheim, B. (1962). The problem of generation. *Daedalus, Winter*, 68–9.

Bidwell, R. J., & Deisher, R. W. (1991). Adolescent sexuality: Current issues. *Pediatric Annals, 6*, 293–302.

Bieber, I., Dain, H. J., Dince, P. R., Drellich, M. G., Grand, H. G., Gundlach, R. H., Kremer, M. W., Rifkin, A. H., Wilbur, C. B., & Bieber, T. B. (1962). *Homosexuality: A Psychoanalytic Study.* New York: Basic Books.

Bingham, C. R., & Crockett, L. J. (1996). Longitudinal adjustment patterns of boys and girls experiencing early, middle and late sexual intercourse. *Developmental Psychology, 32*, 647–58.

Blos, P. (1962). *On Adolescence.* New York: Free Press.

Blos, P. (1988). The inner world of the adolescent. In A. E. Esman (Ed.), *International Annals of Adolescent Psychiatry 1.* Chicago: University of Chicago.

Blum, R. W., & Rinehart, P. M. (1997). Connections that make a difference in the lives of youth. *Youth Studies Australia, 16*, 37–50.

Blum, R. W., & Nelson-Mmari, K. (2004). The health of young people in a global context. *Journal of Adolescent Health, 35*(5), 402–18.

Blumberg, M., & Lester, D. (1991). High school and college students' attitudes toward rape. *Adolescence, 26*, 727–9.

Blyth, D. A., Simmons, R. G., & Zakin, D. (1985). Satisfaction with body image for early adolescent females: The impact of pubertal timing within different school environments. *Journal of Youth and Adolescence, 14*, 207–26.

Bogaert, A. F., & Sadava, S. (2002). Adult attachment and sexual behaviour. *Personal Relationships, 9,* 191–204.

Boldero, J. M., Moore, S. M., & Rosenthal, D. A. (1992). Intention, context, and safe sex: Australian adolescents' responses to AIDS. *Journal of Applied Social Psychology, 22,* 1375–97.

Boocock, R. M., & Trethewie, K. J. (1981). Body image and weight relationships in teenage girls. *Proceedings of the Nutrition Society of Australia, 6,* 166–7.

Boonstra, H. (2002). Teen pregnancy: Trends and lessons learned. *The Guttmacher Report on Public Policy, February 2002,* 7–10.

Boxer, A. M., & Cohler, B. J. (1989). The life course of gay and lesbian youth: An immodest proposal for the study of lives. In G. Herdt (Ed.), *Gay and Lesbian Youth.* New York: Haworth Press.

Bradshaw, Z., & Slade, P. (2003). The effects of induced abortion on emotional experiences and relationships: A critical review of the literature. *Clinical Psychology Review, 23,* 929–58.

Breakwell, G. M., & Fife-Schaw, C. (1994). Commitment to 'safer' sex as a predictor of condom use among 16–20-year-olds. *Journal of Applied Social Psychology, 24,* 189–217.

Breakwell, G. M., Fife-Shaw, C., & Clayden, K. (1991). Risk-taking, control over partner choice and intended use of condoms by virgins. *Journal of Community & Applied Social Psychology. Special Social Dimensions of AIDS, 1*(2), 173–87.

Brook. (2004). www.Brook.org.uk/content.

Brooks-Gunn, J. (1984). The psychological significance of different pubertal events to young girls. *Journal of Early Adolescence, 4*(4), 315–27.

Brooks-Gunn, J., & Warren, M. P. (1985). Measuring physical status and timing in early adolescence: A developmental perspective. *Journal of Youth and Adolescence, 14,* 163–89.

Brooks-Gunn, J., & Furstenberg, F. F. J. (1989). Adolescent sexual behavior. *American Psychologist, 44,* 249–57.

Brooks-Gunn, J., & Warren, M. P. (1989). Biological contributions to affective expression in young adolescent girls. *Child Development, 60,* 372–85.

Brooks-Gunn, J., & Reiter, E. O. (1990). The role of pubertal processes in the early adolescent transition. In S. Feldman, & G. Elliott (Eds), *At the Threshold: The Developing Adolescent.* Cambridge, MA: Harvard University Press.

Brooks-Gunn, J., Warren, M. P., Samelson, M., & Fox, R. (1986). Physical similarity of and disclosure of menarcheal status to friends: Effects of age and pubertal status. *Journal of Early Adolescence, 6,* 3–14.

Brown, B., Larson, R., & Saraswathi, T. S. (Eds) (2002). *The World's Youth: Adolescence in Eight Regions of the Globe.* Cambridge: Cambridge University Press.

Brown, J. C. (1989). Lesbian sexuality in medieval and early modern Europe.

In M. B. Duberman, M. Vicinus, & G. Chauncey Jr. (Eds), *Hidden From History: Reclaiming the Gay and Lesbian Past*. New York: Penguin.

Browne, A., & Finkelhor, D. (1986). Impact of child sexual abuse: A review of the research. *Psychological Bulletin, 99*, 66–77.

Buchanan, C. M., Eccles, J. S., & Becker, J. B. (1992). Are adolescents victims of aging hormones: Evidence for activational effects of hormones on moods and behavior at adolescence. *Psychological Bulletin, 111*, 62–107.

Bury, J. (1984). *Teenage Pregnancy in Britain*. London: Birth Control Trust.

Buss, D. M., & Schmitt, D. P. (1993). Sexual strategies theory: An evolutionary perspective on human mating. *Psychological Review, 100*, 204–32.

Buston, K., & Hart, G. (2001). Heterosexism and homophobia in Scottish school sex education: Exploring the nature of the problem. *Journal of Adolescence, 24*(1), 95–110.

Buzwell, S., & Rosenthal, D. (1995). Exploring the sexual world of the unemployed adolescent. *Journal of Community & Applied Social Psychology, 5*(3), 161–6.

Buzwell, S., Rosenthal, D. A., & Moore, S. M. (1992). Homeless youth: Explorations of sexuality and AIDS risk, *Twenty-sixth Annual Conference of the Australian Psychological Society*, Adelaide.

Byrne, R., & Findlay, B. (2004). Preference for SMS versus telephone calls in initiating romantic relationships. *The Australian Journal of Emerging Technologies and Society, 2*, http://www.swin.edu.au/ajets.

Cameron, J. (2004). Interrelationships between hormones, behavior, and affect during adolescence: Understanding hormonal, physical and brain changes occurring in association with pubertal activation of the reproductive axis. Introduction to Part III. *Annals of the New York Academy of Science, 1021*, 110–23.

Campbell, A. A. (1968). The role of family planning in the reduction of poverty. *Journal of Marriage and the Family, 30*, 236–45.

Canli, T., & Gabrieli, J. D. (2004). Imaging gender differences in sexual arousal. *Nature Neuroscience, 7*, 325–6.

Carmichael, I. (1995). *Rights, duties and obligations in sex education* (Unpublished position paper). Tasmania, Australia: Baptist Churches of Tasmania.

Carpenter, L. M. (1998). From girls into women: Scripts for sexuality and romance in *Seventeen* magazine 1974–1994. *The Journal of Sex Research, 35*, 158–69.

Carr, J. L., & VanDeusen, K. M. (2004). Risk factors for male sexual aggression on college campuses. *Journal of Family Violence, 19*, 279–89.

Carver, K., Joyner, K., & Udry, J. R. (2003). National estimates of adolescent romantic relationships. In P. Florsheim (Ed.), *Adolescent Romantic Relations and Sexual Behavior: Theory, Research and Practical Implications*. Englewood Cliffs, NJ: Lawrence Erlbaum Associates.

Cass, V. (1979). Homosexual identity formation: A theoretical model. *Journal of Homosexuality, 4*, 219–35.

Cass, V. (1984). Homosexual identity: A concept in need of definition. *Journal of Homosexuality*, 9, 105–26.

Cassell, C. (1984). *Swept Away: Why Women Fear Their own Sexuality*. New York: Simon & Schuster.

Catania, J. A., Kegeles, S. M., & Coates, T. J. (1990). Towards an understanding of risk behavior: An AIDS risk reduction model (ARRM). *Health Education Quarterly*, 17, 53–72.

Catholic Archdiocese of Melbourne. (2001). *Directives for Christian Education in Sexuality*. Melbourne: Catholic Archdiocese of Melbourne.

Chandy, J. M., Blum, R. W., & Resnick, M. D. (1996). Female adolescents with a history of sexual abuse: Risk outcome and predictive factors. *Journal of Interpersonal Violence*, 11, 503–18.

Chang, S. C., O'Brien, K. O., Nathanson, M. S., Mancini, J., & Witter, F. R. (2003). Characteristics and risk factors for adverse birth outcomes in pregnant and black adolescents. *Journal of Pediatrics*, 143, 250–7.

Chassin, L., Presson, C. C., & Sherman, S. J. (1989). 'Constructive' vs. 'destructive' deviance in adolescent health-related behaviours. *Journal of Youth and Adolescence*, 18, 245–62.

Cheesebourgh, S., Ingham, R., & Massey, D. (1999). *Reducing the Rate of Teenage Conceptions. A Review of the International Evidence: the United States, Canada, Australia, and New Zealand*. London: Health Education Authority.

Chehab, F. F., Mounzih, K., Lu, R., & Lim, M. E. (1997). Early onset of reproductive function in normal female mice treated with leptin. *Science*, 275, 88–90.

Chesson, H. W., Blandford, J. M., Gift, T. L., Tao, G. Y., & Irwin, K. L. (2004). The estimated direct medical cost of sexually transmitted diseases among American youth, 2000. *Perspectives on Sexual and Reproductive Health*, 36(1), 11–19.

Christoffersen, M. N., & Soothill, K. (2003). The long-term consequences of parental alcohol abuse: A cohort study of children in Denmark. *Journal of Substance Abuse Treatment*, 25, 107–16.

Clausen, J. A. (1975). The social meaning of differential physical and sexual maturation. In S. E. Dragastin, & G. H. Elder (Jr) (Eds), *Adolescence in the Life Cycle*. New York: Halsted.

Colapinto, J. (2000). *Nature Made Him: The Boy who was Raised as a Girl*. New York: Harper Collins.

Coleman, E. (1982). Developmental stages of the coming out process. In W. Paul, J. D. Weinrich, J. C. Gonsiorek, & M. E. Hotvedt (Eds), *Homosexuality: Social, Psychological and Biological Issues*. Beverly Hills, CA: Sage.

Coleman, J. C., & Hendry, L. (1990). *The Nature of Adolescence*, 2nd edn. London: Routledge.

Coleman, J. C., & Schofield, J. (2005). *Key Data on Adolescence*, 5th edn. Brighton: Trust for the Study of Adolescence.

Coles, R., & Stokes, G. (1985). *Sex and the American Teenager*. New York: Harper & Row.

Communicable Diseases Surveillance Australia (2001). *Communicable Diseases Surveillance*. Canberra: Australian Government Department of Health and Ageing.

Condon, J. (1986). Psychological disability in women who relinquish a baby for adoption. *Medical Journal of Australia, 144*, 177–9.

Condon, J. T., Donovan, J., & Corkindale, C. J. (2001). Adolescents' attitudes and beliefs about pregnancy and parenthood: Results from a school-based intervention program. *International Journal of Adolescence & Youth, 9*(2–3), 245–56.

Congleton, G. K., & Calhoun, L. G. (1993). Post-abortion perceptions: A comparison of self-identified distressed and non-distressed populations. *International Journal of Social Psychiatry, 39*, 255–65.

Coppen, A., & Kessel, N. (1963). Menstruation and personality. *British Journal of Psychiatry, 109*, 711–21.

Coyle, K. K., Kirby, D. B., Marin, B. V., Gomez, C. A., & Gregorich, S. E. (2004). Draw the line/respect the line: A randomized trial of a middle school intervention to reduce sexual risk behaviors. *American Journal of Public Health, 94*(5), 843–51.

Crawford, J., Turtle, A., & Kippax, S. (1990). Student-favoured strategies for AIDS avoidance. *Australian Journal of Psychology, 42*(2), 123–37.

Crawford, M., & Popp, D. (2003). Sexual double standards: A review and methodological critique of two decades of research. *The Journal of Sex Research, 40*, 13–26.

Cronin, D. M. (1974). Coming out among lesbians. In E. Goode, & R. R. Troiden (Eds), *Sexual Deviance and Sexual Deviants*. New York: William Morrow & Sons.

Crooks, R., & Baur, K. (1990). *Homosexuality, in Our Sexuality*. San Francisco: Benjamin/Cummings.

Crosby, R. A., & Yarber, W. L. (2001). Perceived versus actual knowledge about correct condom use among U.S. adolescents: Results from a national study. *Journal of Adolescent Health, 28*(5), 415–20.

Crosby, R. A., DiClemente, R. J., Wingood, G. M., Rose, E., & Lang, D. (2003). Correlates of unplanned and unwanted pregnancy among African-American female teens. *American Journal of Preventive Medicine, 25*(3), 225–8.

Crosier, A. (1996). Women's knowledge and awareness of emergency contraception. *The British Journal of Family Planning, 22*, 87–90.

Crowley, A., Moore, S., & Winkler, R. (2004). *Unwanted Sexual Activity Among Young People in the City of Boroondara: The Role of Alcohol and Drugs. Report to City of Boroondara*. Melbourne: Swinburne University.

Cvetkovich, G., & Grote, B. (1980). Psychological development and the social programme of teenage illegitimacy. In C. Childman (Ed.), *Adolescent*

Pregnancy and Childbearing: Findings from Research. Washington, DC: US Department of Health and Human Services.

D'Augelli, A. R., & Hershberger, S. L. (1993). Gay and bisexual youth in community settings: Personal challenges and mental health problems. *American Journal of Community Psychology, 21,* 421–48.

Dailard, C. (2003). *Understanding 'Abstinence': Implications for Individuals, Programs and Policies. The Guttmacher Report on Public Policy.* New York: Alan Guttmacher Institute.

Darling, C. A., & Hicks, M. W. (1982). Parental influence on adolescent sexuality: Implications for parents as educators. *Journal of Youth and Adolescence, 11,* 231–45.

Darling, C. A., Kallen, D. J., & VanDusen, J. E. (1984). Sex in transition, 1900–1980. *Journal of Youth & Adolescence, 13*(5), 385–99.

Darroch, J., & Singh, S. (1999). *Why is Teenage Pregnancy Declining? The Role of Abstinence, Sexual Activity, and Contraceptive Use. Occasional Report No. 1.* New York: Alan Guttmacher Institute.

Darwin, C. (1871). *The Descent of Man and Selection in Relation to Sex.* London: Murray.

Daugherty, L. R., & Burger, J. M. (1984). The influence of parents, church and peers on the sexual attitudes and behaviors of college students. *Archives of Sexual Behavior, 13,* 351–492.

Davies, P., Weatherburn, A., Hickson, F., McManus, T., & Coxon, A. (1992). The sexual behaviour of young gay men in England and Wales. *AIDS Care, 4,* 259–72.

Davis, E. C., & Friel, L. V. (2001). Adolescent sexuality: Disentangling the effects of family structure and family context. *Journal of Marriage and Family, 63,* 669–81.

Davis, G. E., & Leitenberg, H. (1987). Adolescent sexual offenders. *Psychological Bulletin, 101,* 417–27.

Davis, S. M., & Harris, M. B. (1982). Sexual knowledge, sexual interests, and sources of information of rural and urban adolescents from three cultures. *Adolescence, 17,* 471–92.

Davis, T., & Lee, C. (1996). Sexual assault: Myths and stereotypes among Australian adolescents. *Sex Roles, 34,* 787–803.

De Leo, D., & Heller, T. S. (2004). Who are the kids who self-harm? An Australian self-report school survey. *Medical Journal of Australia, 181,* 140–4.

de Visser, R. O., Smith, A. M. A., Rissel, C. E., Richters, J., & Grulich, A. E. (2003). Experiences of sexual coercion among a representative sample of adults. *Australian and New Zealand Journal of Public Health, 27,* 198–203.

DeLamater, J. D., & Hyde, J. S. (1998). Essentialism vs. social construction-ism in the study of human sexuality. *Journal of Sex Research, 35,* 10–18.

Dempsey, D., Hillier, L., & Harrison, L. (2001). Gendered [s]explorations among same sex attracted young people in Australia. *Special Issue on Gay, Lesbian and Bisexual Young People: Journal of Adolescence, 24,* 67–81.

Dennerstein, L., Spencer-Gardner, C., Brown, J. D., Smith, M. A., & Burrows, G. D. (1984). Premenstrual tension-hormonal profiles. *Journal of Psychosomatic Obstetrics and Gynecology*, *3*, 37–51.

Deutsch, H. (1944). *Psychology of Women, Vol. 1*. New York: Grune & Stratton.

Devaney, B. L., & Hubley, K. S. (1981). *The Determinants of Adolescent Pregnancy and Childbearing*. Washington, DC: National Institute of Child Health and Human Development.

Diamond, L. (2004). Emerging perspectives on distinctions between romantic love and sexual desire. *Current Directions in Psychological Science*, *13*(3), 116–19.

Diamond, M., & Sigmundson, G. K. (1997). Sex reassignment at birth: A long term review and clinical implications. *Archives of Pediatrics & Adolescent Medicine*, *151*, 298–308.

Diamond, M., & Sigmundson, G. K. (1999). Sex reassignment at birth. In S. J. Ceci, W. M. Williams, & M. A. Malden (Eds), *Nature–nurture Debate: The Essential Readings*. Boston, MA: Blackwell Publishers.

DiClemente, R. J., Zom, J., & Temoshok, L. (1986). Adolescents and AIDS: A survey of knowledge, attitudes and beliefs about AIDS in San Francisco. *American Journal of Public Health*, *76*, 1443–5.

DiMascolo, E. (1991). *To Have Knowledge and to Hold Power: Adolescents Negotiating Safe Sex*. Melbourne: The University of Melbourne.

Dion, K. K., & Dion, K. L. (1996). Cultural perspectives on romantic love. *Personal Relationships*, *3*, 5–17.

Dummer, G. (1987). Pathogenic weight control behaviors of young competitive swimmers. *Physician and Sports Medicine*, *15*, 75–8.

Duncan, P., Ritter, P., Dornbusch, S., Gross, R., & Carlsmith, J. (1985). The effect of pubertal timing on body image, school behavior and deviance. *Journal of Youth and Adolescence*, *14*, 227–36.

Dunne, M., Donald, M., Lucke, J., Nilsson, R., & Raphael, B. (1993). *National HIV/AIDS Evaluation 1992 HIV Risk and Sexual Behaviour Survey in Australian Secondary Schools: Final Report*. Canberra: Commonwealth Department of Health and Community Services.

Dusek, J. B. (1991). *Adolescent Development and Behavior*, 2nd edn. Englewood Cliffs, NJ: Prentice Hall.

Eagly, A. H., & Wood, W. (1999). The origins of sex differences in human behavior: Evolved dispositions versus social roles. *American Psychologist*, *54*, 408–23.

East, P. L., & Felice, M. E. (1996). *Adolescent Pregnancy and Parenting: Findings from a Racially Diverse Sample*. Englewood Cliffs, NJ: Lawrence Erlbaum Associates.

Eaton, L., Flisher, A. J., & Aaro, L. E. (2003). Unsafe sexual behaviour in South African youth. *Social Science & Medicine*, *56*(1), 149–65.

Eccles, J. S., Miller, C. L., Tucker, M. L., Becker, J., Schramm, W., Midgely, R., Holmes, W., Pasch, L., & Miller, M. (1988). *Hormones and affect at early age adolescence*. Paper presented at the Hormonal Contributions to Adolescent Behavior, a symposium conducted at the second biennial meeting of the Society for Research on Adolescence, Alexandria, VA.

Eder, D., Evans, C. C., & Parker, S. (1995). *Gender and Adolescent Culture*. New Brunswick, NJ: Rutgers University Press.

Edgardh, K. (2002). Adolescent sexual health in Sweden. *Sexually Transmitted Infections*, *78*(5), 352–6.

Edwards, R., & Beech, A. (2004). Treatment programmes for adolescents who commit sexual offences: Dropout and recidivism. *Journal of Sexual Aggression*, *10*, 101–16.

Ehrlich, M. E., Sommer, J., Canas, E., & Unterwald, E. M. (2002). Periadolescent mice show enhanced DeltaFosB upregulation in response to cocaine and amphetamine. *The Journal of Neuroscience*, *22*(21), 9155–9.

Ellertson, C. (1997). Mandatory parental involvement in minors' abortions: Effects of the laws in Minnesota, Missouri, and Indiana. *American Journal of Public Health*, *86*, 1367–74.

Ellickson, P. L., Lara, M. E., Sherbourne, C. D., & Zima, B. (1993). *Forgotten Ages, Forgotten Problems: Adolescents' Health*. Santa Monica, CA: Rand.

Ellis, B. J., & Garber, J. (2000). Psychosocial antecedents of pubertal maturation in girls: Parental psychopathology, stepfather presence, and family and martial stress. *Child Development*, *71*, 485–501.

Ellis, S., & Grey, A. (2004). *Prevention of Sexually Transmitted Infections (STIs): A Review of Reviews into the Effectiveness of Non-clinical Interventions*. London: Health Development Agency.

Ellis, B. J., Bates, J. E., Dodge, K. A., Fergusson, D. M., Horwood, L. J., Pettit, G. S., & Woodward, L. (2003). Does father absence place daughters at special risk for early sexual activity and teenage pregnancy? *Child Development*, *74*(3), 801–21.

Erikson, E. (1959). Identity and the life cycle. *Psychological Issues*, *1*, 1–71.

Erikson, E. (1963). *Childhood and Society*, 2nd edn. New York: Norton.

Erikson, E. (1968). *Identity, Youth and Crisis*. New York: Norton.

Evans, A. (2000). Power and negotiation: Young women's choices about sex and contraception. *Journal of Population Research*, *17*, 143–62.

Evans, A. (2003). The outcome of teenage pregnancy: Temporal and spatial trends. *People and Place*, *11*, 39–49.

Evans, J. K., Holmes, A., Browning, M., & Forster, G. E. (1996). Emergency hormonal contraception usage in genitourinary medicine clinic attenders. *Genitourinary Medicine*, *72*, 217–19.

Eyre, S. L., & Millstein, S. G. (1999). What leads to sex? Adolescent preferred partners and reasons for sex. *Journal of Research on Adolescence*, *9*, 277–309.

Fagot, B. I., Pears, K. C., Capaldi, D. M., Crosby, L., & Leve, C. S. (1998). Becoming an adolescent father: Precursors and parenting. *Developmental Psychology*, *34*, 1209–19.

Fairley, C. K., & Sawyer, S. (2003). What is all the fuss about? Arguments for and against making emergency contraception available over the counter. *Vicdoc*, July, 8–9.

Farr, C., Brown, J., & Beckett, R. (2004). Ability to empathise and masculinity levels: Comparing male adolescent sex offenders with a normative sample of non-offending adolescents. Psychology. *Crime & Law*, *10*, 155–68.

Farrell, C. (1978). *My Mother Said: The Way Young People Learned about Sex and Birth Control*. London: Routledge & Kegan Paul.

Feldman, S. S., & Cauffman, E. (1999a). Sexual betrayal among late adolescents: Perspectives of the perpetrator and the aggrieved. *Journal of Youth and Adolescence*, *28*, 235–58.

Feldman, S. S., & Cauffman, E. (1999b). Your cheatin' heart: Attitudes, behaviors, and correlates of sexual betrayal in late adolescents. *Journal of Research on Adolescence*, *9*, 227–52.

Feldman, S. S., & Rosenthal, D. A. (2000). The effect of communication characteristics on family members' perceptions of parents as sex educators. *Journal of Research on Adolescence*, *10*, 119–50.

Feldman, S. S., Rosenthal, D. A., Brown, N. L., & Canning, R. D. (1995). Predicting sexual experience in adolescent boys from peer acceptance and rejection during childhood. *Journal of Research on Adolescence*, *5*, 387–412.

Fergusson, D. M., & Woodward, L. J. (2002). Mental health, educational, and social role outcomes of adolescents with depression. *Archives of General Psychiatry*, *59*, 225–31.

Fessler, K. B. (2003). Social outcomes of early childbearing: Important considerations for the provision of clinical care. *Journal of Midwifery and Women's Health*, *48*(3), 178–85.

Fine, M. (1988). Sexuality, schooling, and adolescent females: The missing discourse of desire. *Harvard Educational Review*, *58*(1), 29–53.

Fishbein, M., & Ajzen, I. (1975). *Beliefs, Attitudes, Intention, and Behaviour: An Introduction to Theory and Research*. Reading, MA: Addison-Wesley.

Flood, M., & Hamilton, C. (2003a). *Youth and Pornography in Australia: Evidence on the Extent of Exposure and Likely Effects*. Canberra: The Australia Institute.

Flood, M., & Hamilton, C. (2003b). *Regulating Youth Access to Pornography*. Canberra: The Australia Institute.

Flowers, P., & Buston, K. (2001). 'I was terrified of being different': Exploring gay men's accounts of growing-up in a heterosexist society. *Journal of Adolescence*, *24*(1), 51–66.

Ford, N., & Morgan, K. (1989). Heterosexual lifestyles of young people in an English city. *Journal of Population and Social Studies*, *1*, 167–85.

Foucault, M. (1978). *The History of Sexuality, Vol. 1: An Introduction*. New York: Pantheon.

Frankel, L. (2002). 'I've never thought about it': Contradictions and taboos surrounding American males' experiences of first ejaculation (semenarche). *Journal of Men's Studies*, *11*, 37–54.

Freedman, D. S., Khan, L. K., Serdula, M. K., Dietz, W. H., Srinivasan, S. R., & Berenson, G. S. (2002). Relation of age at menarche to race, time period, and anthropometric dimensions: The Bogalusa Heart Study. *110*(4), e43.

Freeman, D. (1983). *Margaret Mead and Samoa: The Making and Unmaking of an Anthropological Myth*. Cambridge, MA: Harvard University Press.

French, D. C., & Dishion, T. (2003). Predictors of early initiation of sexual intercourse among high-risk adolescents. *Journal of Early Adolescence, 23*, 295–315.

Freud, A. (1969). Adolescence as a developmental disturbance. In G. Caplan, & S. Lebovici (Eds), *Adolescence*. New York: Basic Books.

Freud, S. (1924). The passing of the Oedipal complex, in *Collected Papers, Vol. 2*. London: Hogarth.

Freud, S. (1935). *A General Introduction to Psychoanalysis*. New York: Liveright.

Freud, S. (1950). Some psychological consequences of the anatomical distinction between the sexes, in *Collected Papers, Vol. 5*. London: Hogarth.

Freud, S. (1953). Three essays on the theory of sexuality, in *Standard Edition, Vol. VII*. London: Hogarth.

Friedman, S. R., Curtis, R., Jose, B., Neaigus, A., Zenilman, J., Culpepper-Morgan, J., Borg, L., Kreek, M. J., Paone, D., & Des Jarlais, D. C. (1997). Sex, drugs, and infections among youth: Parenterally and sexually transmitted diseases in a high-risk neighborhood. *Sexually Transmitted Diseases, 24*(6), 322–6.

Frisch, R., & Revelle, R. (1970). Height and weight at menarche and a hypothesis of critical body weights and adolescent events. *Science, 169*, 397–9.

Frost, J. J., & Forrest, J. D. (1995). Understanding the impact of effective teenage pregnancy prevention programs. *Family Planning Perspectives, 27*(5), 188–95.

Furstenberg, F. F., Brooks-Gunn, J., & Morgan, S. P. (1987). *Adolescent Mothers in Later Life*. Cambridge: Cambridge University Press.

Furstenberg, F. F. J., Brooks-Gunn, J., & Chase-Lansdale, L. (1989). Teenaged pregnancy and childbearing. *American Psychologist, 44*, 313–20.

Gaddis, A., & Brooks-Gunn, J. (1985). The male experience of pubertal change. *Journal of Youth and Adolescence, 14*, 61–9.

Gagnon, J. H., & Simon, W. (1973). *Sexual Conduct: The Social Sources of Human Sexuality*. Chicago: Aldine.

Gallois, C., & Callan, V. J. (1990). Sexuality in adolescence. In P. Heaven, & V. C. Callan (Eds), *Adolescence: An Australian Perspective*. Sydney: Harcourt Brace Jovanovich.

Gallois, C., McCamish, M., & Kashima, Y. (1989). *Safe and unsafe sexual practices by heterosexual and homosexual men: Predicting intentions and behaviour*. Paper presented at the Australian Conference on Medical and Scientific Aspects of AIDS and HIV infection, Sydney.

Garbarino, J. (Ed.) (1985). *Adolescent Development: An Ecological Perspective*. Columbus, OH: Merrill.

Garland, S. M. (2002). Human papillomavirus update with a particular focus on cervical disease. *Pathology, 34*(3), 213–24.

Gerstel, C. J., Feraios, A. J., & Herdt, G. (1989). Widening circles: An ethnographic profile of a youth group. In G. Herdt (Ed.), *Gay and Lesbian Youth*. New York: Haworth Press.

Gi, X., Conger, R. D., & Elder, G. H. (2001). The relation between puberty and psychological distress in adolescent boys. *Journal of Research on Adolescence, 11*, 49–70.

Giedd, J. N., Blumenthal, J., Jeffries, N. O., Castellanos, F. X., Liu, H., Zijdenbos, A., Paus, T., Evans, A. C., & Rapoport, J. L. (1999). Brain development during childhood and adolescence: A longitudinal MRI study. *Nature Neuroscience, 2*(10), 861–3.

Glasgow, D. H., Horne, L., Calam, R., & Cox, A. (1994). Evidence, incidence, gender and age in sexual abuse of children perpetrated by children: Towards a developmental analysis of child sexual abuse. *Child Abuse Review, 3*, 196–211.

Goggin, M. (1989). *Intimacy, sexuality, and sexual behaviour among young Australian adults*. Unpublished honours thesis, The University of Melbourne.

Gold, R. S., & Skinner, M. J. (1992). Situational factors and thought processes associated with unprotected intercourse in young gay men. *AIDS, 6*, 1021–30.

Gold, R. S., Karmiloff-Smith, A., Skinner, M. J., & Morton, J. (1992). Situational factors and thought processes associated with unprotected intercourse in heterosexual students. *AIDS Care, 4*, 305–23.

Goldman, J. D. G., & Bradley, G. L. (2001). Sexuality education across the lifecycle in the new millennium. *Sex Education, 1*, 197–217.

Graber, J. A., Lewinsohn, P. M., Seeley, M. S., & Brooks-Gunn, J. (1997). Is psychopathology associated with the timing of pubertal development? *Journal of the American Academy of Child and Adolescent Psychiatry, 36*, 1768–76.

Gray, J. (1993). *Men are from Mars, Women are from Venus*. New York: HarperCollins.

Grief, E., & Ulman, K. (1982). The psychological impact of menarche on early adolescent females: A review of the literature. *Child Development, 53*, 1413–30.

Gross, A., Bennett, T., Sloan, L., Marx, B. P., & Juergens, J. (2001). The impact of alcohol and alcohol expectancies on male perception of female sexual arousal in a date rape analogue. *Experimental and Clinical Psychopharmacology, 9*, 380–8.

Gruenert, S. (2003). *Intimacy, fathers and friends: Differences in well being of young adult males*. Unpublished doctoral thesis, Swinburne University of Technology, Melbourne, Australia.

Grunbaum, J., Kann, L., Kinchen, S. A., Williams, B., Ross, J. G., Lowry, R., & Kolbe, L. (2002). Youth risk behavior surveillance: United States, 2001. *Journal of School Health, 72,* 313–28.

Grunseit, A. C., & Richters, J. (2000). Age at first intercourse in an Australian national sample of technical college students. *Australian & New Zealand Journal of Public Health, 24*(1), 11–16.

Grunseit, A., Kippax, S., Aggleton, P., Blado, M., & Slutkin, G. (1997). Sexuality education and young people's sexual behavior: A review of studies. *Journal of Adolescent Research, 12,* 421–53.

Gupta, N., & Mahy, M. (2003). Sexual initiation among adolescent girls and boys: Trends and differentials in sub-Saharan Africa. *Archives of Sexual Behavior, 32*(1), 41–53.

Gyarmathy, V. A., Thomas, R. P., Mikl, J., McNutt, L. A., Morse, D. L., DeHovitz, J., Ujhelyi, E., & Szamado, Sz. (2002). Sexual activity and condom use among Eastern European adolescents: The study of Hungarian adolescent risk behaviours. *International Journal of STD & AIDS, 13*(6), 399–405.

Hall, G. S. (1940). *Adolescence, Vol. 2.* New York: Macmillan.

Halpern, C. T. (2003). Biological influences on adolescent romantic and sexual behavior. In P. Florsheim (Ed.), *Adolescent Romantic Relations and Sexual Behavior.* Mahwah, NJ: Lawrence Erlbaum Associates.

Hamer, D., & Copeland, P. (1994). *The Science of Desire: The Search for the Gay Gene and the Biology of Behavior.* New York: Simon & Schuster.

Harter, S. (1999). *The Construction of the Self.* New York: The Guilford Press.

Hay, R. B., Kegeles, S. M., & Coates, T. J. (1990). High HIV risk-taking among young gay men. *AIDS, 4,* 901–7.

Hayes, C. D. (1987). Adolescent pregnancy and childbearing: An emerging research focus. In S. L. Hofferth, & C. D. Hayes (Eds), *Risking the Future: Adolescent Sexuality, Pregnancy, and Childbearing 2: Working Papers and Statistical Appendices.* Washington, DC: National Academy Press.

Health Development Agency (2004). *Teenage pregnancy and sexual health interventions: Better health for children & young people,* HDA Briefing Number 4, in E. Coleman, & J. Schofield (Eds), *Key Data on Adolescence.* Brighton: TSA.

Health Protection Agency (2004). New diagnoses of chlamydia infections presented at GUM clinics in England, Wales and Northern Ireland among 16–19 year olds, by gender, 1995–2003. In E. Coleman, & J. Schofield (Eds), *Key Data on Adolescence.* Brighton: TSA Ltd.

Henry, S. (1995). No sex please, we're teenagers. *Good Weekend, The Age Magazine,* 42–6.

Henshaw, S. K., & Finer, L. B. (2003). The accessibility of abortion services in the United States, 2001. *Perspectives on Sexual and Reproductive Health, 35*(1), 16–24.

Herdt, G. (1989). Introduction: Gay and lesbian youth, emergent identities, and cultural scenes at home and abroad. In G. Herdt (Ed.), *Gay and Lesbian Youth*. New York: Haworth Press.

Herman-Giddens, M. E., Kaplowitz, P. B., & Wasserman, R. (2004). Navigating the recent articles on girls' puberty in pediatrics: What do we know and where do we go from here? *Pediatrics, 113*, 911–17.

Hiller, J. (2004). Speculations on the links between feelings, emotions and sexual behaviour: Are vasopressin and oxytocin involved? *Sexual and Relationship Therapy, 19*, 393–412.

Hillier, L. (2006). Safe spaces: The upside of the image problem for same sex attracted women playing Australian rules football. *Football Studies* special issue, *8*(2), 51–65.

Hillier, L., & Rosenthal, D. (2001). Editorial: Special issue on gay, lesbian and bisexual youth. *Journal of Adolescence, 24*, 1–4.

Hillier, L., & Harrison, L. (2004). Homophobia and the production of shame: Young people discovering the fault lines in discourse about same sex attraction. *Culture, Health and Sexuality, 6*(1), 79–94.

Hillier, L., Warr, D., & Haste, B. (1996). *The Rural Mural: Sexuality and Diversity in Rural Youth*. Carlton: National Centre in HIV Social Research, La Trobe University.

Hillier, L., Matthews, L., & Dempsey, D. (1997). *A low priority in a hierarchy of needs: A profile of the sexual health of young homeless people in Australia. Monograph Series no. 1*. Carlton: Centre for the Study of Sexually Transmissible Diseases, National Centre in HIV Social Research, La Trobe University.

Hillier, L., Dempsey, D., Harrison, L., Beale, L., Matthews, L., & Rosenthal, D. (1998). *Writing Themselves In: A National Report on the Sexuality, Health and Well-being of Same-sex Attracted Young People*. Carlton: National Centre in HIV Social Research, La Trobe University.

Hingson, R., & Strunin, L. (1992). Monitoring adolescents' responses to the AIDS epidemic: Changes in knowledge, attitudes, beliefs, and behaviors. In R. J. DiClemente (Ed.), *Adolescents and AIDS: A Generation in Jeopardy*. Newbury Park, CA: Sage.

Hingson, R., Strunin, L., Berlin, B., & Heerin, T. (1990). Beliefs about AIDS, use of alcohol and drugs, and unprotected sex among Massachusetts adolescents. *American Journal of Public Health, 80*, 295–9.

Hite, S. (1977). *The Hite Report: A Nationwide Study on Female Sexuality*. Sydney: Summit Books/Paul Hamlyn.

Hockaday, C. M., Crase, S. J., Shelley, M. C., & Stockdale, D. F. (2000). A prospective study of teen pregnancy. *Journal of Adolescence, 23*, 423–38.

Hofferth, S. L. (1987). Factors affecting initiation of sexual intercourse. In S. L. Hofferth, & C. D. Hayes (Eds), *Risking the Future: Adolescent Sexuality, Pregnancy and Childbearing 2: Working Papers and Statistical Appendices*. Washington, DC: National Academy of Science.

Hogben, M., & Dyrne, D. (1998). Using social learning theory to explain individual differences in human sexuality. *Journal of Sex Research, 35,* 58–72.

Holland, J., Ramazanoglu, C., Scott, S., Sharpe, S., & Thomson, R. (1990). *'Don't Die of Ignorance – I Nearly Died of Embarrassment' Condoms in Context, the Women's Risk AIDS Project, Paper no. 2.* London: Tufnell Press.

Holland, J., Ramazanoglu, C., Sharpe, S., & Thomson, R. (1998). *The Male in the Head: Young People, Heterosexuality and Power.* London: Tufnell Press.

Hollway, W. (1984). Women's power in heterosexual sex. *Women's Studies International Forum, 7,* 66–8.

Holmes, S. (Ed.) (1988). *Testimonies: A Collection of Lesbian Coming Out Stories.* Boston, MA: Allyson.

Holschneider, S., & Alexander, C. (2003). Social and psychological influences on HIV preventative behaviors of youth in Haiti. *Journal of Adolescent Health, 33,* 31–40.

Hong, J. H., Fan, M. S., Ng, M. L., Lee, L. K. C., Lui, P. K., & Choy, Y. H. (1994). Sexual attitudes and behaviour of Chinese university students in Shanghai. *Journal of Sex Education and Therapy, 20,* 277–86.

Hudson, F., & Ineichen, B. (1991). *Taking it Lying Down: Sexuality and Teenage Motherhood.* Hong Kong: Macmillan Education Ltd.

Humphrey, J. A., & White, J. W. (2000). Women's vulnerability to sexual assault from adolescence to young adulthood. *Journal of Adolescent Health, 27,* 419–24.

Igra, V. (1998). Pelvic inflammatory disease in adolescents. *AIDS Patient Care STDS, 12*(2), 109–24.

Impett, E. A., & Peplau, L. A. (2002). Why some women consent to unwanted sex with a dating partner: Insights from attachment theory. *Psychology of Women Quarterly, 26,* 360–70.

Inazu, J. K., & Fox, G. L. (1980). Maternal influence on the teen-age daughters. *Journal of Family Issues, 1,* 81–102.

Irwin, C. E. Jr. (1993). Adolescence and risk taking: How are they related. In N. J. Bell, & R. W. Bell (Eds), *Adolescent Risk Taking.* Newbury Park, CA: Sage.

Irwin, C. E. Jr., & Millstein, S. G. (1986). Biopsychosocial correlates of risk-taking behaviors during adolescence. *Journal of Adolescent Health Care, 7,* 82–96.

Irwin, J., Winter, B., Gregoric, M., & Watts, S. (1995). *As Long as I've Got my Doona: A Report on Lesbian and Gay Youth Homelessness.* Sydney: Twenty Ten Association Inc.

Jaccard, J., & Dittus, P. (2000). Adolescent perceptions of maternal approval of birth control and sexual risk behavior. *American Journal of Public Health, 90,* 1426–30.

Jaccard, J., Dodge, T., & Dittus, P. (2002). Parent-adolescent communication about sex and birth control: A conceptual framework. In S. S. Feldman, &

D. A. Rosenthal (Eds), *Talking Sexuality: Parent-adolescent Communication*. San Francisco: Jossey-Bass.

Janz, N. K., & Becker, M. H. (1984). The health belief model a decade later. *Health Education Quarterly, 11*, 1–47.

Jenkins, S. R. (2000). Toward theory development and measure evolution for studying women's relationships and HIV infection. *Sex Roles, 42*, 751–80.

Jessor, S. L., & Jessor, R. (1977). *Problem Behaviour and Psychosocial Development: A Longitudinal Study of Youth*. New York: Academic Press.

Jessor, R., Turbin, M. S., Costa, F. M., QiDong, H. Z., & Wang, C. (2003). Adolescent problem behaviour in China and the United States: A cross national study of psychosocial protective factors. *Journal of Research on Adolescence, 13*, 329–60.

Johnson, A. M., Wadsworth, J., Wellings, K., & Field, J. (1994). *Sexual Attitudes and Lifestyle*. Oxford: Blackwell Scientific.

Johnson, R. A. (1987). *We: Understanding the Psychology of Romantic Love*. London: Arkana.

Jolly, M. C., Sebire, N., Harris, J., Robinson, S., & Regan, L. (2000). Obstetric risks of pregnancy in women less than 18 years old. *Obstetrics and Gynecology, 96*, 962–6.

Jones, J., Mitchell, A., & Walsh, J. (1999). *Talking Sexual Health: A Parents' Guide*. Canberra: ANCARD.

Kaaya, S. F., Flisher, A. J., Mbwambo, J. K., Schaalma, H., Aaro, L. E., & Klepp, K. I. (2002). A review of studies of sexual behaviour of school students in sub-Saharan Africa. *Scandinavian Journal of Public Health, 30*(2), 148–60.

Kandel, D. B. (1990). Parenting styles, drug use, and children's adjustment in families of young adults. *Journal of Marriage and the Family, 52*, 183–96.

Katchadourian, H. (1990). Sexuality. In S. S. Feldman, & G. R. Elliot (Eds), *At the Threshold: The Developing Adolescent*. Cambridge, MA: Harvard University Press.

Keller, S. E., Schleifer, S. J., Bartlett, J. A., & Johnson, R. L. (1988). The sexual behaviour of adolescents and risk of AIDS. *JAMA, 260*, 3586.

Kelly, L., Regan, L., & Burton, S. (1991). *An Exploratory Study of the Prevalence of Sexual Abuse in a Sample of 16/21 Year Olds*. London: Child Abuse Studies Unit, The Polytechnic of London.

Kent, V., Davies, M., Deverall, K., & Gottesman, S. (1990). *Social interaction routines involved in heterosexual encounters: Prelude to first intercourse*. Paper presented at the 4th Conference on Social Aspects of AIDS. London.

Kessler, R. C., Berglund, P. A., Foster, C. L., Saunders, W. B., Stang, P. E., & Walters, E. E. (1997). Social consequences of psychiatric disorders, 2: Teenage parenthood. *American Journal of Public Health, 154*, 1401–11.

Kilmartin, C. T. (2000). *Sexual Assault in Context: Teaching College Men about Gender*. Holmes Beach, FL: Learning Publications.

Kimmel, M., & Plante, R. (Eds) (2004). *Sexualities: Identities, Behaviors, and Society*. New York: Oxford University Press.

Kimura, D. (2002). Sex differences in the brain. *Scientific American, Special Issue 'The Hidden Mind'*, *12*, 32–7.

Kinsey, A. C., Pomeroy, W. B., & Martin, C. E. (1948). *Sexual Behaviour in the Human Male*. Philadelphia: Saunders.

Kinsman, S. B., Romer, D., Furstenberg, F. F., & Schwartz, D. F. (1999). Early sexual initiation: The role of peer norms. *Pediatrics*, *102*, 1185–92.

Kirby, D. (1996). *A Review of Educational Programs Designed to Reduce Sexual Risk-taking Behaviors Among School-aged Youth in the United States*. Washington, DC: The American Psychological Association.

Kirby, D. (2001). *Emerging Answers: Research Findings on Programs to Reduce Teen Pregnancy*. Washington, DC: National Campaign to Prevent Teen Pregnancy.

Kirby, D. (2002). *Do Abstinence-only Programs Delay the Initiation of Sex Among Young People and Reduce Teen Pregnancy?* Washington, DC: National Campaign to Prevent Teen Pregnancy.

Kirby, D., & Coyle, K. (1997). School-based programs to reduce sexual risk-taking behavior. *Children and Youth Services Review*, *19*, 415–36.

Kirby, D., & Miller, B. C. (2002). Interventions designed to promote parent-teen communications about sexuality. In S. S. Feldman, & D. A. Rosenthal (Eds), *Talking Sexuality: Parent-adolescent Communication*. San Francisco: Jossey-Bass.

Kirkman, M., Rosenthal, D., & Smith, A. M. A. (1998a). Adolescent sex and the romantic narrative: Why some young heterosexuals use condoms to prevent pregnancy but not disease. *Psychology, Health & Medicine*, *3*(4), 355–70.

Kirkman, M., Smith, A. M. A., & Rosenthal, D. A. (1998b). Safe sex is not contraception: Reclaiming 'safe sex' for HIV/STD prevention. *Venereology*, *11*(2), 25–8.

Kirkman, M., Rosenthal, D. A., & Feldman, S. S. (2002). Talking to a tiger: Fathers reveal their difficulties in communicating about sexuality with adolescents. In D. A. Rosenthal, & S. S. Feldman (Eds), *Talking Sexuality: Parent-adolescent Communication*. San Francisco: Jossey-Bass.

Kittleson, M. J., & Howard-Barr, E. (2005). *The Truth About Sexual Behaviour and Unplanned Pregnancy*. New York: Facts on File Inc.

Klassen, A. D., Williams, C. J., & Levitt, E. E. (1989). *Sex and Morality in the United States*. Middleton, CT: Wesleyan University Press.

Klein, F., Sepekoff, B., & Wolf, T. J. (1985). Sexual orientation: A multi-variable dynamic process. *Journal of Homosexuality*, *11*, 35–49.

Knee, C. R. (1998). Implicit theories of relationships: Assessment and prediction of romantic relationship initiation, coping, and longevity. *Journal of Personality & Social Psychology*, *74*, 360–70.

Koedt, A. (1973). Myth of the vaginal orgasm. In E. Levine, A. Rapone, & A. Koedt (Eds), *Radical Feminism: Notes from the Second Year*. New York: Quadrangle.

Kosunen, E., Vikat, A., Rimpela, M., Rimpela, A., & Huhtala, H. (1999).

Questionnaire study of use of emergency contraception among teenagers. *British Medical Journal, 319*, 91.

Krahe, B., Scheinberger-Olwig, R., & Bieneck, S. (2003). Men's reports of non-consensual interactions with women: Prevalence and impact. *Archives of Sexual Behavior, 32*, 165–76.

Krstevska-Konstantinova, M., Charlier, C., Craen, M., Du Caju, M., Heinrichs, C., de Beaufort, C., Plomteux, G., & Bourguignon, J. P. (2001). Sexual precocity after immigration from developing countries to Belgium: Evidence of previous exposure to organochlorine pesticides. *Human Reproduction, 16*(5), 1020–6.

Krupnick, J. L., Green, B. L., Stockton, P., Goodman, L., Corcoran, C., & Petty, R. (2004). Mental health effects of adolescent trauma exposure in a female college sample: Exploring differential outcomes based on experiences of unique trauma types and dimensions. *Psychiatry, 67*, 264–79.

Kunkel, D., Eyal, K., Biely, E., Cope-Farrar, K., Donnerstein, E., & Fandrich, R. (2003). *Sex on TV 3: A Biennial Report to the Kaiser Family Foundation*. Menlo Park, CA: Kaiser Family Foundation.

Kuttler, A. F., La Greca, A. M., & Prinstein, M. J. (1999). Friendship qualities and social-emotional functioning of adolescents with close, cross-sex friendships. *Journal of Research on Adolescence, 9*, 339–66.

Lapsley, D. K., Enright, R. D., & Serlin, R. C. (1985). Toward a theoretical perspective on the legislation of adolescence. *Journal of Early Adolescence, 5*, 441–6.

Lapsley, D. K., & Rice, K. G. (1988). History, puberty, and the textbook consensus on adolescent development. *Contemporary Psychology, 33*, 210–13.

Le Vay, S. (1991). A difference in hypothalamic structure between heterosexual and homosexual men. *Science, 253*, 1034–37.

Leadbeater, B. (2001). *Growing up Fast: Transitions to Early Adulthood of Inner-city Adolescent Mothers*. New York: Lawrence Erlbaum Associates.

Lees, S. (1986). *Losing Out: Sexuality and Adolescent Girls*. London: Hutchinson Education.

Lees, S. (1993). *Sugar and Spice: Sexuality and Adolescent Girls*. London: Penguin Books.

Leigh, B. C. (1989). Reasons for having sex: Gender, sexual orientation, and relationship to sexual behavior. *Journal of Sex Research, 26*, 199–209.

Leitenberg, H., Detzer, M., & Srebnik, D. (1993). Gender differences in masturbation and the relation of masturbation experience in preadolescence and/or early adolescence to sexual behaviour and sexual adjustment in young adulthood. *Archives of Sexual Behavior, 22*, 87–98.

Lerner, R. M., & Spanier, G. B. (1980). *Adolescent Development: A Life-span Perspective*. New York: McGraw-Hill.

Lerner, R. M., Orlos, J. B., & Knapp, J. R. (1976). Physical attractiveness, physical effectiveness, and self-concept in late adolescence. *Adolescence, 11*, 313–26.

Lette, K., & Carey, G. (1979). *Puberty Blues*. Melbourne: McPhee, Gribble.

Leung, C., & Moore, S. M. (2003). Individual and cultural gender roles: A comparison of Anglo-Australians and Chinese in Australia. *Current Research in Social Psychology, 8*(21), 1–16.

Levy, A. (2005). *Female Chauvinist Pigs: Women and the Rise of Raunch Culture*. New York: Free Press.

Lewis, R. K., Paine-Andrews, A., Custard, C., Stauffer, M., Harris, K., & Fisher, J. (2001). Are parents in favor or against school-based sexuality education? A report from the mid-west. *Health Promotion Practice, 2*, 155–61.

Lhuede, D., & Moore, S. (1994). AIDS vulnerability of homeless youth. *Venereology, 7*(3), 117–23.

Lindsay, J., Smith, A. M. A., & Rosenthal, D. A. (1997). *Secondary Students, HIV/AIDS & Sexual Health 1997*. Melbourne: Centre for the Study of Sexually Transmissible Diseases, La Trobe University.

Littlejohn, P. (1996). *Young Mothers: A Longitudinal Study of Young Pregnant Women in Victoria*. Melbourne: Youth Research Centre, The University of Melbourne.

Longmore, M. A., Manning, W. D., & Giordano, P. C. (2001). Preadolescent parenting strategies and teens' dating and sexual initiation: A longitudinal analysis. *Journal of Marriage and Family, 63*, 322–35.

Louie, R., Rosenthal, D. A., & Crofts, N. (1996). Injecting and sexual risk-taking among young injecting drug users. *Venereology, 9*(2), 20–4.

Mabray, D., & Labauve, B. J. (2002). A multidimensional approach to sexual education. *Sex Education, 1*, 31–44.

Maccoby, E. E. (1990). Gender and relationships: A developmental account. *American Psychologist, 45*, 515–20.

Maccoby, E. E., & Jacklin, C. N. (1974). *The Psychology of Sex Differences*. Stanford, CA: Stanford University Press.

MacDonald, A. J. (1981). Bisexuality: Some comments on research and theory. *Journal of Homosexuality, 6*, 21–35.

Mackay, J. (2001). Global sex: Sexuality and sexual practices around the world. *Sexual and Relationship Therapy, 16*, 71–82.

MacKenzie, J., Goggin, M., & Rosemeyer, D. (1992). *When You Say Yes Report. Safe Sex Campaign Evaluation of the Victorian AIDS Council Youth Programme*. Melbourne: Victorian AIDS Council.

Mandelblatt, A. L. (1999). Date rape and acquaintance rape attitudes among secondary school students: The influence of a date and acquaintance rape prevention education program. *Dissertation Abstracts International Section A: Humanities and Social Sciences, 60*(5–A), 1451.

Manocha, K. F., & Mezey, G. (1998). British adolescents who sexually abuse: A descriptive study. *Journal of Forensic Psychiatry, 9*, 588–609.

Manzini, N. (2001). Sexual initiation and childbearing among adolescent girls in KwaZulu Natal, South Africa. *Reproductive Health Matters*, 9(17), 44–52.

Marin, B. V., Coyle, K. K., Gomez, C. A., Carvajal, S. C., & Kirby, D. B. (2000). Older boyfriends and girlfriends increase sexual initiation in young adolescents. *Journal of Adolescent Health*, 27, 409–18.

Marshall, D. S., & Suggs, R. C. (Eds) (1971). *Human Sexual Behavior: Variations in the Ethnographic Spectrum*. New York: Basic Books.

Martin, D., & Lyon, P. (1972). *Lesbian Woman*. San Francisco: Glide.

Martin, K. A. (1996). *Puberty, Sexuality and the Self: Girls and Boys at Adolescence*. London: Routledge.

Masters, W. H., & Johnson, V. E. (1979). *Homosexuality in Perspective*. Boston, MA: Little, Brown & Co.

Mays, V. M., & Cochran, S. D. (1993). Ethnic and gender differences in beliefs about sex partner questioning to reduce HIV risk. *Journal of Adolescent Research*, 8, 77–88.

McCabe, M. P., & Collins, J. K. (1990). *Dating, Relating and Sex*. Sydney: Horowitz Grahame.

McCabe, M. P., & Ricciardelli, L. A. (2004). A longitudinal study of pubertal timing and extreme body change behaviors among adolescent boys and girls. *Adolescence*, 39, 145–67.

McGivern, R. F., Andersen, J., Byrd, D., Mutter, K. L., & Reilly, J. (2002). Cognitive efficiency on a match to sample task decreases at the onset of puberty in children. *Brain and Cognition*, 50, 73–89.

McIntosh, M. (1968). The homosexual role. In K. Plummer (Ed.), *The Making of the Modern Homosexual*. London: Hutchinson.

McLaughlin, S. D., Manninen, D. L., & Winges, L. D. (1988). Do adolescents who relinquish their children fare better or worse than those who raise them? *Family Planning Perspectives*, 20, 25–32.

McNeely, C., Shew, M., Beuhring, T., Sieving, R., Miller, B. C., & Blum, R. W. (2002). Mothers' influence on the timing of first sex among 14- and 15-year-olds. *Journal of Adolescent Health*, 31, 256–65.

McRobbie, A. (1982). 'Jackie'; an ideology of adolescent femininity. In B. Waites, T. Bennett, & G. Martin (Eds), *Popular Culture: Past and Present*. London: Croom Helm.

Mead, M. (1939). *From the South Seas: Studies of Adolescence and Sex in Primitive Societies*. New York: William Morrow & Sons.

Mead, M. (1950). *Coming of Age in Samoa*. New York: New American Library.

Meade, C. S., & Ickovics, J. R. (2005). Systematic review of sexual risk among pregnant and mothering teens in the USA: Pregnancy as an opportunity for integrated prevention of STD and repeat pregnancy. *Social Science & Medicine*, 60(4), 661–78.

Medora, N. P., Larson, J. H., & Hortacsu, N. (2002). Perceived attitudes towards romanticism: A cross-cultural study of American, Asian-Indian, and Turkish young adults. *Journal of Comparative Family Studies, 33*, 155–78.

Meekers, D., & Ahmed, G. (2000). Contemporary patterns of adolescent sexuality in urban Botswana. *Journal of Biosocial Science, 32*(4), 467–85.

Melby, T. (2000). Sex education in America (students and parents: What parents want sex educators to teach). *Contemporary Sexuality, 34*(12), 1–3.

Miller, B. C., McCoy, J. K., & Olson, T. D. (1986). Dating age and stage as correlates of adolescent sexual attitudes and behavior. *Journal of Adolescent Research, 1*(3), 361–71.

Miller, K. S., Clark, L. F., & Moore, J. S. (1997). Sexual initiation with older male partners and subsequent HIV risk behavior among female adolescents. *Family Planning Perspectives, 29*, 212–14.

Miller-Johnson, S., Winn, D. M., Coie, J., Maumary-Gremaud, A., Hyman, C., Terry, R., & Lochman, J. (1999). Motherhood during the teen years: A developmental perspective on risk factors for childbearing. *Development and Psychopathology, 11*, 85–100.

Millett, K. (1972). *Sexual Politics.* London: Abacus.

Milligan, D. (1975). Homosexuality: Sexual needs and social problems. In R. Bailey, & M. Brake (Eds), *Radical Social Work.* New York: Pantheon Books.

Milne-Holme, J., Power, A., & Dennis, B. (1996). *Pregnant Futures: Barriers to Employment, Education and Training Amongst Pregnant and Parenting Adolescents. Women's Employment, Education and Training Advisory Group Project.* Canberra: Australian Government Publishing Service.

Minichiello, V. (1992). Gay men discuss social issues and concerns. In E. Timewell, V. Minichiello, & D. Plummet (Eds), *AIDS in Australia.* Sydney: Prentice Hall.

Mitchell, A., Ollis, D., & Watson, J. (2000). Talking sexual health: A national application of the health promoting school framework for HIV/AIDS education in secondary schools. *Journal of School Health, 70*, 262–5.

Mitchell, K., & Wellings, K. (2002). The role of ambiguity in sexual encounters between young people in Britain. *Culture, Health & Sexuality, 4*, 393–408.

Moffat, M. (1989). *Coming of Age in New Jersey.* New Brunswick, NJ: Rutgers University Press.

Moffitt, T. E., & The E-Risk Study Team. (2002). Teen-aged mothers in contemporary Britain. *Journal of Child Psychology and Psychiatry, 43*, 727–42.

Moffitt, T. E., Caspi, A., Belsky, J., & Silva, P. A. (1992). Childhood experience and the onset of menarche: A test of a sociobiological model. *Child Development, 63*, 47–58.

Moir, A., & Jessel, D. (1989). *Brainsex: The Real Difference Between Men and Women.* London: Mandarin.

Money, J. (1968). *Sex Errors of the Body: Dilemmas, Education, Counselling.* Baltimore, MD: The Johns Hopkins University Press.

Money, J., & Ehrhardt, A. A. (1972). *Man and Woman: Boy and Girl.* Baltimore, MD: The Johns Hopkins University Press.

Money, J., & Tucker, P. (1975). *Sexual Signatures.* Boston, MA: Little, Brown & Co.

Monroe, S. M., Rohde, P., Seeley, J. R., & Lewinsohn, P. M. (1999). Life events and depression in adolescence: Relationship loss as a prospective risk factor for first onset of major depressive disorder. *Journal of Abnormal Psychology, 108,* 606–14.

Moore, K. A., & Caldwell, S. (1977). The effect of government policies on out-of-wedlock sex and pregnancy. *Family Planning Perspectives, 9,* 164–9.

Moore, K. A., Peterson, J., & Furstenberg Jr, F. F. (1986). Parental attitudes and the occurrence of early sexual activity. *Journal of Marriage and the Family, 48,* 777–82.

Moore, R. L. (1998). Love and limerance with Chinese characteristics: Student romance in the PRC. In V. C. deMunck (Ed.), *Romantic Love and Sexual Behavior: Perspectives from the Social Sciences.* Westport, CT: Praeger.

Moore, S. M. (1994). *Parents' contributions to girls' sexuality education.* Paper presented at the 29th Annual Conference of the Australian Psychological Society. Wollongong, Australia.

Moore, S. M. (1995). Girls' understanding and social constructions of menarche. *Journal of Adolescence, 18,* 87–104.

Moore, S. M. (2002). *Adolescent sexuality: The last ten years.* Jocelyn Wale lecture, James Cook University, Cairns, Australia.

Moore, S. M., & Boldero, J. (1991). Psychosocial development and friendship functions in young Australian adults. *Sex Roles, 25,* 521–36.

Moore, S. M., & Rosenthal, D. A. (1991a). Condoms and coitus: Adolescents' attitudes to AIDS and safe sex behavior. *Journal of Adolescence, 14*(3), 211–27.

Moore, S. M., & Rosenthal, D. A. (1991b). Adolescent invulnerability and perceptions of AIDS risk. *Journal of Adolescent Research, 6*(2), 164–80.

Moore, S. M., & Rosenthal, D. A. (1991c). Adolescents' perceptions of friends' and parents' attitudes to sex and sexual risk-taking. *Journal of Community and Applied Social Psychology, 1,* 189–200.

Moore, S. M., & Rosenthal, D. A. (1992). The social context of adolescent sexuality: Safe sex implications. *Journal of Adolescence. Special HIV/AIDS and Adolescents: An International Perspective, 15*(4), 415–35.

Moore, S. M., & Rosenthal, D. A. (1993). *Sexuality in Adolescence.* London: Routledge.

Moore, S. M., & Rosenthal, D. A. (1994). Dimensions of adolescent sexual ideology. *Australian Educational and Developmental Psychologist, 11,* 8–14.

Moore, S. M., & Buzwell, S. (2002). *The nature of sexual well-being among young people.* Paper presented at the Third International Conference of Child and Adolescent Mental Health. Brisbane, Australia.

Moore, S. M., & Leung, C. (2002). Young people's romantic attachment styles and their associations with well-being. *Journal of Adolescence*, *25*(2), 243–55.

Moore, S. M., Rosenthal, D. A., & Buzwell, S. (1991). *Adolescent Sexuality, Social Context and AIDS. Report of 1991 Research Activities and Findings.* Report to Commonwealth AIDS Research Grants Committee.

Moore, S. M., Rosenthal, D., & Boldero, J. (1993). Predicting AIDS preventive behaviour among adolescents. In D. J. Terry, C. Gallois, & M. M. McCamish (Eds), *The Theory of Reasoned Action: Its Application to AIDS-preventive Behaviour*. London: Pergamon.

Moore, S. M., Rosenthal, D. A., & Mitchell, A. (1996). *Youth, AIDS, and Sexually Transmitted Diseases*. London: Routledge.

Morrison, D. (1985). Adolescent contraceptive behaviour: A review. *Psychological Bulletin*, *98*, 538–68.

Morrison, L. L., & L'Heureux, J. (2001). Suicide and gay/lesbian/bisexual youth: Implications for clinicians. *Journal of Adolescence*, *24*(1), 39–50.

Mosher, D. L., & Sirkin, M. (1984). Measuring a macho personality constellation. *Journal of Research in Personality*, *18*, 150–63.

Muehlenhard, C. L., & Linton, M. A. (1987). Date rape and sexual aggression in dating situations: Incidence and risk factors. *Journal of Counselling Psychology*, *34*, 186–96.

Mussen, P. H., & Jones, M. C. (1957). Self-concepts, motivations, and interpersonal attitudes of late and early maturing boys. *Child Development*, *28*, 243–56.

Naar-King, S., Silvern, L., Ryan, V., & Sebring, D. (2002). Type and severity of abuse as predictors of psychiatric symptoms in adolescence. *Journal of Family Violence*, *17*, 133–50.

Nassar, A., & Sullivan, E. (2001). *Australia's Mothers and Babies 1999. AIHW Cat No. PER 19*. Sydney: National Perinatal Statistics Unit, Australian Institute of Health and Welfare.

National Centre in HIV Epidemiology and Clinical Research (1998). The status and trends of the HIV/AIDS/STD epidemics in Asia and the Pacific: A report from the Monitoring the AIDS Pandemic (MAP) Network symposium. *Australian HIV Surveillance Report*, *14*, 1–8.

National Institute of Child Health and Human Development (2001). *Virginity Pledge Helps Teens Delay Sexual Activity*. National Institutes of Health (NIH) news release, 4 January 2001.

Newcomer, S. F., & Udry, J. R. (1983a). Adolescent sexual behavior and popularity. *Adolescence*, *18*, 515–22.

Newcomer, S. F., & Udry, J. R. (1983b). Parental marital status effects on adolescent sexual behaviour. *Journal of Marriage and the Family*, *49*, 235–40.

Newcomer, S. F., Gilbert, M., & Udry, J. R. (1980). *Perceived and actual same sex behavior as determinants of adolescent sexual behavior*. Paper presented at the Annual Meeting of the American Psychological Association.

Newman, B. M., & Newman, P. R. (1986). *Adolescent Development.* Columbus, OH: Merrill Publishing Company.

NHS Centre for Reviews and Dissemination (1997). *Effective Healthcare Bulletin*, *3*(1).

Nicholas, J., & Howard, J. (1998). Better dead than gay? Depression, suicide ideation and attempt among a sample of gay and straight-identified males aged 18 to 24. *Youth Studies Australia*, *17*(4), 28–33.

Nielsen, L. (1991). *Adolescence: A Contemporary View.* Fort Worth, TX: Holt, Rinehart & Winston.

Nisbet, I. A., Wilson, P. H., & Smallbone, S. W. (2004). A prospective longitudinal study of sexual recidivism among adolescent sex offenders. *Sexual Abuse: Journal of Research & Treatment*, *16*, 223–34.

Noll, J. G. (2005). Does childhood sexual abuse set in motion a cycle of violence against women? What we know and what we need to learn. *Journal of Interpersonal Violence*, *20*, 455–62.

Nottelmann, E. D., Susman, E. J., Inoff, G. E., Dorn, L. D., Cutler, G. B., Loriaux, D. L., & Chrousos, G. P. (1985). *Hormone level and adjustment and behavior during early adolescence.* Paper presented at the Annual Meeting of the American Association for the Advancement of Science, Los Angeles, CA.

Nottelmann, E. D., Susman, E. J., Blue, J. H., Inoff-Germain, G., Dom, L. D., Loriaux, D. L., & Chroussos, G. P. (1987). Gonadal and adrenal hormone correlates of adjustment in early adolescence. In R. M. Lerner, & T. T. Foch (Eds), *Biological-Psychological Interactions in Early Adolescence.* Hillside, NJ: Lawrence Erlbaum Associates.

O'Donnell, L., O'Donnell, C. R., & Stueve, A. (2001). Early sexual initiation and subsequent sex-related risks among urban minority youth: The reach for health study. *Family Planning Perspectives*, *33*, 268–75.

O'Donnell, L., Myint-U, A., O'Donnell, C. R., & Stueve, A. (2003). Long-term influence of sexual norms and attitudes on timing of sexual initiation among urban minority youth. *Journal of School Health*, *73*, 68–75.

O'Sullivan, L. (2005). Sexual coercion in dating relationships: Conceptual and methodological issues. *Sexual and Relationship Therapy*, *20*, 3–11.

Odimegwu, C. O., Solanke, L. B., & Adedokun, A. (2002). Parental characteristics and adolescent sexual behaviour in Bida Local Government Area of Niger State, Nigeria. *African Journal of Reproductive Health*, *6*(1), 95–106.

Ohring, R., Graber, J. A., & Brooks-Gunn, J. (2002). Girls' recurrent and concurrent body dissatisfaction: Correlates and consequences over 8 years. *International Journal of Eating Disorders*, *31*, 404–15.

Olivardia, R., Pope, H. G., Borowiecki, J. J., & Cohane, G. H. (2004). Biceps and body image: The relationship between muscularity and self-esteem, depression, and eating disorder syndrome. *Psychology of Men and Masculinity*, *5*, 112–20.

Oliver, M. B., & Hyde, J. S. (1993). Gender differences in sexuality: A meta-analysis. *Psychological Bulletin, 114*, 29–51.

Olweus, D. (1986). Aggression and hormones: Behavioral relationships with testosterone and adrenaline. In D. Olweus, J. Block, & M. Radke-Yarrow (Eds), *Development of Antisocial and Prosocial Behavior: Research, Theories and Issues*. San Diego, CA: Academic Press.

Orenstein, P. (1994). *Schoolgirls: Young Women, Self-esteem and the Confidence Gap*. New York: Doubleday.

Orlofsky, J. L., Marcia, J. E., & Lessor, I. M. (1973). Ego identity status and the intimacy versus isolation crisis of young adulthood. *Journal of Personality and Social Psychology, 27*, 211–19.

Ottensen, S., Narring, F., Renteria, S. C., & Michaud, P. A. (2002). Emergency contraception among teenagers in Switzerland: A cross-sectional survey on the sexuality of 16 to 20 year olds. *Journal of Adolescent Health, 31*(1), 101–10.

Ouimette, P. C. (1997). Psychopathology and sexual aggression in non-incarcerated men. *Violence Victims, 12*, 389–95.

Paikoff, R. C., Brooks-Gunn, J., & Warren, M. P. (1991). Effect of girls' hormonal status on depressive and aggressive symptoms over the course of one year. *Journal of Youth and Adolescence, 20*, 191–215.

Parke, R. D., & Neville, B. (1987). Teenage fatherhood. In S. L. Hofferth, & C. D. Hayes (Eds), *Risking the Future: Adolescent Sexuality, Pregnancy, and Childbearing*. Washington, DC: National Academy Press.

Paul, C., Fitzjohn, J., Herbison, P., & Dickson, N. (2000). The determinants of sexual intercourse before age 16. *Journal of Adolescent Health, 27*(2), 136–47.

Payne, K. (Ed.) (1983). *Between Ourselves: Letters between Mothers and Daughters 1750–1982*. Boston, MA: Houghton Mifflin.

Peskin, H. (1967). Pubertal onset and ego functioning. *Journal of Abnormal Psychology, 72*, 1–15.

Peskin, H. (1973). Influence of the developmental schedule of puberty on learning and ego development. *Journal of Youth and Adolescence, 2*, 273–90.

Peterson, C. (1989). *Looking Forward Through the Life Span*. New York: Prentice-Hall.

Pettijohn, T. F., & Jungeberg, B. J. (2004). Playboy playmate curves: Changes in facial and body feature preferences across social and economic conditions. *Personality and Social Psychology Bulletin, 30*, 1186–97.

Phoenix, A. (1991). *Young Mothers?* Cambridge: Polity Press.

Plummer, D. C. (2001). The quest for modern manhood: Masculine stereotypes, peer culture and the social significance of homophobia. *Journal of Adolescence, 24*(1), 15–24.

Pope, L. M., Adler, N. E., & Tschann, J. M. (2001). Postabortion psychological adjustment: Are minors at increased risk? *Journal of Adolescent Health, 29*, 2–11.

Porter, K., & Weeks, J. (Eds) (1991). *Between the Acts: Lives of Homosexual Men 1885–1967*. London: Routledge.

Price-Adams, C., & Greene, A. L. (1990). Secondary attachments and adolescent self concept. *Sex Roles, 22*, 187–98.

Provenzo, E. (1991). *Video Kids: Making Sense of Nintendo*. Cambridge, MA: Harvard University Press.

Quick Hits, Q. (2001). Sex in the news. *Contemporary Sexuality, 35*, 7.

Quick Hits, Q. (2002). Sex in the news. *Contemporary Sexuality, 36*, 8.

Quiles, J. A. (2003). Romantic behaviors of university students: A cross-cultural and gender analysis in Puerto Rico and the United States. *College Student Journal, 37*, 354–67.

Quinlivan, J. A., Peterson, R. W., & Gurrin, L. C. (1999). Adolescent pregnancy: Psychopathology missed. *Australian & New Zealand Journal of Psychiatry, 33*, 864–8.

Quinlivan, J. A., Tan, L. H., Steele, A., & Black, K. (2004). Impact of demographic factors, early family relationships and depressive symptomatology in teenage pregnancy. *Australian & New Zealand Journal of Public Health, 38*, 197–203.

Rector, R. (2002). *The Effectiveness of Abstinence Education Programs to Reduce Teen Pregnancy*. Washington, DC: National Campaign to Prevent Teen Pregnancy.

Remafedi, G. (1987). Homosexual youth: A challenge to contemporary society. *Journal of American Medical Association, 258*, 222–5.

Remafedi, G. (1990). Fundamental issues in the care of homosexual youth. *Medical Clinics of North America, 74*, 1169–79.

Remafedi, G., J., F., & Deisher, R. W. (1991). Risk factors for attempted suicide in gay and bisexual adolescents. *Pediatrics, 87*, 869–75.

Remafedi, G., Resnick, M., Blum, R., & Harris, L. (1992). Demography of sexual orientation in adolescents. *Pediatrics, 89*, 714–21.

Resnick, M. D., Bearman, P. S., Blum, R. W., Bauman, K. E., Harris, K. M., Jones, J., Tabor, J., Beuhring, T., Sieving, R. E., Shew, M., Ireland, M., Bearinger, L. H., & Udry, R. J. (1998). Protecting adolescents from harm: Findings from the National Longitudinal Study of Adolescent Health. In R. E. Muuss, & H. D. Porton (Eds), *Adolescent Behavior and Society: A Book of Readings*, 5th edn. New York: McGraw-Hill.

Richard, R., & van der Pligt, J. (1991). Factors affecting condom use among adolescents. *Journal of Community and Applied Social Psychology, 1*, 105–16.

Richmond, J. (1979). *Statement of the Surgeon General of the US and Assistant Secretary for Health. Adolescent and Pre-adolescent Pregnancy Hearings Before the Select Committee on Population*. Washington, DC: Government Printing Office.

Rickert, V. I., Jay, M. S., & Gottleib, A. (1991). Effects of a peer-counselled AIDS education program on knowledge, attitudes, and satisfaction of adolescents. *Journal of Adolescent Health, 12*, 38–43.

Riono, P., & Jazant, S. (2004). The current situation of the HIV/AIDS epidemic in Indonesia. *AIDS Education and Prevention, 16*, Supplement A, 78–90.

Rissel, C. E., Richters, J., Grulich, A. E., deVisser, R. O., & Smith, A. M. A. (2003). Sex in Australia: First experiences of vaginal intercourse and oral sex among a representative sample of adults. *Australian and New Zealand Journal of Public Health, 27*, 131–7.

Rivers, L. (1995). *Young Person Suicide: Guidelines to Understanding, Preventing and Dealing with the Aftermath.* Wellington: Special Education Service.

Roberts, C., Kippax, S., Sponberg, M., & Crawford, J. (1996). "Going down": Oral sex, imaginary bodies and HIV. *Body and Society, 2*(3): 107–124.

Roberts, D., Foehr, U., Rodeout, V., & Brodie, M. (1999). *Kids and Media at the New Millennium.* Palo Alto, CA: Henry J. Kaiser Family Foundation.

Roberts, G. (1992). Rape OK if led on, say third of boys. *The Age*, Melbourne: 5, September, p. 6.

Roberts, T. A., Auinger, P., & Klein, J. D. (2005). Intimate partner abuse and the reproductive health of sexually active female adolescents. *Journal of Adolescent Health, 36*, 380–5.

Robertson, G. (1972). Parents and child relationships and homosexuality. *British Journal of Psychiatry, 121*, 525–8.

Rogers, D. (1981). *Adolescents and Youth.* Englewood Cliffs, NJ: Prentice Hall.

Rosario, M., Hunter, J., & Gwardz, M. (1997). Exploration of substance abuse among lesbian, gay, and bisexual youth: Prevalence and correlates. *Journal of Adolescent Research, 12*(4), 454–76.

Rosenstock, I. M. (1974). The health belief model and preventive health behavior. *Health Education Monographs, 2*, 354–86.

Rosenthal, D. A. (1997). Understanding sexual coercion among young adolescents: Communicative clarity, pressure and acceptance. *Archives of Sexual Behavior, 26*, 481–94.

Rosenthal, D. A. (2004). *Is adolescence a health risk?* Paper presented at the Nigel Gray Oration, Melbourne.

Rosenthal, D. A., & Collis, F. (1997). Parents' belief about adolescent sexuality and HIV/AIDS. *Journal of HIV Education and Prevention in Children and Adolescents, 1*, 57–72.

Rosenthal, D. A., & Moore, S. M. (1991). Risky business: Adolescents and HIV/AIDS. *The Bulletin for the National Clearinghouse of Youth Studies, 10*, 20–25.

Rosenthal, D. A., & Smith, A. M. A. (1995). Adolescents and sexually transmissible diseases: Information sources, preferences and trust. *Australian Health Promotion Journal, 5*, 38–44.

Rosenthal, D. A., & Feldman, S. S. (1999). The importance of importance:

The differential nature of parent-adolescent communication about sexuality. *Journal of Adolescence, 22*, 835–52.

Rosenthal, D. A., Moore, S. M., & Brumen, I. (1990). Ethnic group differences in adolescents' responses to AIDS. *Australian Journal of Social Issues, 25*, 39–48.

Rosenthal, D., Moore, S., & Flynn, I. (1991). Adolescent self-efficacy, self-esteem and sexual risk-taking. *Journal of Community and Applied Social Psychology, 1*, 77–88.

Rosenthal, D. A., Hall, C., & Moore, S. M. (1992). AIDS, adolescents, and sexual risk taking: A test of the health belief model. *Australian Psychologist, 27*, 166–71.

Rosenthal, D. A., Moore, S. M., & Buzwell, S. (1994). Homeless youths: Sexual and drug-related behaviour, sexual beliefs and HIV/AIDS risk. *AIDS Care, 6*, 83–94.

Rosenthal, D. A., Smith, A. M. A., Reichler, H., & Moore, S. M. (1996). Changes in heterosexual university undergraduates' HIV-related knowledge, attitudes and behaviour: Melbourne, 1989–1994. *Genitourinary Medicine, 72*, 123–7.

Rosenthal, D., Moore, S., & Fernbach, M. (1997). The singles scene: Safe sex practices and attitudes among at-risk heterosexual adults. *Psychology and Health, 12*, 171–82.

Rosenthal, D. A., Feldman, S. S., & Edwards, D. (1998a). 'Mum's the word': Mothers' perspectives on communication about sexuality with adolescents. *Journal of Adolescence, 21*, 727–43.

Rosenthal, D. A., Smith, A. M. A., & Lindsay, J. (1998b). Change over time: High school students' behaviours and beliefs, 1992 to 1997. *Venereology, 11*, 6–13.

Rosenthal, D. A., Senserrick, T., & Feldman, S. S. (2001). A typology approach to describing parents as communicators about sexuality. *Archives of Sexual Behavior, 30*, 463–82.

Ross, M. W. (1988). Perceived parental rearing patterns of homosexual and heterosexual men. *Journal of Sex Research, 24*, 275–81.

Rowe, R., Maughan, B., Worthman, C., Costello, E. J., & Angold, A. (2004). Testosterone, antisocial behavior and social dominance in boys: Pubertal development and biosocial interaction. *Biological Psychiatry, 55*, 546–52.

Rozee, P. D., & Koss, M. P. (2001). Rape: A century of resistance. *Psychology of Women Quarterly, 25*, 295–311.

Ruble, D., & Brooks-Gunn, J. (1982). The experience of menarche. *Child Development, 53*, 1557–66.

Russell, S. (2002). Childhood developmental risk for teen childbearing in Britain. *Journal of Research on Adolescence, 12*, 305–24.

Russell, S. T., Sief, H., & Truong, N. L. (2001). School outcomes of sexual minority youth in the United States: evidence from a national study. *Journal of Adolescence, 24*(1), 111–28.

Sachs, J., Smith, R., & Chant, D. (1991). How adolescents see the media. *Bulletin of the National Clearinghouse for Youth Studies*, *10*, 16–20.

Saghir, M. T., & Robins, E. (1973). *Male and Female Homosexuality: A Comprehensive Investigation*. Baltimore, MD: Williams & Wilkins.

Sanderson, C. A. (2000). The effectiveness of a sexuality education newsletter in influencing teenagers' knowledge and attitudes about sexual involvement and drug use. *Journal of Adolescent Research*, *15*, 674–81.

Sather, L., & Zinn, K. (2002). Effects of abstinence-only education on adolescent attitudes and values concerning premarital sexual intercourse. *Family and Community Health*, *25*, 1–15.

Savin-Williams, R. C. (1990). *Gay and Lesbian Youth: Expressions of Identity*. Washington, DC: Hemisphere.

Savin-Williams, R. C., & Cohen, K. (1996). *The Lives of Lesbians, Gays and Bisexuals: Children to Adults*. Fort Worth, TX: Harcourt Brace.

Savin-Williams, R. C., & Diamond, L. M. (2001). Sexual identity trajectories among sexual-minority youths: Gender comparisons. *Archives of Sexual Behavior*, *29*, 419–40.

Sawyer, R. G., & Smith, N. G. (1996). A survey of situational factors at first intercourse among college students. *American Journal of Health Behavior*, *20*, 208–17.

Scaramella, L. V., Conger, R. D., Simons, R. D., & Whitbeck, L. B. (1998). Predicting risk for pregnancy by adolescence: A social contextual perspective. *Developmental Psychology*, *34*, 1233–45.

Schafer, K. (1976). Sexual and social problems among lesbians. *The Journal of Sex Research*, *12*, 50–69.

Schmitt, D. P., & 118 members of International Sexuality Description Project. (2003). Universal sex differences in the desire for sexual variety: Tests from 52 nations, 6 continents and 13 islands. *Journal of Personality and Social Psychology*, *85*, 85–104.

Schofield, M. (1968). *The Sexual Behaviour of Young People*. Harmondsworth: Penguin.

Schwartz, I. M. (1993). Affective reactions of American and Swedish women to their first premarital coitus: A cross-cultural comparison. *Journal of Sex Research*, *30*(1), 18–26.

Sciarra, D. T. (1999). Assessment and treatment of adolescent sex offenders: A review from a cross-cultural perspective. *Journal of Offender Rehabilitation*, *28*, 103–18.

Scottish Health Education Group. (1990). *Promoting Good Health*. Edinburgh: Scottish Health Education Group.

Seligman, M. E. P. (1993). *What You Can Change and What You Can't*. New York: Random House.

Seminara, S., Messager, S., Chatzidaki, E., Thresher, R., Acierno, J., Shagoury, J., Bo-Abbas, Y., Kuohung, W., Schwinof, K., Hendrick, A., Zahn, D., Dixon, J., Kaiser, U., Slaugenhaupt, S., Gusella, J., O'Rahilly, S., Carlton, M., Crowley, W., Aparicio, S., & Colledge, W. (2003). The

GPR54 gene as a regulator of puberty. *New England Journal of Medicine, 349*, 1614–27.

Shainess, N. (1961). A re-evaluation of some aspects of femininity through a study of menstruation: A preliminary report. *Comprehensive Psychiatry, 2*, 20–6.

Sharpe, S. (1987). *Falling for Love: Teenage Mothers Talk*. London: Virago Press.

Shearer, D. L. (2000). Cognitive ability and its association with early childbearing and second teen births. *Dissertation Abstracts International Section B: The Sciences & Engineering, 60*, 5466.

Shearer, D. L., Mulvihill, B. A., Klerman, L. V., Wallender, J. L., Hovinga, M. A., & Redden, D. T. (2002). Association of early child bearing and low cognitive ability. *Perspectives on Sexual and Reproductive Health, 34*, 236–43.

Sheehan, M., & Ridge, D. (2001). 'You become really close. You talk about the silly things you did, and we laugh': The role of binge drinking in female secondary students' lives. *Substance Use and Misuse, 36*, 347–72.

Sheeran, P., Abraham, C. and Orbell, S. (1999). Psychosocial correlates of heterosexual condom use: A meta-analysis. *Psychological Bulletin, 125*, 90–132.

Sheridan, A., McKeown, K., & Cherry, J. (1998). Perspectives on treatment outcome in adolescent sexual offending: A study of a community-based treatment programme. *Irish Journal of Psychology, Special issue: Understanding, Assessing and Treating Juvenile and Adult Sex Offenders, 19*, 168–80.

Shulman, S. (2003). Conflict and negotiation in adolescent romantic relationships. In P. Florsheim (Ed.), *Adolescent Romantic Relations and Sexual Behavior: Theory, Research and Practical Implications*. Englewood Cliffe, NJ: Lawrence Erlbaum Associates.

Siedlecky, S. (1984). Defusing a new teenage baby boom. *Education News, 18*, 20–3.

Siedlecky, S. (1985). Trends in teenage births – dispelling some myths. *New Doctor, 38*, 14–19.

Siedlecky, S. (1996). Contraception and abortion in Australia: a review of the last decade. *On the Level, 4*(2), 44–50.

Silbereisen, R. K., & Kracke, B. (1997). Self reported maturational timing and adaptation in adolescence. In J. Schulenberg, J. L. Maggs, & K. Hurrelmann (Eds), *Health Risks and Developmental Transitions During Adolescence*. Cambridge: Cambridge University Press.

Simmons, R. G., Blyth, D. A., & McKinney, K. L. (1983). The social and psychological effects of puberty on white females. In J. Brooks-Gunn, & A. C. Petersen (Eds), *Girls at Puberty*. New York: Plenum.

Simms, M., & Smith, C. (1986). *Teenage Mothers and Their Partners*. London: HMSO.

Simon, S., & Paxton, S. (2004). Sexual risk attitudes and behaviours among young adult Indonesians. *Culture, Health & Sexuality, 6,* 393–409.

Singh, S., Darroch, J. E., & Bankole, A. (2003). *A, B and C in Uganda: The Roles of Abstinence, Monogamy and Condom Use in HIV Decline, Occasional Report No. 9.* New York: Alan Guttmacher Institute.

Sisk, C., & Foster, D. (2004). The neural basis of puberty and adolescence. *Nature Neuroscience, 7,* 1040–7.

Sloane, B., & Zimmer, C. (1993). The power of peer health education. *Journal of American College Health, 41,* 241–5.

Slonim-Nevo, V. (1992). First pre-marital intercourse among Mexican American and Anglo-American adolescent women. *Journal of Adolescent Health, 7,* 332–51.

Smith, A. M. A., & Rosenthal, D. A. (1998). Revisiting adolescents' sexual styles: Patterns of adolescents' self perceptions. *Psychological Reports, 83,* 65–6.

Smith, A. M. A., Rosenthal, D. A., & Tesoriero, A. (1995). Adolescents and sexually transmissible diseases: Patterns of knowledge in Victorian high schools. *Venereology, 8,* 83–8.

Smith, A. M. A., Rosenthal, D., & Reichler, H. (1996). 'High schoolers' masturbatory practices: Their relationship to sexual intercourse and personal characteristics. *Psychological Reports, 79,* 499–509.

Smith, A. M. A., Lindsay, J., & Rosenthal, D. A. (1999). Same-sex attraction, drug injection and binge drinking among Australian adolescents: Results of a national survey. *Australian and New Zealand Journal of Public Health, 23*(6), 643–6.

Smith, A. M. A., Agius, P., Dyson, S., Mitchell, A., & Pitts, M. (2003a). *Secondary Students & Sexual Health 2002, Results of the 3rd National Survey of Australian Secondary Students, HIV/AIDS and Sexual Health.* Melbourne: Australian Research Centre in Sex, Health and Society, La Trobe University.

Smith, A. M. A., Rissel, C. E., Richters, J., Grulich, A. E., & de Visser, R. O. (2003b). Sex in Australia: Reproductive experiences and reproductive health among a representative sample of women. *Australian & New Zealand Journal of Public Health, 27*(2), 204–9.

Smith, D. F., & Hokland, M. (1988). Love and salutinogenesis in late adolescence: A preliminary investigation. *Psychology: A Journal of Human Behavior, 25,* 44–9.

Smith, E. (1989). A biosocial model of adolescent sexual behavior. In G. R. Adams, R. Montemayor, & T. P. Gullotta (Eds), *Biology of Adolescent Behavior and Development.* Newbury Park, CA: Sage.

Smith, E. A., Udry, J. R., & Morris, N. M. (1985). Pubertal development and friends: A biosocial explanation of adolescent sexual behaviour. *Journal of Health and Social Behavior, 26,* 183–92.

Smith, M., Gertz, E., Alvarez, S., & Lurie, P. (2000). The content and accessibility of sex education information on the internet. *Health Education and Behavior*, *27*, 684–94.

Sneed, C. D., Marisky, D. E., Rotherum-Borus, M. J., Ebin, V., Marlotte, C. K., Lyde, M., & Gill, J. K. (2001). 'Don't know' and 'didn't think if it': Condom use at first intercourse by Latino adolescents. *AIDS Care*, *13*(3), 303–8.

Sobo, E. J. (1993). Inner city women and AIDS: The psycho-social benefits of unsafe sex. *Culture, Medicine and Psychiatry*, *17*, 455–85.

Sorenson, R. E. (1973). *Adolescent Sexuality in Contemporary America*. New York: World.

Sowell, E. R., Thompson P. M., Holmes, C. J., Jernigan, T. L., & Toga, A. W. (1999). In vivo evidence for post-adolescent brain maturation in frontal and striatal regions. *Nature Neuroscience*, *2*(10), 859–61.

Spanier, G. B. (1976). Formal and informal sex education as determinants of premarital sexual behavior. *Archives of Sexual Behavior*, *5*, 39–67.

Spitzer, P. G., & Weiner, N. J. (1989). Transmission of HIV infection from a woman to a man by oral sex. *New England Journal of Medicine*, *320*(4), 251.

Spitzer, R. L. (1981). The diagnostic status of homosexuality in DSM III: A reformulation of the issues. *American Journal of Psychiatry*, *138*, 210–15.

Starkman, N., & Rajani, N. (2002). The case for comprehensive sex education. *AIDS Patient Care and STDs*, *16*, 313–18.

Stice, E., & Whitenton, K. (2002). Risk factors for body dissatisfaction in adolescent girls: A longitudinal investigation. *Developmental Psychology*, *38*, 669–78.

Stice, E., Presnell, K., & Bearman, S. K. (2001). Relation of early menarche to depression, eating disorders, substance abuse, and comorbid psychopathology among adolescent girls. *Developmental Psychology*, *37*, 608–19.

Strobino, D. M. (1987). The health and medical consequences of adolescent sexuality and pregnancy: A review of the literature. In S. L. Hofferth, & C. D. Hayes (Eds), *Risking the Future: Adolescent Sexuality, Pregnancy, and Childbearing*. Washington, DC: National Academy Press.

Strunin, L., & Hingson, R. (1987). Acquired immunodeficiency syndrome and adolescents: Knowledge, beliefs, attitudes and behaviours. *Pediatrics*, *79*, 825–32.

Sulak, P. (2004). Adolescent sexual health. *The Journal of Family Practice Supplement*, *S3–S4*.

Susman, E. J., Dorn, L. D., & Chrousos, G. P. (1991). Negative affect and hormone levels in young adolescents: Concurrent and predictive perspectives. *Journal of Youth and Adolescence*, *20*, 167–90.

Sutton, H. (1944). *Lectures on Preventive Medicine*. Sydney: Consolidated Press.

Swann, C., Bowe, K., McCormick, G., & Kosmin, M. (2003). *Teenage Pregnancy and Parenthood: A Review of Reviews, Evidence Briefing*. London: Health Development Agency, Department of Health.

Tannen, D. (1990). *You Just Don't Understand: Women and Men in Conversation*. Australia: Random House.

Tanner, J. M. (1966). The secular trend towards earlier physical maturation. *Tijdschrift Voor Sociale Geneeskunde, 44*, 524–38.

Tanner, J. M. (1970). Physical growth. In P. H. Mussen (Ed.), *Carmichael's Manual of Child Psychology*, Vol. 1. New York: Wiley.

Tanzman, E. S. (1992). Unwanted sexual activity: The prevalence in college women. *Journal of American College Health, 40*, 167–71.

Tarr, C. M., & Aggleton, P. (1999). Young people and HIV in Cambodia: Meanings, contexts and sexual cultures. *AIDS Care, 11*, 375–84.

Terry, J. (1997). The seductive power of science in the making of deviant subjectivities. In V. Rosario (Ed.), *Science and Homosexualities*. New York: Routledge.

The Herald-Sun (2003). Drinking spike on increase, May, 3.

Thompson, J. K., Heinberg, L. J., Altabe, M., & Tantleff-Dunn, S. (1999). *Exacting Beauty: Theory, Assessment and Treatment of Body Image Disturbance*. Washington, DC: American Psychological Association.

Thompson, S. (1990). Putting a big thing into a little hole: Teenage girls' accounts of sexual initiation. *The Journal Of Sex Research, 27*(3), 341–61.

Thornburg, H. D. (1975). Adolescent sources of initial sex information. In R. E. Grinder (Ed.), *Studies in Adolescence*, 3rd edn. London: Collier-Macmillan.

Thornburg, H. D. (1981). The amount of sex information learning obtained during early adolescence. *Journal of Early Adolescence, 1*, 71–183.

Thornton, A., & Camburn, D. (1987). The influence of the family on premarital sexual attitudes and behavior. *Demography, 24*, 323–40.

Thurlow, C. (2001). Naming the 'outsider within': homophobic pejoratives and the verbal abuse of lesbian, gay and bisexual high-school pupils. *Journal of Adolescence, 24*(1), 25–38.

Tolman, D. L. (2002). *Dilemmas of Desire: Teenage Girls Talk About Sexuality*. Cambridge, MA: Harvard University Press.

Tolman, D. L., & Higgins, T. (1996). How being a good girl can be bad for girls. In N. B. Maglin, & D. Perry (Eds), *Good Girls/Bad Girls: Women, Sex, Violence and Power in the 1990s*. New Brunswick, NJ: Rutgers University Press.

Tomas, P. (2005). Mapping brain maturation and cognitive development during adolescence. *Trends in Cognitive Sciences, 9*, 60–8.

Toups, M., & Holmes, W. (2002). Effectiveness of abstinence-based sex education curricula: A review. *Counseling and Values, 46*, 237–40.

Townsend, S. (1982). *The Secret Diary of Adrian Mole Aged 13¾*. London: Methuen.

Tracy, J. L., Shaver, P. R., Albino, A. W., & Cooper, M. L. (2003). Attachment styles and adolescent sexuality. In P. Florsheim (Ed.), *Adolescent Romantic Relations and Sexual Behavior: Theory, Research and Practical Implications*. Englewood Cliffs, NJ: Lawrence Erlbaum Associates.

Trivers, R. (1972). Parental investment and sexual selection. In B. Campbell (Ed.), *Sexual Selection and the Descent of Man*. Chicago: Aldine-Atherton.

Troiden, R. R. (1989). The formation of homosexual identities. In G. Herdt (Ed.), *Gay and Lesbian Youth*. New York: Haworth Press.

Trussell, J. (1988). Teenage pregnancy in the United States. *Family Planning Perspectives*, 20, 262–72.

Turner, K. M. (2004). Young women's views on teenage motherhood: a possible explanation for the relationship between socio-economic background and teenage pregnancy outcome? *Journal of Youth Studies*, 7(2), 221–38.

Turtle, A. M., Ford, B., Habgood, R., Grant, M., Bekiaris, J., Constantinou, C., Macek, M., & Polyzoidis, H. (1989). AIDS-related beliefs and behaviours of Australian university students. *Medical Journal of Australia*, 150, 371–6.

Tyler, K. A., Hoyt, D. R., & Whitbeck, L. B. (1998). Coercive sexual strategies. *Violence Victims*, 13, 47–61.

Udry, J. R. (1985). Androgenic hormones motivate serum sexual behavior in boys. *Fertility and Sterility*, 43, 90–4.

Udry, J. R. (1988). Biological predispositions and social control in adolescent sexual behavior. *American Sociological Review*, 53, 709–22.

Udry, J. R. (1993). The politics of sex research. *The Journal of Sex Research*, 30, 103–10.

Udry, J. R. (2000). Biological limits of gender construction. *American Sociological Review*, 65, 443–57.

Udry, J. R., & Billy, J. O. G. (1987). Initiation of coitus in early adolescence, *American Sociological Review*, 52, 841–55.

Udry, J. R., Talbert, L. M., & Morris, N. M. (1986). Biosocial foundations for adolescent female sexuality. *Demography*, 23(2), 217–30.

UNICEF (2001). *Early Marriage: Child Spouses*. Florence: United Nations Children's Fund, Innocenti Research Centre.

UNICEF (2002). *Young People and HIV/AIDS: Opportunity and Crisis*. New York: United Nations Children's Fund, Joint United Nations Programme on HIV/AIDS and World Health Organization.

Urberg, K. A. (1982). A theoretical framework for studying adolescent contraceptive use. *Adolescence*, 17, 527–40.

van der Klis, K. A., Westenberg, L., Chan, A., Dekker, G., & Keane, R. J. (2002). Teenage pregnancy: Trends, characteristics and outcomes in South Australia and Australia. *Australian & New Zealand Journal of Public Health*, 26(2), 125–31.

Vicary, J. R., Klingaman, L. R., & Harkness, W. L. (1995). Risk factors associated with date rape and sexual assault of adolescent girls. *Journal of Adolescence*, 18, 289–306.

Victorian Government Department of Health and Community Services (1993). *Are You at Risk of STD's? A Simple Guide to Understanding and*

Preventing Sexually Transmitted Diseases. Melbourne: Victorian Government Department of Health and Community Services.

Vinovskis, M. A. (2003). Historical perspectives on adolescent pregnancy and education in the United States. *History of the Family, 8,* 399–421.

Waldner-Haugrud, L. K., & Magruder, B. (1995). Male and female sexual victimization in dating relationships: Gender differences in coercion techniques and outcomes. *Violence and Victims, 10,* 203–15.

Walkerdine, V. (1984). Some day my prince will come: Young girls and the preparation for adolescent sexuality. In A. McRobbie, & M. Nava (Eds), *Gender and Generation.* Basingstoke: Macmillan.

Wallis, Y. (1992). *The Victorian Community's Attitudes to Child Sexual Abuse.* Victoria: Protective Services for Children and Young People, Community Services.

Ward, L. M. (1995). Talking about sex: Common themes about sexuality in the prime-time television programs children and adolescents view most. *Journal of Youth and Adolescence, 24,* 595–615.

Ward, L. M. (2003). Understanding the role of entertainment in the sexual socialization of America's youth: A review of empirical research. *Developmental Review, 23,* 347–88.

Warwick, I., & Aggleton, P. (1990). Adolescents, young people and AIDS research. In P. Aggleton, P. Davies, & G. Hart (Eds), *AIDS: Individual, Cultural and Policy Dimensions.* Lewes: Falmer Press.

Warwick, I., Aggleton, P., & Douglas, N. (2001). Playing it safe: Addressing the emotional and physical health of lesbian and gay pupils in the UK. *Journal of Adolescence, 24*(1), 129–40.

Watts, R. H., & Borders, L. D. (2005). Boys' perceptions of the male role: Understanding gender role conflict in adolescent males. *The Journal of Men's Studies, 13,* 267–80.

Weeks, J. (1977). *Coming Out: Homosexual Politics in Britain from the Nineteenth Century to the Present.* London: Quartet.

Weideger, P. (1976). *Menstruation and Menopause.* New York: Knopf.

Wekerle, C., & Avgoustis, E. (2003). *Child Maltreatment, Adolescent Dating and Adolescent Dating Violence.* Englewood Cliffs, NJ: Lawrence Erlbaum Associates.

Wellings, K., Wadsworth, J., Johnson, A., Field, J., & Macdowall, W. (1999). Teenage fertility and life chances. *Reviews of Reproduction, 4,* 184–90.

Wellings, K., Nanchahal, K., Macdowall, W., McManus, S., Erens, B., Mercer, C. H., Johnson, A. M., Copas, A. J., Korovessis, C., Fenton, K. A., & Field, J. (2001). Sexual behaviour in Britain: Early heterosexual experience. *The Lancet, 358,* 1843–50.

Welsh, D. P., Grello, C. P., & Harper, M. S. (2003). When love hurts: Depression and adolescent romantic relationships. In P. Florsheim (Ed.), *Adolescent Romantic Relations and Sexual Behavior: Theory, Research and Practical Implications.* Englewood Cliffs, NJ: Lawrence Erlbaum Associates.

Werner, B. (1988). Fertility trends in the UK and in thirteen other developed countries, 1966–86. *Population Trends, 51*, 18–24.

Weston, C. (1988). *Girltalk about Guys: Real Questions and Real Answers.* New York: Harper & Row.

Whitefield, K. (1999). Violence, rape and sexual coercion: Everyday love in a South African township. *Gender and Development, 5*, 41–6.

Widmer, E. D. (1997). Influence of older siblings on initiation of sexual intercourse. *Journal of Marriage and the Family, 59*, 928–38.

Widmer, E. D., Treas, J., & Newcomb, R. (1998). Attitudes toward non-marital sex in 24 countries. *Journal of Sex Research, 35*, 349–58.

Wielandt, H., Boldsen, J., & Jeune, B. (1989). Age of partners at first intercourse among Danish males and females. *Archives of Sexual Behaviour, 18*, 449–54.

Wiemann, C. M., Rickert, V. I., Berenson, A. B., & Volk, R. J. (2005). Are pregnant adolescents stigmatized by pregnancy? *Journal of Adolescent Health, 36*, 352, e351–352, e357.

Wilcox, B. L. (1999). Sexual obsessions: Public policy and adolescent girls. In N. Johnson, M. Roberts, & J. Worrell (Eds), *Beyond Appearance: A New Look at Adolescent Girls.* Washington, DC: American Psychological Association.

Williams, H., & Davidson, S. (2004). Improving adolescent sexual and reproductive health. A view from Australia: Learning from world's best practice. *Sexual Health, 1*, 95–105.

Wilton, T. (2000). *Sexualities in Health and Social Care: A Textbook.* Buckingham: Open University Press.

Woodward, L. J., & Fergusson, D. M. (2001). Life course outcomes of young people with anxiety disorders in adolescence. *Journal of the American Academy of Child and Adolescent Psychiatry, 40*, 1086–93.

Woodward, L. J., Fergusson, D. M., & Horwood, L. J. (2001). Risk factor and life processes associated with teenage pregnancy: Results of a prospective study from birth to 20 years. *Journal of Marriage and Family, 63*, 1170–84.

Woody, J. D., DeSouza, H. J., & Russel, R. (2003). Emotions and motivations in first adolescent intercourse: An exploratory study based on object relations theory. *The Canadian Journal of Human Sexuality, 12*, 35–51.

Worling, J. R. (2001). Personality-based typology of adolescent male sexual offenders: Differences in recidivism rates, victim-selection characteristics, and personal victimisation histories. *Sexual Abuse: A Journal of Research and Treatment, 13*, 149–66.

Wu, D. (2003). Survey reveals sexual behavior and attitudes, *Taipei Times*, 19 December, 4.

Wyn, J., & Stewart, F. (1991). *Young Women and Sexually Transmitted Diseases, Working Paper No. 7.* Melbourne: Youth Research Centre.

Yampolskaya, S., Brown, E. C., & Greenbaum, P. E. (2002). Early pregnancy among adolescent females with serious emotional disturbances: Risk factors and outcomes. *Journal of Emotional and Behavioral Disorders, 10,* 108–15.

Yankelovich, D. (1974). *The New Morality: A Profile of American Youth in the 1970s.* New York: McGraw-Hill.

Youn, G. (1996). Sexual activities and attitudes of adolescent Koreans. *Archives of Sexual Behavior, 25*(6), 629–43.

Young, S. (1994). Nine out of 10 parents support sex lessons, *Times Educational Supplement,* 15.

Youth Risk Behavior Surveillances (YRBS) (2004). *Youth Risk Behavior Surveillance – United States, 2003: Morbidity and Mortality Weekly Report, 53,* No. SS–2.

Zabin, L. S., Astone, N. M., & Emerson, M. R. (1993). Do adolescents want babies? *Journal of Research on Adolescence, 3,* 67–86.

Zawacki, T., Abbey, A., Buck, P. O., McAuslan, P., & Clinton-Sherrod, A. M. (2003). Perpetrators of alcohol-involved sexual assaults: How do they differ from other sexual assault perpetrators and nonperpetrators? *Aggressive Behavior, 29,* 366–80.

Zelnik, M., Kantner, J., & Ford, K. (1981). *Sex and Pregnancy in Adolescence.* Beverly Hills, CA: Sage.

Zelnik, M., & Shah, K. F. (1983). First intercourse among young Americans. *Family Planning Perspectives, 15,* 64–70.

Index